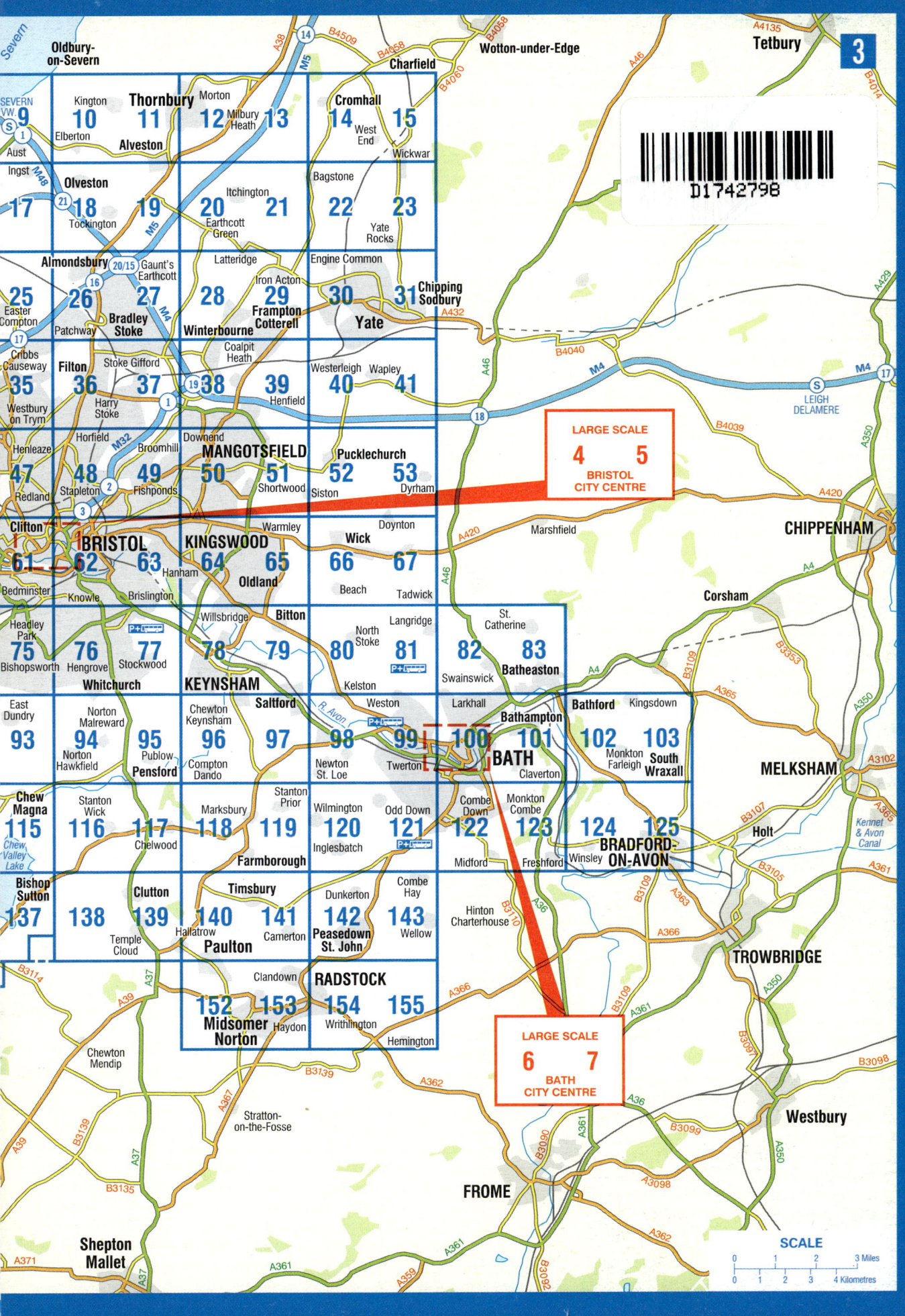

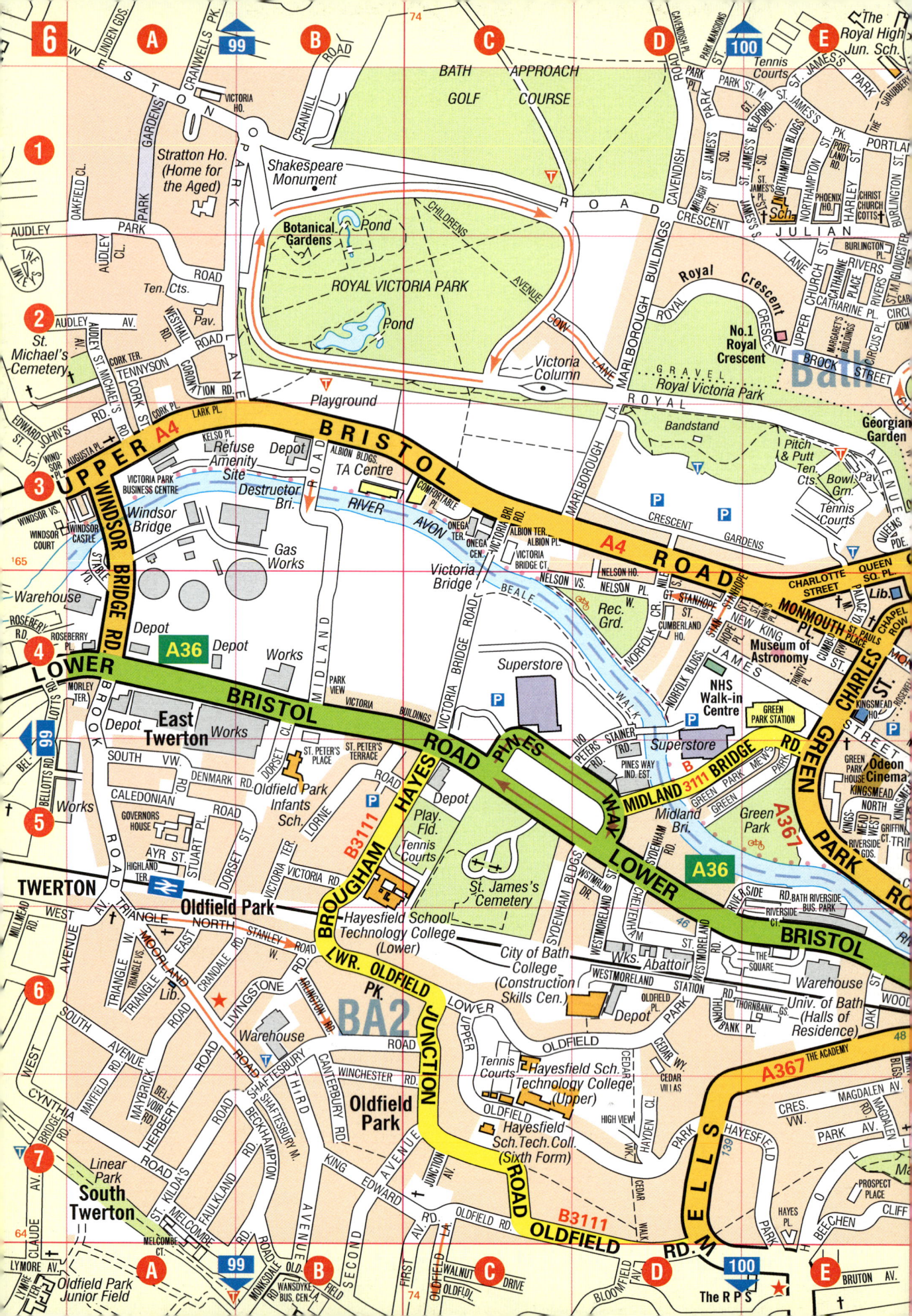

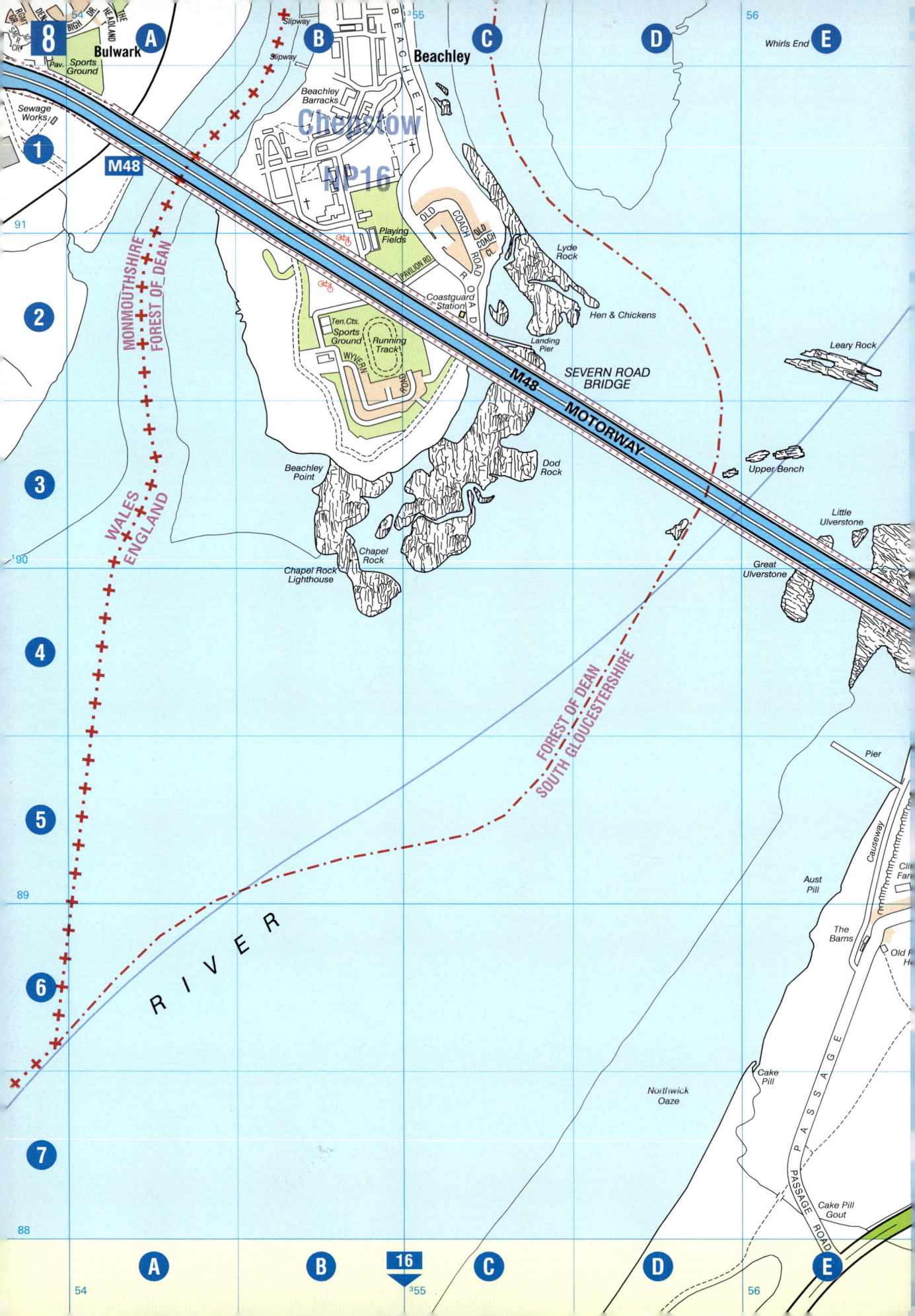

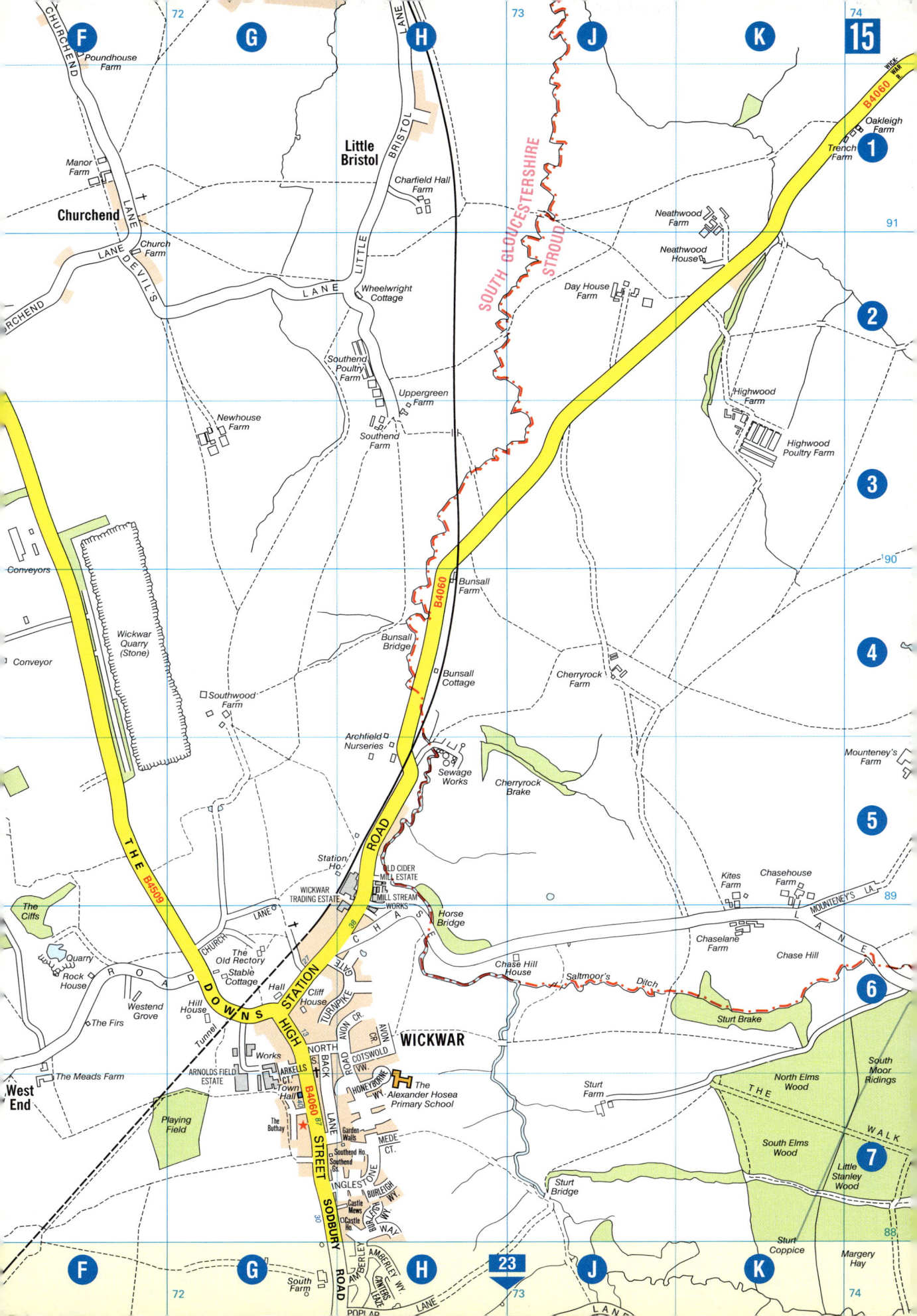

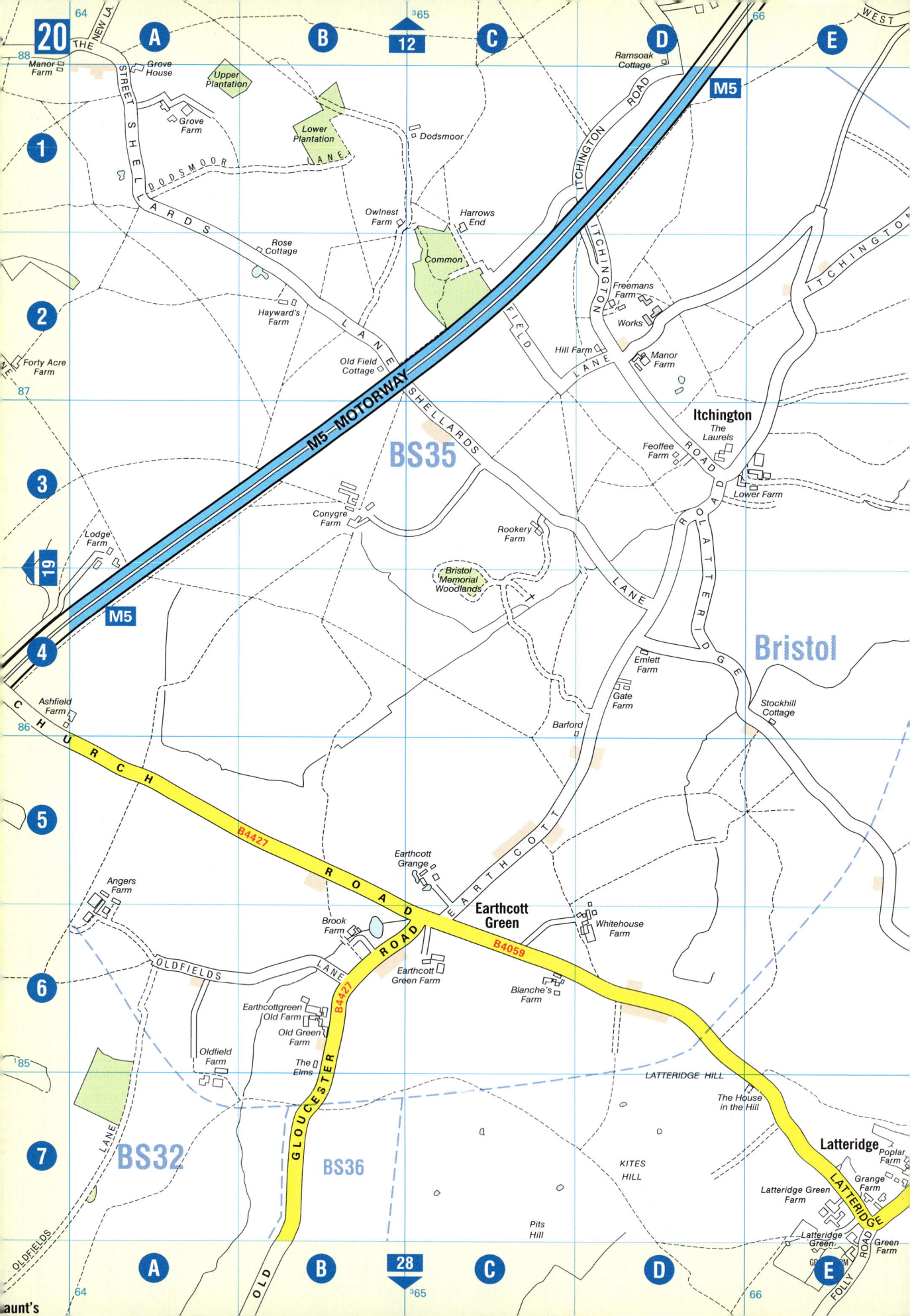

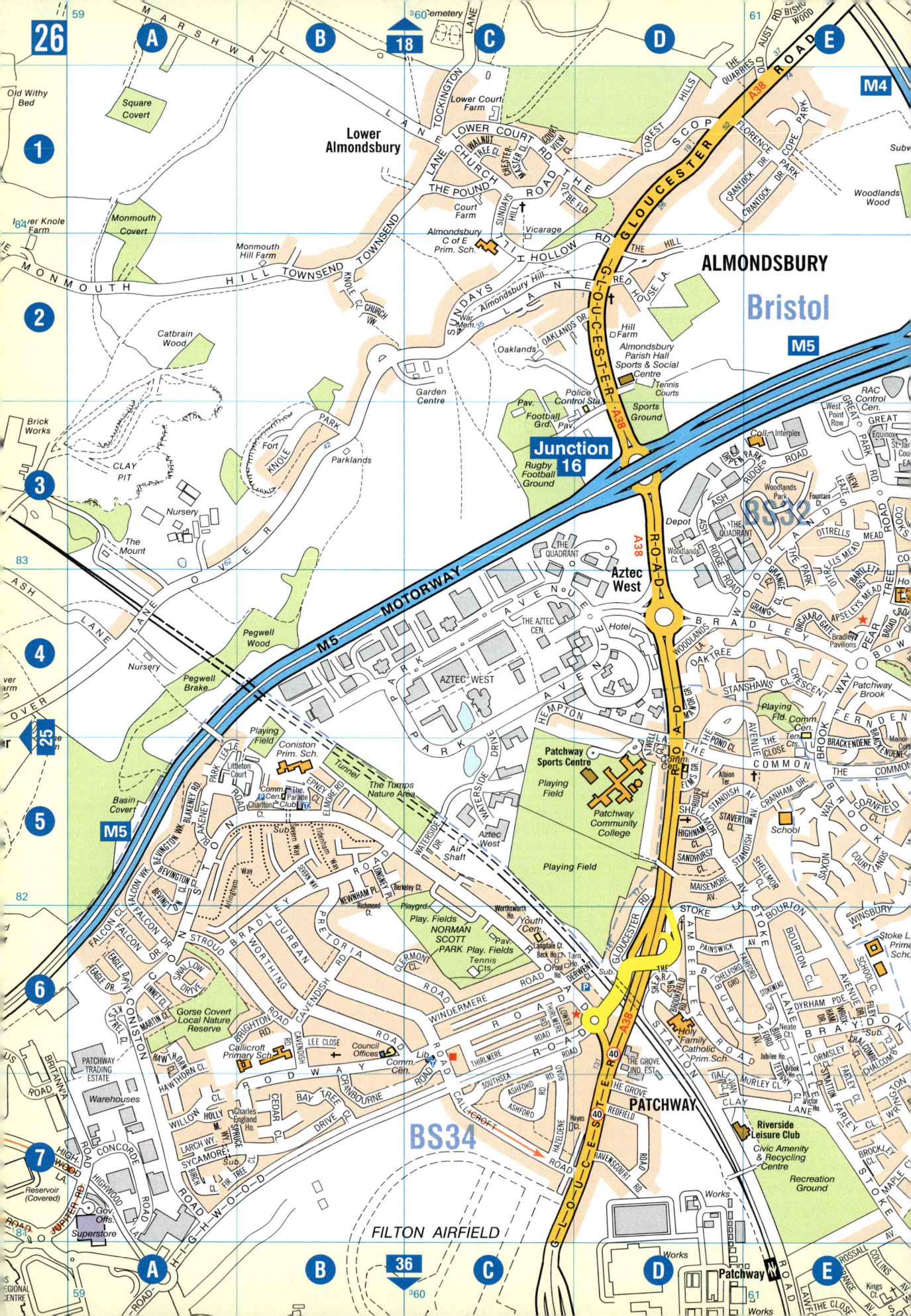

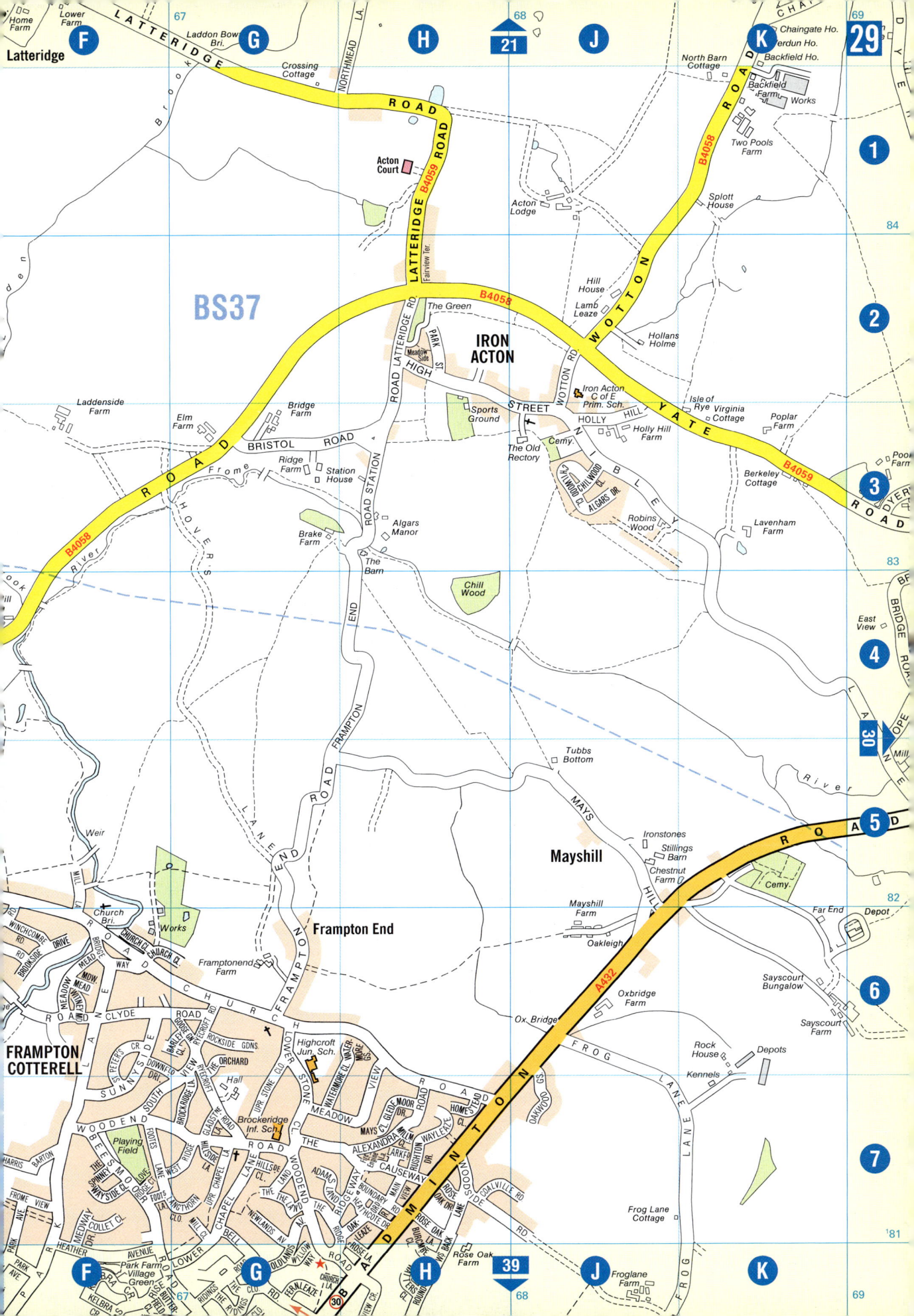

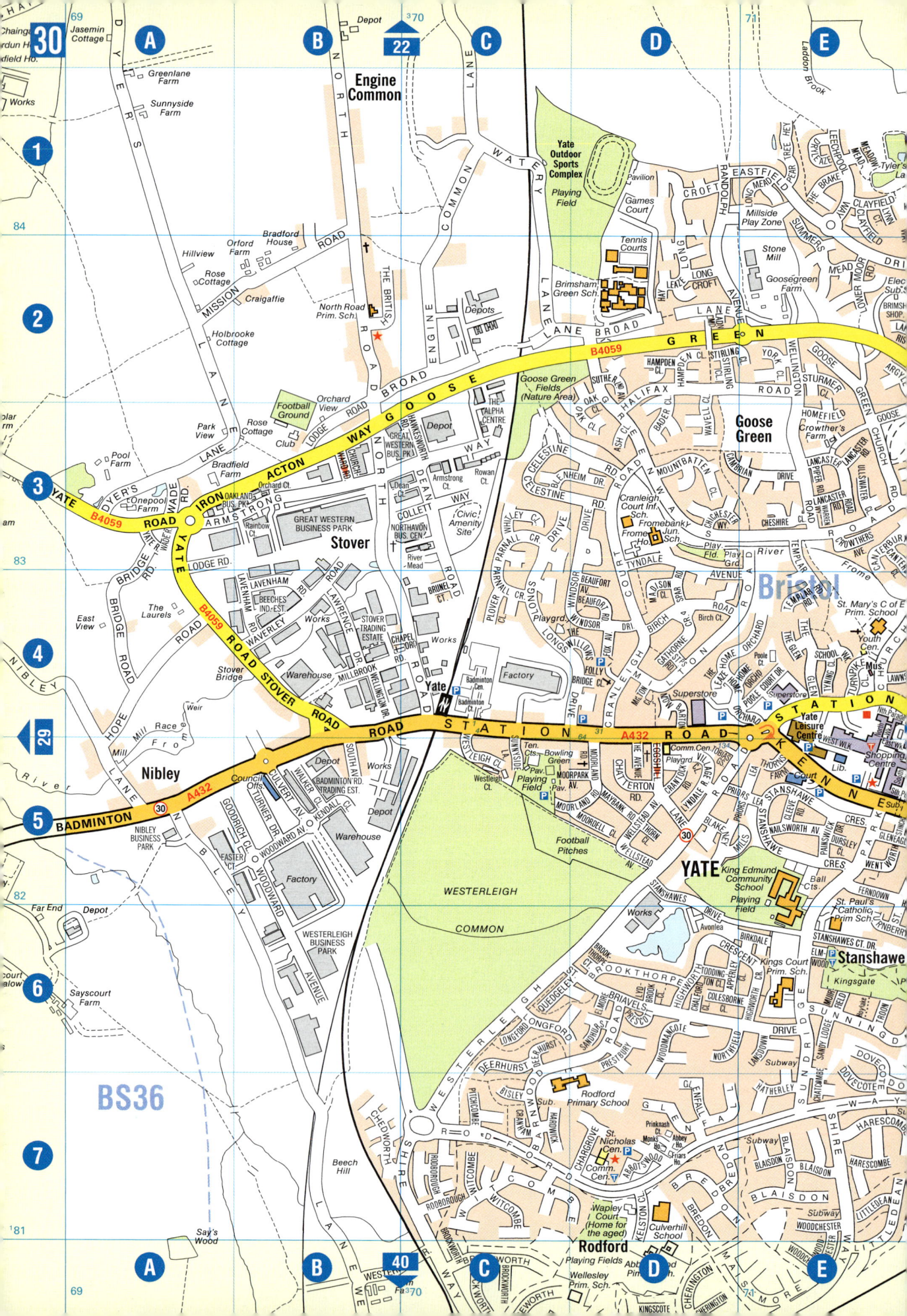

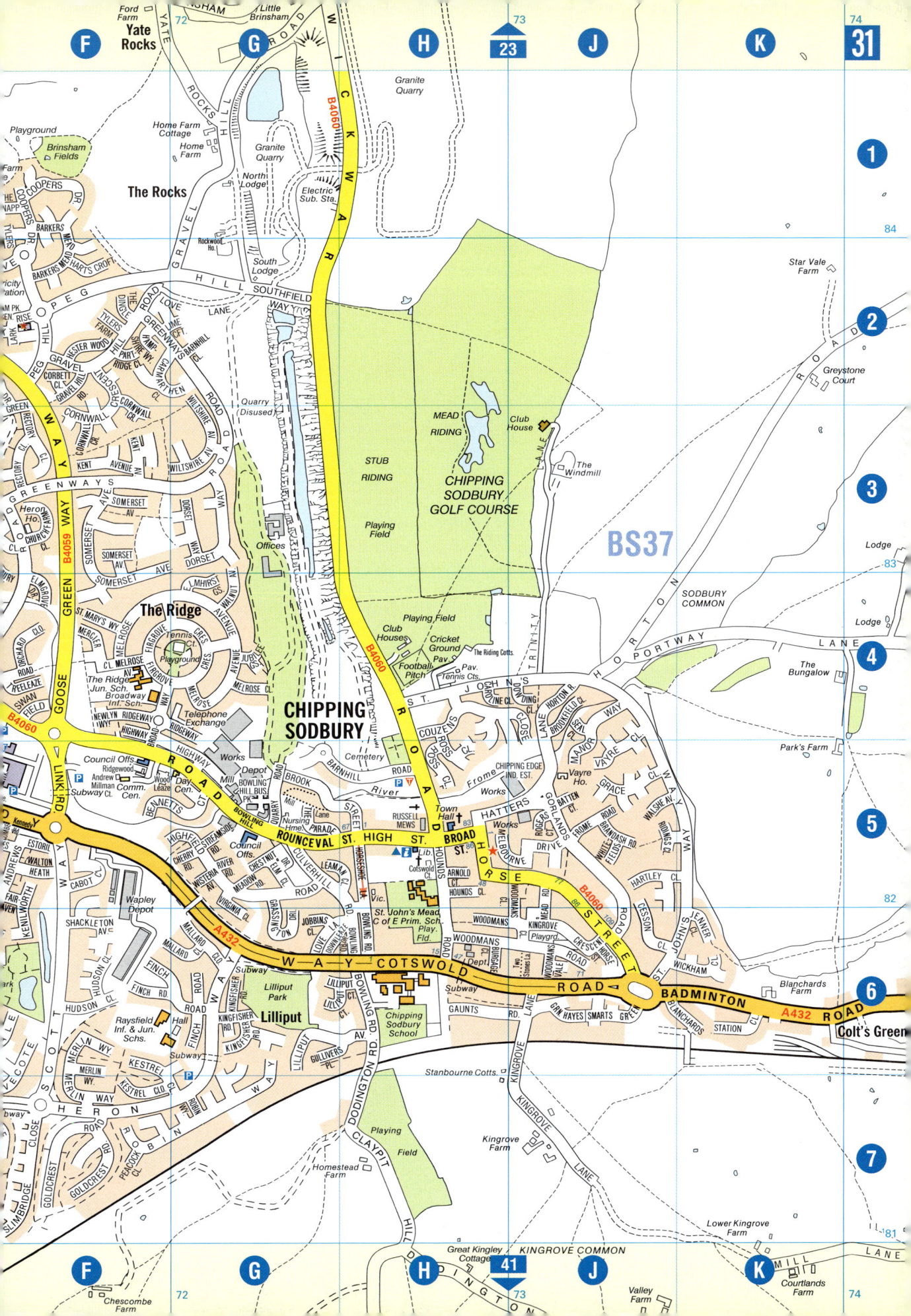

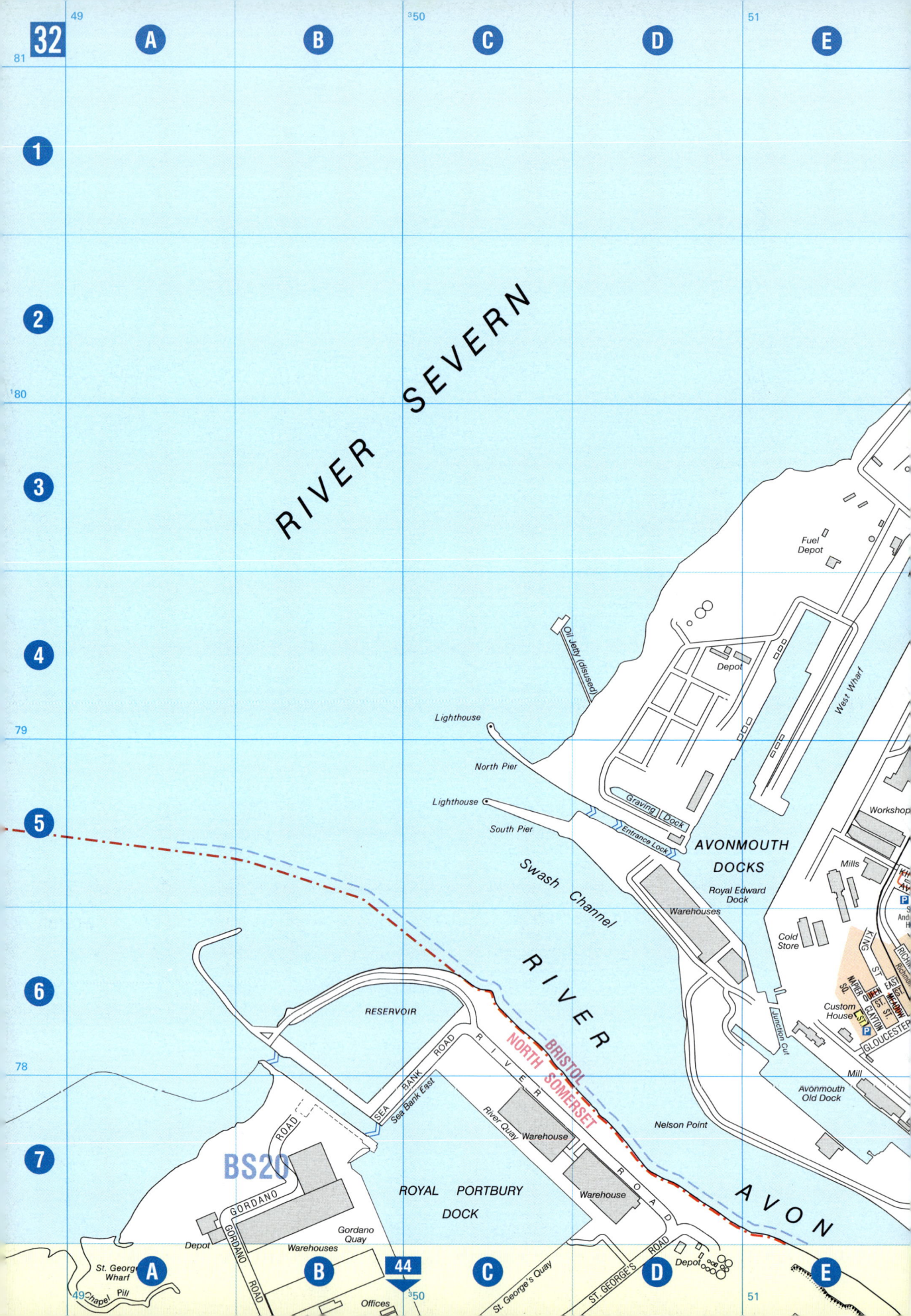

32

A   B   C   D   E

RIVER SEVERN

Fuel
Depot

Oil Jetty (disused)

Lighthouse

North Pier

West Wharf

Lighthouse

South Pier

Graving Dock

Entrance Lock

Workshop

Swash Channel

AVONMOUTH
DOCKS

Mills

Royal Edward
Dock

Warehouses

Cold
Store

RIVER

Custom
House

GLOUCESTER

RESERVOIR

BRISTOL

NORTH SOMERSET

Junction Cut

Mill

Avonmouth
Old Dock

Nelson Point

SEA BANK ROAD

Sea Bank East

RIVER

River Quay

Warehouse

ROAD

AVON

BS20

GORDANO ROAD

ROYAL PORTBURY

DOCK

Warehouse

Depot

Gordano Quay

Warehouses

44

St. George's Quay

ST. GEORGE'S ROAD

Depot

St. George
Wharf

Chapel Pill

Offices

A   B   C   D   E

1
2
3
4
5
6
7

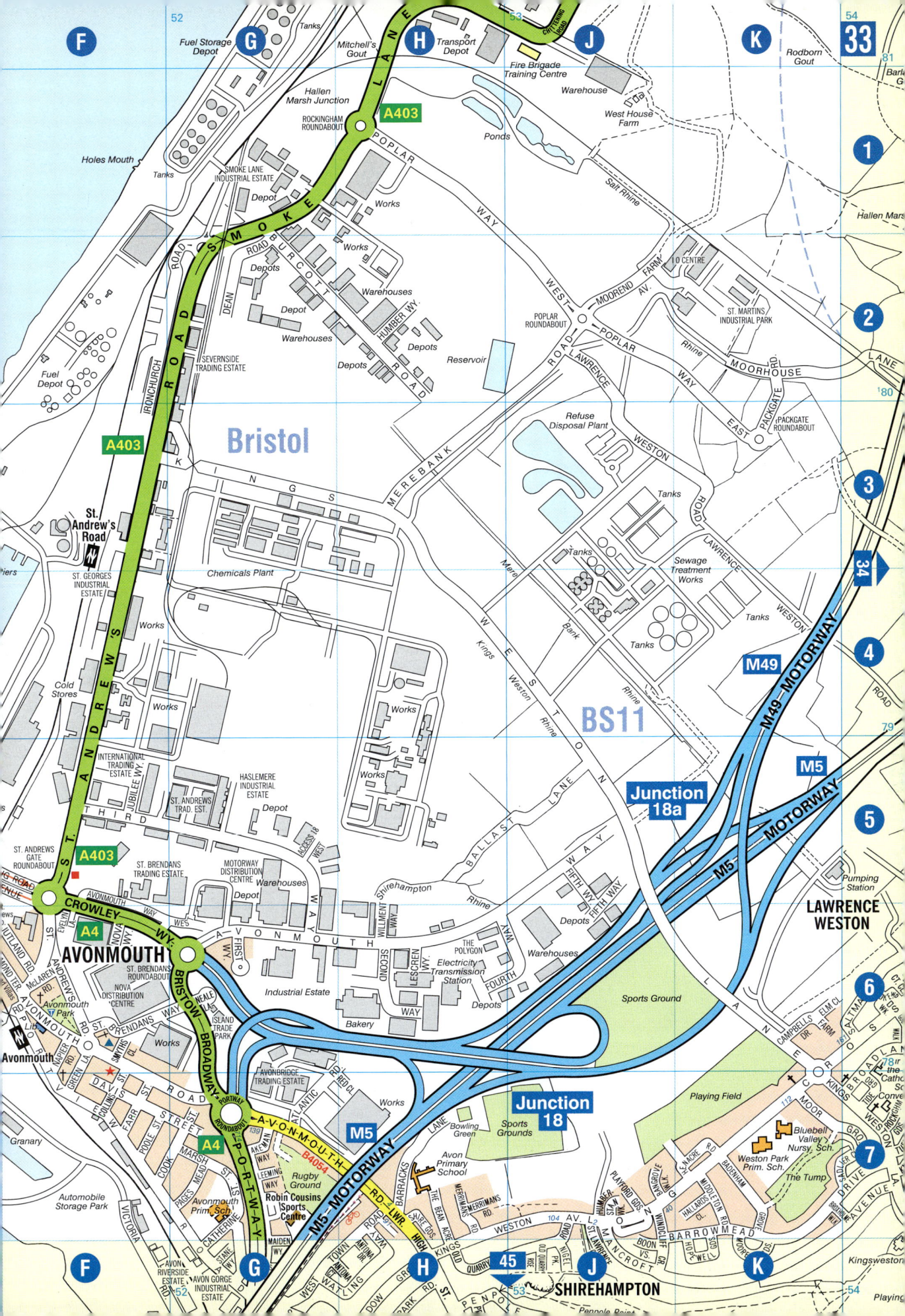

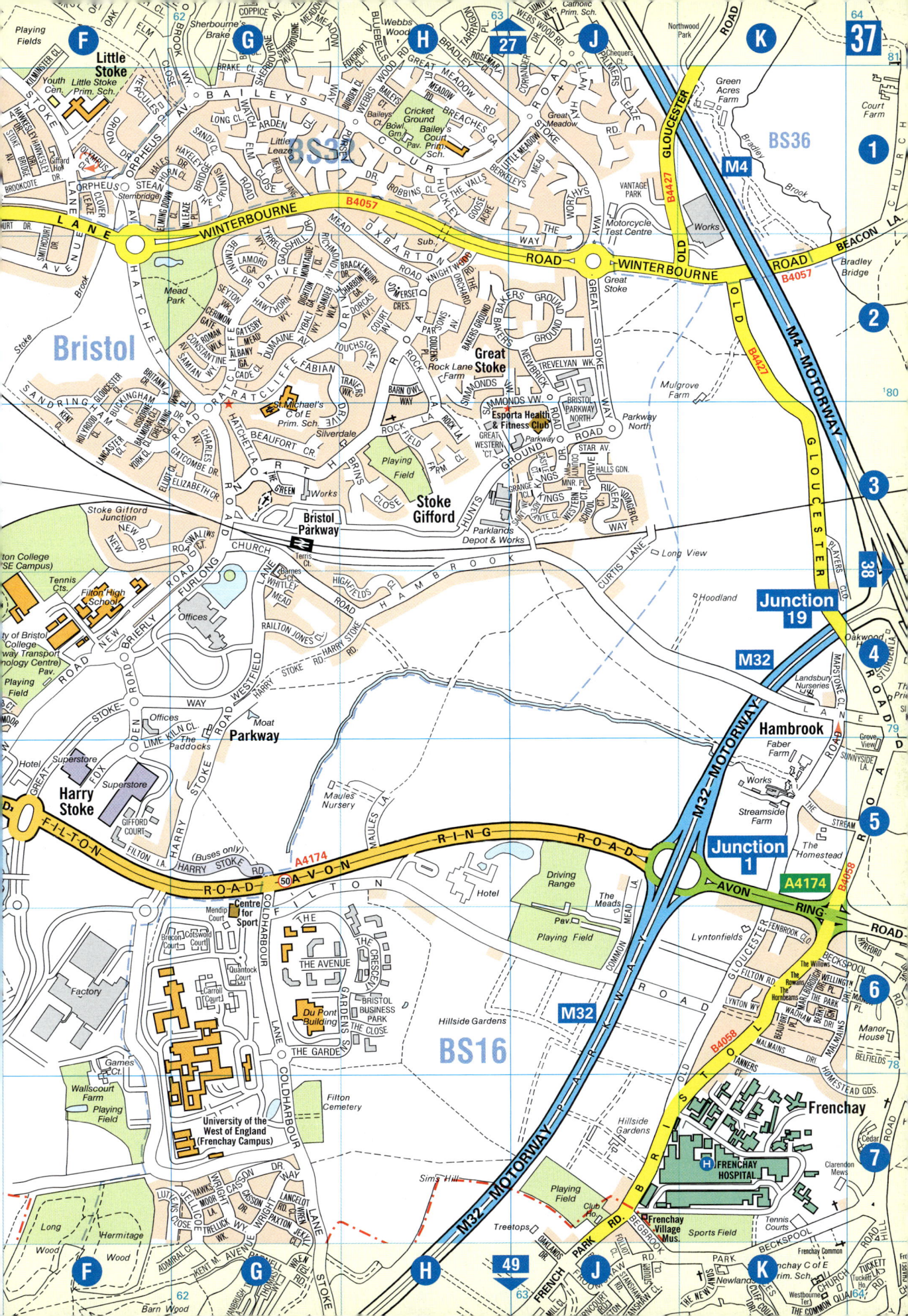

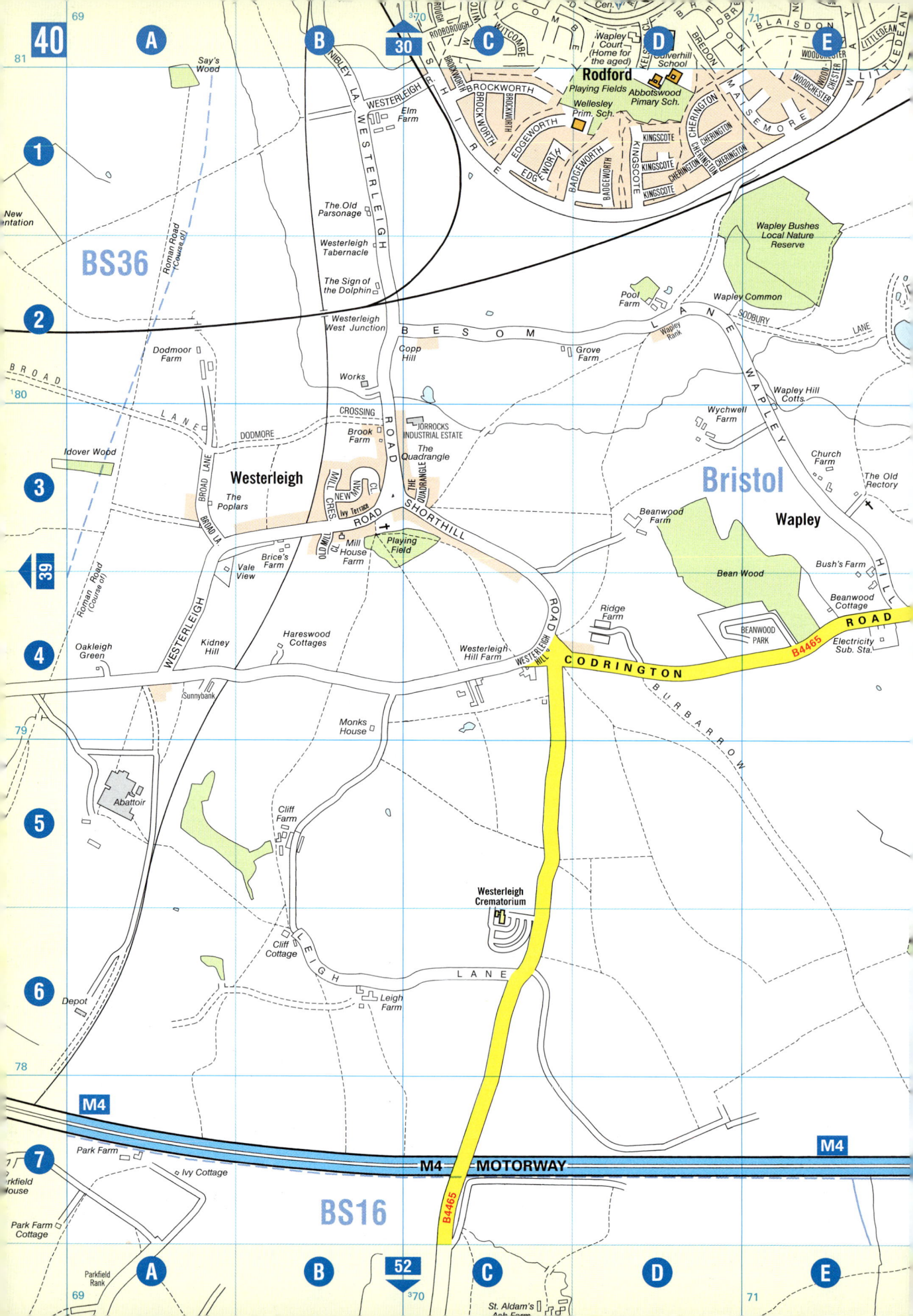

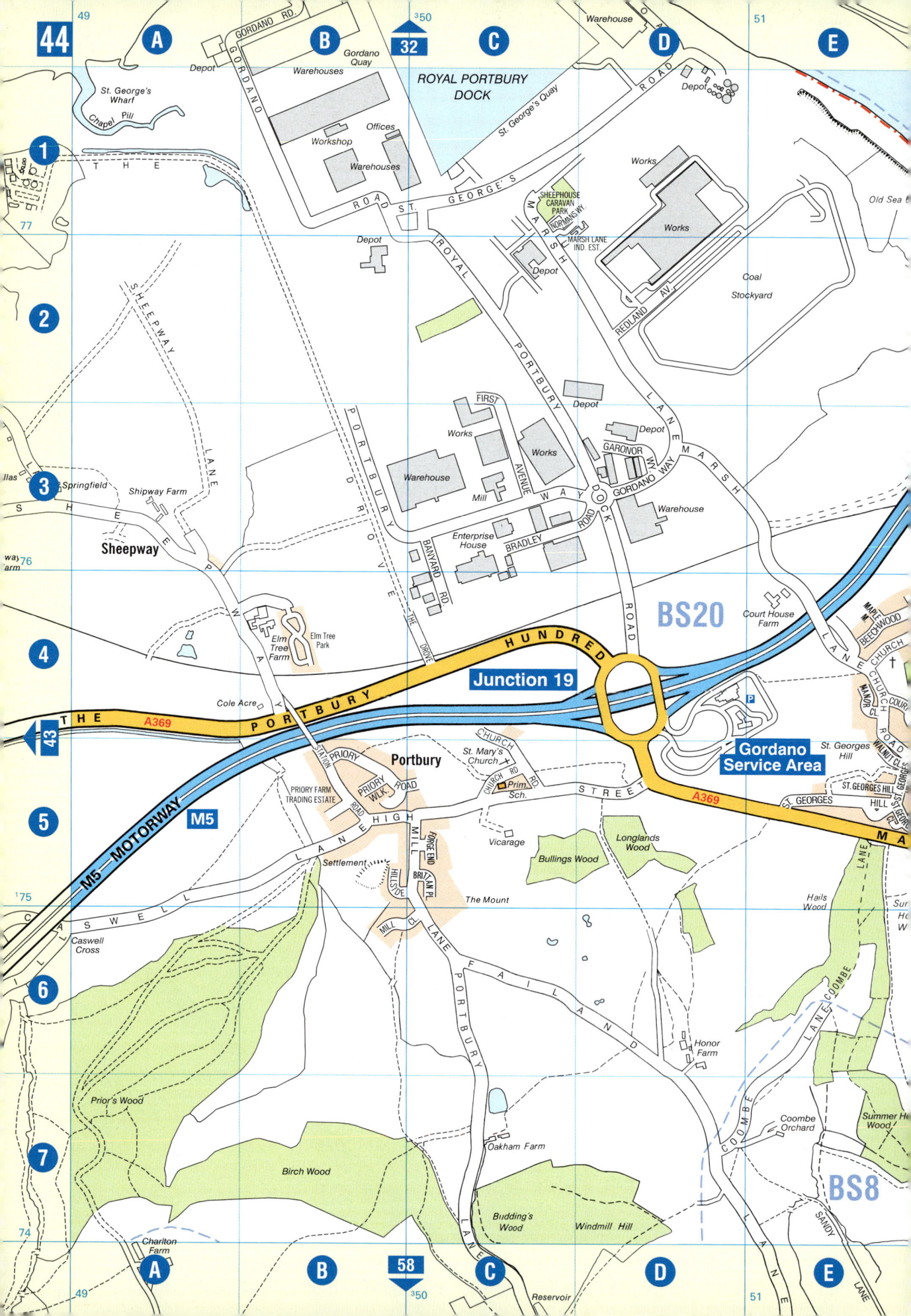

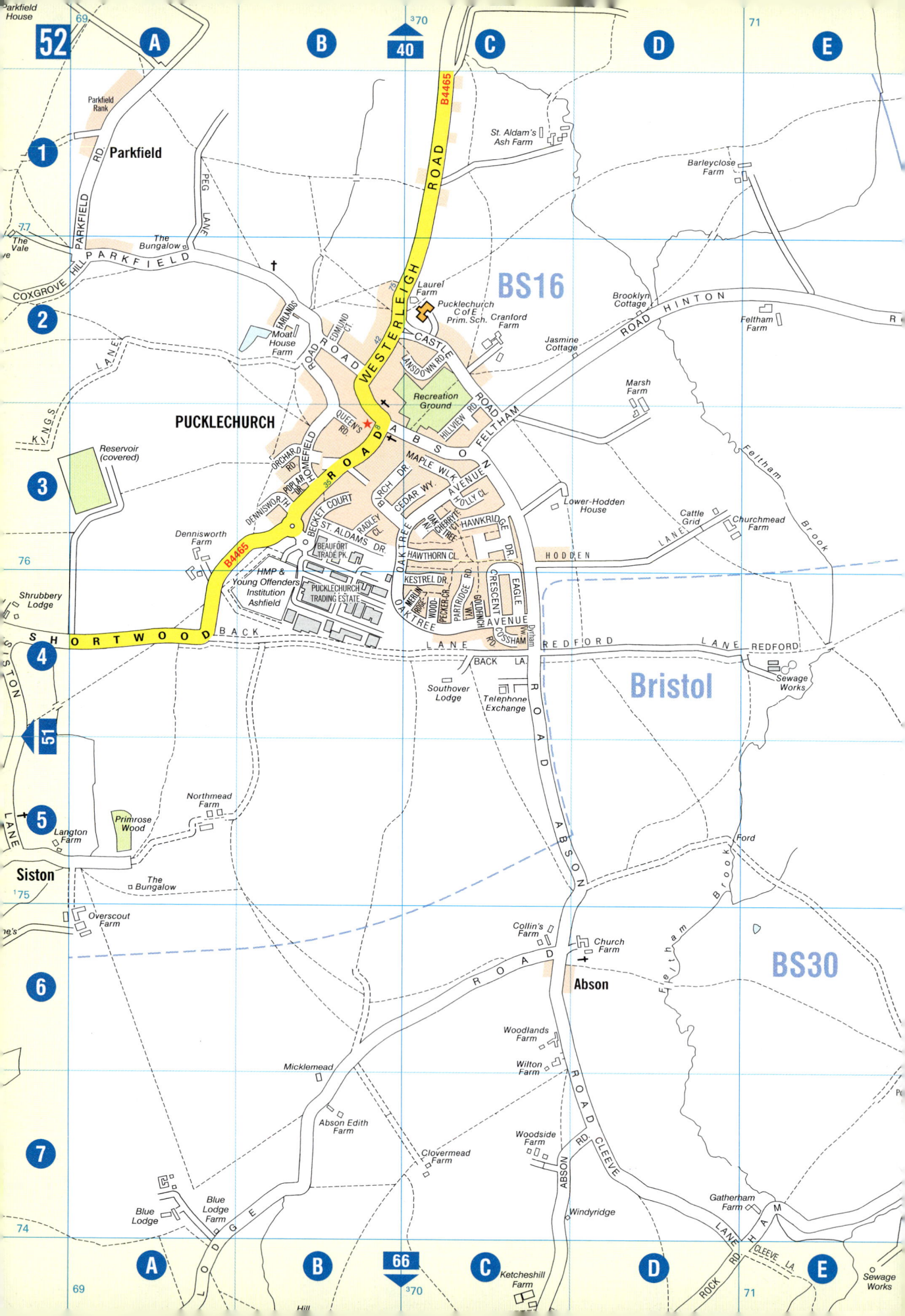

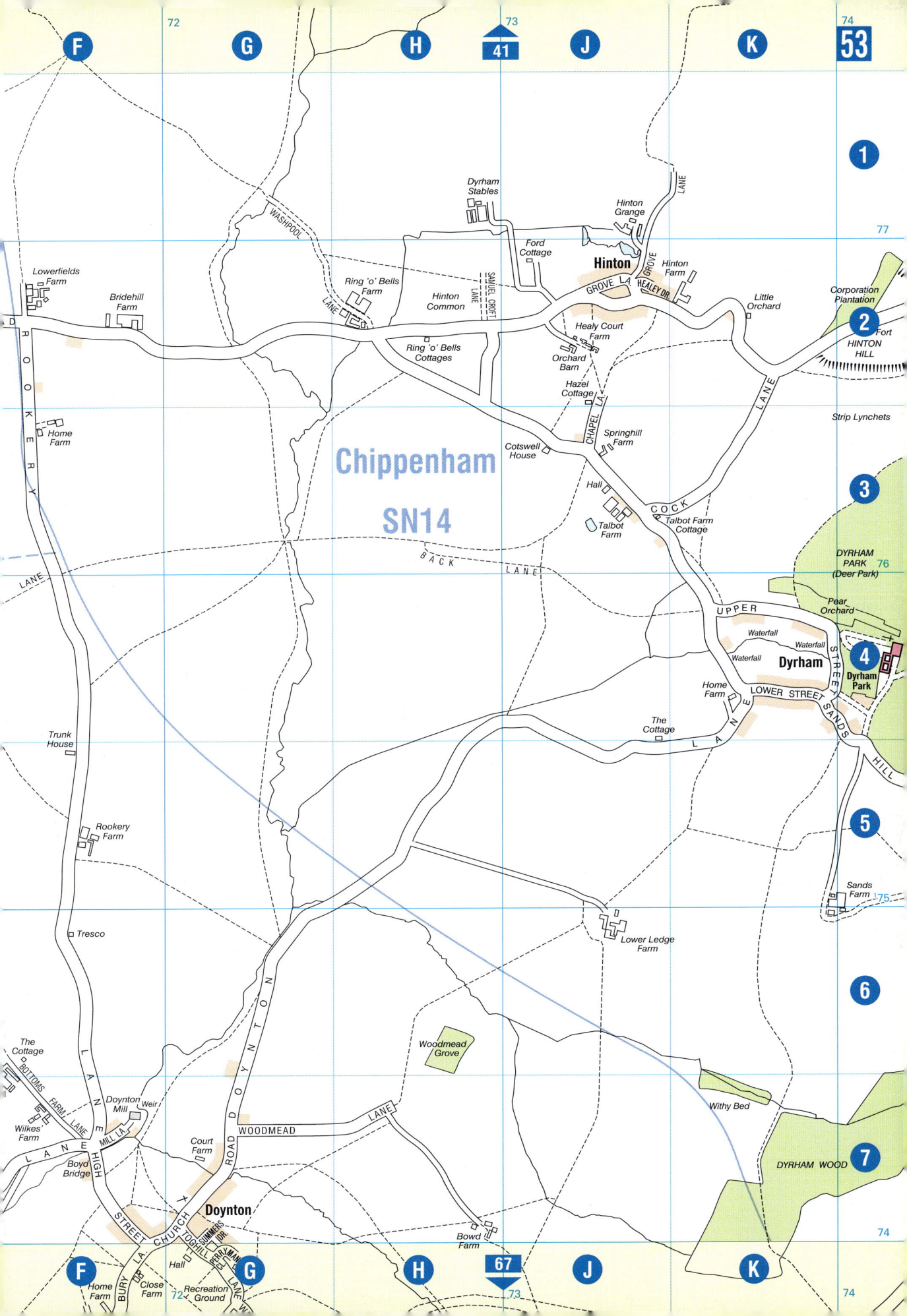

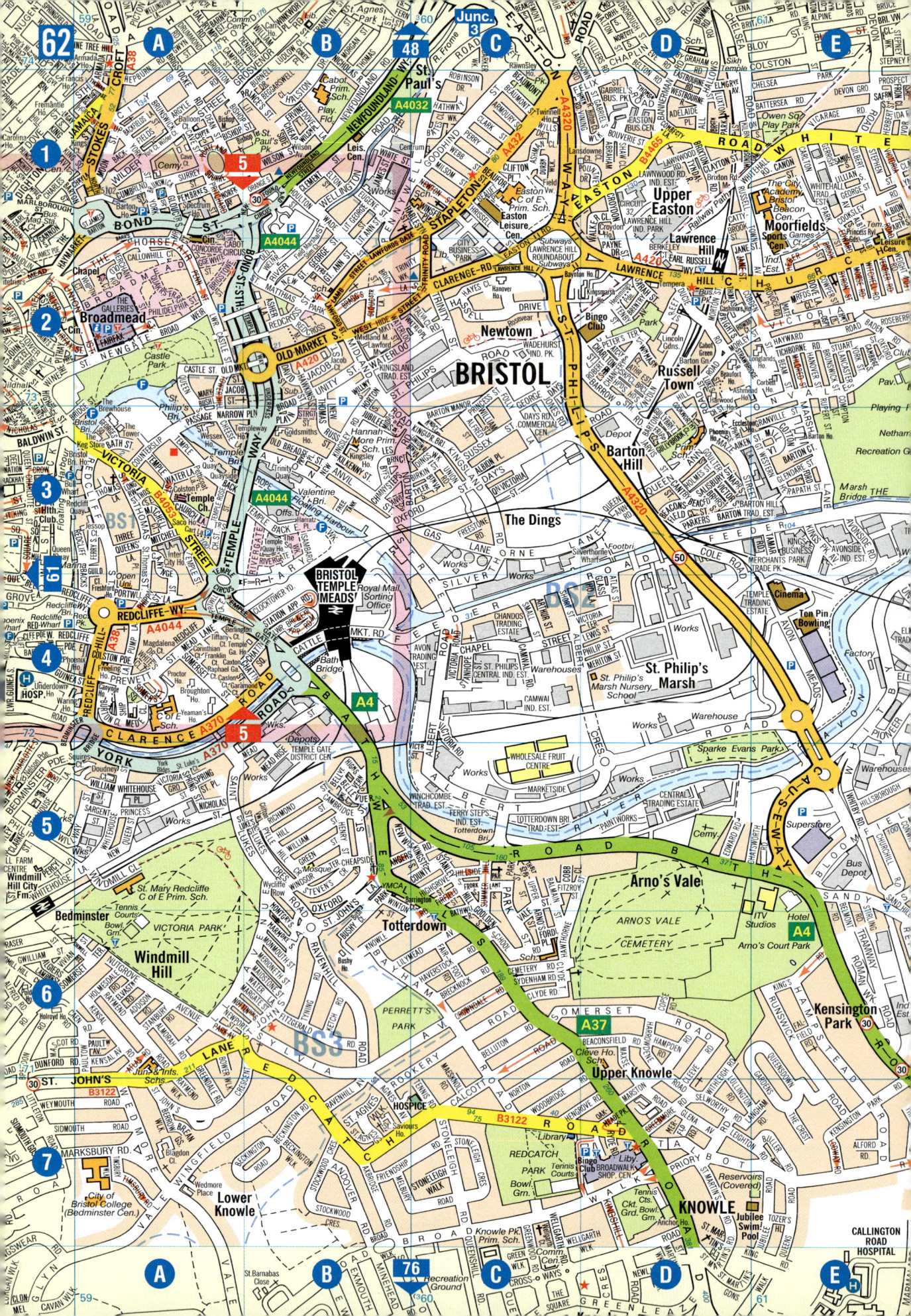

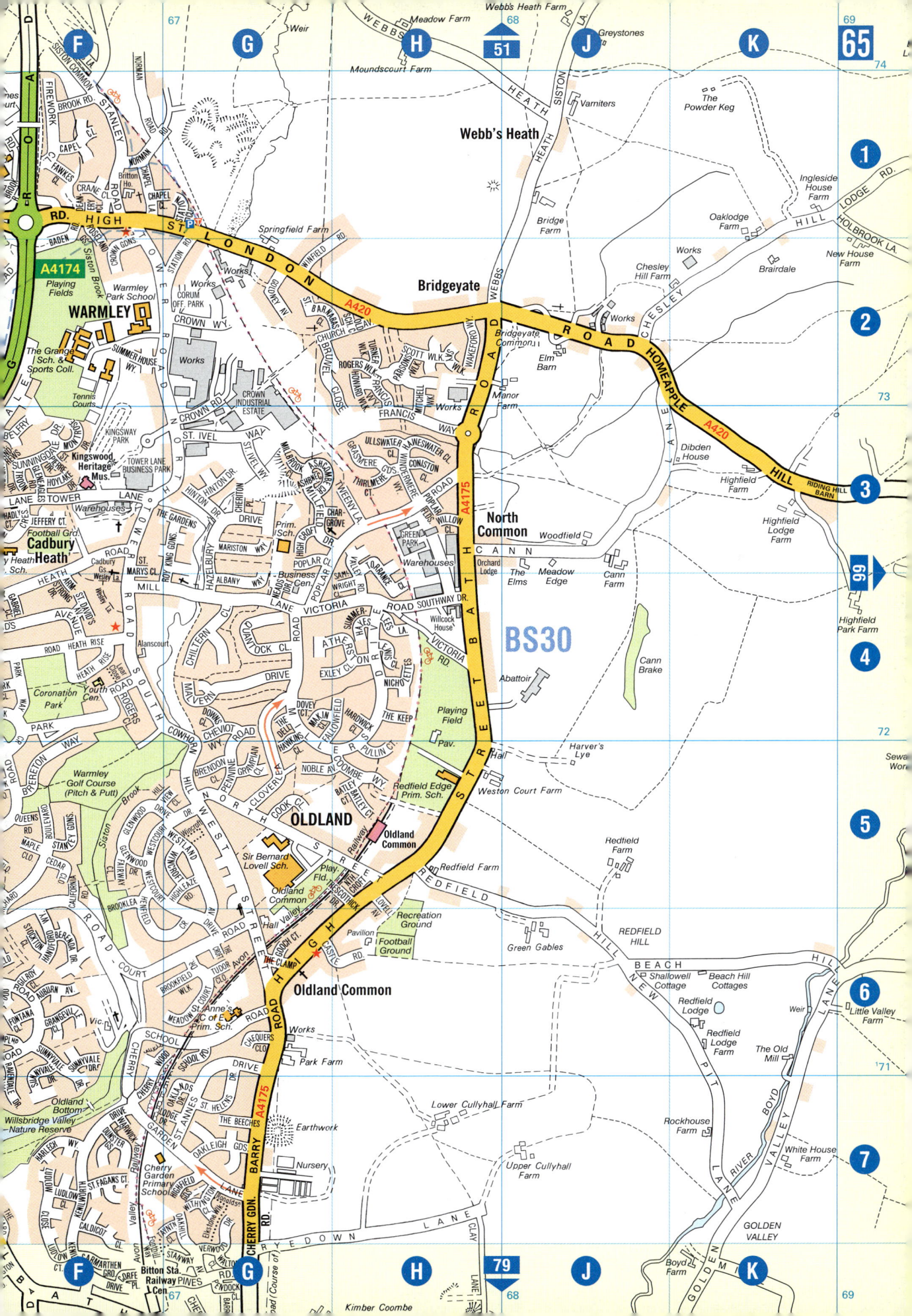

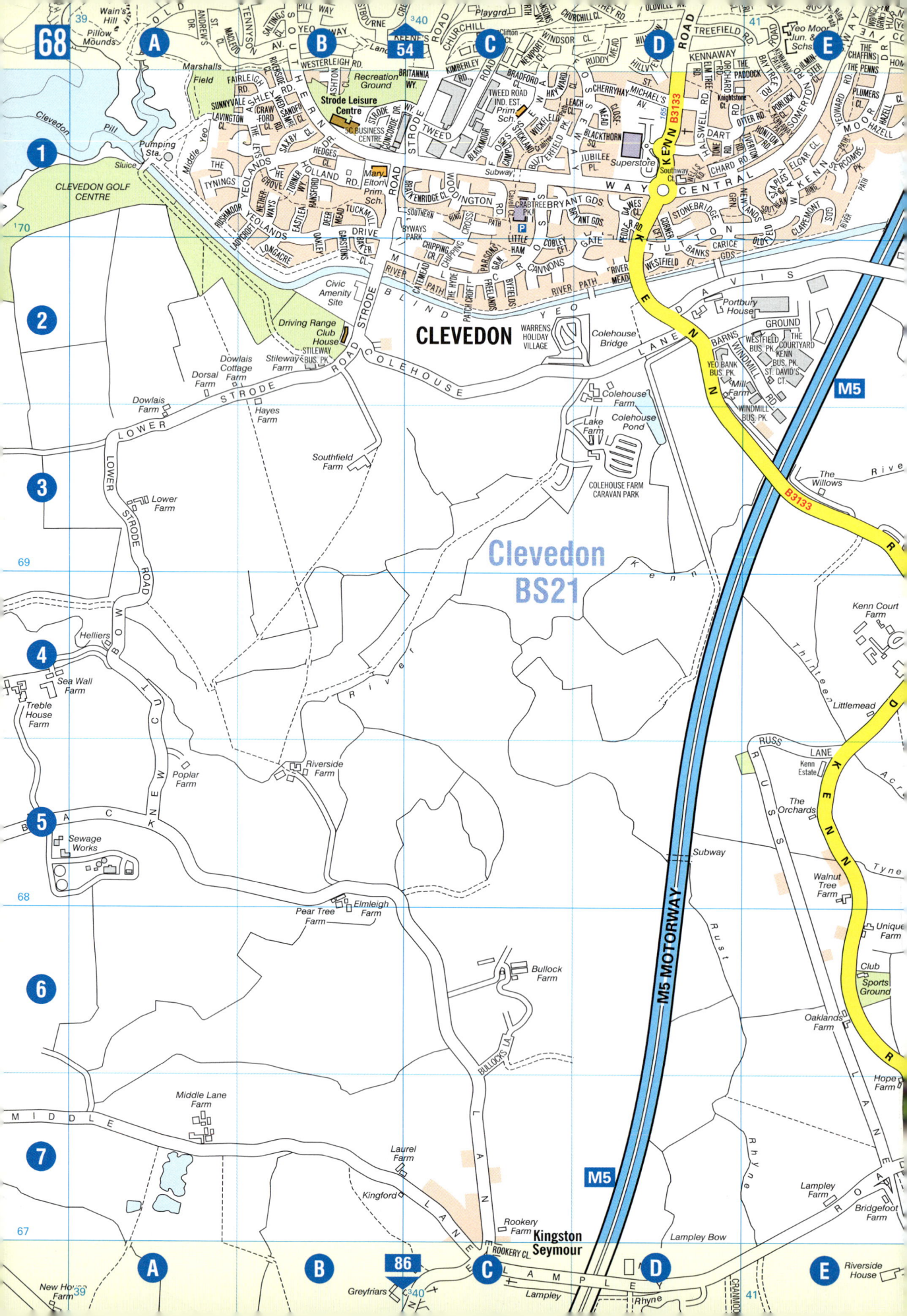

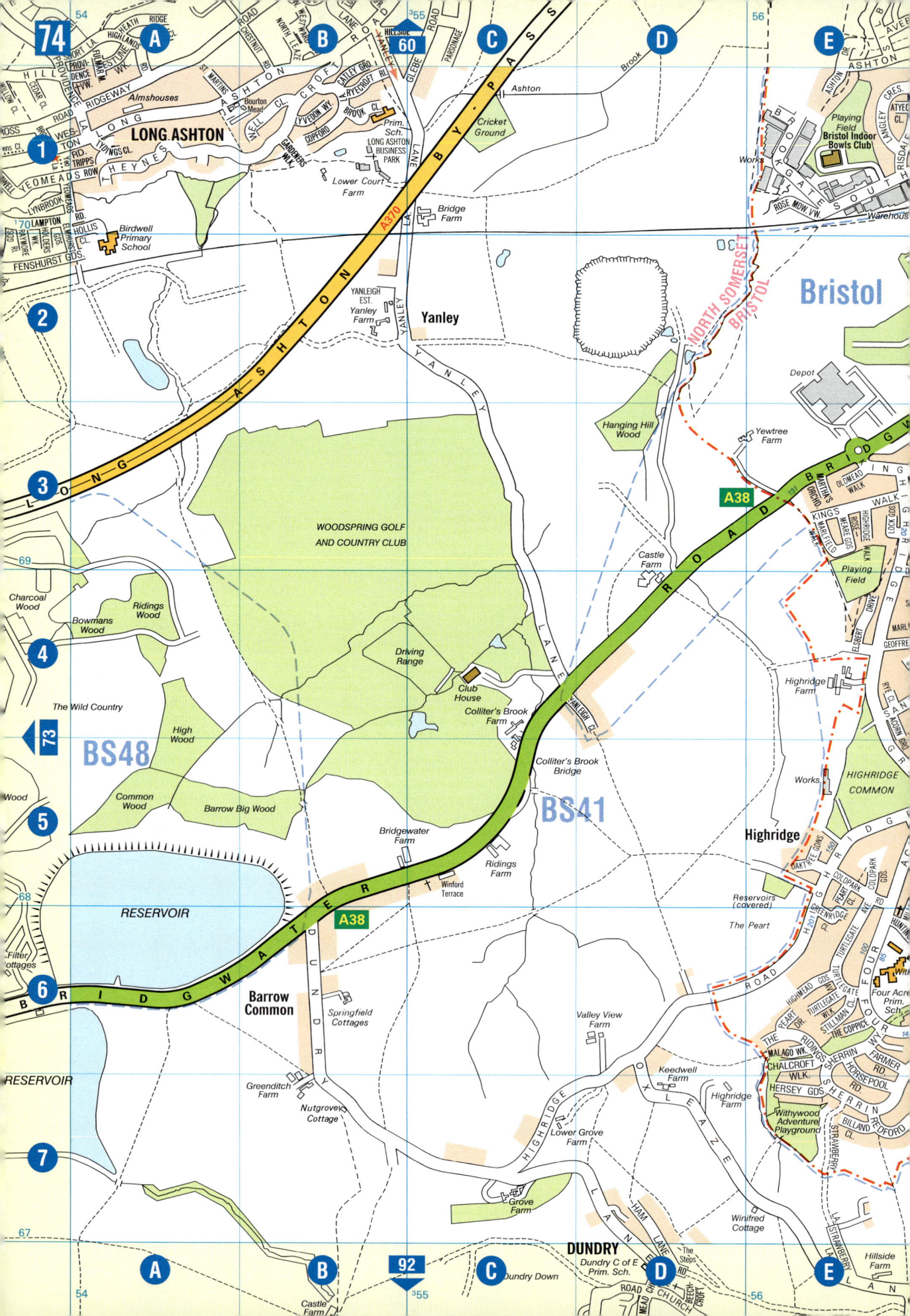

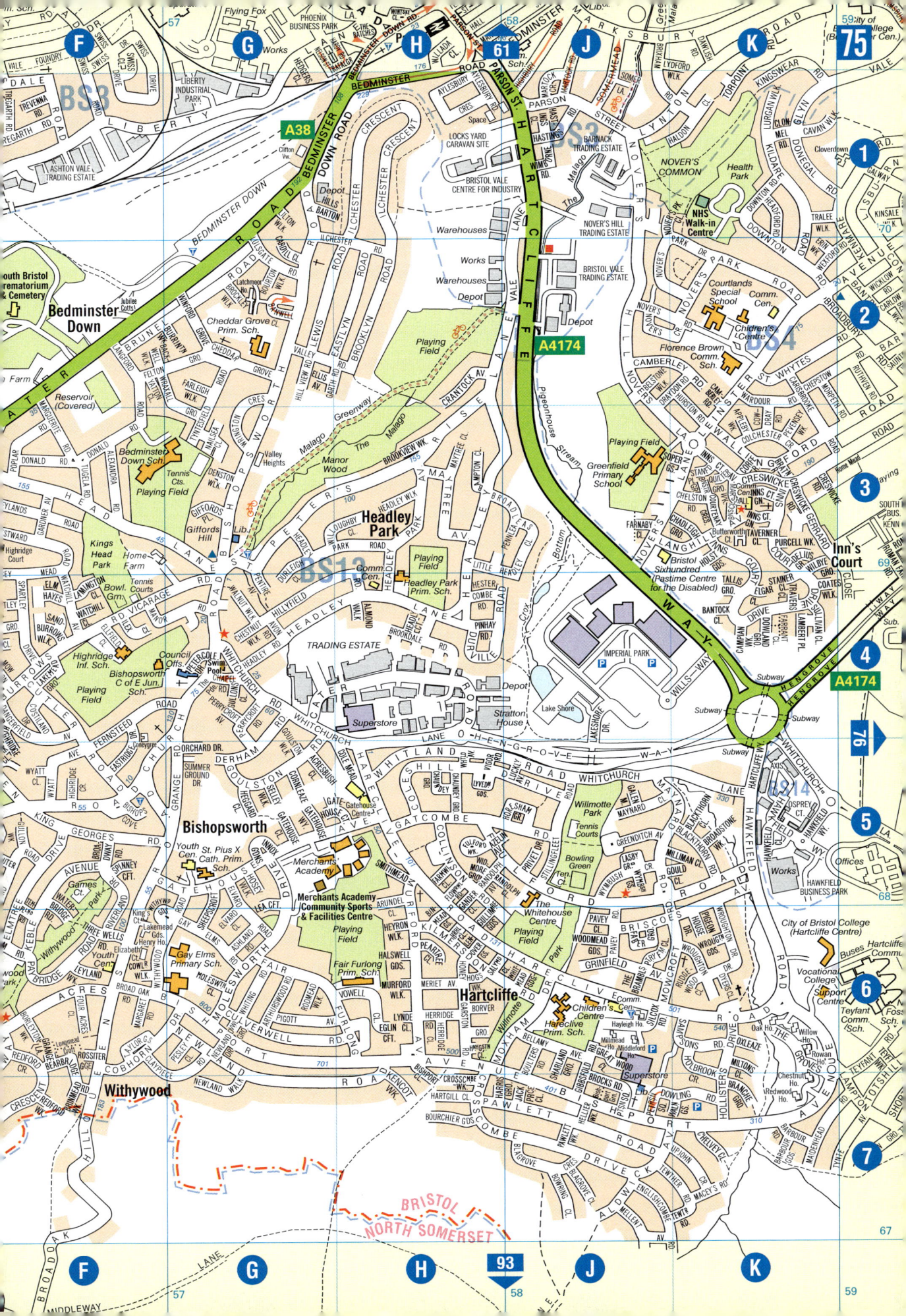

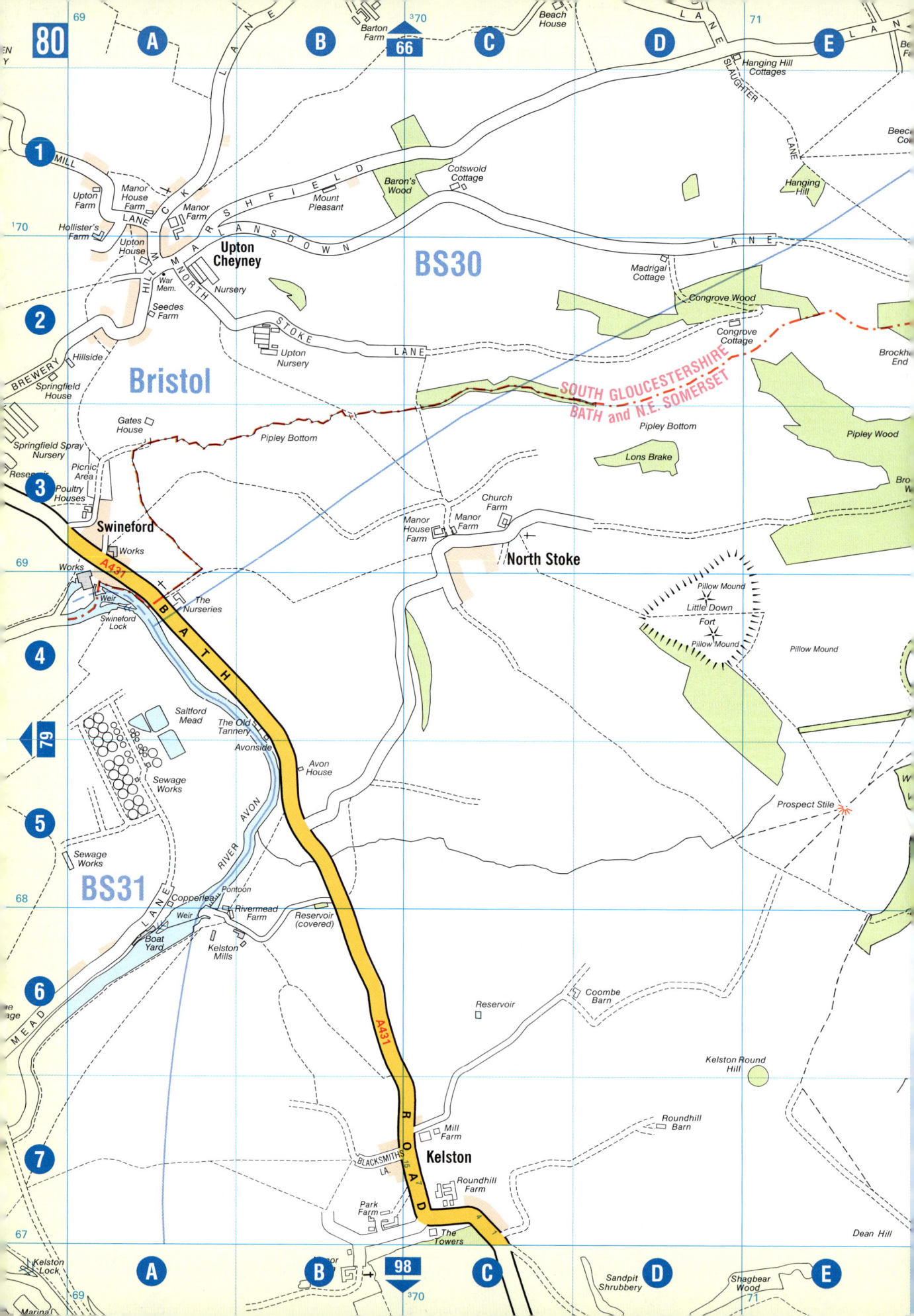

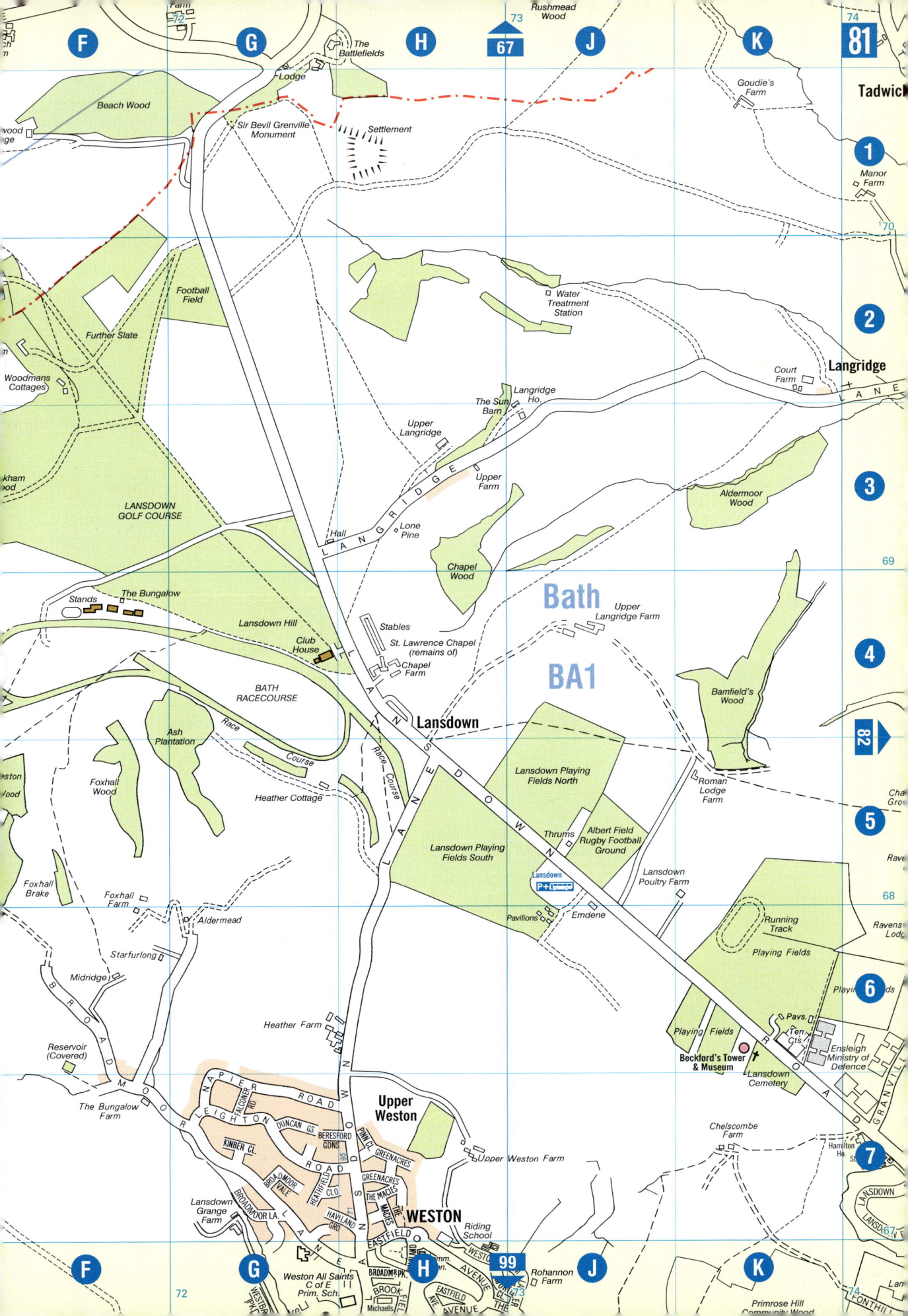

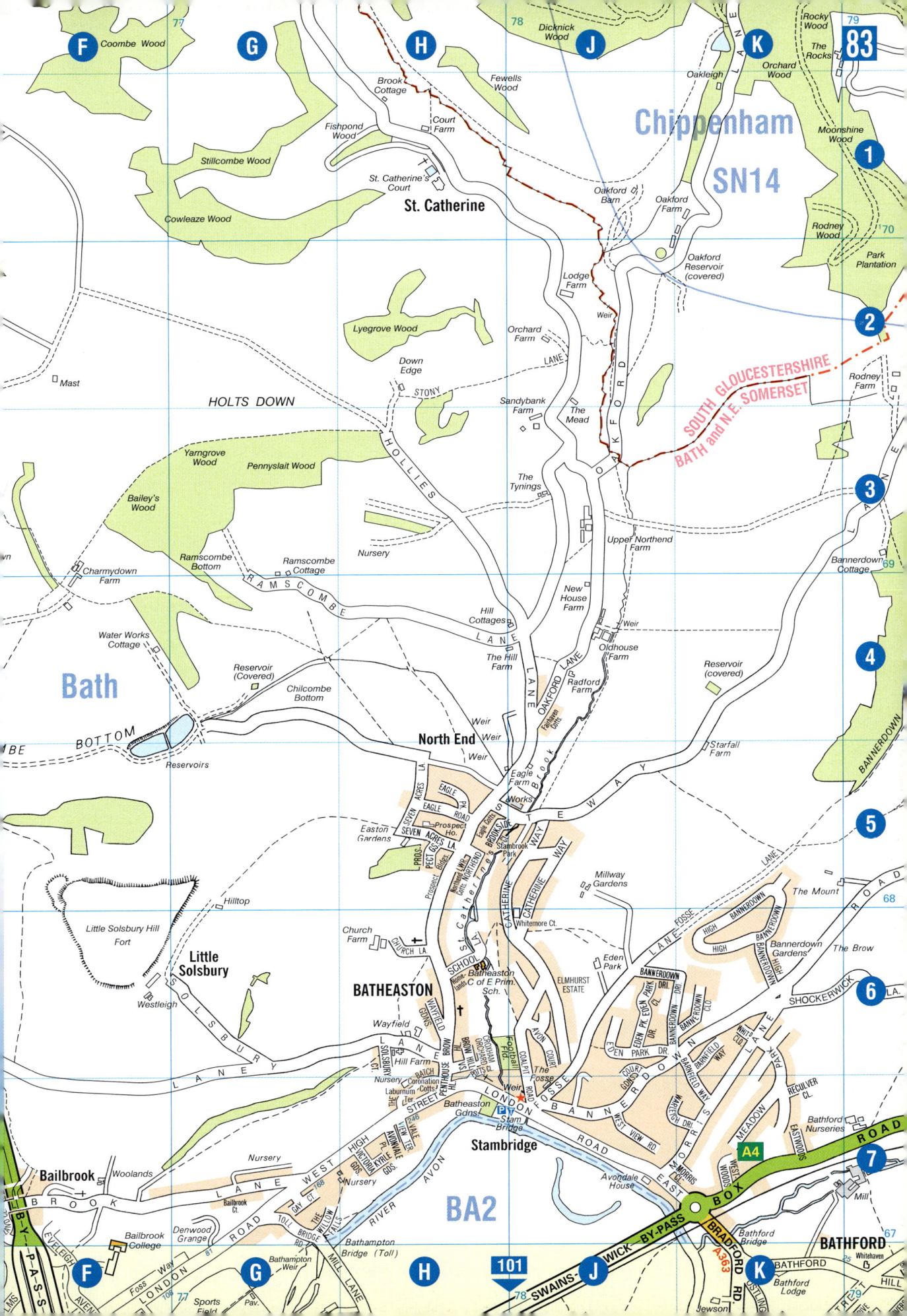

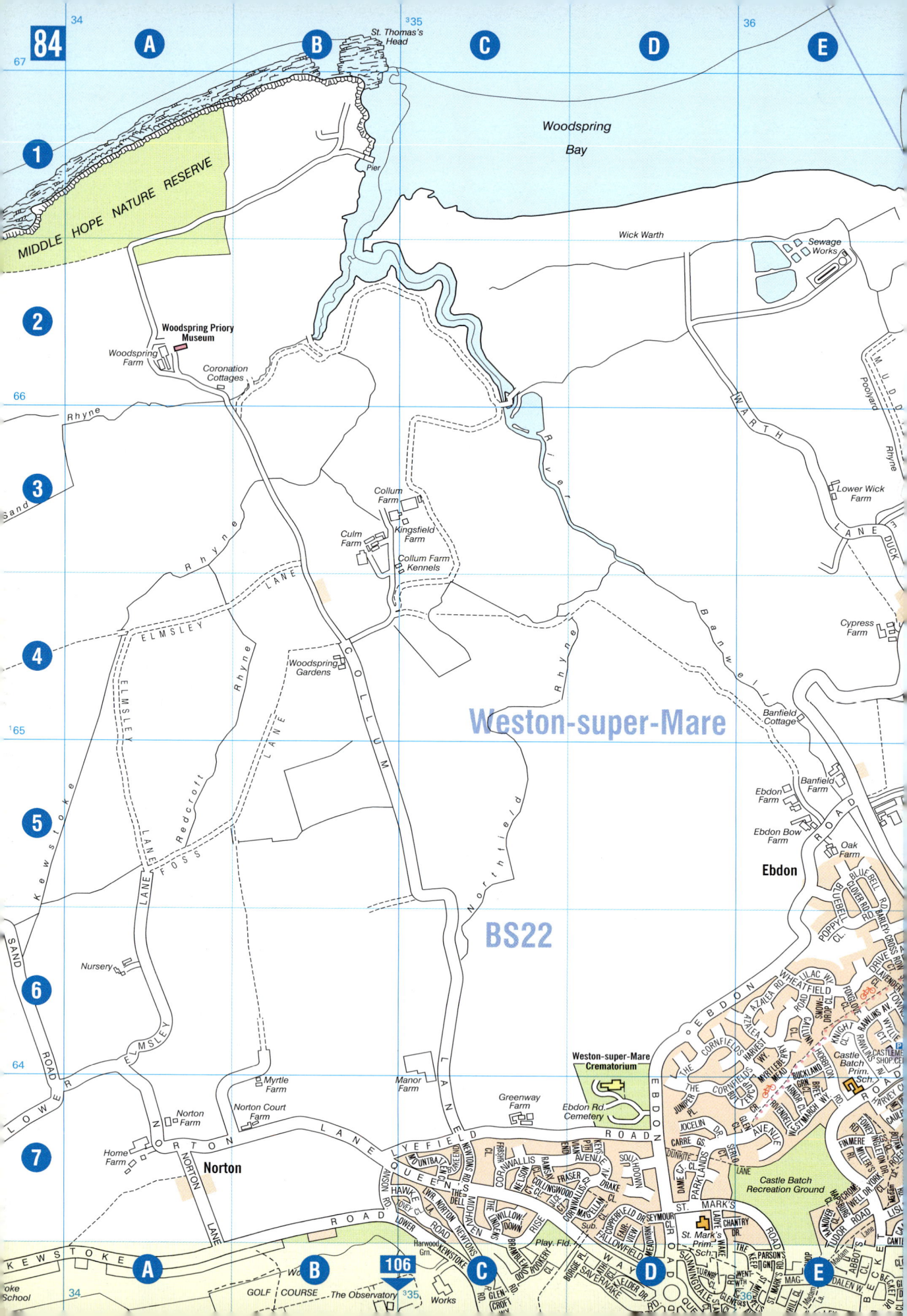

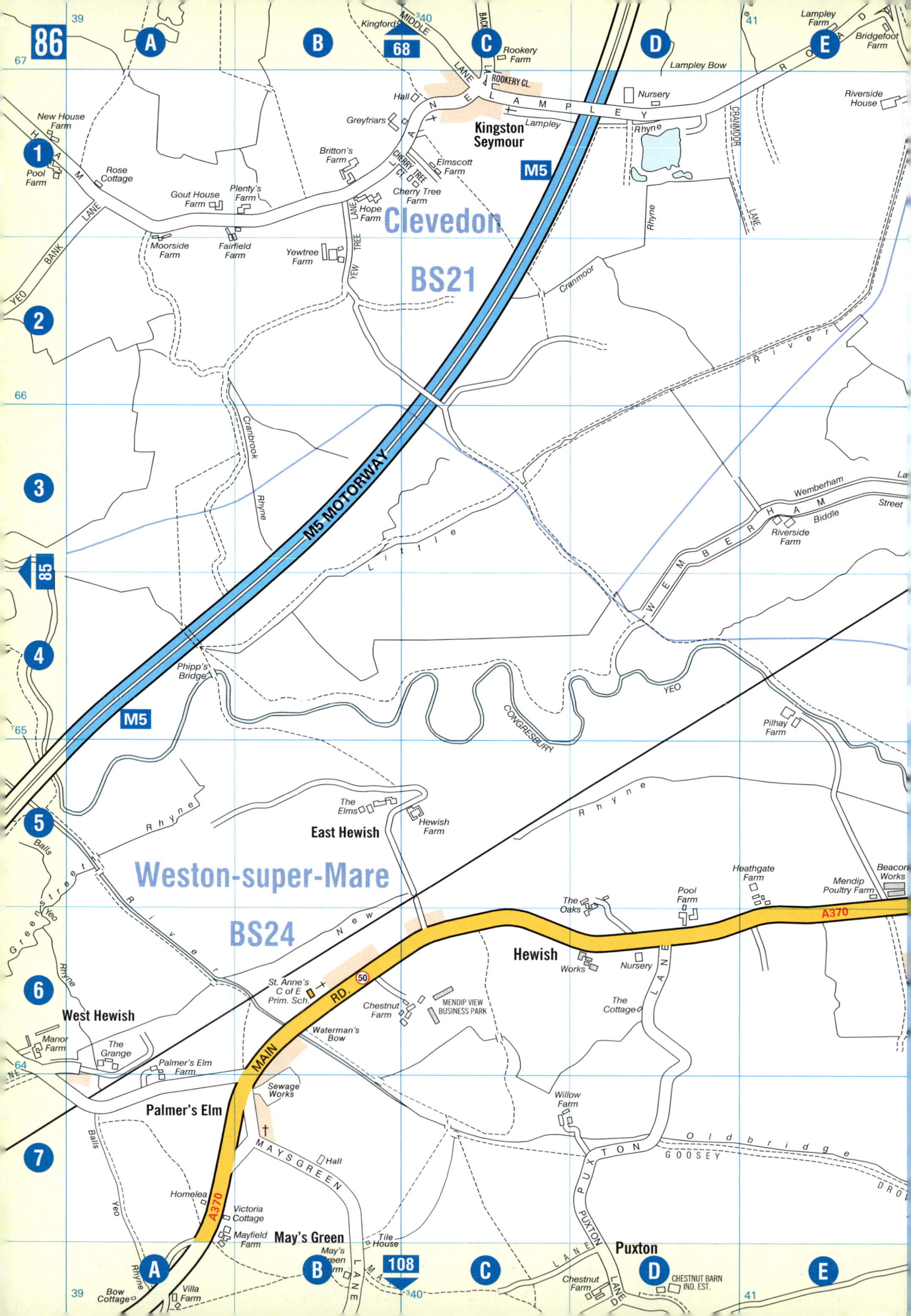

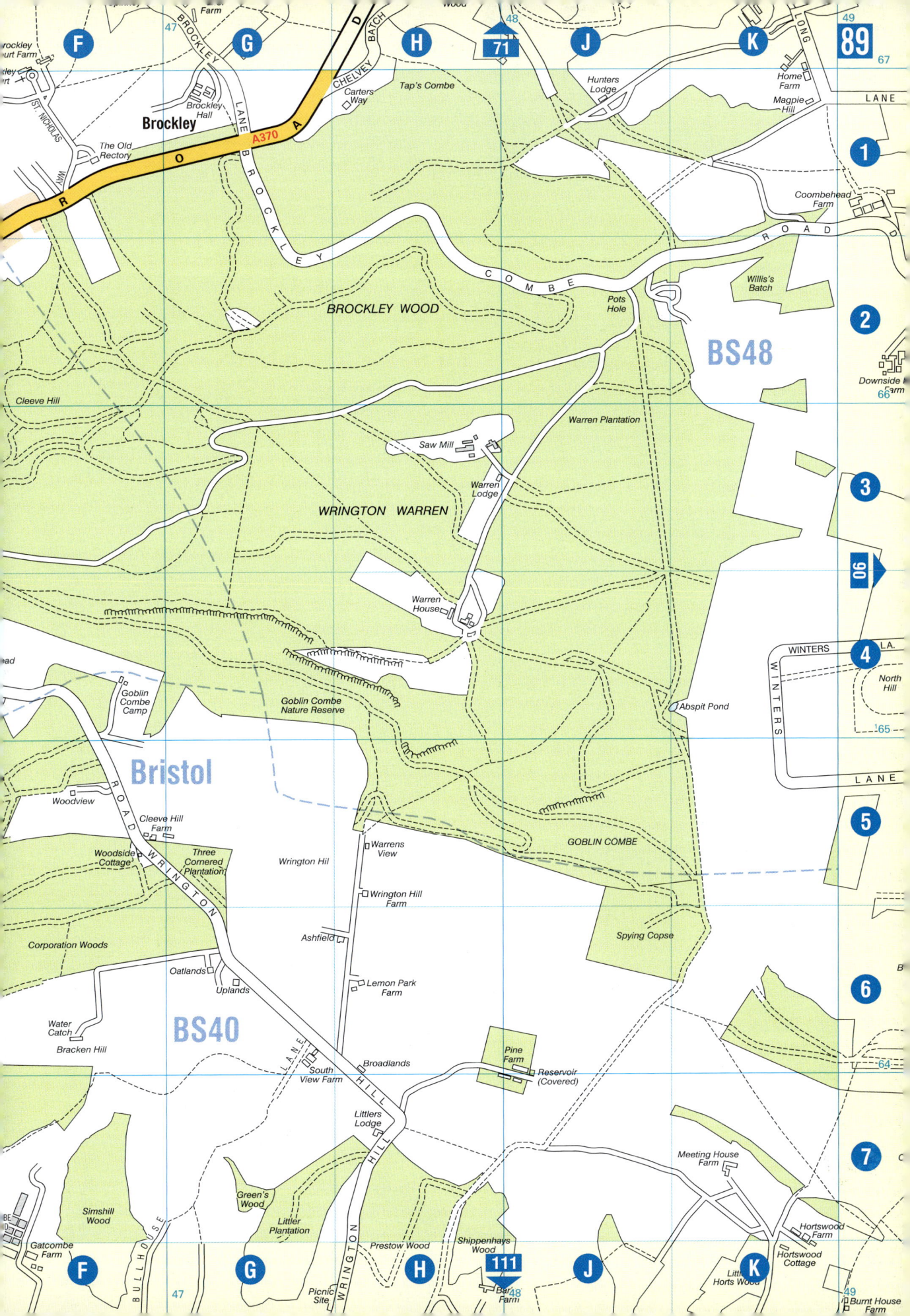

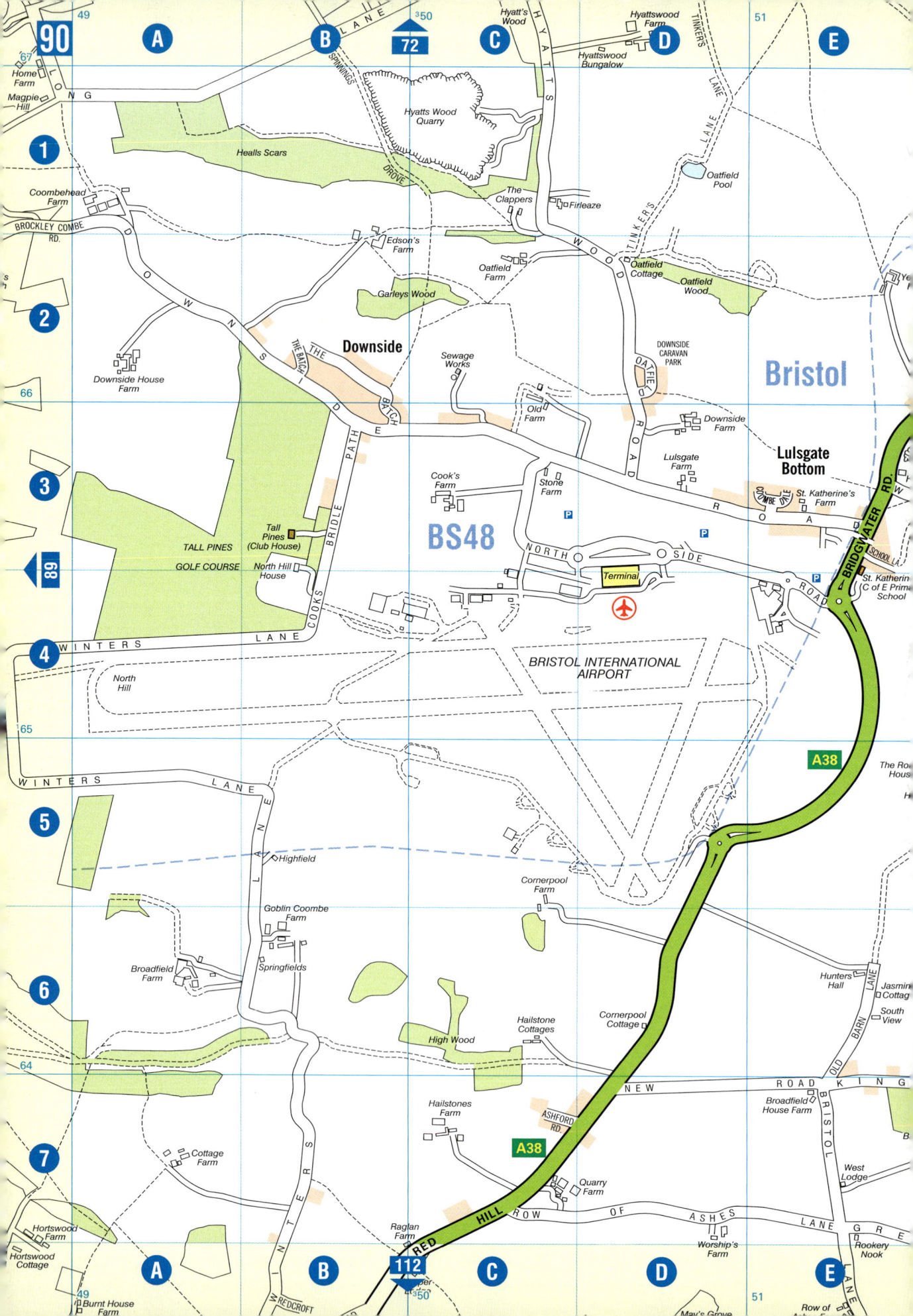

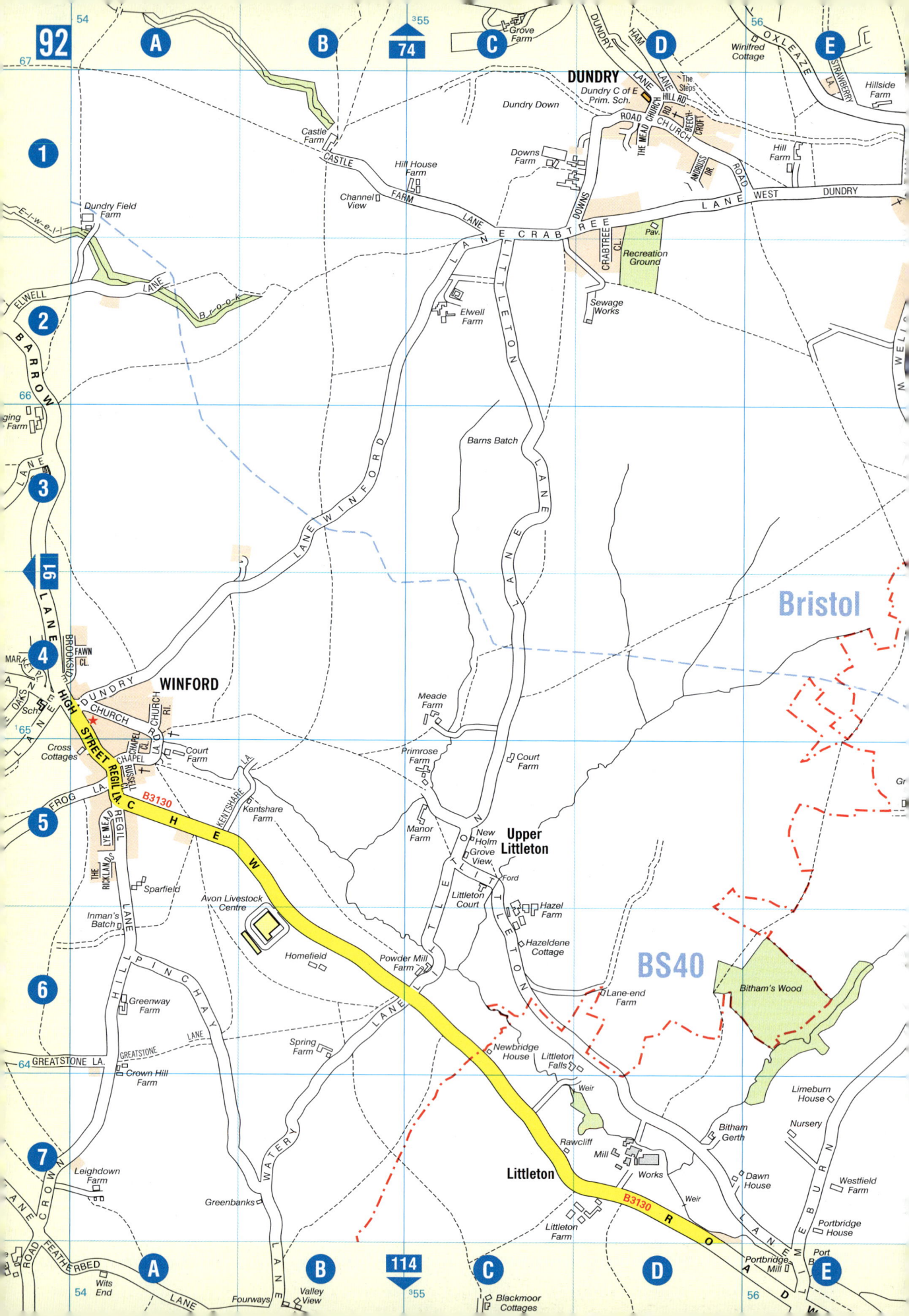

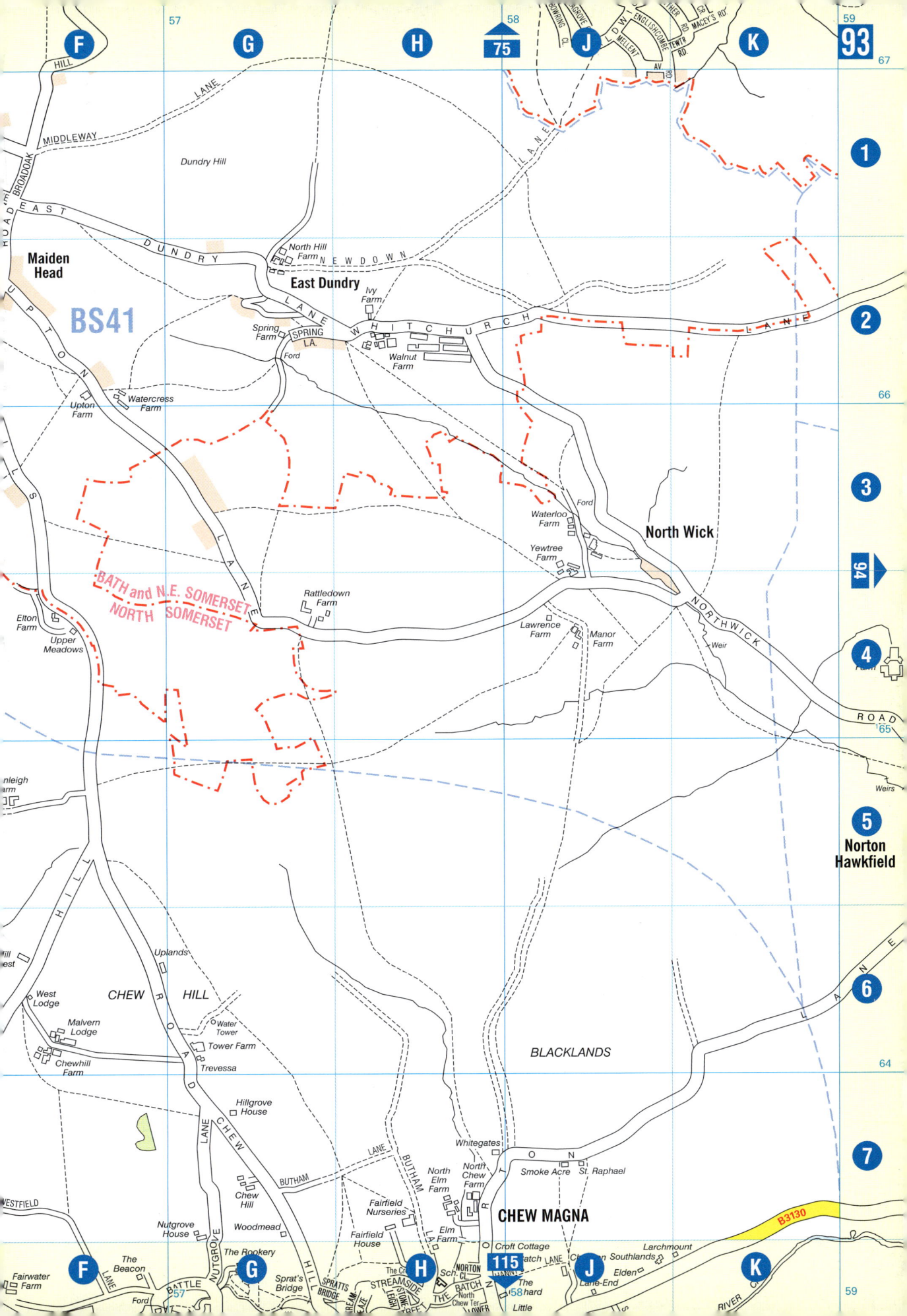

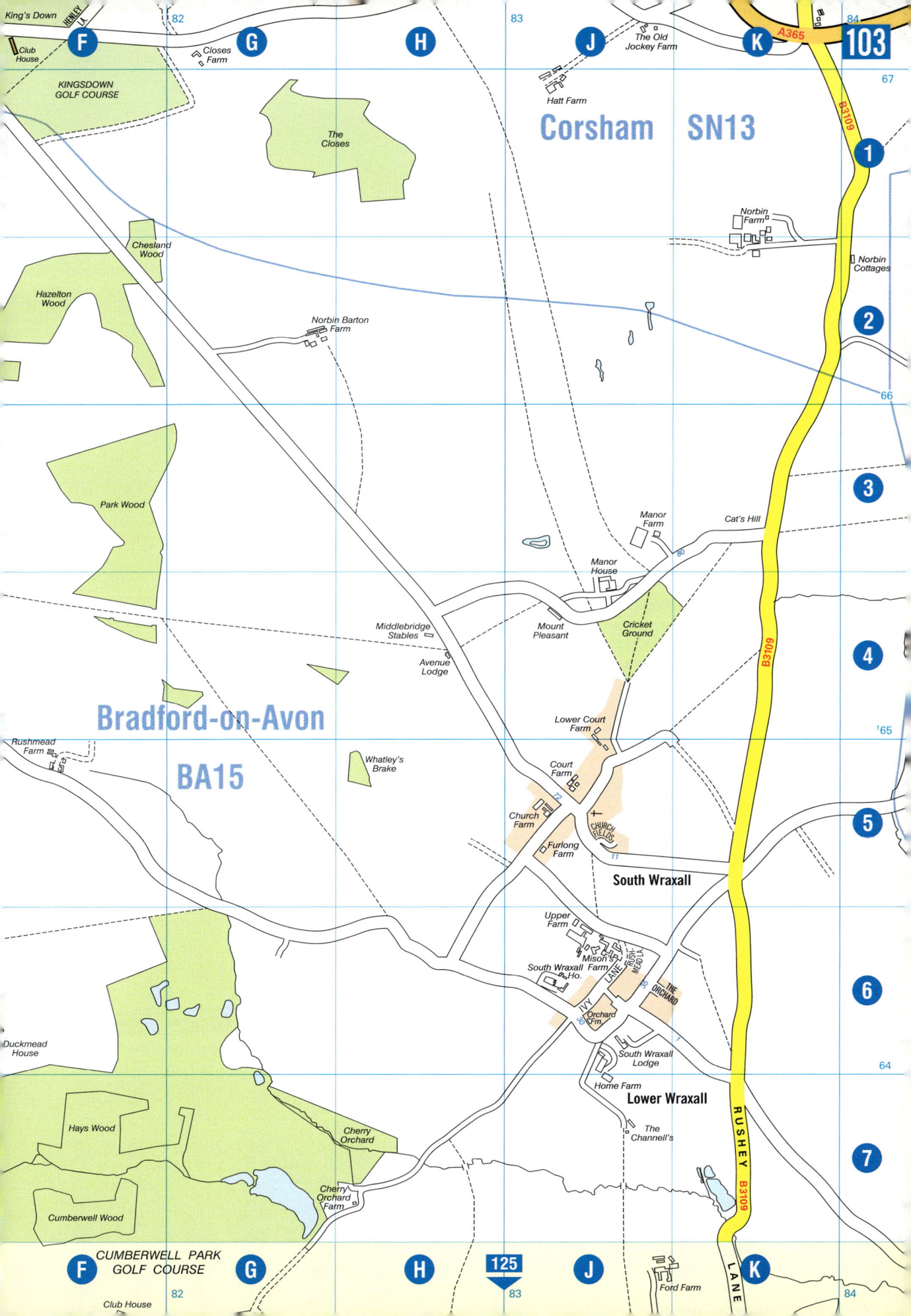

MOUTH OF THE SEVERN

Birnbeck
Pier

BIRNBECK
ISLAND

Spring Cove

Lifeboat
Sta.

Pier

Toll
Gate

Worlebury WORLEBURY
Hill Fort CAMP

Rainham Ct.

TRINITY

Boating Slip

Atlantic Ct.

Anchor Head

ATLANTIC
BUS PARK

Villa
Rosa

Parade

Madeira
Cove

MANILLA

Marine
Lake

Glentworth Bay

Yacht Club
HQ

The
Pavilion

The Beacon
The Baths
Centre
Ho. Dr. Fox's

CAUSEWAY

KNIGHTSTONE

Pavilion

WESTON-SUPER-MARE

WESTON BAY

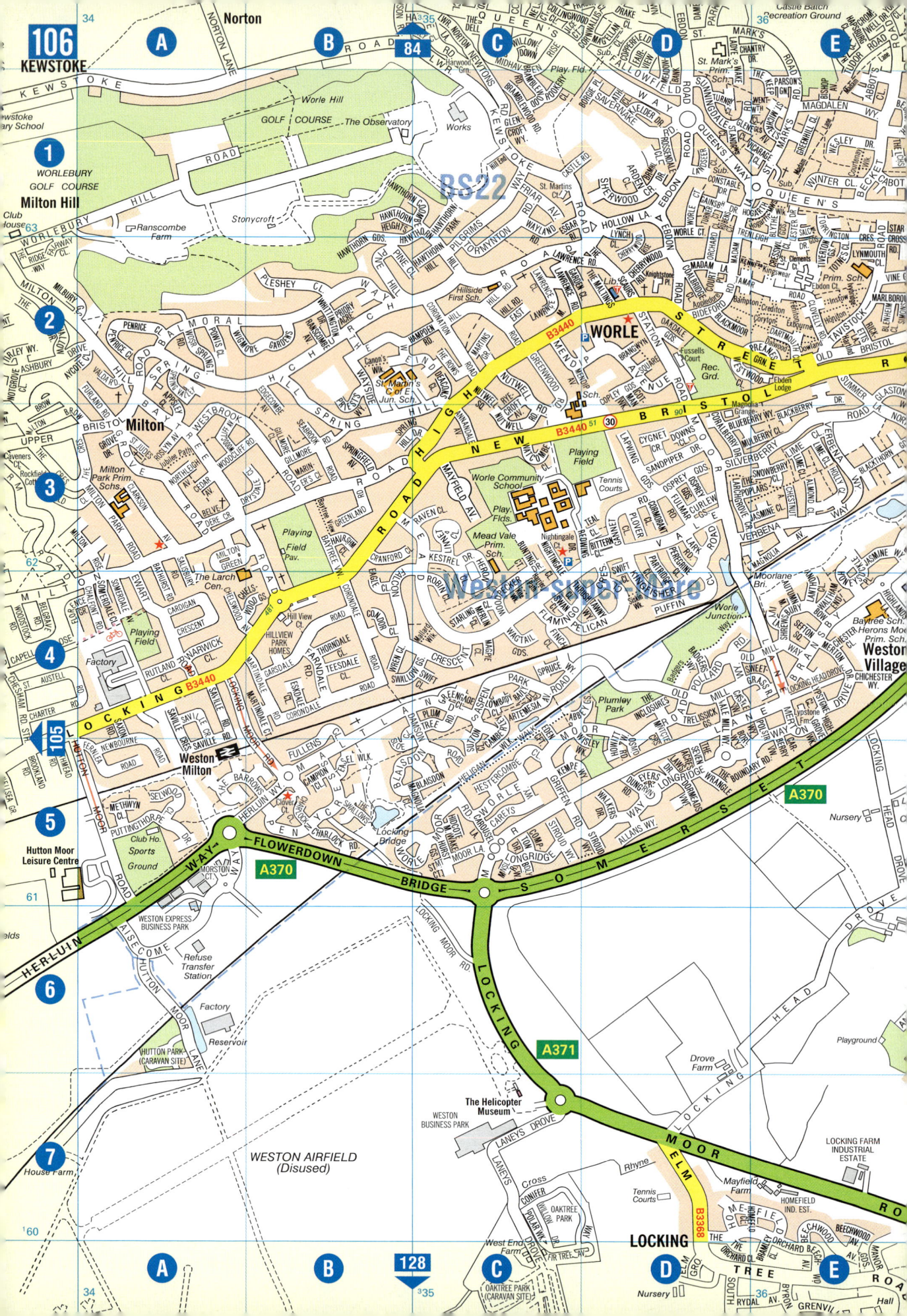

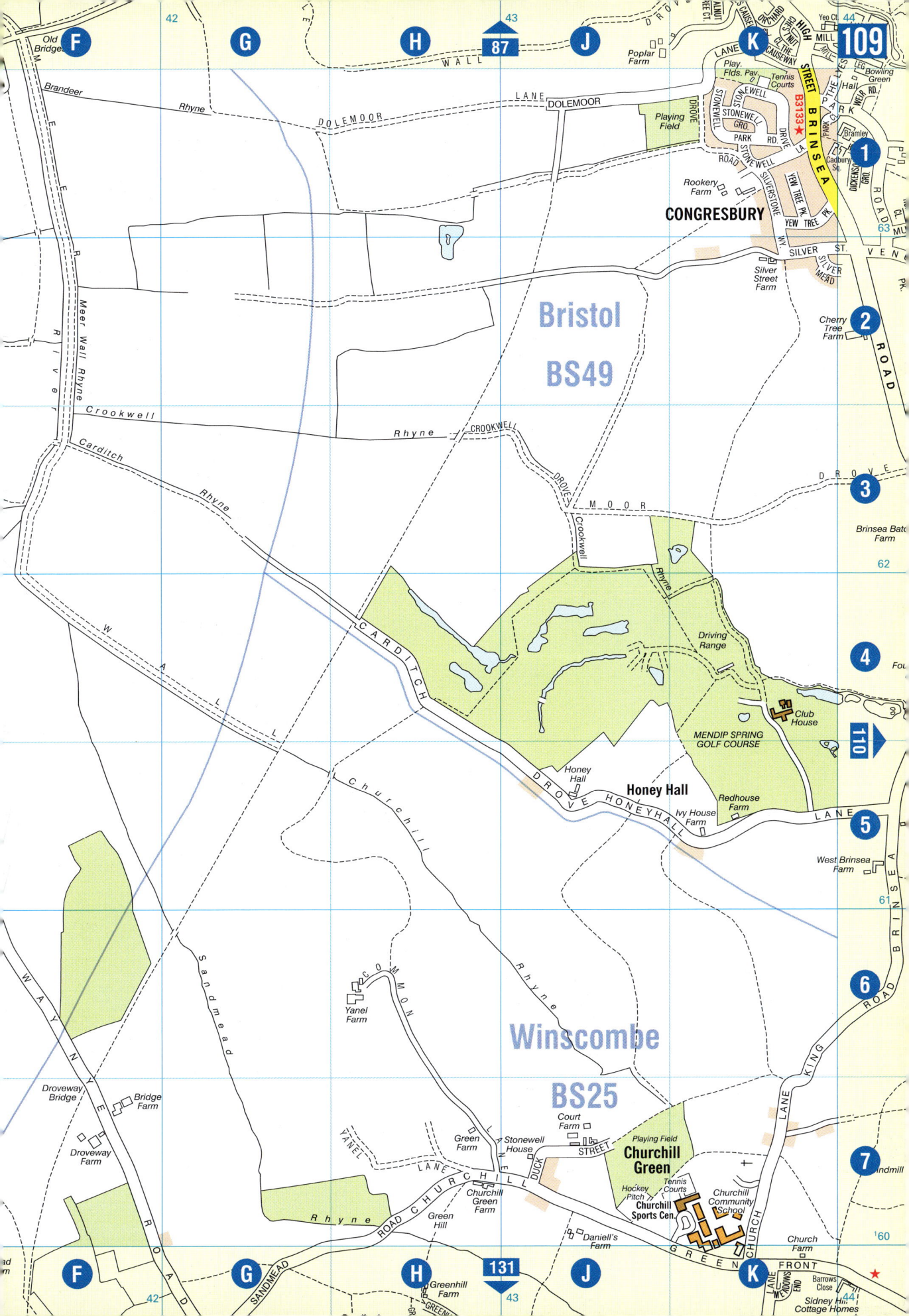

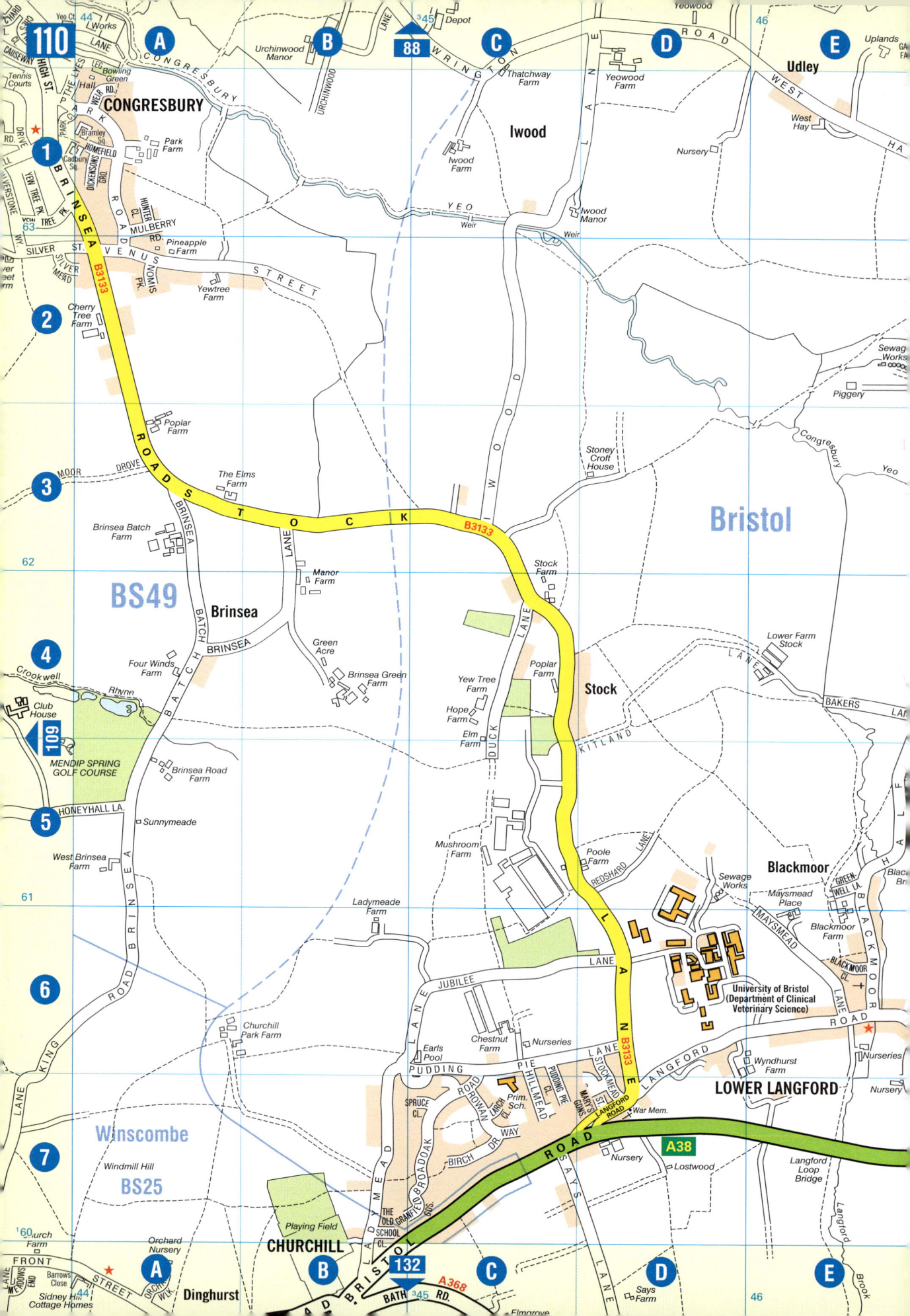

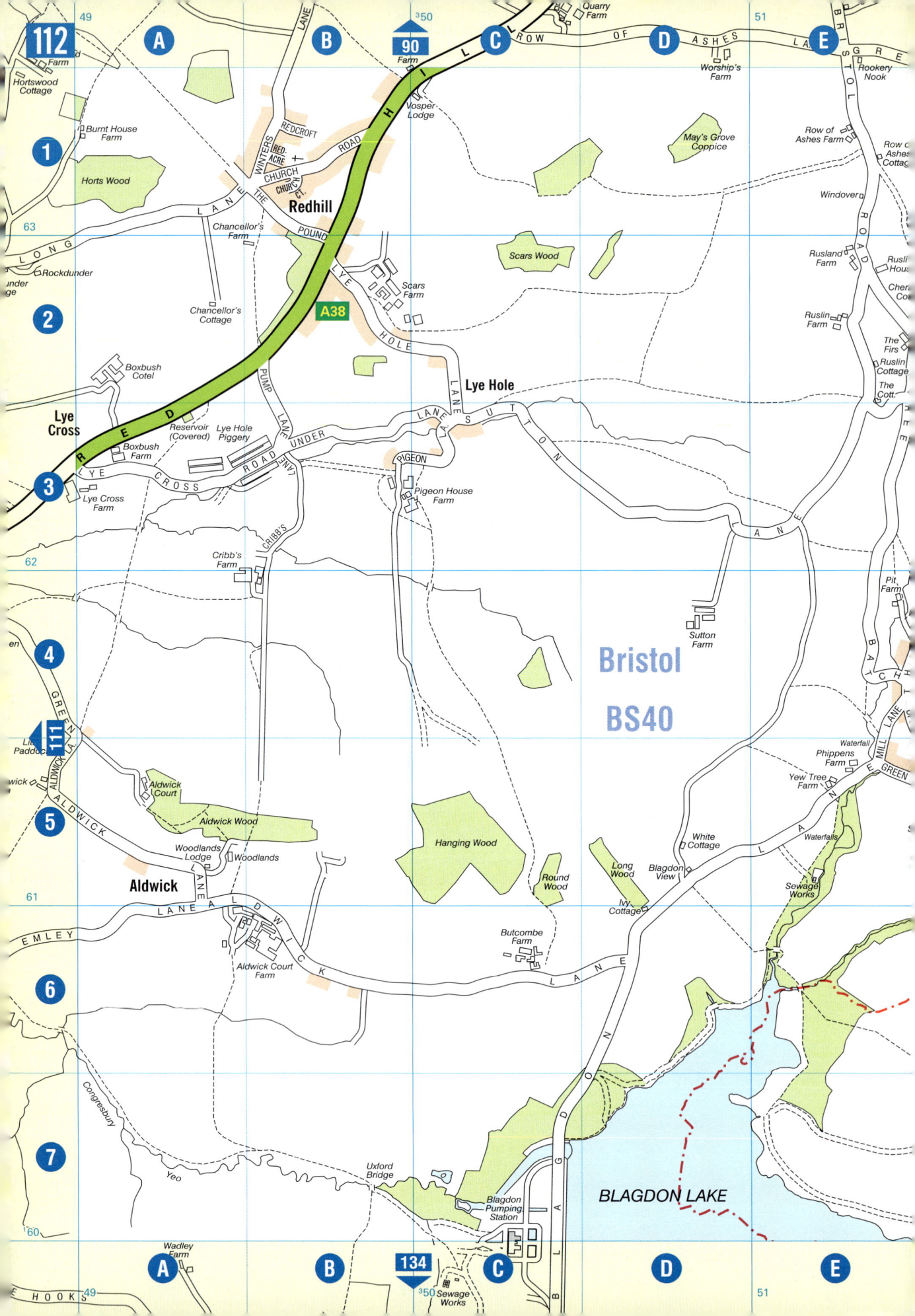

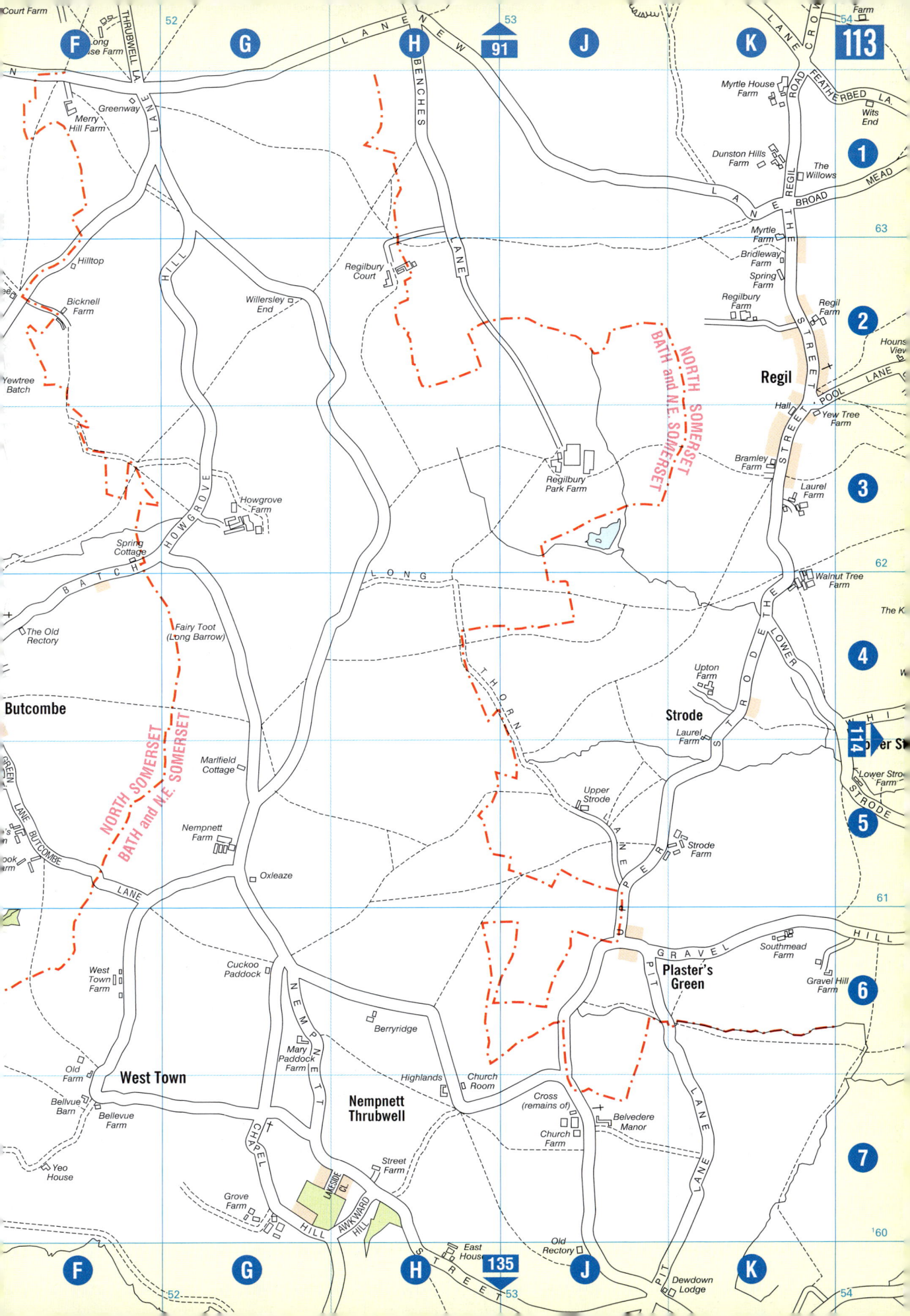

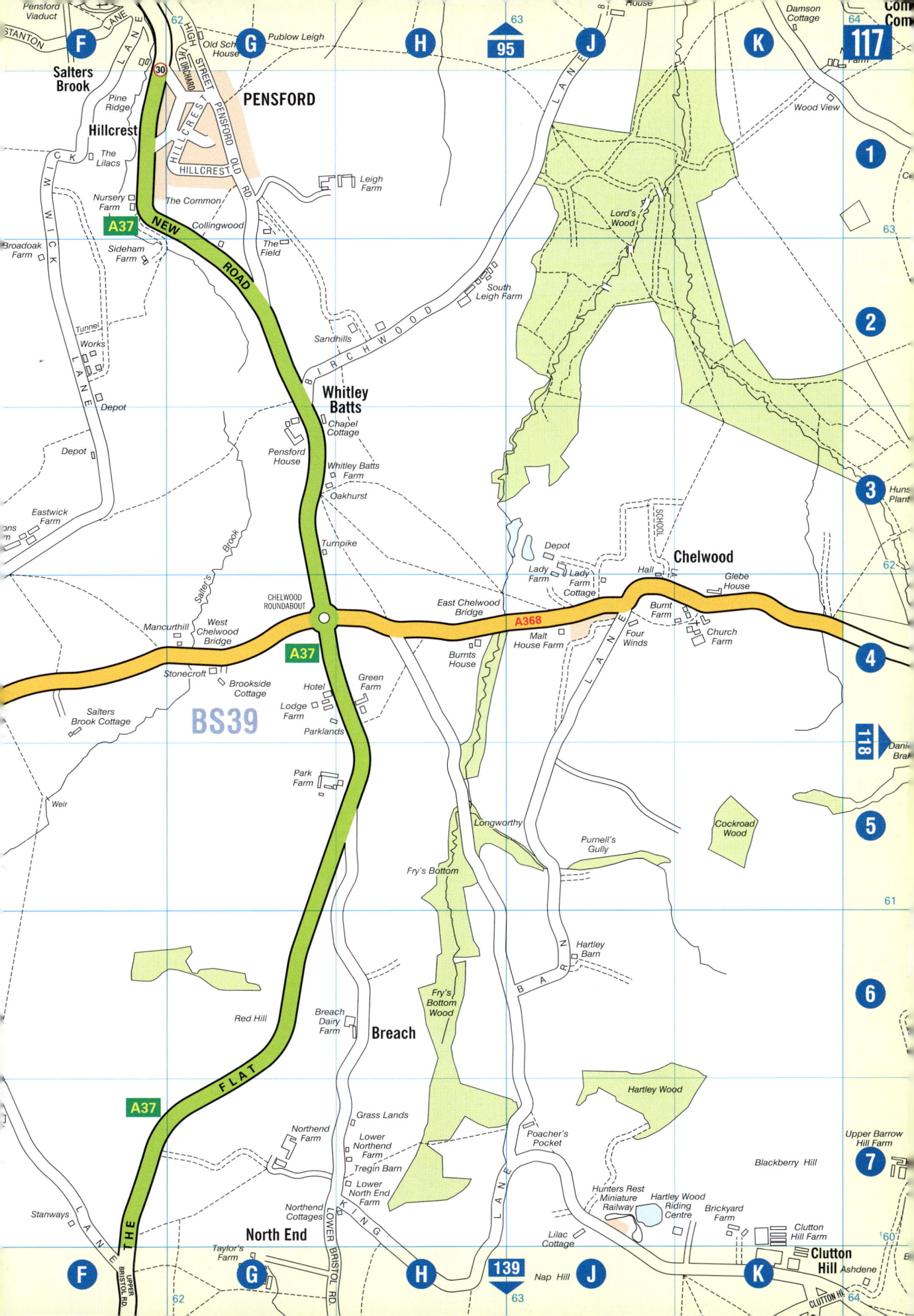

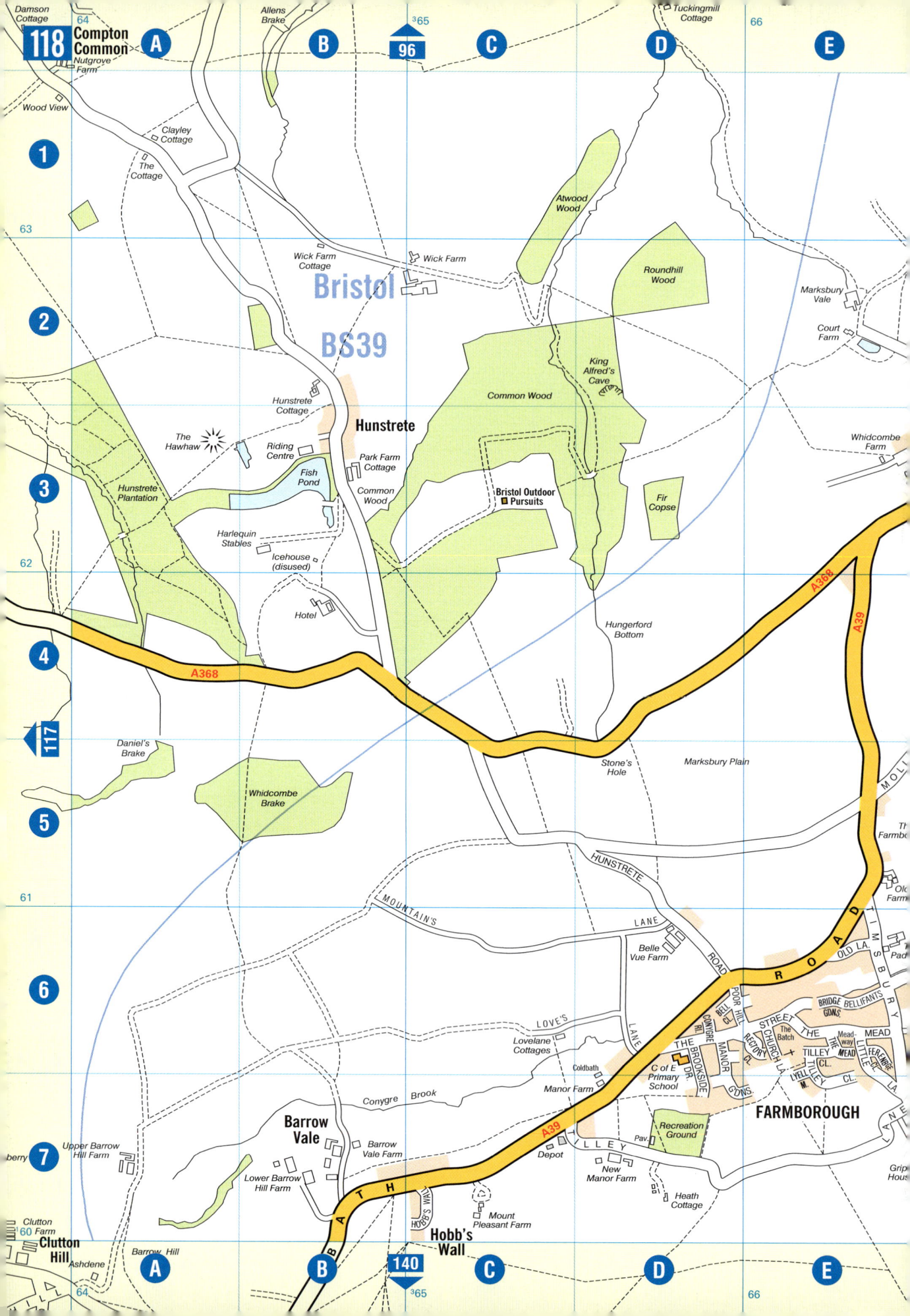

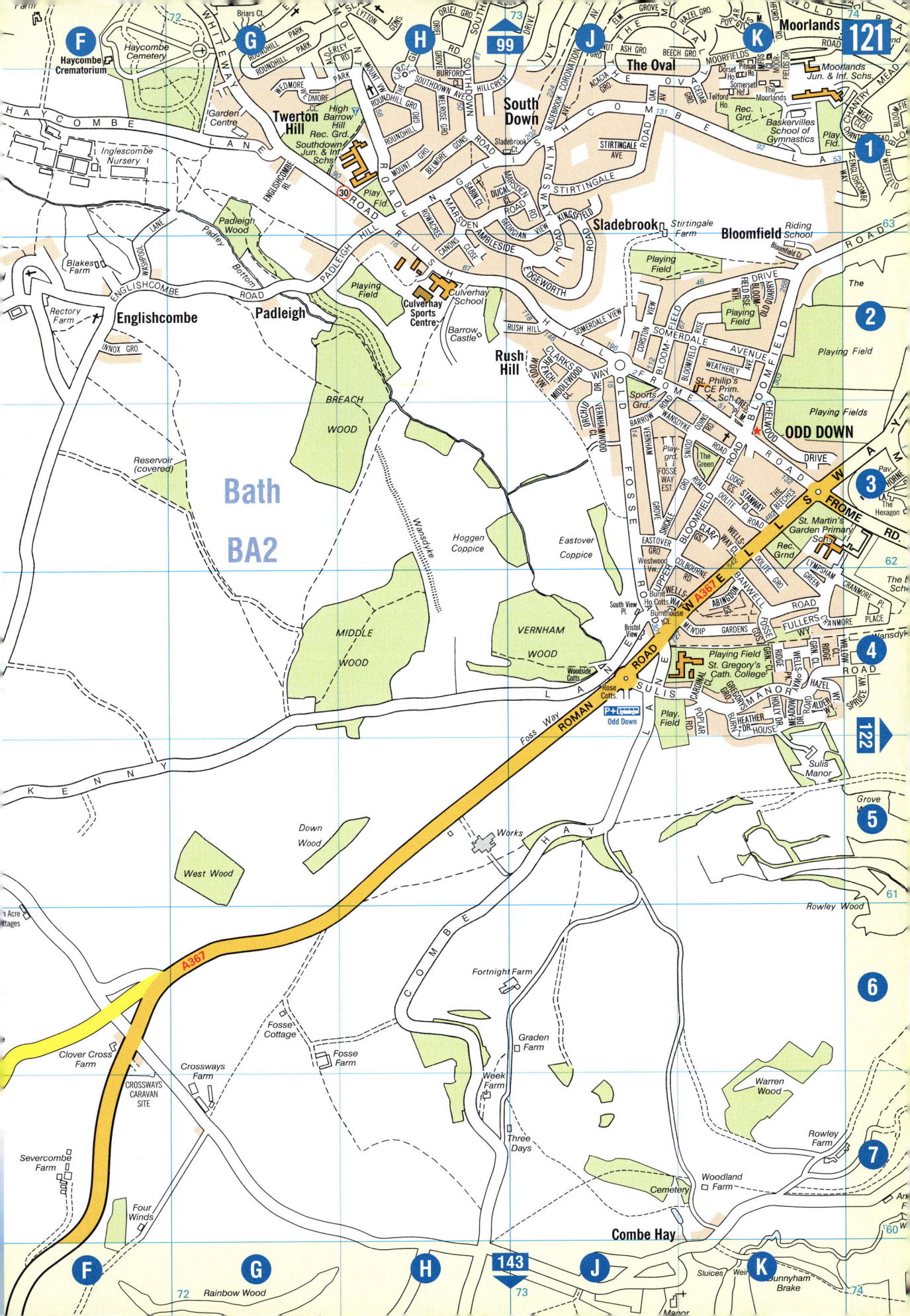

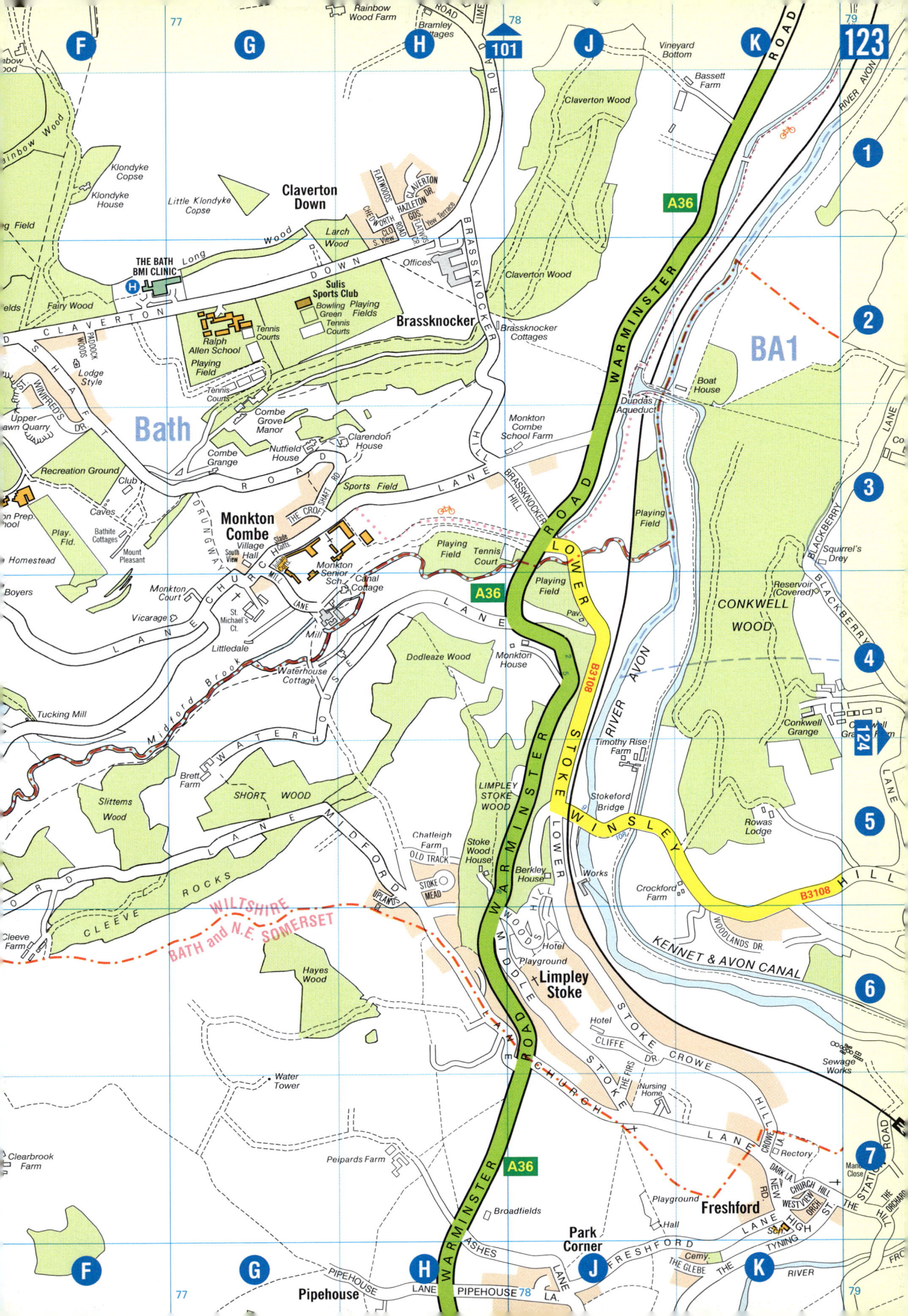

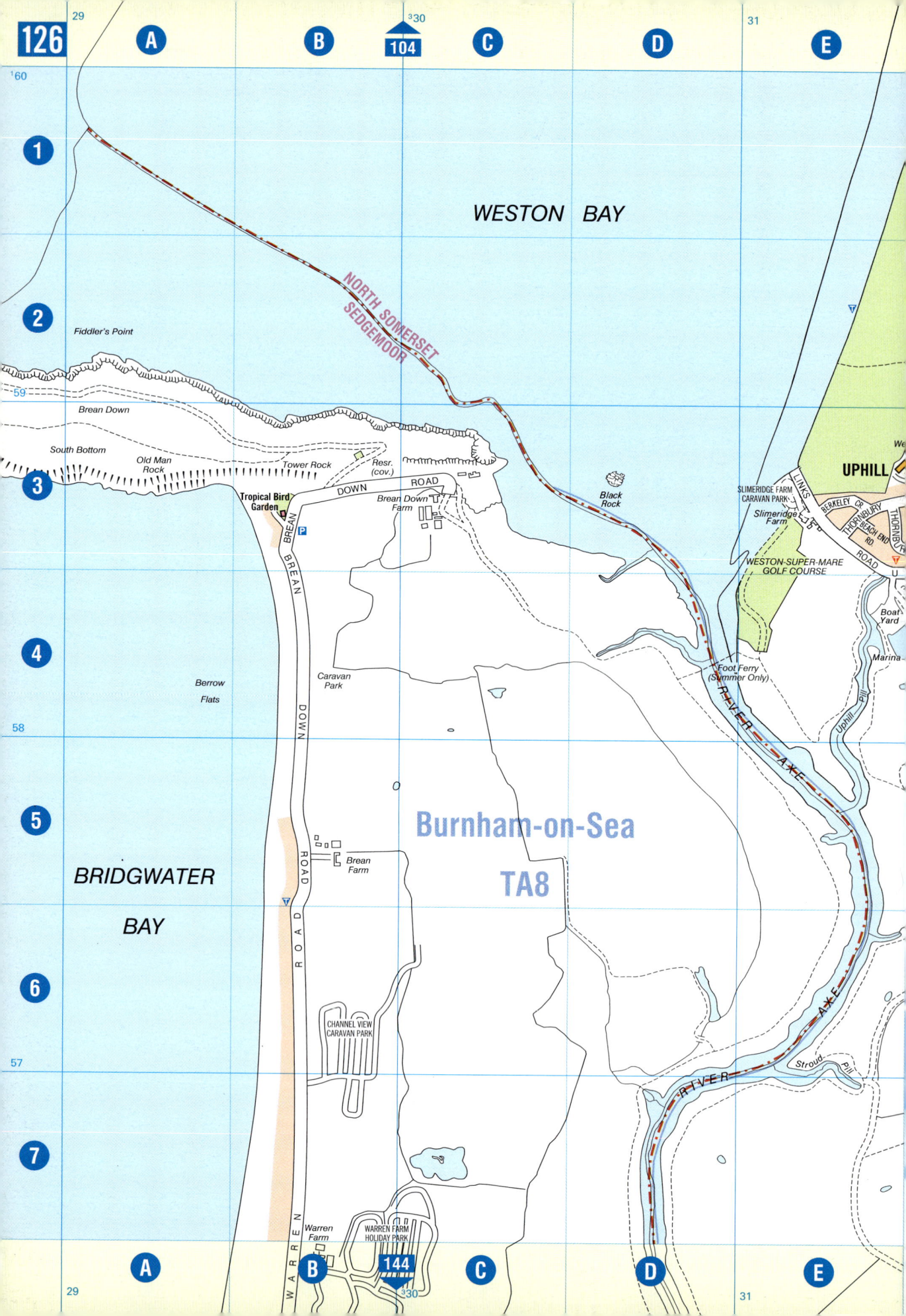

WESTON BAY

NORTH SOMERSET SEDGEMOOR

Fiddler's Point

Brean Down

South Bottom

Old Man Rock

Tower Rock

Resr. (cov.)

Black Rock

UPHILL

SLIMERIDGE FARM CARAVAN PARK

Slimeridge Farm

LINKS

BERKELEY CR

THORNBURY

BEACH END.

THORNBURY RD.

WESTON-SUPER-MARE GOLF COURSE

Boat Yard

Marina

Tropical Bird Garden

BREAN DOWN ROAD

Brean Down Farm

BREAN

DOWN

ROAD

Caravan Park

Berrow Flats

Foot Ferry (Summer Only)

RIVER AXE

Burnham-on-Sea

TA8

BRIDGWATER

BAY

Brean Farm

WARREN ROAD

CHANNEL VIEW CARAVAN PARK

RIVER AXE

Stroud Pill

RIVER AXE

Warren Farm

WARREN FARM HOLIDAY PARK

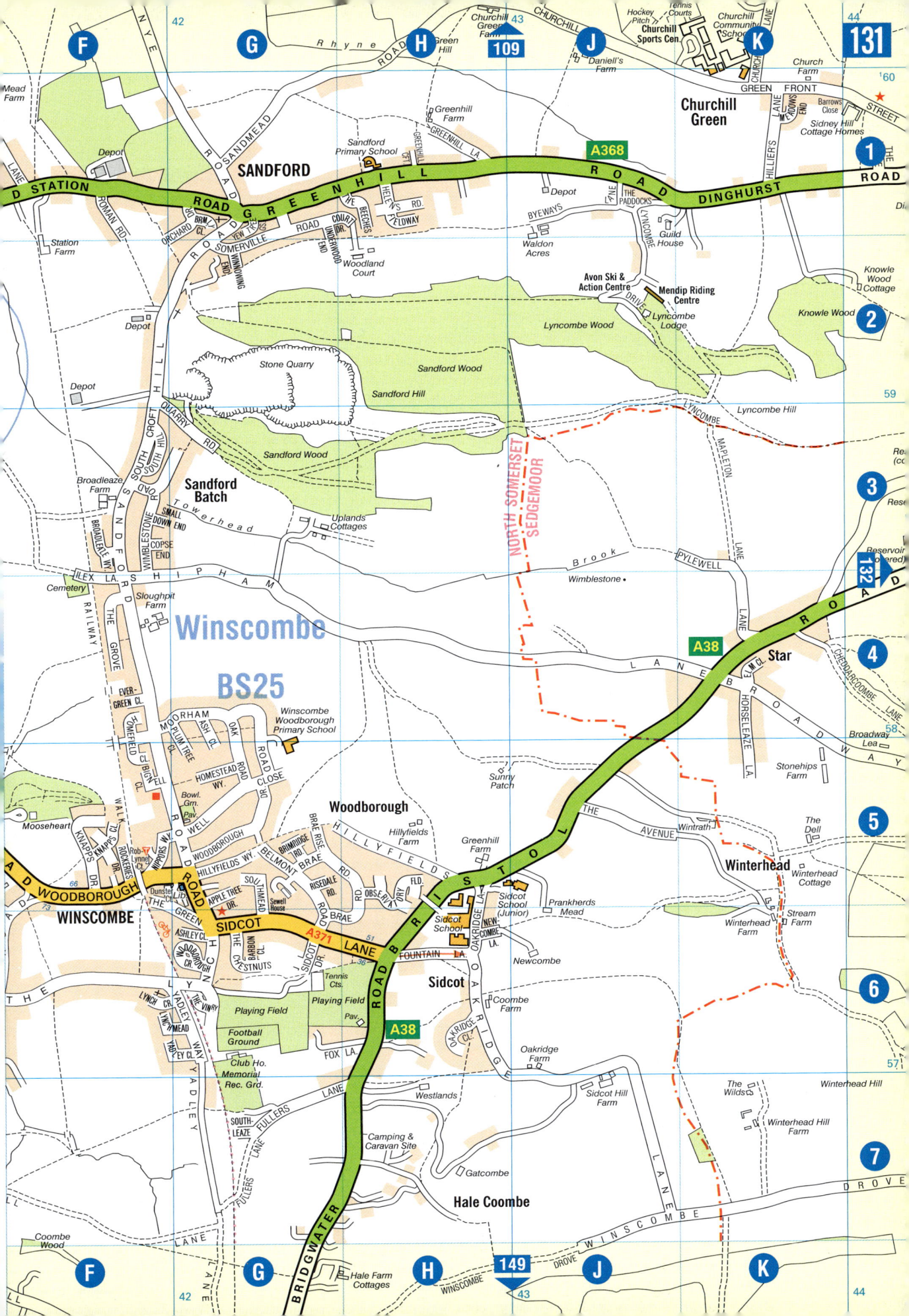

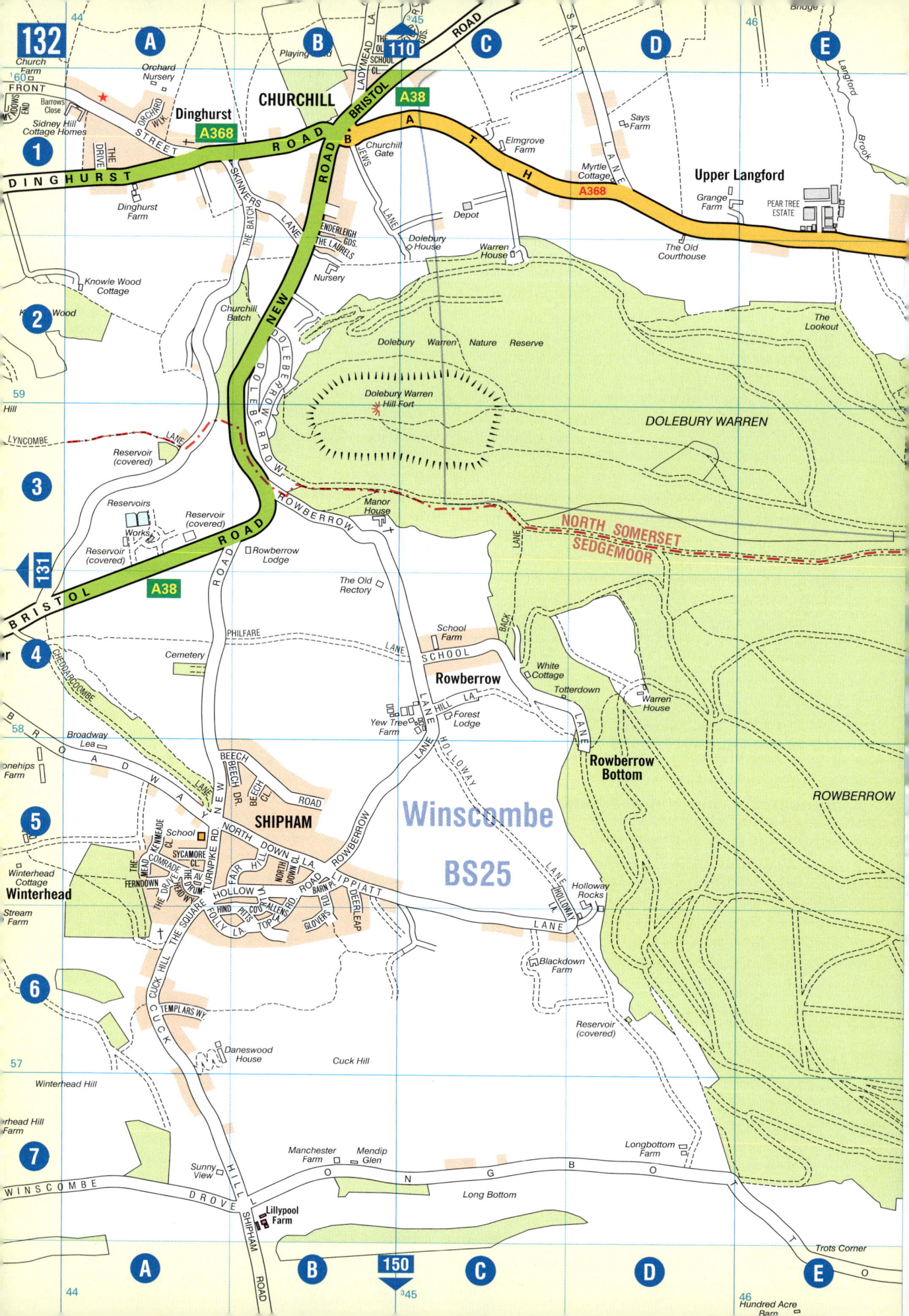

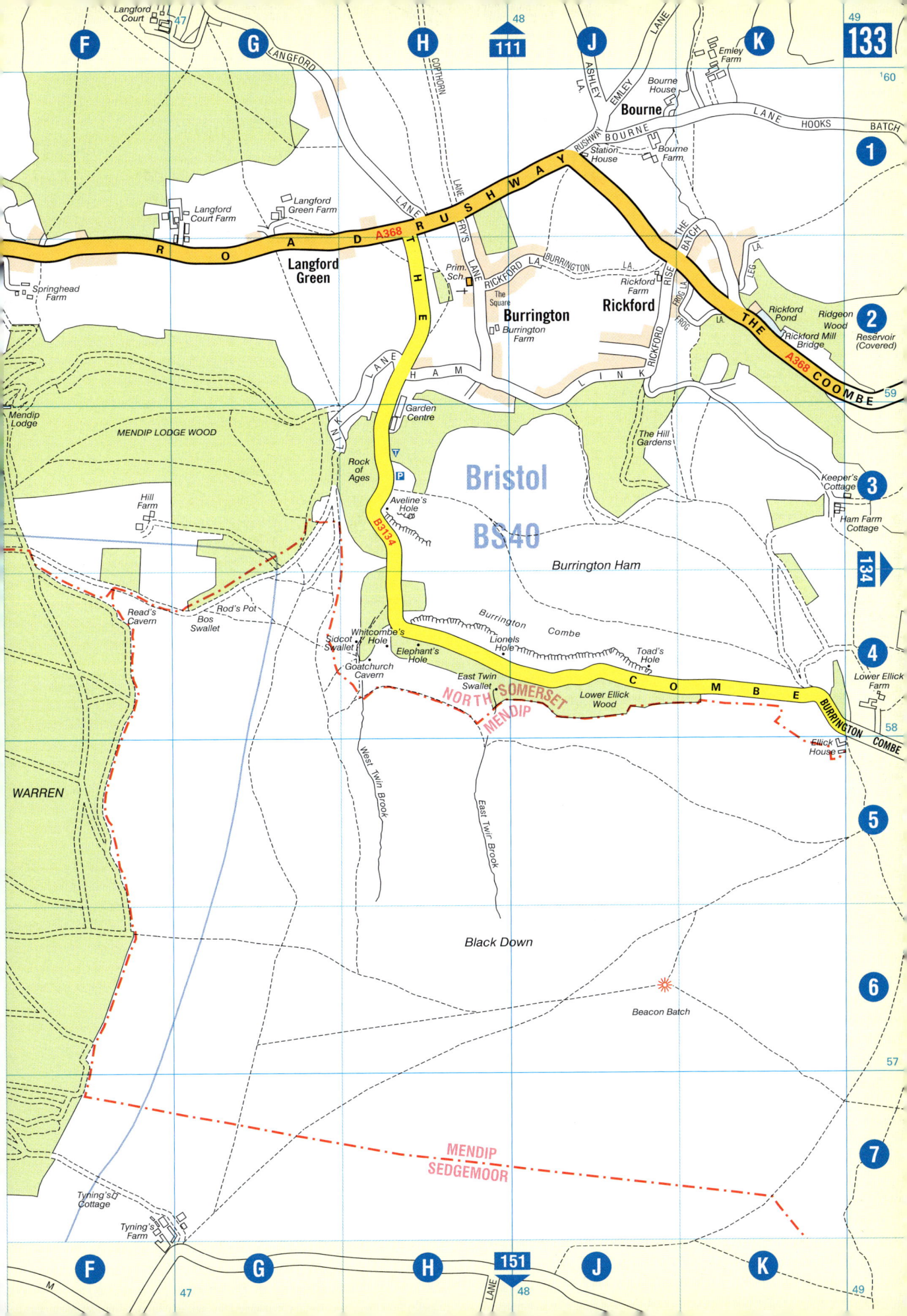

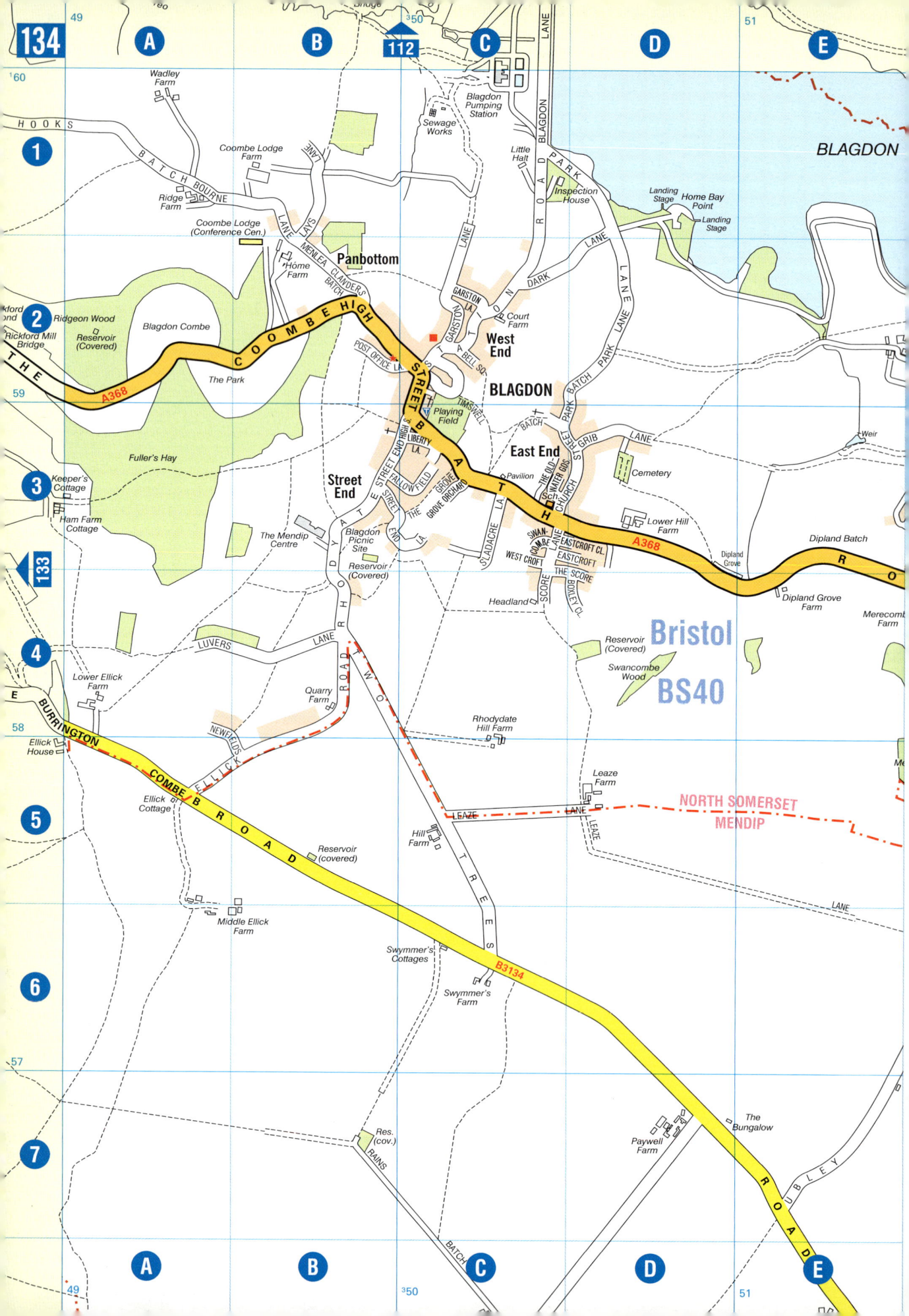

54

A

'60

Breach Hill Common

CAPLE

B

Caple Farm

114

KINGSHILL

355

C

Kingsley Paddocks

D

Villice Bay

55

56

E

Nunnery Copse

1

Breach Hill

Breach Hill Farm

Herons Green Farm

LANE

Herons Green

B3114

Moreton Point

2

Ubley Park House

Herons Green Bay

Moreton Cottage

Moreton LANE

59

3

Woodbridge Farm

dbri dge

LANE

VILLICE

Moat

Moat Farm

Bickfield Farm

LANE

Oakleaze

LANE

135

Bristol

4

RIVER

YEO

Bickfield House Farm

Woodwick Farm

Summerlea Farm

NEW CLOSE

OLDBARN LA.

STRATFORD

58

5

LANE VILLICE

BICKFIELD LANE

BS40

Lug Fall

Park Spring

Lug Fall

White Cross Cottage

White Cross Farm

White Cross House

Mendip View

MENDIP VILLAS

THE

UNDERTOWN

YEW TREE LA.

VILLICE

UNDERTOWN

MILL LA.

TINKERS LA.

LANE

Rose Cottage

Easton Mons Cottage

B3114

A368

BATH

6

A368

THE COOMBE

HAZEL BARRON

STREET

THE REDDINGS

THE BARTON

The Barton

COMPTON

MARTIN

WEST HARPTREE

Jarmadene

NEWTON

PARSONGE CL.

Parsonage Farm

WHISTLEY

57

COMPTON MARTIN

THE BATCH

RECTORY LANE

HILL LANE

Fairash Bungalow

Fairash Poultry Farm

Tilly Manor

Hall

Gournay Court

ROAD

WEST

RIDGE CR.

The Courtyard

B3114

7

Browning's Tump

Compton Combe

HIGHFIELD

Fairash

Rock House

COWLEAZE

Beaconsfield Farm

RIDGEWAY CL.

Bungalow Farm

BATH HA

The Wrangle

A

54

B

355

C

D

RIDGE

56

E INSET

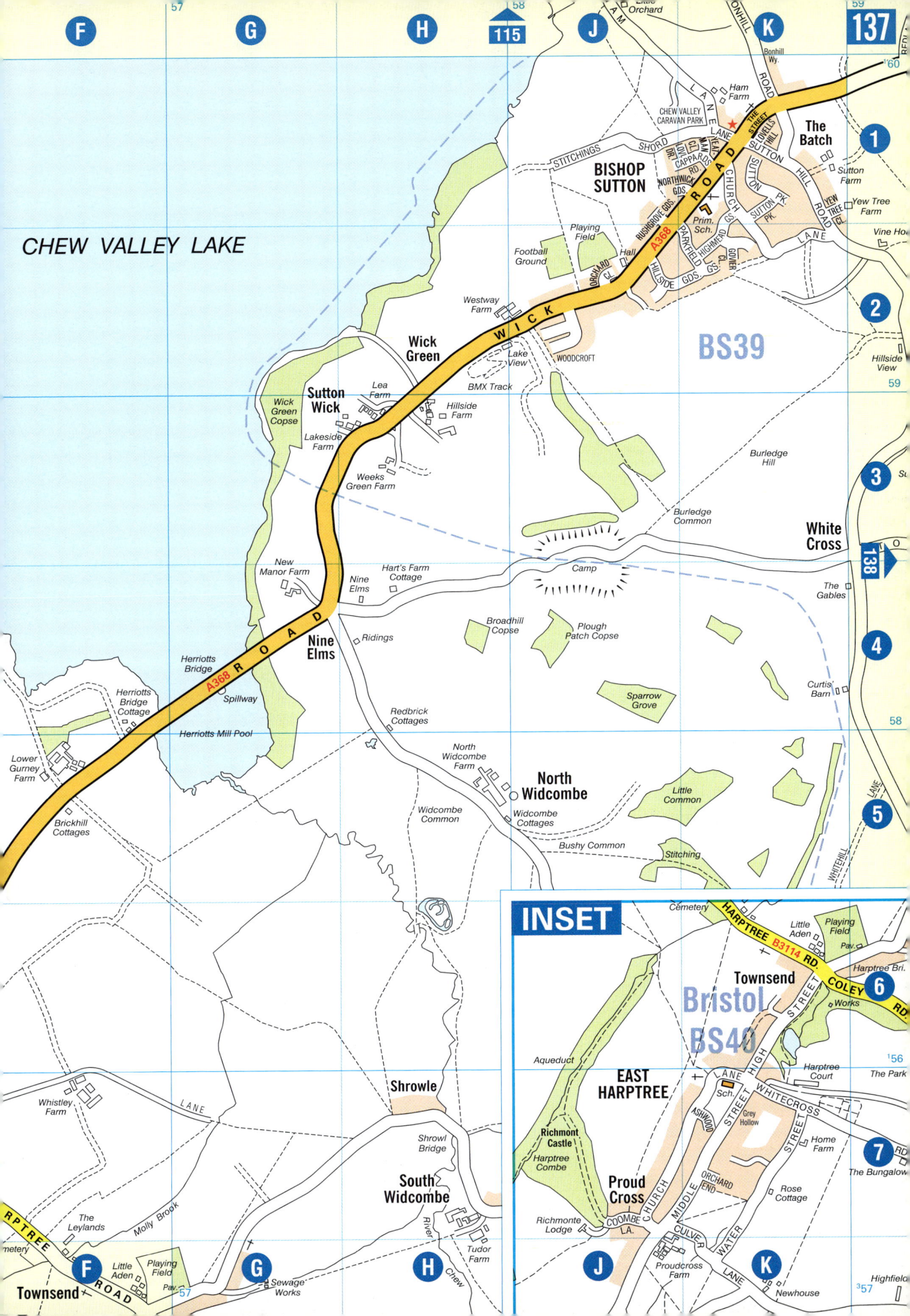

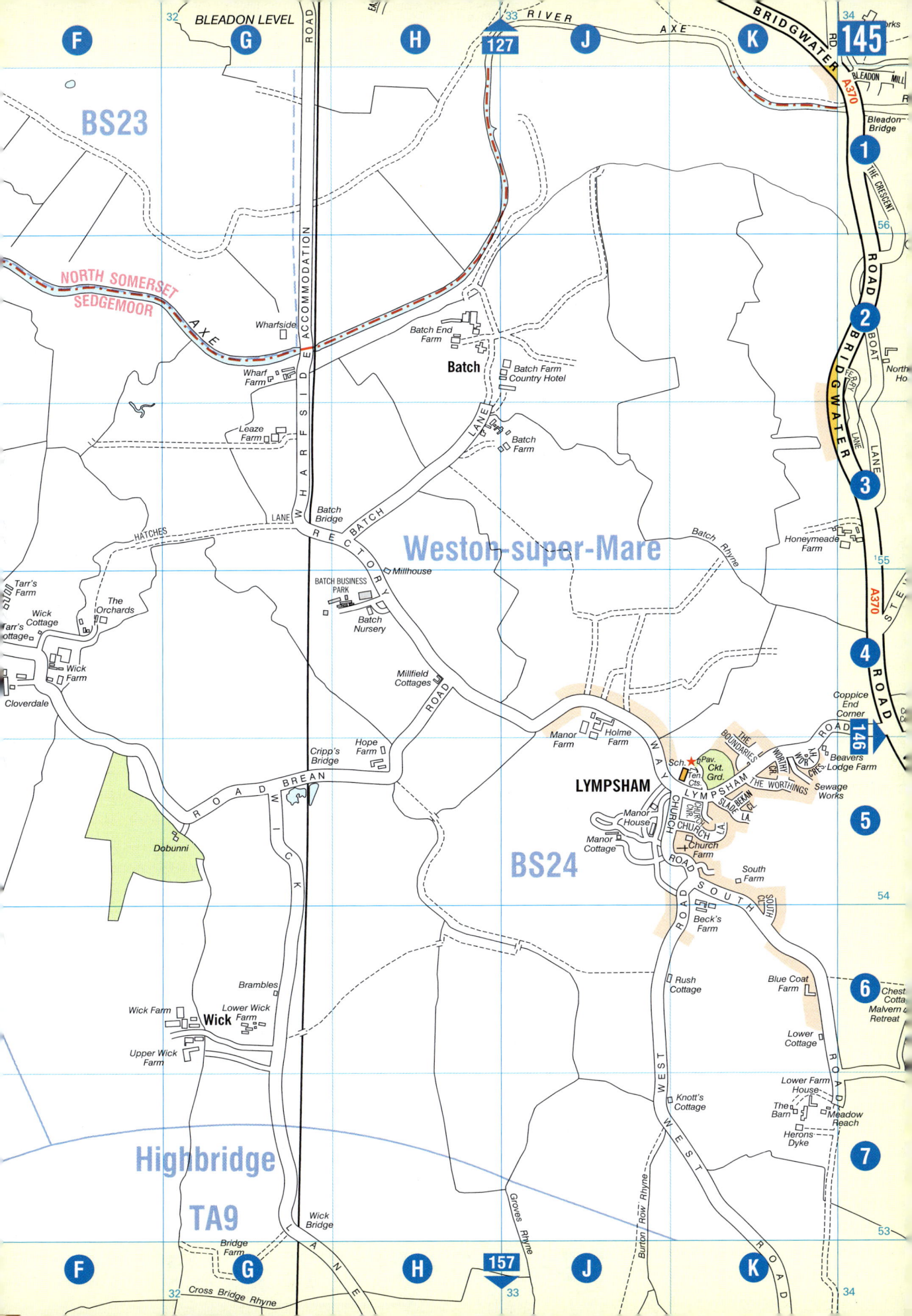

A · B · 128 · C · D · E

Works
South Hill
South Hill Farm
Court Farm
Shiplate

BRIDGWATER A370

BLEADON MILL
RIVER AXE
Bleadon Bridge
Lake Farm
Shiplate Farm
Shiplate Manor Farm

1

56

2

THE CRESCENT
BOAT
North Farm House
Warehouse
Baytree House
White Gate Farm
Rhynemoor Farm

FERRY LANE
LANE

3

White House Farm
Riversmeet Farm

Honeymeade Farm
Appledore Farm

Weston-super-Mare

¹55

BS24

STEVENS ROAD WESTON

Chestnut Farm
White House Kennels

HOUSE

4

Coppice End Corner
Copse Corner
Walnut Farm
Eastertown Farm
Depot

NORTH ROAD

Eastertown

145
YMPSHAM RD.
Beavers Lodge Farm
WORTHY CRES
WORTHINGS
Sewage Works
East Farm
Stonebow Farm

North Yeo Farm
River Yeo Farm

5

50

ROWBERROW LANE

Poplar Farm

WHITE HOUSE LANE

54

SOUTH ROAD

Willlow Farm

6

Blue Co Farm
Chestnut Cottage
Malvern Retreat

PURVING ROW

Lower Cottage
Mendip View Farm

Lower Farm House
The Barn
Meadow Reach
Herons Dyke

DELHORN

Delhorne
EDINGWORTH

LANE
Brent House Farm

Laurel Farm

MENDIP ROAD

Yor Hou
Yo Cotte
ROOKS

7

DELHORN LANE
Dulhorn Farm
A370 ROAD

DULHORN FARM CAMPING SITE

Old Holt Farm
Badger Manor
Rookery Farm

M5 MOTORWAY

M5

Edingworth

ROOKERY CL.
Cooter Farm

53

A · B · C · **Sedgemoor Service Area** · D · MENDIP · E

34 · ³35 · 36

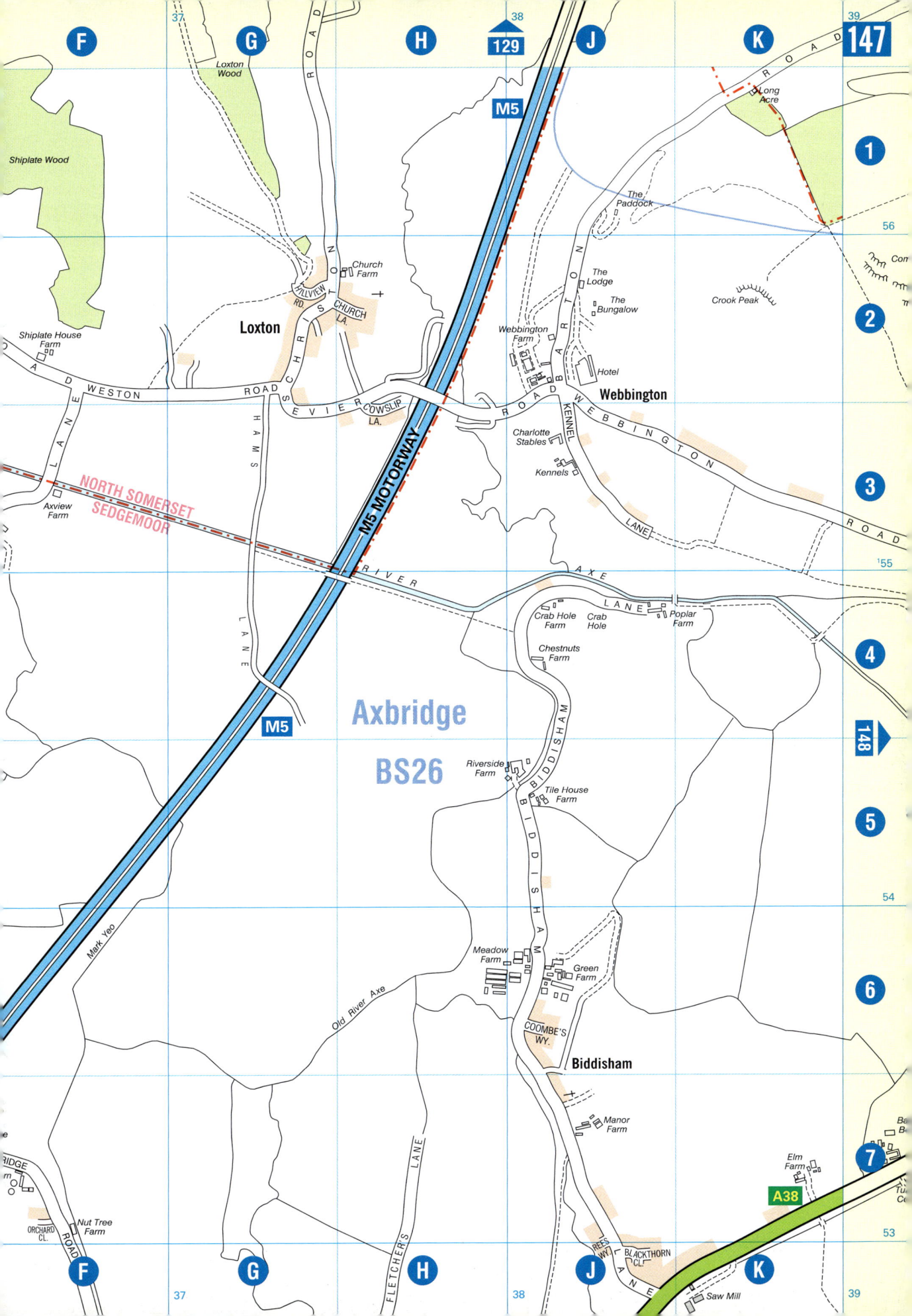

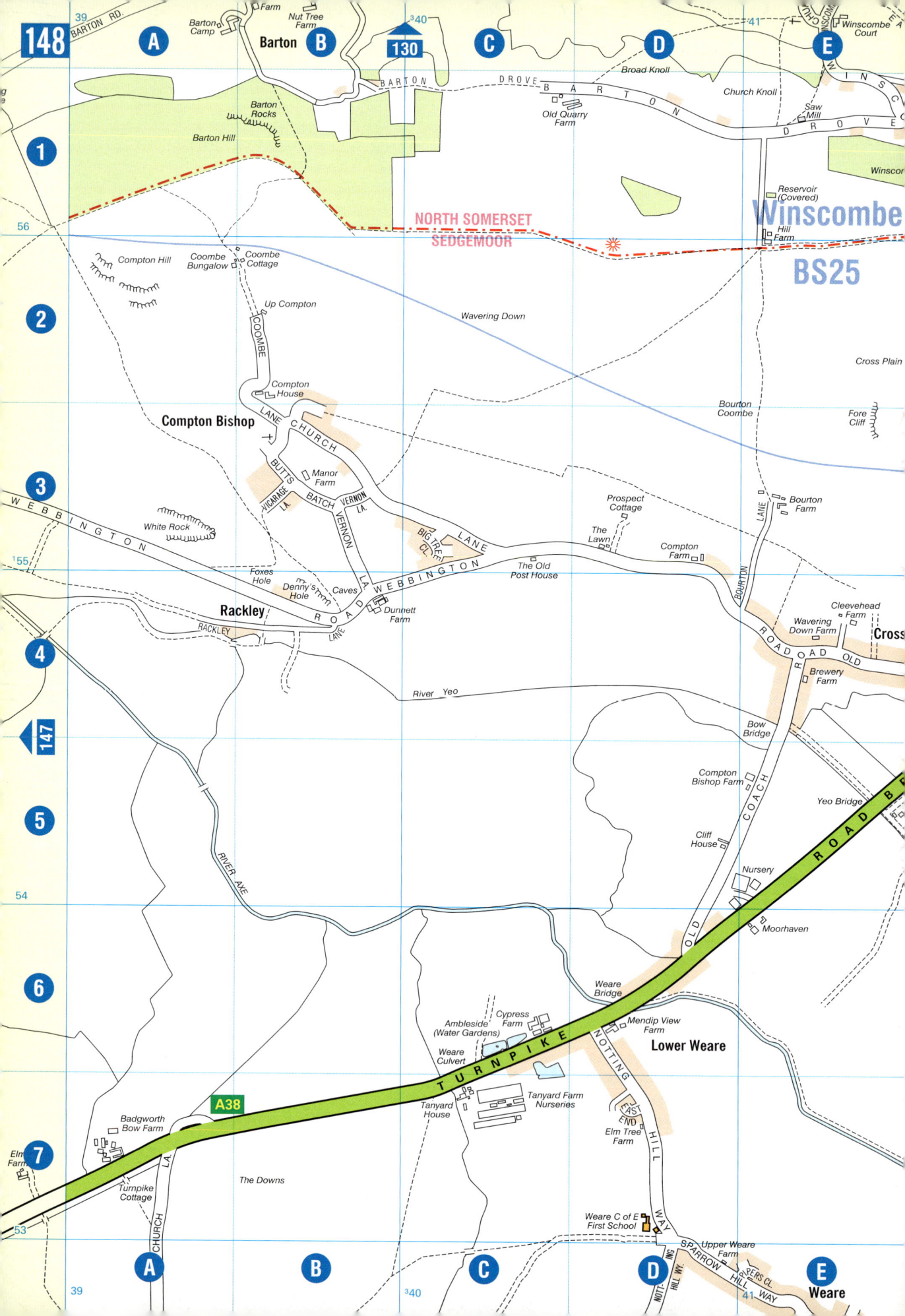

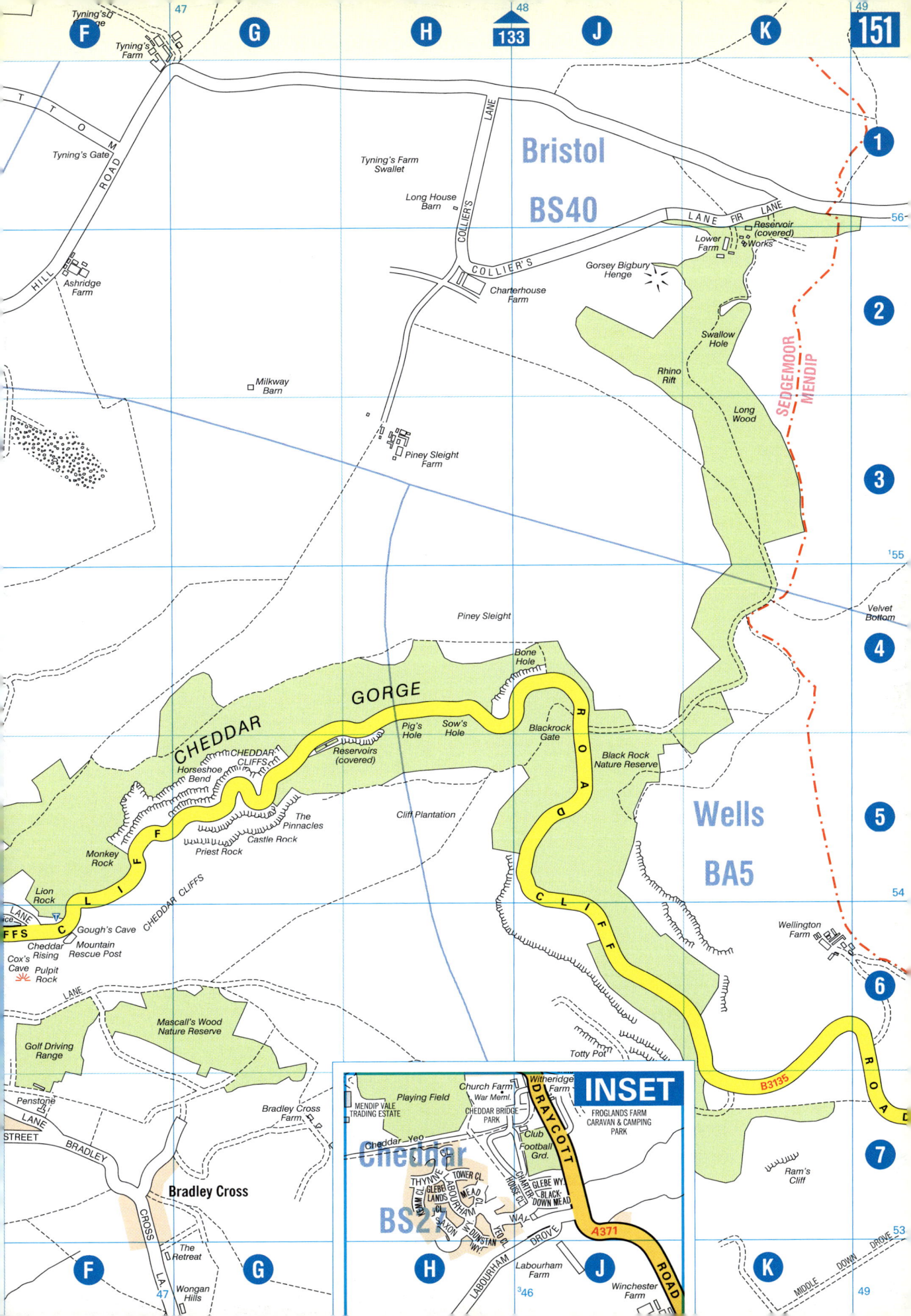

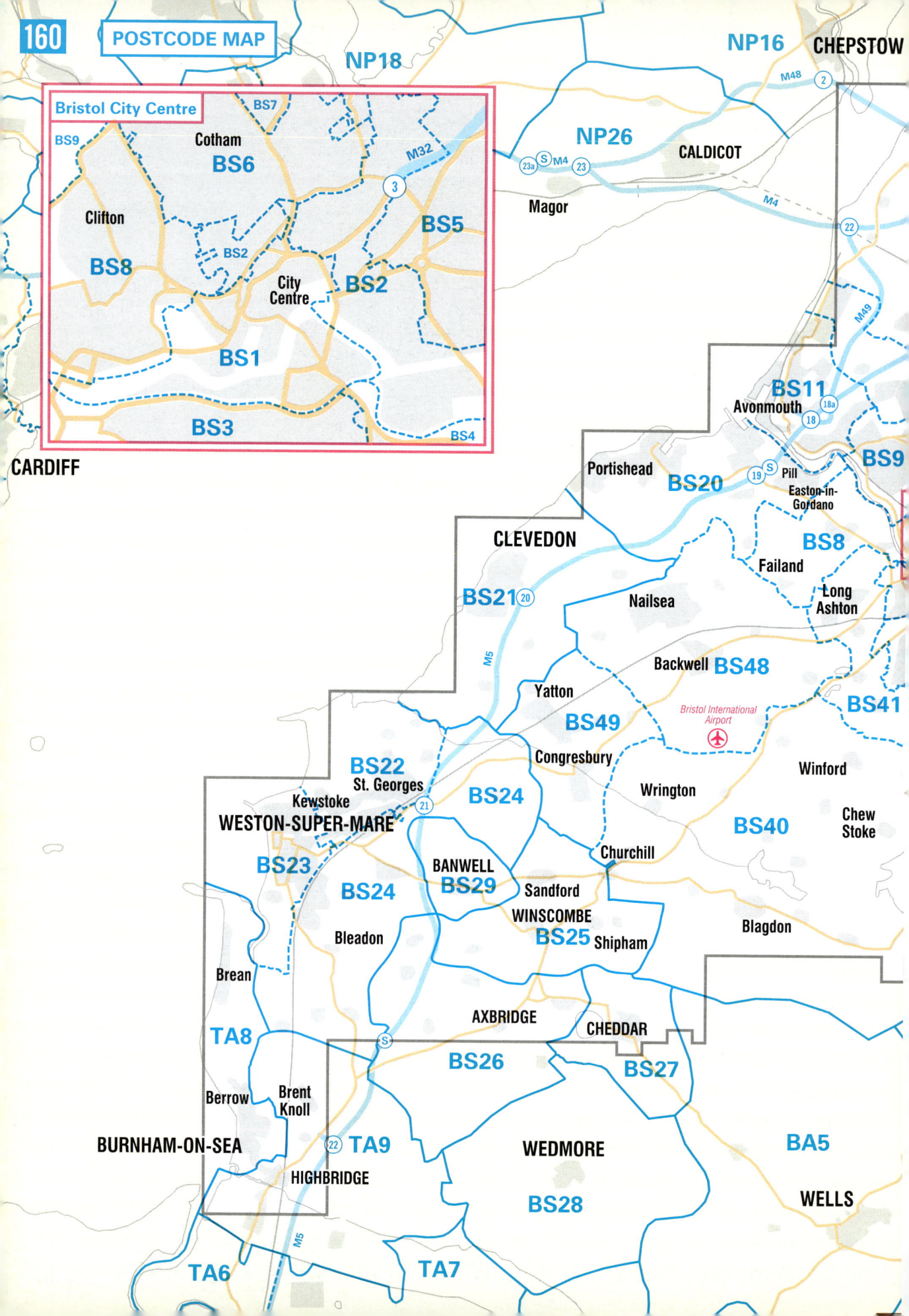

Bristol City Centre

Cotham

BS7

BS9

BS6

M32

3

Clifton

BS8

BS2

BS5

City
Centre

BS2

BS1

BS3

BS4

CARDIFF

NP18

NP16

CHEPSTOW

M48

2

NP26

CALDICOT

23a S M4 23

Magor

M4

M4

22

M49

BS11

Avonmouth

18a

18

BS9

Portishead

BS20

19 S Pill

Easton-in-
Gordano

CLEVEDON

BS8

Failand

BS21 20

Nailsea

Long
Ashton

M5

Backwell BS48

BS41

Yatton

BS49

Bristol International
Airport

Congresbury

Winford

BS22

Wrington

Chew
Stoke

St. Georges

BS24

BS40

Kewstoke

21

WESTON-SUPER-MARE

Churchill

BS23

BANWELL

Sandford

BS24

BS29

WINSCOMBE

Blagdon

Bleadon

BS25

Shipham

Brean

AXBRIDGE

CHEDDAR

TA8

BS26

BS27

BA5

Berrow

Brent
Knoll

BURNHAM-ON-SEA

22

TA9

WEDMORE

WELLS

HIGHBRIDGE

BS28

M5

TA6

TA7

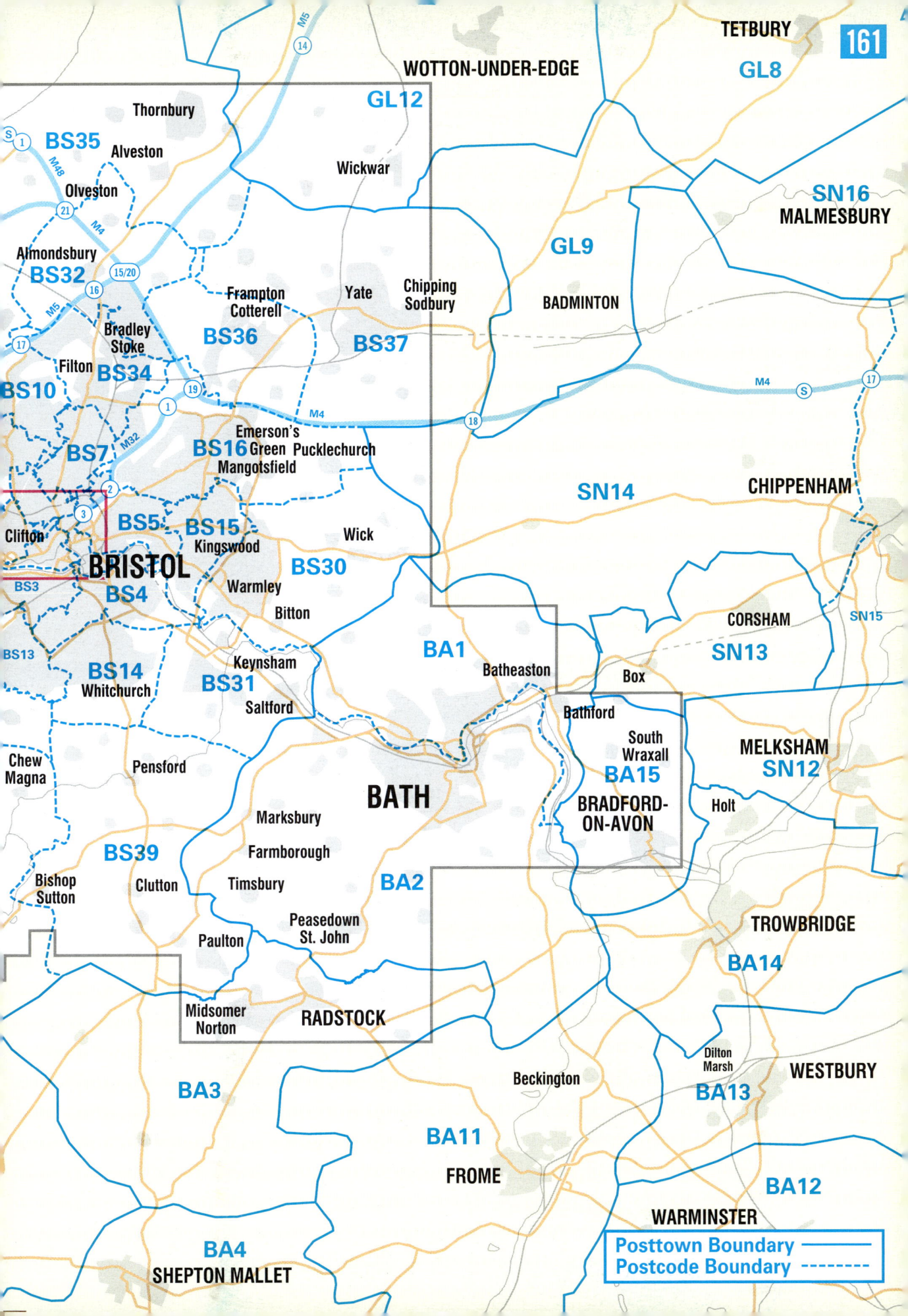

INDEX

Including Streets, Places & Areas, Industrial Estates,
Selected Flats & Walkways, Service Areas, Stations and Selected Places of Interest.

HOW TO USE THIS INDEX

1. Each street name is followed by its Postcode District and then by its Locality abbreviation(s) and then by its map reference; e.g. **Abbey Rd.** BS9: W Trym . . . .2F **47** is in the BS9 Postcode District and the Westbury-on-Trym Locality and is to be found in square 2F on page **47**. The page number is shown in bold type.

2. A strict alphabetical order is followed in which Av., Rd., St., etc. (though abbreviated) are read in full and as part of the street name; e.g. **Abbeygate St.** appears after **Abbey Gdns.** but before **Abbey Grn.**

3. Streets and a selection of flats and walkways too small to be shown on the maps, appear in the index with the thoroughfare to which it is connected shown in brackets; e.g. **Abbey Chambers** BA1: Bath . . . .5G **7** (off York St.)

4. Addresses that are in more than one part are referred to as not continuous.

5. Places and areas are shown in the index in BLUE TYPE and the map reference is to the actual map square in which the town centre or area is located and not to the place name shown on the map; e.g. **ALMONDSBURY** 2C **26**

6. An example of a selected place of interest is **American Mus. in Britain, The** 6J **101**

7. An example of a station is **Avoncliff Station (Rail)** . . . .7C **124**. Included are Rail **(Rail)** and Park & Ride e.g. **Ashton Vale (Park & Ride)** 7D **60**

8. Junction names and Service Areas are shown in the index in BOLD CAPITAL TYPE; e.g. **GORDANO SERVICE AREA** 4D **44**

9. Map references for entries that appear on large scale pages **4-7** are shown first, with small scale map references shown in brackets; e.g. **Abbey Ct.** BA2: Bath 3J **7** (4D **100**)

GENERAL ABBREVIATIONS

All. : Alley	**Cotts.** : Cottages	**La.** : Lane	**Ri.** : Rise
App. : Approach	**Ct.** : Court	**Lit.** : Little	**Rd.** : Road
Arc. : Arcade	**Cres.** : Crescent	**Lwr.** : Lower	**Rdbt.** : Roundabout
Av. : Avenue	**Cft.** : Croft	**Mnr.** : Manor	**Shop.** : Shopping
Bk. : Back	**Dr.** : Drive	**Mans.** : Mansions	**Sth.** : South
Blvd. : Boulevard	**E.** : East	**Mkt.** : Market	**Sq.** : Square
Bri. : Bridge	**Ent.** : Enterprise	**Mdw.** : Meadow	**Sta.** : Station
B'way. : Broadway	**Est.** : Estate	**Mdws.** : Meadows	**St.** : Street
Bldgs. : Buildings	**Fld.** : Field	**M.** : Mews	**Ter.** : Terrace
Bungs. : Bungalows	**Flds.** : Fields	**Mt.** : Mount	**Twr.** : Tower
Bus. : Business	**Gdn.** : Garden	**Mus.** : Museum	**Trad.** : Trading
Cvn. : Caravan	**Gdns.** : Gardens	**Nth.** : North	**Up.** : Upper
C'way. : Causeway	**Ga.** : Gate	**No.** : Number	**Va.** : Vale
Cen. : Centre	**Gt.** : Great	**Pde.** : Parade	**Vw.** : View
Chu. : Church	**Grn.** : Green	**Pk.** : Park	**Vs.** : Villas
Circ. : Circle	**Gro.** : Grove	**Pas.** : Passage	**Vis.** : Visitors
Cir. : Circus	**Hgts.** : Heights	**Pl.** : Place	**Wlk.** : Walk
Cl. : Close	**Ho.** : House	**Pct.** : Precinct	**W.** : West
Comn. : Common	**Ho's.** : Houses	**Prom.** : Promenade	**Yd.** : Yard
Cnr. : Corner	**Ind.** : Industrial	**Quad.** : Quadrant	
Cott. : Cottage	**Info.** : Information	**Res.** : Residential	

LOCALITY ABBREVIATIONS

Abb L : **Abbots Leigh**	**Bur S** : **Burnham-on-Sea**	**F Brnt** : **East Brent**	**Ing C** : **Inglestone Common**
Abson : **Abson**	**Burr** : **Burrington**	**E Harp** : **East Harptree**	**Ingst** : **Ingst**
A'wck : **Aldwick**	**But** : **Butcombe**	**E Hunt** : **East Huntspill**	**Iron A** : **Iron Acton**
Alm : **Almondsbury**	**C Hth** : **Cadbury Heath**	**E Rols** : **East Rolstone**	**Itch** : **Itchington**
Alv : **Alveston**	**Came** : **Cameley**	**E Comp** : **Easter Compton**	**Iwood** : **Iwood**
Ash G : **Ashton Gate**	**Cam** : **Camerton**	**E'tn** : **Easton**	**Kel** : **Kelston**
Ash V : **Ashton Vale**	**Char** : **Charfield**	**Eas** : **Easton-in-Gordano**	**Kenn** : **Kenn**
Ash : **Ashwicke**	**Charl** : **Charlcombe**	**Eastv** : **Eastville**	**Kew** : **Kewstoke**
Aust : **Aust**	**C'hse** : **Charterhouse**	**E'wth** : **Edingworth**	**Key** : **Keynsham**
Avon : **Avoncliff**	**Ched** : **Cheddar**	**Edith** : **Edithmead**	**Kil** : **Kilmersdon**
A'mth : **Avonmouth**	**C'vey** : **Chelvey**	**Elbton** : **Elberton**	**Kings** : **Kingsdown**
Axb : **Axbridge**	**C'wd** : **Chelwood**	**Elbgh** : **Elborough**	**Kings S** : **Kingston Seymour**
Back : **Backwell**	**Chew M** : **Chew Magna**	**Emer G** : **Emersons Green**	**K'wd** : **Kingswood**
Badg : **Badgworth**	**Chew S** : **Chew Stoke**	**Eng** : **Englishcombe**	**King** : **Kington**
Bag : **Bagstone**	**Chip S** : **Chipping Sodbury**	**Fail** : **Failand**	**Know** : **Knowle**
Ban : **Banwell**	**Chit** : **Chittening**	**Fal** : **Falfield**	**L'frd** : **Langford**
Bar G : **Barrow Gurney**	**Chri** : **Christon**	**F'boro** : **Farmborough**	**L'rdge** : **Langridge**
Bar C : **Barrs Court**	**C'hll** : **Churchill**	**Far G** : **Farrington Gurney**	**L'dwn** : **Lansdown**
Bart : **Barton**	**Clan** : **Clandown**	**Faul** : **Faulkland**	**Law W** : **Lawrence Weston**
Bar H : **Barton Hill**	**C'tn** : **Clapton**	**F'tn** : **Felton**	**L Wds** : **Leigh Woods**
Bath : **Bath**	**Clap G** : **Clapton in Gordano**	**Fil** : **Filton**	**Ley** : **Leyhill**
B'ptn : **Bathampton**	**Clav** : **Claverham**	**Fish** : **Fishponds**	**Lim S** : **Limpley Stoke**
Bathe : **Batheaston**	**C'ton** : **Claverton**	**Flax B** : **Flax Bourton**	**Lit A** : **Little Ashley**
Bathf : **Bathford**	**Clav D** : **Claverton Down**	**Fox** : **Foxcote**	**Lit S** : **Little Stoke**
Beach : **Beach**	**C've** : **Cleeve**	**Fram C** : **Frampton Cotterell**	**L Sev** : **Littleton-upon-Severn**
B'ly : **Beachley**	**Clev** : **Clevedon**	**Fren** : **Frenchay**	**Lock** : **Locking**
Bedm : **Bedminster**	**Clif** : **Clifton**	**F'frd** : **Freshford**	**L'lze** : **Lockleaze**
Berr : **Berrow**	**Clut** : **Clutton**	**Gau E** : **Gaunt's Earthcott**	**L Ash** : **Long Ashton**
Bidd : **Biddisham**	**Coal H** : **Coalpit Heath**	**Grov** : **Grovesend**	**L Grn** : **Longwell Green**
B'stn : **Bishopston**	**Cod** : **Codrington**	**Hall** : **Hallatrow**	**L Ham** : **Lower Hamswell**
Bis S : **Bishop Sutton**	**C Ash** : **Cold Ashton**	**H'len** : **Hallen**	**L Wrax** : **Lower South Wraxall**
Bis : **Bishopsworth**	**C Down** : **Combe Down**	**H End** : **Hall End**	**L Wre** : **Lower Weare**
Bit : **Bitton**	**C Hay** : **Combe Hay**	**Ham** : **Hambrook**	**Lox** : **Loxton**
Blag : **Blagdon**	**Comp B** : **Compton Bishop**	**Han** : **Hanham**	**Lym** : **Lympsham**
B'don : **Bleadon**	**Comp D** : **Compton Dando**	**Hart** : **Hartcliffe**	**Mang** : **Mangotsfield**
Bwr A : **Bower Ashton**	**Comp M** : **Compton Martin**	**Hay** : **Haydon**	**Mark** : **Marksbury**
Brad L : **Bradford Leigh**	**Cong** : **Congresbury**	**Hem** : **Hemington**	**Mid** : **Midford**
Brad A : **Bradford-on-Avon**	**C Din** : **Coombe Dingle**	**Hen** : **Henbury**	**Mid N** : **Midsomer Norton**
Brad S : **Bradley Stoke**	**Cor** : **Corston**	**H'fld** : **Henfield**	**Mon C** : **Monkton Combe**
Brean : **Brean**	**Cot** : **Cotham**	**H'gro** : **Hengrove**	**Mon F** : **Monkton Farleigh**
Bre K : **Brent Knoll**	**C'hill** : **Cowhill**	**Henle** : **Henleaze**	**Nail** : **Nailsea**
Bren : **Brentry**	**Crom** : **Cromhall**	**Hew** : **Hewish**	**Nem T** : **Nempnett Thrubwell**
B'yte : **Bridgeyate**	**Cross** : **Cross**	**High** : **Highbridge**	**New L** : **Newton St Loe**
Brisl : **Brislington**	**Dod** : **Dodington**	**High L** : **High Littleton**	**N Wick** : **North Wick**
Bris : **Bristol**	**Down** : **Downend**	**Hin** : **Hinton**	**N'wick** : **Northwick**
B'ley : **Brockley**	**Doy** : **Doynton**	**Hin B** : **Hinton Blewett**	**N Wid** : **North Widcombe**
B'hll : **Broomhill**	**Dun** : **Dundry**	**Hor** : **Horfield**	**Nor H** : **Norton Hawkfield**
Buck : **Buckover**	**Dunk** : **Dunkerton**	**Hort** : **Horton**	**Nor M** : **Norton Malreward**
Bulw : **Bulwark**	**Dyr** : **Dyrham**	**Hut** : **Hutton**	**Nye** : **Nye**
Burn : **Burnett**	**E Grn** : **Earthcott Green**	**Ing** : **Inglesbatch**	**Odd D** : **Odd Down**

5C Bus. Cen.—Alveston Wlk.

Old D : Old Down
Old C : Oldland Common
Old S : Old Sodbury
Olv : Olveston
Pat : Patchway
Paul : Paulton
Pea J : Peasedown St John
Pens : Pensford
Pill : Pill
Piln : Pilning
P'bry : Portbury
P'head : Portishead
Pris : Priston
Pub : Publow
Puck : Pucklechurch
Pux : Puxton
Q Char : Queen Charlton
Rads : Radstock
Rang : Rangeworthy
Redf : Redfield
Redh : Redhill
Redl : Redland
Redw : Redwick
Regil : Regil
R'frd : Rickford
Rook : Rooksbridge
Row : Rowberrow
Rudg : Rudgeway
St Ap : St Annes Park
St C : St Catherine
St G : St George
St Geo : St George's
Salt : Saltford
Sandf : Sandford
Sea M : Sea Mills
Sev B : Severn Beach
S'ham : Shipham
Shire : Shirehampton
Sho : Shockerwick
Short : Shortwood
Shos : Shoscombe
Sis : Siston
Soun : Soundwell
S'mead : Southmead
S'ske : Southstoke
S'wll : Speedwell
Stan D : Stanton Drew
Stan P : Stanton Prior
Stan W : Stanton Wick
Stap H : Staple Hill
Stap : Stapleton
Star : Star
Stoc : Stockwood
Stok B : Stoke Bishop
Stok G : Stoke Gifford
Ston L : Stoney Littleton
Stow : Stowey
Stratt F : Stratton-on-the-Fosse
Swa : Swainswick
S'frd : Swineford
Tad : Tadwick
Temp C : Temple Cloud
T'bry : Thornbury
Tic : Tickenham
Tim : Timsbury
Toc : Tockington
Tun : Tunley
Tur : Turleigh
Tyth : Tytherington
Ubl : Ubley
Udl : Udley
Uph : Uphill
Up S Wra : Upper South Wraxall
Up Str : Upper Strode
Up Swa : Upper Swainswick
Upton C : Upton Cheyney
Walt G : Walton-in-Gordano
Warl : Warleigh
Warm : Warmley
W'fld : Watchfield
Weare : Weare
Webb : Webbington
W Hth : Webbs Heath
Wel : Wellow
W Har : West Harptree
W Hunt : West Huntspill
W Wick : West Wick
W Trym : Westbury-on-Trym
W'lgh : Westerleigh
W'ton : Weston
Wes : Weston in Gordano
W Mare : Weston-Super-Mare
W'ton V : Weston Village
Whit : Whitchurch
W'hall : Whitehall
Wick : Wick
Wick L : Wick St Lawrence
Wickw : Wickwar
Will : Willsbridge
Wind H : Windmill Hill
Winf : Winford
Wins : Winscombe
W'ley : Winsley
Wint : Winterbourne
Wint D : Winterbourne Down
Withy : Withywood
Wool : Woollard
W'ly : Woolley
Wor : Worle
Wrax : Wraxall
Wrin : Wrington
Writ : Writhlington
Yate : Yate
Yat : Yatton

5C Bus. Cen. BS21: Clev . . . 1B 68
21 West *BS3: Bedm* . . . *6J 61*
(off Skypark Rd.)
100 Steps BS15: Han . . . 4J 63
5102 BS1: Bris . . . 1G 5 (1A 62)

A

Abbey Chambers *BA1: Bath* . . . *5G 7*
(off York St.)
Abbey Chu. Ho. *BA1: Bath* . . . *5J 100*
(off Hetling Ct.)
Abbey Church Yd. *BA1: Bath* . . . *4G 7*
(off Cheap St.)
Abbey Cl. BS31: Key . . . 4D 78
Abbey Ct. BA2: Bath . . . 3J 7 (4D 100)
BS4: St Ap . . . 4H 63
Abbeydale BS36: Wint . . . 1C 38
Abbey Gdns. BS24: W'ton V . . . 4C 106
Abbeygate St. BA1: Bath . . . 5G 7 (5C 100)
Abbey Grn. BA1: Bath . . . 5G 7 (5C 100)
Abbey Ho. BS37: Yate . . . 7D 30
Abbey La. BS35: Grov . . . 5A 12
Abbey Mill BA15: Brad A . . . 6H 125
Abbey Pk. BS31: Key . . . 4D 78
Abbey Retail Pk. BS34: Fil . . . 5E 36
Abbey Rd. BS9: W Trym . . . 2F 47
Abbey St. *BA1: Bath* . . . *5G 7*
(off York St.)
Abbey Vw. BA2: Bath . . . 6K 7 (6D 100)
BA3: Rads . . . 3A 154
Abbey Vw. Gdns.
BA2: Bath . . . 6J 7 (6D 100)
Abbeywood Dr. BS9: Stok B . . . 3C 46
Abbeywood Pk. BS34: Fil . . . 5D 36
Abbots Av. BS15: Han . . . 5A 64
Abbotsbury Rd. BS48: Nail . . . 1F 71
Abbots Cl. BS14: Whit . . . 7C 76
BS22: Wor . . . 1E 106
TA8: Bur S . . . 2D 158
Abbotsford Rd. BS6: Cot . . . 7H 47
Abbots Horn BS48: Nail . . . 7F 57
ABBOTSIDE . . . 2K 13
ABBOTS LEIGH . . . 1A 60
Abbots Leigh Rd. BS8: Abb L, L Wds . . . 1A 60
Abbots Rd. BS15: Han . . . 6A 64
Abbots Way BS9: Henle . . . 2K 47
Abbotswood BS15: K'wd . . . 2B 64
BS37: Yate . . . 7D 30
Abbott Rd. BS35: Sev B . . . 1A 24
Abbotts Farm Cl. BS39: Paul . . . 1B 152
Aberdeen Rd. BS6: Cot . . . 1H 61
Abi Clay Ct. *BS2: Bris* . . . *6B 48*
(off Sevier St.)
Abingdon Gdns. BA2: Odd D . . . 4K 121
Abingdon Rd. BS16: Fish . . . 5J 49
Abingdon St. TA8: Bur S . . . 2C 158
Ableton Ct. BS35: Sev B . . . 7A 16
Ableton La. BS10: H'len . . . 6A 24
BS35: Sev B . . . 7A 16
Ableton Wlk. BS9: Sea M . . . 3C 46
Abona Ct. BS9: Sea M . . . 2C 46
Abon Ho. BS9: Sea M . . . 4C 46
Abraham Cl. BS5: E'tn . . . 1D 62
Abraham Fry Ho. BS15: K'wd . . . 2C 64
ABSON . . . 6D 52
Abson Rd. BS16: Puck . . . 3C 52
BS30: Abson . . . 5C 52
Acacia Av. BS16: Stap H . . . 4A 50
BS23: W Mare . . . 4K 105
Acacia Cl. BS16: Stap H . . . 5B 50
Acacia Ct. BS31: Key . . . 6A 78
Acacia Gro. BA2: Bath . . . 1J 121
Acacia M. BS16: Stap H . . . 4B 50
Acacia Rd. BA3: Rads . . . 5J 153
BS16: Stap H . . . 4B 50
Academy, The BA2: Bath . . . 6E 6 (6B 100)
Access 18 West BS11: A'mth . . . 5G 33
Accommodation Rd.
BS24: B'don . . . 2G 145
Acer Cres. BS32: Alm . . . 1G 27
Acer Village BS14: H'gro . . . 3E 76
Aconite Cl. BS22: Wick L . . . 6F 85
Acorn Cl. TA9: High . . . 4F 159
Acorn Gro. BS13: Bis . . . 4E 74
Acraman's Rd. BS3: Bedm . . . 7D 4 (5J 61)
Acresbush Cl. BS13: Bis . . . 5G 75
Acton Court . . . 1H 29
Acton Rd. BS16: Fish . . . 5J 49
Adams Cl. BA2: Pea J . . . 5D 142
TA9: W Hunt . . . 6E 158
Adams Ct. *BS8: Clif* . . . *3F 61*
(off Cumberland Pl.)
Adams Hay BS4: Brisl . . . 1F 77
Adams Land BS36: Coal H . . . 7G 29
Adam St. TA8: Bur S . . . 2D 158
Adastral Rd. BS24: Lock . . . 1H 129
Adderly Ga. BS16: Emer G . . . 1F 51
Addicott Rd. BS23: W Mare . . . 6G 105
Addiscombe Rd. BS14: Whit . . . 5D 76
BS23: W Mare . . . 1G 127
Addison Rd. BS3: Wind H . . . 6A 62
Adelaide Pl. BA2: Bath . . . 4K 7 (5D 100)
BS5: E'tn . . . 1D 62
BS16: Fish . . . 4H 49
Adelaide Ter. BS16: Fish . . . 4J 49
Adelante Cl. BS34: Stok G . . . 3J 37
Admiral Cl. BS16: Stap . . . 1F 49
Admirals Wlk. BS20: P'head . . . 3D 42
Aelfric Mdw. BS20: P'head . . . 4H 43
Agate St. BS3: Bedm . . . 6H 61
Aiken St. BS5: Bar H . . . 3D 62
Ainslie's Belvedere *BA1: Bath* . . . *1F 7*
(off Caroline Pl.)
Aintree Dr. BS16: Down . . . 6D 38
Air Balloon Rd. BS5: St G . . . 2J 63
Airpoint BS3: Bedm . . . 6J 61
Airport Rd. BS14: H'gro . . . 3E 76
Aisecome Way BS22: W Mare . . . 6A 106
Akeman Way BS11: Shire . . . 7G 33
Alanscourt BS30: C Hth . . . 4F 65
Alard Rd. BS4: Know . . . 3B 76
Albany Bldgs. BS3: Bedm . . . 5J 61
Albany Ct. BA2: Bath . . . 5H 99
Albany Ga. BS34: Stok G . . . 2G 37
Albany Rd. BA2: Bath . . . 5H 99
BS6: Bris . . . 7B 48
Albany St. BS15: K'wd . . . 1A 64
Albany Way BS30: Old C . . . 4G 65
Albermarle Row BS8: Clif . . . 3F 61
Albermarle Ter. *BS8: Clif* . . . *3F 61*
(off Cumberland Pl.)
Albert Av. BA2: Pea J . . . 6C 142
BS23: W Mare . . . 6G 105
Albert Cres. BS2: Bris . . . 4C 62
Albert Gro. BS5: St G . . . 1H 63
Albert Gro. Sth. BS5: St G . . . 1H 63
Albert Mill BS31: Key . . . 6D 78
Alberton Rd. BS16: B'hll . . . 2H 49
Albert Pde. BS5: Redf . . . 1F 63
Albert Pk. BS6: Bris . . . 7B 48
Albert Pk. Pl. BS6: Bris . . . 7A 48
Albert Pl. BA2: C Down . . . 3E 122
BS3: Bedm . . . 6J 61
BS9: W Trym . . . 1G 47
Albert Quad. BS23: W Mare . . . 4G 105
Albert Rd. BS2: Bris . . . 7K 5 (5C 62)
BS15: Han . . . 4B 64
BS16: Stap H . . . 4C 50
BS20: P'head . . . 3F 43
BS21: Clev . . . 6C 54
BS23: W Mare . . . 6G 105
BS31: Key . . . 5C 78
BS35: Sev B . . . 7A 16
Albert St. BS5: Redf . . . 1E 62
Albert Ter. BA2: Bath . . . 5J 99
BS16: Fish . . . 4H 49
Albion Bldgs. BA1: Bath . . . 3B 6 (4K 99)
Albion Chambers BS1: Bris . . . 3F 5
Albion Cl. BS16: Mang . . . 3D 50
Albion Dockside Est.
BS1: Bris . . . 6B 4 (4H 61)
Albion Pl. BA1: Bath . . . 3C 6 (4A 100)
BS2: Bris . . . 3C 62
(Kingsland Rd.)
BS2: Bris . . . 2J 5
(Lawford St.)
Albion Rd. BS5: E'tn . . . 7D 48
Albion St. BS5: Redf . . . 1E 62
Albion Ter. BA1: Bath . . . 3C 6 (4A 100)
BS27: Ched . . . *7D 150*
(off Wesley M.)
BS34: Pat . . . 5D 26
Alburys BS40: Wrin . . . 1F 111
Alcove Rd. BS16: Fish . . . 5G 49
Aldercombe Rd. BS9: C Din . . . 7C 34
Alder Ct. BS14: H'gro . . . 5D 76
Alderdown Cl. BS11: Law W . . . 7A 34
Alder Dr. BS5: W'hall . . . 7G 49
Alderley Rd. BA2: Bath . . . 7G 99
Aldermoor Way BS30: L Grn . . . 5C 64
(not continuous)
Alderney Av. BS4: Brisl . . . 5H 63
Alders, The *BS16: Fren* . . . *6K 37*
(off Marlborough Dr.)
Alder Ter. BA3: Rads . . . 4J 153
Alderton Rd. BS7: Hor . . . 7A 36
Alder Way BA2: Odd D . . . 4K 121
Aldhelm Ct. BA15: Brad A . . . 7J 125
ALDWICK . . . 5A 112
Aldwick Av. BS13: Hart . . . 7J 75
Aldwick La. BS40: A'wck, But . . . 5K 111
Aldwych Cl. TA8: Bur S . . . 3E 158
Alec Ricketts Cl. BA2: Bath . . . 6F 99
Alexander Bldgs. BA1: Bath . . . 2D 100
Alexander Hall BA2: Lim S . . . 6A 124
Alexander Way BS49: Yat . . . 4H 87
Alexandra Cl. BS16: Stap H . . . 4B 50
Alexandra Ct. BS16: Fish . . . 4H 49
BS21: Clev . . . 5C 54
Alexandra Gdns. BS16: Stap H . . . 4B 50
Alexandra Pde. BS23: W Mare . . . 5G 105
Alexandra Pk. BS6: Redl . . . 6J 47
BS16: Fish . . . 4H 49
BS39: Paul . . . 1C 152
Alexandra Pl. BA2: C Down . . . 3E 122
BS16: Stap H . . . 4B 50
Alexandra Rd. BA2: Bath . . . 7G 7 (6C 100)
BS8: Clif . . . 1A 4 (1H 61)
BS10: W Trym . . . 7J 35
BS13: Bis . . . 3F 75
BS15: Han . . . 4B 64
BS21: Clev . . . 5C 54
BS36: Coal H . . . 7H 29
Alexandra Ter. BS39: Paul . . . 1C 152
Alexandra Way BS35: T'bry . . . 1K 11
Alford Rd. BS4: Brisl . . . 7E 62
Alfred Ct. BS23: W Mare . . . 5G 105
Alfred Hill BS2: Bris . . . 1E 4 (1K 61)
Alfred Lovell Gdns. BS30: C Hth . . . 5E 64
Alfred Pde. BS2: Bris . . . 1E 4 (1K 61)
Alfred Pl. BS1: Bris . . . 7F 5 (4K 61)
BS2: Bris . . . 1D 4 (1J 61)
Alfred Rd. BS3: Wind H . . . 6K 61
BS6: Henle . . . 4G 47
Alfred St. BA1: Bath . . . 2F 7 (4B 100)
BS2: Bris . . . 3C 62
BS5: Redf . . . 1E 62
BS23: W Mare . . . 5G 105
Algars Dr. BS37: Iron A . . . 3J 29
Algiers St. BS3: Wind H . . . 6K 61
Alison Gdns. BS48: Back . . . 3J 71
Allandale Rd. TA8: Bur S . . . 7C 156
Allanmead Rd. BS14: H'gro . . . 2D 76
Allans Way BS24: W'ton V . . . 5D 106
Allens La. BS25: S'ham . . . 6B 132
Aller BS24: W Mare . . . 3J 127
Aller Pde. BS24: W Mare . . . 3J 127
Allerton Cres. BS14: Whit . . . 6D 76
Allerton Gdns. BS14: H'gro . . . 5D 76
Allerton Rd. BS14: Whit . . . 6C 76
Allfoxton Rd. BS7: Eastv . . . 5C 48
All Hallows Rd. BS5: E'tn . . . 1D 62
Allington Dr. BS30: Bar C . . . 5D 64
Allington Gdns. BS48: Nail . . . 2E 70
Allington Rd. BS3: Bris . . . 7C 4 (4J 61)
Allison Av. BS4: Brisl . . . 6G 63
Allison Rd. BS4: Brisl . . . 6F 63
All Saints Cl. BS30: L Grn . . . 6E 64
All Saints Ct. BS1: Bris . . . 3F 5 (3K 61)
All Saints Gdns. BS8: Clif . . . 1G 61
All Saints La. BS1: Bris . . . 3F 5 (2K 61)
BS21: Clev . . . 5F 55
All Saints Pl. BA2: Clav D . . . 6F 101
All Saints Rd. BA1: Bath . . . 3B 100
BS8: Clif . . . 1G 61
BS23: W Mare . . . 3G 105
All Saints St. BS1: Bris . . . 3F 5 (2K 61)
Alma Cl. BS15: K'wd . . . 1C 64
Alma Ct. BS8: Clif . . . 7H 47
Alma Rd. BS8: Clif . . . 1G 61
BS15: K'wd . . . 7C 50
Alma Rd. Av. BS8: Clif . . . 1H 61
Alma St. BS23: W Mare . . . 5G 105
Alma Va. Rd. BS8: Clif . . . 1G 61
Almeda Rd. BS5: St G . . . 3J 63
Almond Cl. BS22: Wor . . . 3E 106
ALMONDSBURY . . . 2C 26
Almondsbury Bus. Cen.
BS32: Brad S . . . 2F 27
Almond Wlk. BS13: Bis . . . 4H 75
Almond Way BS16: Mang . . . 3D 50
Almorah Rd. BS3: Wind H . . . 6A 62
Alonzo Pl. BS21: Clev . . . 5D 54
Alpha Cen., The BS37: Yate . . . 3C 30
Alpha Ho. TA9: High . . . 5G 159
Alpha Rd. BS3: Bedm . . . 7E 4 (5K 61)
Alpine Cl. BS39: Paul . . . 2D 152
Alpine Gdns. BA1: Bath . . . 1G 7 (3C 100)
Alpine Rd. BS5: E'tn . . . 7E 48
BS39: Paul . . . 2D 152
Alsop Rd. BS15: K'wd . . . 1B 64
ALSTONE . . . 6E 158
Alstone Gdns. TA9: W Hunt . . . 6E 158
Alstone La. TA9: W Hunt . . . 6E 158
Alstone Rd. TA9: W Hunt . . . 6E 158
Alstone Wildlife Pk. . . . 6E 158
Alton Pl. BA2: Bath . . . 7G 7 (6C 100)
Alton Rd. BS7: Hor . . . 3B 48
Altringham Rd. BS5: W'hall . . . 7F 49
Alverstoke BS14: H'gro . . . 3B 76
ALVESTON . . . 7J 11
ALVESTON DOWN . . . 7H 11
Alveston Hill BS35: T'bry . . . 6J 11
Alveston Rd. BS32: Old D . . . 2E 18
Alveston Wlk. BS9: Sea M . . . 1B 46

Alwins Ct.—Avondown Cl.

Alwins Ct. BS30: Bar C 5D **64**
Ambares Ct. BA3: Mid N 6D **152**
Amberey Rd. BS23: W Mare 7H **105**
Amberlands Cl. BS48: Back 3J **71**
Amberley Cl. BS16: Down 1B **50**
BS31: Key 6C **78**
Amberley Gdns. BS48: Nail 1F **71**
Amberley Rd. BS16: Down 1B **50**
BS34: Pat 6D **26**
Amberley Way GL12: Wickw 1H **23**
Amble Cl. BS15: K'wd 2D **64**
Ambleside Av. BS10: S'mead 6H **35**
Ambleside Rd. BA2: Bath 2H **121**
Ambra Ct. BS8: Clif 3G **61**
Ambra Ter. BS8: Clif 3G **61**
Ambra Va. BS8: Clif 3G **61**
Ambra Va. E. BS8: Clif 3G **61**
Ambra Va. Sth. BS8: Clif 3G **61**
Ambra Va. W. BS8: Clif 3G **61**
Ambrose Rd. BS8: Clif 3G **61**
Ambury BA1: Bath 6F **7** (6B **100**)
Amelia Ct. BS1: Bris 4E **4** (3K **61**)
Amercombe Wlk. BS14: Stoc 3F **77**
American Mus. in Britain, The 6J **101**
Amery La. BA1: Bath 5F **7** (5C **100**)
AMESBURY 3D **140**
Amesbury Dr. BS24: B'don 7K **127**
AMF Bowling
Weston-Super-Mare 5F **105**
Amis Wlk. BS7: Hor 7C **36**
Ammerdown Pk. 7E **154**
Ammerdown Ter. BA3: Hem 7F **155**
Anchorage, The
BS20: P'head 2G **43**
Anchor Cl. BS5: St G 3H **63**
Anchor Ho. BS4: Know 7D **62**
Anchor La. BS1: Bris 5D **4** (3J **61**)
Anchor Rd. BA1: W'ton 2H **99**
BS1: Bris 5B **4** (3H **61**)
BS15: K'wd 7E **50**
Anchor Sq. BS1: Bris 5D **4** (3J **61**)
Anchor Way BS20: Pill 4H **45**
Ancliff Sq. BA15: Avon 7C **124**
Andereach Cl. BS14: H'gro 2D **76**
Andover Rd. BS4: Know 7B **62**
Andrew Millman Ct. BS37: Yate 5F **31**
Andruss Dr. BS41: Dun 1D **92**
Angels Ground BS4: St Ap 3H **63**
Angers Rd. BS4: Wind H 5B **62**
Anglesea Pl. BS8: Clif 6G **47**
Anglo Office Pk. BS15: K'wd 6K **49**
Anglo Ter. BA1: Bath 1H **7**
Animal Farm Country Pk. 4D **144**
Ankatel Cl. BS23: W Mare 7J **105**
Annaly Rd. BS27: Ched 7C **150**
Annandale Av. BS22: Wor 3C **106**
Annie Scott Cl. BS16: Fish 4H **49**
Anson Cl. BS31: Salt 1H **97**
Anson Rd. BS22: Kew 7B **84**
BS24: Lock 6E **106**
Anstey's Cl. BS15: Han 4K **63**
Anstey's Rd. BS15: Han 4K **63**
Anstey St. BS5: E'tn 7D **48**
Anthea Rd. BS5: S'wll 6G **49**
Antona Ct. BS11: Shire 1H **45**
Antona Dr. BS11: Shire 1H **45**
Antrim Rd. BS9: Henle 2H **47**
Anvil Rd. BS49: Clav 2B **88**
Anvil St. BS2: Bris 4K **5** (3B **62**)
Apex Ct. BS32: Brad S 3F **27**
Apex Dr. TA9: High 4E **158**
Apex Leisure & Wildlife Pk. 4D **158**
Apollo Apartments BS1: Bris 4F **5**
Apperley Cl. BS37: Yate 6D **30**
Appleby Wlk. BS4: Know 3K **75**
Applecroft BA2: Shos 7E **142**
Appledore BS22: Wor 2D **106**
Appledore Cl. BS14: H'gro 2D **76**
Apple Farm La. BS24: W Wick 3F **107**
Applegate BS10: Bren 4H **35**
Applehayes Ri. BS20: Eas 5F **45**
Appletree Ct. BS22: Wor 2F **107**
Apple Tree Dr. BS25: Wins 5G **131**
Appletree M. BS22: Wor 2F **107**
Applin Grn. BS16: Emer G 2G **51**
Appsley Cl. BS22: W Mare 2A **106**
Apseleys Mead BS32: Brad S 4E **26**
Apsley Ct. BA1: Bath 4H **99**
Apsley Rd. BA1: Bath 4G **99**
BS8: Clif 7G **47**
Apsley St. BS5: Eastv 6E **48**
Apsley Vs. BS6: Bris 7K **47**
Arbutus Dr. BS9: C Din 1C **46**
Arbutus Wlk. BS9: C Din 6D **34**
Arcade, The BS1: Bris 2G **5**
Arch Cl. BS41: L Ash 1K **73**
Archer Ct. BS30: L Grn 6D **64**
Archer Dr. TA8: Bur S 2E **158**
Archer's Ct. BS21: Clev 5D **54**
Archer Wlk. BS14: Stoc 4G **77**
Archfield Rd. BS6: Cot 7J **47**
Arch Gro. BS41: L Ash 1K **73**
Architectural Cen., The *BS1: Bris* *6E 4*
(off Narrow Quay)
Archway St. BA2: Bath 6J **7** (6D **100**)
Ardagh Ct. BS7: Hor 1B **48**
Arden Cl. BS22: Wor 1D **106**
BS32: Brad S 1G **37**
Ardenton Wlk. BS10: Bren 4G **35**
Ardern Cl. BS9: C Din 7B **34**
Ardnave Holiday Pk.
BS22: Kew 1J **105**
Argus Ct. BS3: Bedm 7J **61**
Argus Rd. BS3: Bedm 6J **61**
Argyle Av. BS5: Eastv 6E **48**
BS23: W Mare 1H **127**
Argyle Dr. BS37: Yate 2E **30**
Argyle Pl. BS8: Clif 5A **4** (3G **61**)
Argyle Rd. BS2: Bris 1A **62**
BS16: Fish 6K **49**
BS21: Clev 4D **54**
Argyle St. BA2: Bath 4H **7** (5C **100**)
BS3: Bedm 5J **61**
BS5: Eastv 6E **48**
Argyle Ter. BA2: Bath 5J **99**
Arkells Ct. GL12: Wickw 6G **15**
Arley Cotts. BS6: Cot 7K **47**
Arley Ct. BS6: Cot 7K **47**
Arley Hill BS6: Cot 7K **47**
Arley Pk. BS6: Cot 7K **47**
Arley Ter. BS5: W'hall 7G **49**
Arlingham Way BS34: Pat 5A **26**
Arlington Rd. BA2: Bath 6B **6** (6K **99**)
BS4: St Ap 3F **63**
Arlington Vs. BS8: Clif 2A **4** (2H **61**)
Armada Ho. BS1: Bris 7A **48**
Armadale Av. BS6: Bris 7A **48**
Armada Pl. BS1: Bris 7A **48**
Armada Rd. BS14: Whit 4C **76**
Armes Ct. BA2: Bath 7H **7** (6C **100**)
Armoury Sq. BS5: E'tn 1C **62**
Armstrong Cl. BS35: T'bry 5B **12**
Armstrong Ct. BS37: Yate 3C **30**
Armstrong Dr. BS30: C Hth 4F **65**
Armstrong Way BS37: Yate 3A **30**
Arnall Dr. BS10: Hen 6F **35**
Arncliffe BS10: S'mead 7J **35**
Arnold Ct. BS37: Chip S 5H **31**
Arnold Rd. BS16: Mang, Sis 5F **51**
Arnolds Fld. Est. GL12: Wickw 6G **15**
Arnold's Way BS49: Yat 2F **87**
Arnolfini 6E **4** (4J **61**)
Arnor Cl. BS22: Wor 7E **84**
Arno's St. BS4: Wind H 6C **62**
ARNO'S VALE 5D **62**
Arnside Rd. BS10: S'mead 6J **35**
Arrowfield Cl. BS14: Whit 1C **94**
Artemesia Av. BS22: W Mare 4C **106**
Arthurs Cl. BS16: Emer G 2G **51**
Arthur Skemp Cl. BS5: Bar H 2D **62**
Arthur St. BS2: Bris 4C **62**
BS5: Redf 1E **62**
Arthurswood Rd. BS13: Withy 6G **75**
Arundel Cl. BS13: Hart 5H **75**
Arundel Ct. BS7: B'stn 5K **47**
Arundell Ct. BS23: W Mare 4G **105**
Arundell Rd. BS23: W Mare 4G **105**
Arundel Rd. BA1: Bath 2C **100**
BS7: B'stn 5K **47**
BS21: Clev 6D **54**
Arundel Wlk. BS31: Key 5B **78**
Ascension Ho. BA2: Bath 7K **99**
Ascot Cl. BS16: Down 6D **38**
Ascot Rd. BS10: S'mead 5K **35**
Ashbourne Cl. BS30: Old C 3G **65**
Ashburton Rd. BS10: S'mead 6J **35**
Ashbury Dr. BS22: W Mare 2K **105**
Ash Cl. BS16: Fish 5A **50**
BS22: St Geo 2H **107**
BS25: Wins 4G **131**
BS34: Lit S 7F **27**
BS37: Yate 3D **30**
Ashcombe Cres. BS30: Old C 3G **65**
Ashcombe Gdns.
BS23: W Mare 3J **105**
Ashcombe Ho. TA8: Bur S 4C **156**
Ashcombe Pk. Rd.
BS23: W Mare 3J **105**
Ashcombe Pl. BS23: W Mare 5H **105**
Ashcombe Rd. BS23: W Mare 5H **105**
Ashcott BS14: H'gro 3B **76**
Ashcott Cl. TA8: Bur S 2E **158**
Ashcott Dr. TA8: Bur S 2E **158**
Ashcott Pl. TA8: Bur S 1E **158**
Ash Ct. BS14: Whit 4C **76**
Ashcroft BS24: W Mare 3K **127**
Ashcroft Av. BS31: Key 5B **78**
Ashcroft Rd. BS9: Sea M 1C **46**
Ashdene Av. BS5: Eastv 5F **49**
Ashdene Rd. BS23: W Mare 3J **105**
Ashdown Rd. BS20: P'head 2C **42**
Asher La. BS2: Bris 2J **5** (2B **62**)
Ashes La. BA2: F'frd 7H **123**
Ashey La. BS27: Ched 6D **150**
Ashfield Pl. BS6: Bris 7B **48**
Ashfield Rd. BS3: Bedm 6H **61**
Ashford Dr. BS24: W Mare 4J **127**
Ashford Rd. BA2: Bath 7K **99**
BS34: Pat 7C **26**
BS40: Redh 7C **90**
Ashford Way BS15: K'wd 2E **64**
ASHGROVE 5D **142**
Ash Gro. BA2: Bath 7J **99**
BS16: Fish 5A **50**
BS21: Clev 5E **54**
BS23: Uph 3G **127**
Ashgrove BA2: Pea J 5D **142**
BS35: T'bry 3A **12**
Ashgrove Av. BS7: B'stn 4B **48**
BS8: Abb L 2B **60**
Ashgrove Cl. BS7: B'stn 4B **48**
Ashgrove Pl. BS7: B'stn 4B **48**
Ashgrove Rd. BS3: Bedm 6H **61**
BS6: Redl 7H **47**
BS7: B'stn 4B **48**
Ash Hayes Dr. BS48: Nail 1G **71**
Ash Hayes Rd. BS48: Nail 1G **71**
Ashland Rd. BS13: Withy 6G **75**
Ash La. BS32: Alm 3K **25**
Ashleigh Cl. BS23: W Mare 4J **105**
BS39: Paul 7C **140**
Ashleigh Cres. BS49: Yat 3H **87**
Ashleigh Ho. BS39: Paul 1C **152**
Ashleigh Rd. BS23: W Mare 4J **105**
BS49: Yat 3H **87**
Ashley BS15: K'wd 1D **64**
Ashley Apartments BS6: Bris 6B **48**
Ashley Av. BA1: Bath 4J **99**
TA8: Bur S 2D **158**
Ashley Cl. BA15: Brad A 4F **125**
(not continuous)
BS7: B'stn 4B **48**
BS25: Wins 6G **131**
Ashley Ct. BS6: Bris 7B **48**
Ashley Ct. Rd. BS7: Bris 6B **48**
ASHLEY DOWN 4B **48**
Ashley Down Rd. BS7: B'stn, Bris 5B **48**
BS7: B'stn, Hor 3A **48**
Ashley Gro. Rd. BS2: Bris 6B **48**
Ashley Hill BS6: Bris 5B **48**
BS7: Bris 5B **48**
Ashley La. BA15: W'ley 5D **124**
BS40: Burr, L'frd 6H **111**
Ashley Pde. BS2: Bris 6B **48**
Ashley Pk. BS6: Bris 5B **48**
Ashley Rd. BA1: Bathf 1A **102**
BA15: Brad A, Lit A 3F **125**
BS6: Bris 7A **48**
BS21: Clev 1B **68**
Ashley St. BS2: Bris 7C **48**
Ashley Ter. BA1: Bath 4J **99**
Ashley Trad. Est. BS2: Bris 6B **48**
Ashman Cl. BS5: E'tn 1C **62**
Ashmans Ga. BS39: Paul 1B **152**
Ashmans Yd. BA1: Bath 5H **99**
Ashmead BS39: Temp C 4G **139**
Ashmead Ho. BS5: Bar H 2D **62**
Ashmead Ind. Est. BS31: Key 5F **79**
Ashmead Pk. BS31: Key 5F **79**
Ashmead Rd. BS31: Key 5F **79**
Ashmead Way BS1: Bris 4F **61**
Ash Ridge Rd. BS32: Brad S 3D **26**
Ash Rd. BS7: Hor 3A **48**
BS29: Ban 2J **129**
Ashton *BS16: Fren* *6A 38*
(off Harford Dr.)
Ashton Av. BS1: Bris 4G **61**
Ashton Cl. BS21: Clev 1B **68**
Ashton Ct. BS41: L Ash 5D **60**
Ashton Court Nature Reserve 5C **60**
Ashton Court Vis. Cen. 5D **60**
Ashton Cres. BS48: Nail 1F **71**
Ashton Dr. BS3: Ash V 1E **74**
ASHTON GATE 5G **61**
Ashton Ga. Rd. BS3: Bris 5G **61**
Ashton Gate Stadium 6F **61**
Ashton Ga. Ter. BS3: Bris 5G **61**
Ashton Ga. Trad. Est. BS3: Ash V 6E **60**
Ashton Ga. Underpass
BS3: Ash V, Bwr A 5F **61**
ASHTON HILL 3J **97**
Ashton Hill BA2: Cor 4A **98**
Ashton Pk. Sports Cen. 5E **60**
Ashton Rd. BS3: Ash G 5F **61**
BS3: Ash V 6F **61**
BS41: L Ash 6C **60**
ASHTON VALE 7F **61**
Ashton Vale (Park & Ride) 7D **60**
Ashton Va. Rd. BS3: Ash V 6E **60**
Ashton Va. Trad. Est. BS3: Ash V 1F **75**
ASHTON WATERING 2H **73**
Ashton Way BS31: Key 4C **78**
Ash Tree Cl. BS24: B'don 7A **128**
TA8: Bur S 4C **156**
Ash Tree Ct. BA3: Rads 5J **153**
Ash Tree Cres. TA8: Bur S 4C **156**
Ash Tree Pl. TA8: Bur S 4C **156**
Ash Tree Rd. TA8: Bur S 4C **156**
Ashvale Cl. BS48: Nail 7J **57**
Ashville Pk. BS35: T'bry 5K **11**
Ashville Rd. BS3: Ash G 5G **61**
Ash Wlk. BS10: Bren 4H **35**
Ashwell Cl. BS14: Stoc 4G **77**
Ashwicke BS14: H'gro 4C **76**
Ashwood BS40: E Harp 7K **137**
Aspects Leisure Pk.
BS15: K'wd 4C **64**
Aspen Pk. Rd. BS22: W Mare 4C **106**
Assembly Rooms
Bath 2F **7**
Assembly Rooms La.
BS1: Bris 5E **4** (3K **61**)
Aston Ga. Depot BS3: Ash G 5F **61**
Aston Ho. BS1: Bris 7G **5**
Astry Cl. BS11: Law W 6A **34**
Atchley St. BS5: Bar H 2D **62**
Atherston BS30: Old C 4H **65**
Athlone Wlk. BS4: Know 1A **76**
Atholl Cl. BS22: Wor 1D **106**
Atkins Cl. BS14: Stoc 4G **77**
Atlanta Key TA8: Bur S 7C **156**
Atlantic Bus. Pk. BS23: W Mare 3E **104**
Atlantic Ct. BS23: W Mare 3E **104**
Atlantic Cres. TA8: Bur S 3D **158**
Atlantic Rd. BS11: Shire 7G **33**
BS23: W Mare 3E **104**
Atlantic Rd. Sth. BS23: W Mare 3E **104**
Atlas Cl. BS5: S'wll 6J **49**
Atlas Rd. BS3: Wind H 6A **62**
Atlas St. BS2: Bris 4D **62**
Atlay Ct. BS49: Yat 2H **87**
Atrium, The *BS2: Bris* *5K 5*
(off Anvil St.)
Attewell Ct. BA2: Bath 7B **100**
Atwell Cl. BS32: Alm 5D **26**
Atwood Dr. BS11: Law W 5B **34**
Atyeo Cl. BS3: Ash V 1E **74**
TA8: Bur S 7E **156**
Aubrey Meads BS30: Bit 2J **79**
Aubrey Rd. BS3: Bedm 6H **61**
Auburn Av. BS30: L Grn 6F **65**
Auburn Rd. BS6: Redl 6H **47**
Auckland Cl. BS23: W Mare 2H **127**
Auden Mead BS7: Hor 7C **36**
Audley Av. BA1: Bath 2A **6** (4J **99**)
Audley Cl. BA1: Bath 2A **6** (4K **99**)
BS37: Rang 5A **22**
Audley Gro. BA1: Bath 4J **99**
Audley Pk. Rd. BA1: Bath 1A **6** (3J **99**)
Audrey Wlk. BS9: Henle 1K **47**
Augusta Pl. BA1: Bath 3A **6** (4K **99**)
Aumery Gdns. BS39: High L 4B **140**
AUST 5G **9**
Austen Dr. BS22: Wor 7F **85**
Austen Gro. BS7: Hor 7C **36**
Austen Ho. BS7: Hor 7C **36**
Austen Pl. BS11: Shire 1J **45**
Aust La. BS9: W Trym 7G **35**
Aust Rd. BS35: Elbton, Olv 7K **9**
BS35: N'wick 2D **16**
Autumn M. BS24: W'ton V 4E **106**
Avalon Cl. BS49: Yat 2G **87**
Avalon Ho. BS48: Nail 1E **70**
Avalon La. BS5: St G 3K **63**
Avalon Rd. BS5: St G 4K **63**
TA9: High 4G **159**
Avebury Cl. TA8: Bur S 7F **157**
Avebury Rd. BS3: Ash V 7E **60**
Aveline's Hole 3H **133**
Avening Cl. BS48: Nail 2H **71**
Avening Rd. BS15: K'wd 1J **63**
Avenue, The BA2: C Down 3D **122**
BA2: Clav D 6G **101**
(not continuous)
BA2: Tim 3F **141**
BS5: St G 2G **63**
BS7: B'stn 5A **48**
BS8: Clif 7F **47**
BS9: Stok B 6D **46**
BS16: Fren 6G **37**
BS21: Clev 4D **54**
BS22: St Geo 1G **107**
BS25: Wins 5J **131**
BS31: Key 4C **78**
BS34: Lit S 1E **36**
BS34: Pat 4D **26**
BS37: Yate 5D **30**
BS48: Back 3J **71**
BS49: Yat 3H **87**
Avenue Pl. BA2: C Down 3D **122**
Averay Rd. BS16: Stap 4E **48**
Averill Ct. BS21: Clev 5D **54**
Avonbank Ind. Est. BS11: A'mth 1F **45**
Avonbridge Trad. Est. BS11: Shire 7G **33**
Avon Bus. Pk. BS16: Fish 5H **49**
AVONCLIFF 7D **124**
Avoncliff Station (Rail) 7C **124**
Avon Cl. BA15: Brad A 7J **125**
BS5: St G 3H **63**
BS23: W Mare 3H **127**
BS31: Key 4D **78**
Avon Ct. BA1: Bathe 6J **83**
BS16: Fish 3K **49**
Avon Cres. BS1: Bris 4G **61**
GL12: Wickw 6H **15**
(not continuous)
Avondale Bldgs. BA1: Bath 1D **100**
Avondale Bus. Cen. BS15: K'wd 6A **50**
Avondale Ct. BA1: Bath 4H **99**
BS9: Stok B 6D **46**
BS30: L Grn 6D **64**
Avondale Rd. BA1: Bath 4H **99**
Avondale Works BS15: K'wd 6A **50**
Avondown Cl. BS10: S'mead 5K **35**

Avondown Ct.—Bath Racecourse

Avondown Ct. BS3: Bedm 7J **61**
Avondown Ho. BA2: Bath 6H **99**
Avonfield Av. BA15: Brad A 7J **125**
Avon Gorge Ind. Est. BS11: A'mth 1G **45**
Avon Gro. BS9: Stok B 6D **46**
Avon Hgts. BA2: Lim S 6A **124**
Avon La. BS31: Salt 6K **79**
Avonlea BS15: Han 4A **64**
BS37: Yate 6D **30**
Avonleaze BS9: Sea M 3B **46**
Avonleigh Rd. BS3: Bedm 7H **61**
Avon Meads BS2: Bris 4E **62**
Avon Mill La. BS31: Key 4D **78**
AVONMOUTH 6F **33**
Avonmouth Rd. BS11: A'mth 6F **33**
BS11: Shire 7G **33**
Avonmouth Station (Rail) 6F **33**
Avonmouth Way BS10: Hen 4E **34**
BS11: A'mth 6G **33**
Avonmouth Way W. BS11: A'mth 5F **33**
Avon Pk. BA1: Bath 4G **99**
BS5: Redf 2F **63**
Avon Ring Rd. BS4: Key 2A **78**
BS15: Han 2A **78**
BS15: Warm, Sis 1F **65**
BS16: Down 6B **38**
BS16: Emer G, Mang, Sis 5E **38**
BS16: Ham 5G **37**
BS30: Bar C, Han 2A **78**
BS30: Sis .6F **51**
Avon Riverside Est. BS11: A'mth 1F **45**
Avon Rd. BS13: Bis 4G **75**
BS20: Pill .3G **45**
BS31: Key .5D **78**
Avonside Ind. Est. BS2: Bris 3E **62**
Avonside Rd. BS2: Bris 3E **62**
Avonside Way BS4: St Ap 3H **63**
Avon Ski & Action Cen. 2J **131**
Avonsmere Res. Pk. BS34: Stok G 4E **36**
Avon St. BA1: Bath 6F **7** (5B **100**)
BS2: Bris 4J **5** (3B **62**)
Avon Trad. Est. BS2: Bris 7K **5** (4C **62**)
Avon Va. BS9: Stok B 4D **46**
Avonvale Pl. BA1: Bathe 7H **83**
Avonvale Rd. BS5: Bar H, Redf 3D **62**
Avon Valley Bus. Pk. BS4: St Ap 3G **63**
Avon Valley Country Pk. 4G **79**
Avon Valley Farm Bus. Pk.
BS31: Key .5H **79**
Avon Valley Pk. 5K **63**
Avon Valley Railway
Bitton Station 1F **79**
Oldland Common Station 5H **65**
Avon Vw. BS15: Han 6K **63**
Avon Way BS9: Stok B 3C **46**
BS10: S'mead 7K **35**
BS20: P'head 3D **42**
BS35: T'bry 4A **12**
Avonwood Cl. BS11: Shire 2J **45**
Awdelett Cl. BS11: Law W 6B **34**
AWKLEY 5A **18**
Awkley La. BS32: Toc 4A **18**
BS35: Olv 4A **18**
Awkward Hill BS40: Nem T 7H **113**
AXBRIDGE 4J **149**
Axbridge Cl. BS48: Nail 2G **71**
TA8: Bur S 7E **156**
Axbridge Moor Drove BS26: Axb 7J **149**
Axbridge Mus.
(King John's Hunting Lodge) 4J **149**
Axbridge Rd. BA2: C Down 2C **122**
BS4: Know 7B **62**
BS27: Ched 4A **150**
Axe Cl. BS23: W Mare 7J **105**
Axe Ct. BS35: T'bry 4K **11**
Axford Way BA2: Pea J 5D **142**
Axis BS14: Hart 5K **75**
Ayckbourn Cl. TA8: Bur S 2E **158**
Aycote Cl. BS22: W Mare 2K **105**
Aylesbury Cres. BS3: Bedm 1H **75**
Aylesbury Rd. BS3: Bedm 1H **75**
Aylmer Cres. BS14: H'gro 4D **76**
Aylminton Wlk. BS11: Law W 5B **34**
Ayr St. BA2: Bath 5A **6** (5K **99**)
Azalea Rd. BS22: Wick L 6E **84**
Azelin Av. BS13: Hart 5H **75**
Aztec Cen., The BS32: Alm 4C **26**
AZTEC WEST .4C **26**
Aztec W. BS32: Alm 4C **26**
Azure, The *BS6: Bris* *7A* ***48***
(off Bath Bldgs.)

B

Backfields BS2: Bris 1G **5** (1A **62**)
Backfields Ct. *BS2: Bris* *1A* ***62***
(off Backfields La.)
Backfields La. BS2: Bris 1G **5** (1A **62**)
Back La. BS16: Puck 4A **52**
BS20: Pill .3G **45**
(not continuous)
BS21: Kings S 5A **68**
BS25: Row 4C **132**
BS26: Axb 4J **149**
BS27: Ched 7C **150**
Back La. BS31: Key 4C **78**
BS36: Coal H 1H **39**
GL12: Wickw 6G **15**
SN14: Dyr 3H **53**
Bk. of Kingsdown Pde. BS6: Bris 1K **61**
Back Rd. BS3: Bris 5G **61**
Bk. Stoke La. BS9: W Trym 2F **47**
Back St. BS23: W Mare 5G **105**
BACKWELL 4K **71**
Backwell Bow BS48: Back 1K **71**
BACKWELL COMMON 2J **71**
Backwell Comn. BS48: Back 3J **71**
BACKWELL GREEN 2B **72**
BACKWELL HILL 6C **72**
Backwell Hill Rd. BS48: Back 3B **72**
Backwell Leisure Cen. 4K **71**
Backwell Vw. BS48: Wrax 5A **58**
Backwell Wlk. BS13: Bis 2F **75**
Badenham Gro. BS11: Law W 7K **33**
Baden Hill Rd. GL12: Tyth 7F **13**
Baden Rd. BS5: Redf 2E **62**
BS15: K'wd 2E **64**
BS15: Warm 1F **65**
Bader Cl. BS37: Yate 3D **30**
Badger Cl. BS30: L Grn 6D **64**
Badger Ri. BS20: P'head 5A **42**
Badgers, The BS22: St Geo 1G **107**
Badgers Cl. BS32: Brad S 3F **27**
Badgers Dr. BS10: Bren 3A **36**
Badger Sett BS5: St G 2K **63**
Badgers Holt BS14: H'gro 4E **76**
Badger's La. BS32: Alm 3J **25**
Badgers Wlk. BS4: Brisl 7F **63**
Badgers Way BS24: W'ton V 4D **106**
Badgeworth BS37: Yate 1D **40**
Badman Cl. BS39: Paul 1B **152**
Badminton *BS16: Fren* *6A* ***38***
(off Penn Dr.)
Badminton Cen. BS37: Yate 4C **30**
Badminton Ct. BS37: Yate 4C **30**
Badminton Gdns. BA1: Bath 3J **99**
Badminton Rd. BS2: Bris 7B **48**
BS16: Down 2C **50**
BS36: Coal H, Wint, Wint D 5E **38**
BS36: Fram C 6J **29**
BS37: Chip S 6K **31**
BS37: Yate 5E **38**
Badminton Rd. Trad. Est. BS37: Yate . . .5B **30**
Badminton Wlk. BS16: Down 1C **50**
Badock Hall BS9: Stok B 4E **46**
Baglyn Av. BS15: Soun 5D **50**
Bagnell Cl. BS14: Stoc 5G **77**
Bagnell Rd. BS14: Stoc 5G **77**
BAGSTONE 2K **21**
Bagstone Rd. GL12: Bag 3K **21**
Bagworth Dr. BS30: L Grn 6D **64**
BAILBROOK 7F **83**
Bailbrook Ct. BA1: Swa 7G **83**
Bailbrook Gro. BA1: Swa 7E **82**
Bailbrook La. BA1: Swa 7E **82**
Baildon Ct. BS23: W Mare 1H **127**
Baildon Cres. BS23: W Mare 1J **127**
Baildon Rd. BS23: W Mare 1H **127**
Bailey Cl. BS22: W Mare 4C **106**
Bailey Ct. BS20: P'head 2H **43**
Baileys Barn BA15: Brad A 7H **125**
Baileys Ct. BS32: Brad S 1H **37**
Baileys Ct. Rd. BS32: Brad S 1G **37**
Baileys Mead Rd. BS16: Stap 3E **48**
Bailiffs Cl. BS26: Axb 5J **149**
Bailiffs' Wall BS26: Axb 6H **149**
Bainton Cl. BA15: Brad A 5J **125**
Baker Cl. BS21: Clev 2B **68**
Baker's Bldgs. BS40: Wrin 2F **111**
Bakersfield BS30: L Grn 6E **64**
Bakers Ground BS34: Stok G 2H **37**
Bakers La. BS40: L'frd 4E **110**
Bakers Pde. BA2: Tim 3F **141**
Baker St. BS23: W Mare 4G **105**
Balaclava Rd. BS16: Fish 5H **49**
Baldwin St. BS1: Bris 4E **4** (3K **61**)
Balfour Rd. BS3: Ash G 6H **61**
Ballance St. BA1: Bath 1F **7** (3B **100**)
Ballast La. BS11: A'mth 5H **33**
Balloon Ct. BS2: Bris 1H **5** (1A **62**)
Balls Barn La. BS24: E Rols 3A **108**
Ballstreet La. BS35: N'wick 4C **16**
Balmain St. BS4: Wind H 5C **62**
Balmoral Cl. BS34: Stok G 3F **37**
Balmoral Ct. BS16: Mang 3E **50**
Balmoral Dr. TA8: Bur S 6D **156**
Balmoral Ho. BS1: Bris 6C **4**
Balmoral Rd. BS7: Bris 6B **48**
BS30: L Grn 7D **64**
BS31: Key .6C **78**
Balmoral Way BS22: W Mare, Wor 2A **106**
Baltic Pl. BS20: Pill 4H **45**
Baltic Wharf Water Leisure Cen. 4G **61**
Balustrade *BA1: Bath* *2D* ***100***
(off St Saviours Rd.)
Bamfield BS14: Whit, H'gro 3B **76**
Bampton BS22: Wor 2D **106**
Bampton Cl. BS13: Bis 3H **75**
BS16: Emer G 2G **51**
Bampton Cft. BS16: Emer G 2G **51**
Bampton Dr. BS16: Down 7B **38**
Bancroft BA15: Brad A 5H **125**
Banfield Cl. BS11: Law W 7A **34**
Bangor Gro. BS4: St Ap 4H **63**
Bangrove Wlk. BS11: Law W 7J **33**
Banister Gro. BS4: Know 3K **75**
Bank Pl. BS20: Pill 4H **45**
Bank Rd. BS15: K'wd 1B **64**
BS35: Piln 6D **16**
Banks Cl. BS21: Clev 2D **68**
Bankside BS16: Stap H 4D **50**
Bankside Rd. BS4: Brisl 6F **63**
Bank St. TA9: High 5F **159**
Bannerdown Cl. BA1: Bathe 6K **83**
Bannerdown Dr. BA1: Bathe 6J **83**
Bannerdown Rd. BA1: Bathe 7J **83**
Bannerleigh La. BS8: L Wds 3E **60**
Bannerleigh Rd. BS8: L Wds 3E **60**
Bannerman Rd. BS5: E'tn 1D **62**
(not continuous)
Banner Rd. BS6: Bris 7A **48**
Bannetts Tree Cres. BS35: Alv 7J **11**
Bantock Cl. BS4: Know 4K **75**
Bantry Rd. BS4: Know 2A **76**
BANWELL 2B **130**
Banwell Cl. BS13: Bis 2G **75**
BS31: Key .1E **96**
Banwell Rd. BA2: Odd D 4K **121**
BS3: Ash G 6G **61**
BS24: Elbgh, Hut 3D **128**
BS25: Chri 6J **129**
BS25: Wins 4D **130**
BS26: Chri 6J **129**
BS29: Ban 6J **129**
Banyard Rd. BS20: P'bry 3C **44**
BAPTIST MILLS 6C **48**
Baptist St. BS5: E'tn 7C **48**
Barberry Farm Rd. BS49: Yat 2H **87**
Barbour Gdns. BS13: Hart 7K **75**
Barbour Rd. BS13: Hart 7K **75**
Barcroft Cl. BS15: K'wd 1A **64**
Barkers Mead BS37: Yate 1F **31**
Barker Wlk. BS5: E'tn 7C **48**
Barkleys Hill BS16: Stap 4E **48**
Barlands Ho. BS10: Hen 4F **35**
Barley Cl. BS16: Mang 2E **50**
BS36: Fram C 6G **29**
Barley Cft. BS9: W Trym 3F **47**
Barley Cross BS22: Wick L 6E **84**
Barleyfields BS2: Bris 4K **5** (3B **62**)
Barnabas Cl. BS26: Axb 4K **149**
Barnabas St. BS2: Bris 7A **48**
Barnaby Cl. BA3: Mid N 4E **152**
Barnack Trad. Est. BS3: Bedm 1J **75**
Barnard Cl. BS49: Yat 3J **87**
Barnard Wlk. BS31: Key 6B **78**
Barn Cl. BS16: Emer G 2F **51**
Barnes Ct. BS34: Stok G 3G **37**
Barnes St. BS5: St G 1F **63**
Barnfield Way BA1: Bathe 6K **83**
Barn Hill BA2: Shos 7F **143**
Barnhill Cl. BS37: Yate 2G **31**
Barnhill Rd. BS37: Chip S 5G **31**
Barn La. BS39: C'wd 6J **117**
Barn Owl Way BS34: Stok G 2H **37**
Barn Piece BA15: Brad A 7H **125**
Barn Pool BS25: S'ham 5B **132**
Barns Cl. BS48: Bar G 6H **73**
BS48: Nail 7G **57**
Barns Ground BS21: Clev 2D **68**
Barnstaple Ct. BS4: Know 2A **76**
Barnstaple Rd. BS4: Know 2A **76**
Barnstaple Wlk. BS4: Know 2B **76**
Barnwell Cl. BS10: Bren 3G **35**
Barnwood Cl. BS15: K'wd 1D **64**
Barnwood Ct. BS48: Nail 1D **70**
Barnwood Rd. BS37: Yate 7C **30**
Baron Cl. BS30: Bit 2J **79**
Barons Cl. BS3: Ash V 6F **61**
Barossa Pl. BS1: Bris 6F **5** (4K **61**)
Barracks La. BS11: Shire 7H **33**
Barratt St. BS5: E'tn 7D **48**
Barrie Way TA8: Bur S 2E **158**
Barrington Cl. BS15: Soun 6D **50**
Barrington Ct. BS4: Wind H 5B **62**
BS15: Soun 7C **50**
Barrington Rd. TA8: Bur S 7E **156**
BARROW COMMON 6B **74**
Barrow Ct. BS21: Tic 5B **56**
Barrow Ct. La. BS48: Bar G 6F **73**
BARROW GURNEY 6H **73**
Barrow Hill BS30: Wick 3B **66**
Barrow Hill Cres. BS11: Shire 1G **45**
Barrow Hill Rd. BS11: Shire 2G **45**
Barrow La. BS40: Winf 1J **91**
Barrowmead Dr. BS11: Law W 7K **33**
Barrow Rd. BA2: Odd D 3J **121**
BS5: Bar H 2D **62**
BS24: Hut 3C **128**
BARROWS 6C **150**
Barrows, The BS22: W Mare 5A **106**
BS27: Ched 5C **150**
Barrows Cl. BS25: C'hll 1K **131**
Barrows Cft. BS27: Ched 6C **150**
Barrows Pk. BS27: Ched 6C **150**
Barrows Rd. BS27: Ched 6C **150**
Barrow St. BS48: Bar G 4G **73**
BARROW VALE 7B **118**
Barrow Vw. BA2: F'boro 1F **141**
BARRS COURT 4D **64**
Barr's Ct. BS1: Bris 1G **5** (1A **62**)
Barrs Ct. Av. BS30: Bar C 4E **64**
Barrs Ct. Rd. BS30: Bar C 4E **64**
Barry Cl. BS24: W Mare 4J **127**
BS30: Bit .1G **79**
Barry Rd. BS30: Old C 7G **65**
Barstaple Ho. BS2: Bris 3K **5**
Barter Cl. BS15: K'wd 1B **64**
Bartholomew Row BA2: Tim 3F **141**
Bartholomews Sq. BS7: Hor 1B **48**
Bartlett's Rd. BS3: Bedm 7J **61**
Bartlett St. BA1: Bath 3F **7** (4B **100**)
Bartletts Way BS24: Lock 1F **129**
Bartley Ct. BS5: St G 2F **63**
Bartley St. BS3: Bedm 5K **61**
BARTON 7B **130**
Barton, The BA2: Cor 4A **98**
BS15: Han 5A **64**
BS24: B'don 7A **128**
BS39: Stan D 1C **116**
BS40: Comp M 6B **136**
Barton Bldgs. BA1: Bath 3F **7** (4B **100**)
Barton Cl. BS4: St Ap 3H **63**
BS35: Alv .7J **11**
BS36: Wint 2C **38**
TA8: Berr .2B **156**
Barton Ct. *BA1: Bath* *4G* ***7***
(off Up. Borough Walls)
BS5: Bar H 3E **62**
Barton Drove BS25: Wins 1B **148**
Barton Farm Country Pk. 7E **124**
Barton Grn. BS5: Bar H 2D **62**
BARTON HILL 3D **62**
Barton Hill Rd. BS5: Bar H 3D **62**
Barton Hill Trad. Est. BS5: Bar H 3D **62**
Barton Ho. BS1: Bris 1G **5** (1A **62**)
BS5: Redf .3E **62**
Bartonia Gro. BS4: Brisl 1F **77**
Barton Mnr. BS2: Bris 4K **5** (3C **62**)
Barton Mdw. Est. BS16: Fish 2A **50**
Barton Orchard BA15: Brad A 6G **125**
Barton Rd. BS2: Bris 5K **5** (3B **62**)
BS25: Bart, Wins 2J **147**
BS26: Bart, Webb 2J **147**
TA8: Berr .3B **156**
Barton St. BA1: Bath 4F **7** (5B **100**)
BS1: Bris 1F **5** (1K **61**)
Barton Va. BS2: Bris 4K **5** (3C **62**)
(not continuous)
Barwick Ho. BS11: Shire 1J **45**
Bassetts Pasture *BA15: Brad A* *7H* ***125***
(off Southway Rd.)
BATCH 2H **145**
BATCH, THE
BS39, Bishop Sutton 1K **137**
BS39, Paulton 1C **152**
Batch, The BA1: Bathe 7H **83**
BA2: F'boro 6E **118**
BA2: Wel .4K **143**
BS25: C'hll 2B **132**
BS31: Salt 7K **79**
BS39: High L 4B **140**
BS40: But .4E **112**
BS40: Chew M 1H **115**
BS40: Comp M 6A **136**
BS40: R'frd 1K **133**
BS48: Back 2B **90**
(not continuous)
BS49: Yat .4H **87**
Batch Bus. Pk. BS24: Lym 4G **145**
Batches, The BS3: Bedm 7H **61**
Batch La. BS24: Lym 3H **145**
BS39: Clut 2H **139**
Bates Cl. BS5: E'tn 1K **5** (1C **62**)
BATH 4G **7** (5C **100**)
Bath Abbey 4G **7** (5C **100**)
Bath Abbey Heritage Vaults *5G* ***7***
(within Bath Abbey)
BATHAMPTON 2H **101**
Bathampton La. BA2: B'ptn 2G **101**
Bath Aqua Theatre of Glass . . .1G **7** (4C **100**)
Bath Bldgs. BS6: Bris 7A **48**
Bath Bus. Cen. *BA1: Bath* *4G* ***7***
(off Up. Borough Walls)
Bath Bus. Pk. BA2: Pea J 6E **142**
Bath City FC .5H **99**
Bath County Court 5G **7**
BATHEASTON 7H **83**
Batheaston Swainswick By-Pass
BA1: Bath, Swa, Up Swa 4D **82**
BA2: B'ptn 2F **101**
Bath Festival Maze, The 4H **7** (5C **100**)
BATHFORD 1A **102**
Bathford Hill BA1: Bathf 1K **101**
BS39: Comp D 5B **96**
Bath Hill BA2: Wel 3J **143**
BS31: Key .4D **78**
Bathings, The BS35: T'bry 4A **12**
Bathite Cotts. BA2: Mon C 3F **123**
Bath Marina & Cvn. Pk. BA1: Bath 3F **99**
Bath New Rd. BA3: Clan, Rads 2J **153**
Bath Old Rd. BA3: Rads 3K **153**
Bath Racecourse 4G **81**

Bath Riverside Bus. Pk.—Berrow Grn.

Bath Riverside Bus. Pk.
BA2: Bath . . . 5E 6 (5B 100)
Bath Rd. BA1: Kel, S'frd . . . 4A 80
BA2: Cor . . . 5F 79
BA2: F'boro . . . 1B 140
BA2: Pea J . . . 6B 142
BA15: Brad A . . . 3G 125
BS4: Bris, Wind H . . . 7K 5 (4B 62)
BS4: Brisl . . . 1G 77
(Bonville Rd.)
BS4: Brisl . . . 7F 63
(Eagle Rd.)
BS25: C'hll . . . 1B 132
BS30: Bit, Will . . . 1F 79
BS30: B'yte, Old C . . . 4H 65
BS30: L Grn . . . 5C 64
BS30: Wick . . . 3E 66
BS31: Key, Salt . . . 5D 78
BS35: T'bry . . . 4K 11
BS39: Paul . . . 7C 140
BS40: Blag . . . 3C 134
BS40: L'frd . . . 1B 132
BS40: N Wid, W Har . . . 7E 136
Bath Road (Park & Ride) . . . 2H 77
Bath RUFC . . . 4H 7 (5C 100)
Baths, The BS23: W Mare . . . 4E 104
Bath Spa Station (Rail) . . . 6H 7 (6C 100)
Bath Spa University
Newton Pk. Campus . . . 6A 98
Bath Spa University College . . . 2A 100
Bath Sports & Leisure Cen. . . . 4H 7 (5C 100)
Bath St. BA1: Bath . . . 5F 7 (5B 100)
BS1: Bris . . . 4G 5 (3A 62)
BS3: Ash G . . . 5G 61
BS16: Stap H . . . 4C 50
BS27: Ched . . . 7D 150
Bathurst Cl. TA8: Bur S . . . 7F 157
Bathurst Pde. BS1: Bris . . . 7E 4 (4K 61)
Bathurst Rd. BS22: W Mare . . . 3A 106
Bathurst Ter. BS1: Bris . . . 7E 4
(off Commercial Rd.)
Bathview Pk. BA1: Up Swa . . . 1C 82
Bathwell Rd. BS4: Wind H . . . 6C 62
BATHWICK . . . 2J 7 (4D 100)
Bathwick Hill
BA2: Bath, Clav D . . . 3J 7 (5D 100)
Bathwick Ri. BA2: Bath . . . 2K 7 (3E 100)
Bathwick St. BA2: Bath . . . 1H 7 (3C 100)
Bathwick Ter. BA2: Bath . . . 4K 7
Batley Ct. BS30: Old C . . . 5H 65
Bat Stall La. BA2: Bath . . . 4G 7
(off Orange Gro.)
Batstone Cl. BA1: Bath . . . 1D 100
Batt Cl. BS32: Alm . . . 1G 27
Battenburg Rd. BS5: St G . . . 1J 63
Batten Ct. BS37: Chip S . . . 5J 31
Batten Rd. BS5: St G . . . 2K 63
Batten's La. BS5: St G . . . 3J 63
Battersby Way BS10: Hen . . . 5E 34
Battersea Rd. BS5: E'tn . . . 1E 62
Battery La. BS20: P'head . . . 2F 43
Battery Rd. BS20: P'head . . . 2F 43
Battleborough La. TA9: Bre K . . . 6K 157
Battle La. BS40: Chew M . . . 1G 115
Battson Rd. BS14: Stoc . . . 5G 77
Baugh Gdns. BS16: Down . . . 6C 38
Baugh Rd. BS16: Down . . . 6C 38
Baxter Cl. BS15: K'wd . . . 1D 64
Bay Gdns. BS5: Eastv . . . 6E 48
Bayham Rd. BS4: Know, Wind H . . . 6B 62
Bayleys Dr. BS15: K'wd . . . 3A 64
Baynham Ct. BS15: Han . . . 4K 63
(off Henbury Rd.)
Baynton Ho. BS5: E'tn . . . 2C 62
Baynton Mdw. BS16: Emer G . . . 2G 51
Baynton Rd. BS3: Ash G . . . 5G 61
Bay Rd. BS21: Clev . . . 3D 54
Bays, The BS27: Ched . . . 6E 150
Bayswater Av. BS6: Henle . . . 4H 47
Bayswater Rd. BS7: Hor . . . 1B 48
Bay Tree Cl. BS34: Pat . . . 7B 26
Bay Tree Rd. BA1: Bath . . . 1C 100
BS21: Clev . . . 7E 54
Baytree Rd. BS22: W Mare . . . 3A 106
Baytree Vw. BS22: W Mare . . . 3B 106
Bay Vw. Gdns. TA8: Bur S . . . 3D 158
Bay Willow Dr. BS6: Redl . . . 6H 47
BEACH . . . 7C 66
Beach, The BS21: Clev . . . 5C 54
Beach Av. BS21: Clev . . . 7C 54
BS35: Sev B . . . 6A 16
Beach End Rd. BS23: Uph . . . 3E 126
Beachgrove Gdns. BS16: Fish . . . 4A 50
Beachgrove Rd. BS16: Fish . . . 4K 49
Beach Hill BS20: P'head . . . 2E 42
BS30: Bit . . . 6J 65
Beach La. BS30: Beach . . . 6B 66
BEACHLEY . . . 1C 8
Beachley Rd. NP16: B'ly . . . 1B 8
Beachley Wlk. BS11: Shire . . . 1H 45
Beach Rd. BS22: Kew . . . 1H 105
BS23: W Mare . . . 7F 105
BS35: Sev B . . . 6A 16
Beach Rd. E. BS20: P'head . . . 2F 43
Beach Rd. W. BS20: P'head . . . 2E 42
Beacon, The BS23: W Mare . . . 4E 104
BEACON HILL . . . 2D 100
Beacon Ho. BS8: Clif . . . 2B 4
Beacon La. BS36: Wint . . . 2A 38
Beaconlea BS15: K'wd . . . 3B 64
Beacon Rd. BA1: Bath . . . 2C 100
Beaconsfield Cl. BS5: Bar H . . . 3D 62
Beaconsfield Ct. BS8: Clif . . . 7G 47
(off Beaconsfield Rd.)
Beaconsfield Rd. BS4: Know . . . 6D 62
BS5: St G . . . 1G 63
BS8: Clif . . . 7G 47
BS21: Clev . . . 7E 54
BS23: W Mare . . . 5G 105
Beaconsfield St. BS5: Bar H . . . 3D 62
Beale Cl. BS14: Stoc . . . 4G 77
Beale Wlk. BA2: Bath . . . 4C 6 (5A 100)
Beale Way TA8: Bur S . . . 3F 159
BEAM BRIDGE . . . 3F 111
Beam St. BS5: Redf . . . 2E 62
Bean Acre, The BS11: Shire . . . 7H 33
Beanhill Cres. BS35: Alv . . . 7J 11
Bean St. BS5: E'tn . . . 7C 48
Beanwood Pk. BS37: W'lgh . . . 4E 40
Bearbridge Rd. BS13: Withy . . . 6F 75
Bear Cl. BA15: Brad A . . . 5F 125
Bearfield Bldgs. BA15: Brad A . . . 4G 125
BEAR FLAT . . . 7A 100
Bear Yd. M. BS8: Clif . . . 3G 61
(off Charles Pl.)
Beatrix Pl. BS7: Hor . . . 7C 36
Beatty Way TA8: Bur S . . . 1E 158
Beauchamp Rd. BS7: B'stn . . . 4K 47
Beauford Sq. BA1: Bath . . . 4F 7 (5B 100)
Beaufort BS16: Fren . . . 6A 38
(off Harford Dr.)
Beaufort All. BS5: St G . . . 3H 63
Beaufort Av. BA3: Mid N . . . 4E 152
BS37: Yate . . . 4D 30
Beaufort Bldgs. BS8: Clif . . . 2F 61
Beaufort Cl. BS5: St G . . . 2F 63
BS24: Elbgh . . . 2G 129
Beaufort Ct. BS16: Down . . . 7E 38
BS21: Clev . . . 4C 54
TA8: Bur S . . . 7D 156
Beaufort Cres. BS34: Stok G . . . 3G 37
Beaufort E. BA1: Bath . . . 2E 100
Beaufort Gdns. BS48: Nail . . . 1F 71
Beaufort Hgts. BS5: St G . . . 2G 63
Beaufort Ho. BS5: Bar H . . . 2D 62
Beaufort M. BA1: Bath . . . 2E 100
BS8: Clif . . . 2F 61
Beaufort Pk. BS32: Brad S . . . 3F 27
Beaufort Pl. BA1: Bath . . . 2E 100
BS5: E'tn . . . 1C 62
BS16: Fren . . . 6K 37
Beaufort Rd. BS5: St G . . . 2F 63
BS7: Hor . . . 2B 48
BS8: Clif . . . 7G 47
BS15: K'wd . . . 7A 50
BS16: Down . . . 1E 50
BS16: Stap H . . . 4C 50
BS23: W Mare . . . 4H 105
BS36: Fram C . . . 6E 28
BS37: Yate . . . 4D 30
Beaufort St. BS3: Bedm . . . 7J 61
BS5: E'tn . . . 1C 62
Beaufort Trade Pk. BS16: Puck . . . 3B 52
Beaufort Vs. BA1: Bath . . . 2D 100
Beaufort Way BS10: S'mead . . . 7K 35
Beaufort W. BA1: Bath . . . 2D 100
Beauley Rd. BS3: Bris . . . 7B 4 (4H 61)
Beaumont Cl. BS23: W Mare . . . 1H 127
BS30: L Grn . . . 6E 64
Beaumont St. BS5: E'tn . . . 1C 62
Beaumont Ter. BS5: E'tn . . . 1C 62
Beau St. BA1: Bath . . . 5F 7 (5B 100)
Beaver Cl. BS36: Wint . . . 7D 28
Beazer Cl. BS16: Soun . . . 5B 50
Beck Cl. BS16: Emer G . . . 2G 51
Becket Ct. BS16: Puck . . . 3B 52
Becket Dr. BS22: Wor . . . 1E 106
Becket Rd. BS22: Wor . . . 1E 106
Becket's La. BS48: Nail . . . 2G 71
Beckford Ct. BA2: Bath . . . 2K 7
(off Darlington Rd.)
Beckford Gdns. BA2: Bath . . . 2K 7 (3D 100)
BS14: Whit . . . 7C 76
Beckford Rd. BA2: Bath . . . 2J 7 (4D 100)
Beckford's Tower & Mus. . . . 6K 81
Beckhampton Rd. BA2: Bath . . . 7B 6 (6K 99)
Beck Ho. BS34: Pat . . . 6C 26
Beckington BS24: W Mare . . . 3J 127
Beckington Rd. BS3: Know . . . 7B 62
Beckington Wlk. BS3: Know . . . 7B 62
Becks Bus. Pk. BS23: W Mare . . . 5J 105
Beckspool Rd. BS16: Fren . . . 1K 49
Beddoe Cl. BA15: Brad A . . . 7J 125
Bedford Ct. BA1: Bath . . . 3C 100
Bedford Cres. BS7: Hor . . . 3B 48
Bedford Pl. BS2: Bris . . . 1E 4 (1K 61)
Bedford Rd. BS23: W Mare . . . 1G 127
Bedford St. BA1: Bath . . . 3C 100
BEDMINSTER . . . 6J 61
Bedminster Bri. BS1: Bris . . . 7F 5 (4K 61)
BS3: Bris . . . 7F 5 (4K 61)
BEDMINSTER DOWN . . . 2G 75
Bedminster Down Rd.
BS13: Bedm, Bis . . . 1G 75
Bedminster Pde. BS3: Bedm . . . 5K 61
Bedminster Pl. BS3: Bedm . . . 5K 61
Bedminster Rd. BS3: Bedm . . . 1H 75
Bedminster Station (Rail) . . . 5K 61
Bedminster Trade Pk. BS3: Bedm . . . 6J 61
Bedwin Cl. BS20: P'head . . . 4B 42
Beechacres BS35: T'bry . . . 2A 12
Beech Av. BA2: Clav D . . . 6G 101
Beech Cl. BS25: S'ham . . . 5B 132
BS30: Bar C . . . 4E 64
BS35: Alv . . . 7J 11
Beech Ct. BS14: Whit . . . 5C 76
Beech Cft. BS14: H'gro . . . 5D 76
Beechcroft BS41: Dun . . . 1D 92
Beechcroft Wlk. BS7: Hor . . . 7C 36
Beech Dr. BS25: S'ham . . . 5B 132
BS48: Nail . . . 6J 57
BEECHEN CLIFF . . . 7F 7 (6B 100)
Beechen Cliff Rd. BA2: Bath . . . 7E 6 (6B 100)
Beechen Dr. BS16: Fish . . . 6K 49
Beeches, The BA2: Odd D . . . 3K 121
BS4: St Ap . . . 4G 63
BS9: Stok B . . . 5D 46
BS25: Sandf . . . 1H 131
BS30: Old C . . . 7G 65
BS32: Brad S . . . 6F 27
Beeches Gro. BS4: Brisl . . . 7F 63
Beeches Ind. Est. BS37: Yate . . . 4B 30
Beechfield Cl. BS41: L Ash . . . 7C 60
Beechfield Gro. BS9: C Din . . . 7C 34
Beech Gro. BA2: Bath . . . 7J 99
Beech Ho. BS16: Stap . . . 3E 48
Beech Leaze BS35: Alv . . . 7J 11
Beechmount Cl. BS24: W Mare . . . 4H 127
Beechmount Ct. BS14: H'gro . . . 2D 76
Beechmount Dr. BS24: W Mare . . . 4J 127
Beechmount Gro. BS14: H'gro . . . 2D 76
Beech Rd. BS7: Hor . . . 3A 48
BS25: S'ham . . . 5B 132
BS31: Salt . . . 7J 79
BS49: Yat . . . 3J 87
Beech Ter. BA3: Rads . . . 5H 153
Beech Vw. BA2: Clav D . . . 6F 101
Beechwood Av. BS15: Han . . . 4B 64
BS24: Lock . . . 7E 106
Beechwood Cl. BS14: Stoc . . . 2E 76
Beechwood Dr. BS20: P'head . . . 3A 42
Beechwood Rd. BA2: C Down . . . 3D 122
BS16: Fish . . . 4J 49
BS20: Eas . . . 4E 44
BS20: P'head . . . 3A 42
BS48: Nail . . . 7F 57
Beehive Trad. Est. BS5: St G . . . 2G 63
Beehive Yd. BA1: Bath . . . 3G 7 (4C 100)
Beesmoor Rd. BS36: Coal H, Fram C . . . 7F 29
Begbrook Dr. BS16: B'hll . . . 2H 49
Begbrook La. BS16: B'hll . . . 2H 49
Begbrook Pk. BS16: Fren . . . 7J 37
Beggar Bush La. BS8: Abb L, Fail . . . 5H 59
Beggarswell Cl. BS2: Bris . . . 1B 62
Belcombe Pl. BA15: Brad A . . . 6G 125
Belcombe Rd. BA15: Brad A . . . 6F 125
Belfast Wlk. BS4: Know . . . 2A 76
Belfield Ct. TA8: Bur S . . . 7C 156
Belfields La. BS16: Fren . . . 6A 38
Belfry BS30: Warm . . . 3F 65
Belfry All. BS5: St G . . . 1J 63
Belfry Av. BS5: St G . . . 1J 63
Belgrave Cres. BA1: Bath . . . 3C 100
Belgrave Hill BS8: Clif . . . 6G 47
Belgrave Pl. BA1: Bath . . . 2C 100
BS8: Clif . . . 2G 61
Belgrave Rd. BA1: Bath . . . 2D 100
BS8: Clif . . . 1B 4 (1H 61)
BS22: W Mare . . . 4K 105
Belgrave Ter. BA1: Bath . . . 2C 100
Bellamy Av. BS13: Hart . . . 6J 75
Bellamy Cl. BS15: St G . . . 4J 63
Belland Dr. BS14: Whit . . . 6B 76
Bell Av. BS1: Bris . . . 6F 5 (4K 61)
Bella Vista Rd. BA1: Bath . . . 3B 100
Bell Barn Rd. BS9: Stok B . . . 2D 46
Bell Cl. BA2: F'boro . . . 6D 118
BS10: Hor . . . 1A 48
BELLE VUE . . . 3F 153
Belle Vue BA3: Mid N . . . 3F 153
Bellevue BS8: Clif . . . 4A 4 (3H 61)
Belle Vue Cl. BA2: Pea J . . . 5D 142
Bellevue Cl. BS15: K'wd . . . 2C 64
Bellevue Cotts. BS8: Clif . . . 5A 4 (3H 61)
BS9: W Trym . . . 1G 47
Bellevue Ct. BS8: Clif . . . 4A 4 (3H 61)
Bellevue Cres. BS8: Clif . . . 4A 4 (3H 61)
Bellevue Mans. BS21: Clev . . . 5D 54
Bellevue Pk. BS4: Brisl . . . 7F 63
Belle Vue Rd. BS5: E'tn . . . 6E 48
Bellevue Rd. BS4: Wind H . . . 5B 62
BS5: St G . . . 1J 63
BS15: K'wd . . . 2D 64
BS21: Clev . . . 5D 54
Bellevue Ter. BS4: Brisl . . . 7F 63
BS4: Wind H . . . 5B 62
BS8: Clif . . . 4A 4 (3H 61)
Bell Hill BS16: Stap . . . 4E 48
Bell Hill Rd. BS5: St G . . . 1J 63
Bellhouse Wlk. BS11: Law W . . . 6B 34
Bellifants BA2: F'boro . . . 6E 118
Bell La. BS1: Bris . . . 3E 4 (2K 61)
(not continuous)
BS32: Alm, Piln . . . 1H 25
BS35: Piln . . . 1H 25
Bellotts Rd. BA2: Bath . . . 5A 6 (5J 99)
Bell Pit Brow BS48: Wrax . . . 7K 57
Bell Rd. BS36: Coal H . . . 7G 29
Bell Sq. BS40: Blag . . . 2C 134
Bell's Wlk. BS40: Wrin . . . 2G 111
BELLUTON . . . 6E 94
Belluton La. BS39: Pens . . . 6F 95
Belluton Rd. BS4: Know . . . 6C 62
Belmont BA1: Bath . . . 2F 7 (4B 100)
Belmont, The BS21: Clev . . . 6D 54
Belmont Dr. BS8: Fail . . . 6F 59
BS34: Stok G . . . 2G 37
Belmont Hill BS48: Fail, Flax B . . . 1E 72
Belmont Pk. BS7: Fil . . . 6B 36
Belmont Rd. BA2: C Down . . . 3E 122
BS4: Brisl . . . 5E 62
BS6: Bris . . . 6A 48
BS25: Wins . . . 5G 131
Belmont St. BS5: E'tn . . . 7D 48
Belmore Gdns. BA2: Bath . . . 1H 121
Beloe Rd. BS7: Hor . . . 3A 48
Belroyal Av. BS4: Brisl . . . 6H 63
Belsher Dr. BS15: K'wd . . . 3E 64
Belstone Wlk. BS4: Know . . . 2J 75
Belton Ct. BA1: W'ton . . . 1H 99
Belton Ho. BA1: W'ton . . . 1H 99
Belton Rd. BS5: E'tn . . . 7D 48
BS20: P'head . . . 2C 42
Belvedere BA1: Bath . . . 2F 7 (4B 100)
Belvedere Cres. BS22: W Mare . . . 3A 106
Belvedere Pl. BA1: Bath . . . 1F 7
(off Morford St.)
Belvedere Rd. BS6: Redl . . . 5G 47
Belvedere Vs. BA1: Bath . . . 1F 7 (3B 100)
Belvoir Rd. BA2: Bath . . . 7A 6 (6K 99)
BS6: Bris . . . 6A 48
Bence Ct. BS15: Han . . . 4K 63
(off Memorial Rd.)
Benches La. BS40: Winf . . . 7H 91
Bendalls Bri. BS39: Clut . . . 3G 139
Benford Cl. BS16: Fish . . . 2A 50
Bengough's Almshouses
BS2: Bris . . . 2D 4 (2J 61)
BENGROVE . . . 4K 141
Bennett Rd. BS5: St G . . . 2G 63
TA9: High . . . 5H 159
Bennetts Ct. BS37: Yate . . . 5F 31
Bennett's La. BA1: Bath . . . 2C 100
Bennett's Rd. BA1: Swa . . . 7E 82
Bennett St. BA1: Bath . . . 2F 7 (4B 100)
Bennetts Way BS21: Clev . . . 4E 54
Bennett Way BS8: Clif . . . 4F 61
Bensaunt Gro. BS10: Bren . . . 3K 35
Bentley Cl. BS14: Whit . . . 7B 76
Bentley Rd. BS22: Wor . . . 1F 107
Ben Travers Way TA8: Bur S . . . 2E 158
Benville Av. BS9: C Din . . . 7C 34
Berchel Ho. BS3: Bedm . . . 5J 61
Berenda Dr. BS30: L Grn . . . 6F 65
Beresford Cl. BS31: Salt . . . 1J 97
TA8: Bur S . . . 1E 158
Beresford Gdns. BA1: W'ton . . . 7G 81
Berkeley Av. BA3: Mid N . . . 4E 152
BS7: B'stn . . . 5K 47
BS8: Clif . . . 3C 4 (2J 61)
Berkeley Cl. BS16: Down . . . 7D 38
Berkeley Ct. BA2: Bath . . . 4K 7 (5E 100)
BS5: E'tn . . . 2D 62
BS7: B'stn . . . 5K 47
BS34: Pat . . . 5B 26
Berkeley Cres. BS8: Clif . . . 3B 4 (2H 61)
BS23: Uph . . . 3E 126
Berkeley Gdns. BS31: Key . . . 6B 78
Berkeley Grn. BS16: Fren . . . 6K 37
Berkeley Grn. Rd. BS5: Eastv . . . 6E 48
Berkeley Gro. BS5: Eastv . . . 6E 48
Berkeley Ho. BA1: Bath . . . 3C 100
BS1: Bris . . . 4C 4 (3H 61)
BS16: Stap H . . . 3B 50
Berkeley Pl. BA1: Bath . . . 1G 7 (3C 100)
BA2: C Down . . . 2E 122
BS8: Clif . . . 3A 4 (2H 61)
Berkeley Rd. BS6: Henle . . . 4G 47
BS7: B'stn . . . 5K 47
BS15: K'wd . . . 2C 64
BS16: Fish . . . 6J 49
BS16: Stap H . . . 4B 50
Berkeleys Mead BS32: Brad S . . . 1H 37
Berkeley Sq. BS8: Clif . . . 3B 4 (2J 61)
Berkeley St. BS5: Eastv . . . 6E 48
(off Berkeley Grn. Rd.)
BS5: Eastv . . . 5E 48
(Gadshill Rd.)
Berkeley Way BS16: Emer G . . . 1F 51
Berkshire Rd. BS7: B'stn . . . 5K 47
Berlington Ct. BS1: Bris . . . 6H 5 (4A 62)
Berners Cl. BS4: Know . . . 3K 75
BERROW . . . 2B 156
Berrow Grn. TA8: Berr . . . 3B 156

Berrow Lodge—Brackenwood Rd.

Berrow Lodge BS23: W Mare 7G **105**
Berrow Rd. TA8: Bur S 3B **156**
Berrows Mead BS37: Rang 5A **22**
Berrow Wlk. BS3: Wind H 7A **62**
Berry Cft. BS3: Bedm 5K **61**
Berryfield Rd. BA15: Brad A 5H **125**
Berry Hill Cl. BS10: S'mead 6K **35**
Berry La. BS7: Hor 2B **48**
Bertha Ter. TA9: High 5F **159**
BERWICK 1D **34**
Berwick Cl. BS35: E Comp 6D **24**
Berwick Ct. BS10: H'len 2B **34**
Berwick Dr. BS10: Hen 2E **34**
Berwick La. BS10: H'len 2C **34**
BS35: E Comp 6E **24**
Berwick Rd. BS5: Eastv 6D **48**
Beryl Gro. BS14: H'gro 2E **76**
Beryl Rd. BS3: Bedm 6H **61**
Besom La. BS37: W'lgh 2C **40**
Bess Ho. BS21: Clev 7C **54**
Bethell Ct. BA15: Brad A 5G **125**
Bethel Rd. BS5: St G 1H **63**
Betjeman Ct. BS30: Bar C 4E **64**
Betts Grn. BS16: Emer G 1G **51**
Bevan Ct. BS34: Fil 5C **36**
Beverley Av. BS16: Down 6D **38**
Beverley Cl. BS5: St G 3K **63**
Beverley Gdns. BS9: W Trym 1D **46**
Beverley Rd. BS7: Hor 7B **36**
Beverstone BS15: K'wd 1A **64**
Beverston Gdns. BS11: Law W 5B **34**
Bevington Cl. BS34: Pat 5A **26**
Bevington Wlk. BS34: Pat 5A **26**
Bewdley Rd. BA2: Bath 7J **7** (7D **100**)
Bexley Rd. BS16: Fish 5K **49**
BIBSTONE 1B **14**
Bibstone BS15: K'wd 1E **64**
Bibury Av. BS34: Pat 6D **26**
Bibury Cl. BS9: Henle 1K **47**
BS48: Nail 1J **71**
Bibury Cres. BS9: Henle 1K **47**
BS15: Han 4A **64**
Bickerton Cl. BS10: Hen 4F **35**
Bickfield La. BS40: Comp M 6B **136**
Bickford Cl. BS30: Bar C 3E **64**
Bickley Cl. BS15: Han 7K **63**
Biddestone Rd. BS7: Hor 7A **36**
BIDDISHAM 6J **147**
Biddisham Cl. BS48: Nail 1G **71**
Biddisham La. BS26: Bidd 5J **147**
Biddle St. BS49: Yat 4G **87**
Bideford Cres. BS4: Know 2B **76**
Bideford Rd. BS22: Wor 2D **106**
Bidwell Cl. BS10: Bren 4H **35**
Bifield Cl. BS14: Stoc 5H **77**
Bifield Gdns. BS14: Stoc 5G **77**
(not continuous)
Bifield Rd. BS14: Stoc 6G **77**
Bignell Cl. BS25: Wins 5F **131**
Big Tree Cl. BS26: Comp B 3C **148**
Bigwood La. BS1: Bris 4C **4** (3J **61**)
Bilberry Cl. BS9: C Din 7C **34**
Bilbie Cl. BS10: Hor 1A **48**
BS40: Chew S 4E **114**
Bilbie Rd. BS22: Wor 1F **107**
BS40: Chew S 4E **114**
Bilbury Ho. BA1: W'ton 1H **99**
Bilbury La. BA1: Bath 5G **7** (5C **100**)
Billand Cl. BS13: Withy 7E **74**
Bilsham La. BS35: N'wick 4E **16**
Binces La. BA2: Stan P 1J **119**
Bince's Lodge La. BA3: Mid N 2E **152**
Bindon Dr. BS10: Bren 3K **35**
Binhay Rd. BS49: Yat 4H **87**
Binley Gro. BS14: Stoc 5F **77**
Binmead Gdns. BS13: Hart 6H **75**
Birbeck Rd. BS9: Stok B 3E **46**
Birchall Rd. BS6: Redl 4J **47**
Birch Av. BS21: Clev 5E **54**
BS24: B'don 7A **128**
Birch Cl. BS24: Lock 1F **129**
BS27: Ched 6E **150**
BS34: Pat 7A **26**
Birch Ct. BS22: St Geo 2G **107**
BS31: Key 6A **78**
BS37: Yate 4D **30**
Birch Cft. BS14: Whit 7C **76**
Birchdale Rd. BS14: H'gro 2C **76**
Birchdene BS48: Nail 7J **57**
Birch Dr. BS16: Puck 3B **52**
BS35: Alv 1H **19**
BS40: L'frd 7C **110**
Birches, The BS48: Nail 7J **57**
Birch Gro. BS20: P'head 4E **42**
Birch Hill BS27: Ched 6E **150**
Birchills Trad. Est. BS4: Brisl 1H **77**
Birch Lawn TA8: Bur S 2D **158**
Birch Rd. BA3: Rads 5J **153**
BS3: Bris 5H **61**
BS15: Soun 5C **50**
BS37: Yate 4D **30**
Birchwood Av. BS23: W Mare 5J **105**
Birchwood Ct. BS4: St Ap 3H **63**
Birchwood Dr. BS8: Fail 6F **59**
Birchwood La. BS39: Pens, Wool 2G **117**
Birchwood Rd. BS4: Brisl, St Ap 6G **63**
Birdale Cl. BS10: Hen 4E **34**
Birdcombe Cl. BS48: Nail 6G **57**
Birdlip Cl. BS48: Nail 2J **71**
Birdwell La. BS41: L Ash 1K **73**
Birdwell Rd. BS41: L Ash 1K **73**
Birdwood BS15: Han 3B **64**
Birkdale BS30: Warm 3E **64**
BS37: Yate 6E **30**
Birkett Rd. BS23: W Mare 3D **104**
Birkin St. BS2: Bris 4K **5** (3C **62**)
Birnbeck Ct. BS23: W Mare 5F **105**
Birnbeck Rd. BS23: W Mare 3D **104**
Biscay Dr. BS20: P'head 2H **43**
Bisdee Rd. BS24: Hut 3B **128**
Bishop Av. BS22: Wor 1E **106**
Bishop La. BS7: B'stn 4A **48**
Bishop Mnr. Rd. BS10: Hor 1K **47**
Bishop M. BS2: Bris 1H **5** (1A **62**)
Bishop Monk BS16: Fish 3J **49**
Bishop Rd. BS7: B'stn 4J **47**
BS16: Emer G 2G **51**
Bishops Cl. BS9: Stok B 5E **46**
Bishops Ct. BS9: Stok B 5C **46**
Bishops Cove BS13: Bis 5F **75**
Bishops Knoll BS9: Stok B 5C **46**
Bishops Knoll Nature Reserve 6D **46**
Bishops Mead BS49: C've 3C **88**
Bishop's Path TA8: Bur S 2D **158**
Bishops Rd. BS49: Clav, C've 2B **88**
BISHOPSTON 5K **47**
Bishop St. BA3: Faul 4K **155**
BS2: Bris 1H **5** (1A **62**)
BISHOP SUTTON 1K **137**
Bishops Wood BS32: Alm 7E **18**
BISHOPSWORTH 4G **75**
Bishopsworth Rd. BS13: Bis 3G **75**
Bishopsworth Swimming Pool 4G **75**
Bishop Ter. BS2: Bris 1B **62**
Bishopthorpe Rd. BS10: Hor 1K **47**
Bishport Av. BS13: Hart, Withy 6G **75**
Bishport Cl. BS13: Hart 6H **75**
Bishport Grn. BS13: Hart 7J **75**
Bisley BS37: Yate 7C **30**
Bissex Mead BS16: Emer G 3F **51**
Bittern Av. BS20: P'head 1H **43**
Bittern Cl. BS22: Wor 3D **106**
Bitterwell Cl. BS36: H'fld 4H **39**
Bittle Mead BS13: Hart 6B **76**
BITTON 2J **79**
Bitton Station
Avon Valley Railway 1F **79**
Bitton Station Railway Cen. 1F **79**
Blackacre BS14: Whit 6E **76**
Blackberry Av. BS16: Stap 3G **49**
Blackberry Dr. BS22: Wor 3E **106**
BS36: Fram C 1F **39**
Blackberry Hill BS16: Stap 3G **49**
Blackberry La. BA1: Lim S 4K **123**
BA2: Lim S 4K **123**
BA15: W'ley 3K **123**
BS20: P'head 6B **42**
Blackberry Way BA3: Mid N 3D **152**
Blackbird Cl. BA3: Mid N 6F **153**
Black Boy Hill BS8: Clif 6G **47**
Blackcurrant Dr. BS41: L Ash 2J **73**
Blackdown Ct. BS14: Whit 5D **76**
Blackdown Mead BS27: Ched 7J **151**
Blackdown Rd. BS20: P'head 3C **42**
(not continuous)
Blackfriars BS1: Bris 2E **4** (2K **61**)
Blackfriars Rd. BS48: Nail 1D **70**
BLACKHORSE 7E **38**
Blackhorse Cl. BS16: Emer G 7E **38**
Blackhorse Ct. BS15: K'wd 1A **64**
Blackhorse Hill BS10: Pat 6H **25**
BS35: E Comp 6H **25**
Blackhorse La. BS16: Down 6D **38**
Blackhorse Pl. BS16: Mang 2E **50**
Blackhorse Rd. BS15: K'wd 1B **64**
BS16: Mang 1E **50**
Black La. BS27: Ched 4A **150**
BLACKMOOR
BS40, Chew Stoke 1C **114**
BS40, Lower Langford 6E **110**
Blackmoor BS21: Clev 1C **68**
BS22: Wor 2D **106**
BS40: L'frd 6E **110**
Blackmoor Cl. BS40: L'frd 6E **110**
Blackmoor Rd. BS8: Abb L 7J **45**
Blackmoors La. BS3: Bwr A 5E **60**
Blackmore Dr. BA2: Bath 6H **99**
Black Nore Point BS20: P'head 3B **42**
BLACKROCK 3G **95**
Blackrock La. BS14: Whit 3G **95**
BS39: Pub 3G **95**
Black Rock Nature Reserve 5J **151**
Blacksmith La. BA1: Up Swa 4D **82**
Blacksmiths La. BA1: Kel 7B **80**
Blackswarth Rd. BS5: St G 2F **63**
Blackthorn Cl. BS13: Hart 5K **75**
BS26: Bidd 7J **147**
Blackthorn Dr. BS20: P'head 3G **43**
(not continuous)
BS32: Brad S 7F **27**
Blackthorne Ter. BS22: Wor 3E **106**
Blackthorn Gdns. BS22: Wor 3E **106**
Blackthorn Rd. BS13: Hart 5K **75**
Blackthorn Sq. BS21: Clev 1D **68**
Blackthorn Wlk. BS15: K'wd 6C **50**
Blackthorn Way BS48: Nail 7J **57**
Bladen Cl. BS20: P'head 4G **43**
Bladud Bldgs. BA1: Bath 3G **7** (4C **100**)
BLAGDON 2C **134**
Blagdon Cl. BS3: Wind H 7A **62**
BS24: W Mare 4H **127**
Blagdon La. BS40: Blag, But 1C **134**
Blagdon Pk. BA2: Bath 7G **99**
Blagdon Picnic Site 3B **134**
Blagrove Cl. BS13: Hart 7J **75**
Blagrove Cres. BS13: Hart 7J **75**
Blaisdon BS22: W Mare 5B **106**
BS37: Yate 7E **30**
Blaisdon Cl. BS10: Hen 6G **35**
Blaise Castle Folly 6D **34**
Blaise Castle House Mus. 5E **34**
Blaisedell Vw. BS10: Hen 4D **34**
BLAISE HAMLET 5C **34**
Blaise Hamlet 5D **34**
Blaise Wlk. BS9: Sea M 1C **46**
Blaise Weston Ct. BS11: Law W 6A **34**
Blake End BS22: Kew 7C **84**
Blakeney Gro. BS48: Nail 2E **70**
Blakeney Mills BS37: Yate 5D **30**
Blakeney Rd. BS7: Hor 2C **48**
BS34: Pat 5A **26**
Blake Rd. BS7: L'lze 2D **48**
Blake's Cres. TA9: High 3G **159**
Blakes Rd. BS35: T'bry 3K **11**
Blanchards BS37: Chip S 6J **31**
Blandamour Way BS10: S'mead 5K **35**
Blandford Cl. BS9: W Trym 2H **47**
BS48: Nail 1F **71**
Blands Row BS35: Redw 4B **16**
BLEADON 7A **128**
Bleadon Hill BS24: W Mare 4H **127**
Bleadon Mill BS24: B'don 1A **146**
Bleadon Rd. BS24: B'don 6J **127**
Blencathara Ct. TA8: Bur S 7C **156**
Blenheim Cl. BA2: Pea J 6D **142**
BS22: Wor 2E **106**
Blenheim Ct. BS1: Bris 1F **5**
Blenheim Dr. BS34: Fil 3D **36**
BS37: Yate 3C **30**
Blenheim Gdns. BA1: Bath 1C **100**
Blenheim Rd. BS6: Redl 5H **47**
Blenheim St. BS5: E'tn 7C **48**
Blenheim Way BS20: P'head 3G **43**
Blenman Cl. BS16: B'hll 1J **49**
Blethwin Cl. BS10: Hen 6F **35**
Blind La. BA1: W'ton 1J **99**
BA2: Bath 7D **100**
BA2: Tun 2A **142**
BS40: Chew S 4E **114**
BS49: Cong 4B **88**
BS49: C've 4B **88**
BLOOMFIELD
BA2, Bath 2K **121**
BA2, Timsbury 2F **141**
BS39 1C **152**
Bloomfield BS24: W Mare 3J **127**
Bloomfield Av. BA2: Bath 7D **6** (7A **100**)
BA2: Tim 2F **141**
Bloomfield Cl. BA2: Tim 2F **141**
Bloomfield Cres. BA2: Bath 2K **121**
Bloomfield Dr. BA2: Odd D 2J **121**
Bloomfield Gro. BA2: Bath 1A **122**
Bloomfield La. BS39: Paul 1C **152**
Bloomfield Pk. BA2: Bath 1A **122**
Bloomfield Pk. Rd. BA2: Tim 2F **141**
Bloomfield Pl. BA2: Dunk 7D **120**
Bloomfield Ri. BA2: Odd D 2K **121**
Bloomfield Ri. Nth. BA2: Odd D 2K **121**
Bloomfield Rd. BA2: Bath, Odd D 2K **121**
BA2: Tim 1F **141**
BS4: Brisl 5E **62**
(not continuous)
Bloomfield Tennis & Bowling Club 1A **122**
Bloomfield Ter. BA2: Pea J 6C **142**
Bloy St. BS5: E'tn 7E **48**
(not continuous)
Bluebell Cl. BS9: Sea M 2B **46**
BS35: T'bry 2B **12**
Bluebell Ri. BA3: Mid N 3E **152**
Bluebell Rd. BS22: Wick L 5E **84**
Bluebells, The BS32: Brad S 7G **27**
Blueberry Way BS22: Wor 3D **106**
Blue Falcon Rd. BS15: K'wd 6C **50**
Blue Water Dr. BS24: Elbgh 2G **129**
Blythe Gdns. BS22: Wor 1E **106**
Blythe Way TA8: Bur S 4C **156**
Boarding Ho. La. BS32: Alm 7J **17**
Board's La. TA8: Bur S 2F **159**
Boat La. BS24: Lym 2A **146**
Bockenem Cl. BS35: T'bry 5B **12**
Bodey Cl. BS30: C Hth 3E **64**
Bodley Way BS24: W'ton V 5C **106**
Bodmin Wlk. BS4: Know 2B **76**
Bodyce Rd. BS35: Alv 7J **11**
Boiling Wells La. BS2: Bris 5C **48**
BS7: Eastv 5C **48**
Bolton Cl. TA9: High 4H **159**
Bolton Rd. BS7: B'stn 5A **48**
Bond La. BS35: King, T'bry 4E **10**
Bond St. BS1: Bris 1G **5** (1A **62**)
BS2: Bris 1G **5** (1A **62**)
Bond St. Sth. BS1: Bris 2J **5** (2B **62**)
Bonhill La. BS39: Bis S 6J **115**
Bonhill Rd. BS39: Bis S 7K **115**
Bonhill Way BS39: Bis S 7K **115**
Boniface Wlk. TA8: Bur S 2D **158**
Bonnington Wlk. BS7: L'lze 7D **36**
Bonville Bus. Cen. BS4: Brisl 7H **63**
Bonville Rd. BS4: Brisl 1G **77**
Bonville Trad. Est. BS4: Brisl 7H **63**
Boon Vs. BS11: Law W 1J **45**
Booth Rd. BS3: Bedm 5J **61**
Boot La. BS3: Bedm 5K **61**
Bordesley Rd. BS14: Whit 7C **76**
Boreal Way BS24: W'ton V 4D **106**
Borgie Pl. BS22: Wor 1D **106**
Borleyton Wlk. BS13: Withy 6F **75**
Borver Gro. BS13: Hart 6H **75**
(not continuous)
Boscombe Cres. BS16: Down 7D **38**
Boston Rd. BS7: Hor 7B **36**
Boswell St. BS5: Eastv 6E **48**
Botanical Gdns.
Bath 1B **6** (4K **99**)
BOTANY BAY 3F **35**
Botham Cl. BS22: Wor 7E **84**
Botham Dr. BS4: Brisl 1F **77**
Bottoms Farm La. BS30: Doy 6F **53**
Boucher Pl. BS2: Bris 6C **48**
Boulevard BS23: W Mare 4G **105**
Boulters Rd. BS13: Hart 6J **75**
Boultons La. BS15: K'wd 1B **64**
Boultons Rd. BS15: K'wd 1B **64**
Boundaries, The BS24: Lym 5K **145**
Boundary Cl. BA3: Mid N 7F **153**
BS23: W Mare 2G **127**
Boundary Rd. BS24: W'ton V 5D **106**
BS36: Coal H 7H **29**
Bourchier Gdns. BS13: Hart 7H **75**
BOURNE 1J **133**
Bourne Cl. BS15: K'wd 1K **63**
BS36: Wint 7C **28**
Bourne La. BS5: Eastv 6D **48**
BS40: Blag 1A **134**
BS40: Burr 1J **133**
Bourne Rd. BS15: K'wd 1J **63**
Bourneville Rd. BS5: W'hall 1F **63**
Bournville Rd. BS23: W Mare 7H **105**
Boursland Cl. BS32: Brad S 4F **27**
BOURTON 5J **85**
Bourton Av. BS34: Pat 6E **26**
Bourton Cl. BS34: Pat 6E **26**
Bourton Combe BS48: Flax B 3D **72**
Bourton La. BS22: Hew, St Geo 1H **107**
BS26: Comp B 4E **148**
Bourton Mead BS41: L Ash 1B **74**
BS48: Flax B 2D **72**
Bourton Wlk. BS13: Bis 2G **75**
Bouverie St. BS5: E'tn 1D **62**
Boverton Rd. BS34: Fil 4D **36**
Bow Cotts. *BS20: Pill 4H **45***
(off Water La.)
Bowden Cl. BS9: C Din 7C **34**
Bowden Pl. BS16: Down 1D **50**
Bowden Rd. BS5: W'hall 7G **49**
Bowden Way BS8: Fail 6F **59**
Bowen Rd. BS24: Lock 1G **129**
BOWER ASHTON 5E **60**
Bower Ashton Ter. BS3: Ash G 5F **61**
Bowerleaze BS9: Sea M 3C **46**
Bower Rd. BS3: Bedm 6G **61**
Bower Wlk. BS3: Wind H 6A **62**
Bowlditch La. BA3: Mid N 2F **153**
Bowling Hill BS37: Chip S 5G **31**
Bowling Hill Bus. Pk. BS37: Chip S 5G **31**
Bowling Rd. BS37: Chip S 6H **31**
(not continuous)
Bowlplex
Kingswood 4C **64**
Bow Mead BS14: Stoc 5G **77**
Bowood *BS16: Fren 6A **38***
(off Avon Ring Rd.)
Bowring Cl. BS13: Hart 7J **75**
Bowsland BS32: Brad S 4G **27**
Bowsland Way BS32: Brad S 4E **26**
Bowstreet La. BS35: E Comp 6G **25**
Boxbury Hill BS39: Paul 3C **152**
Box Bush La. BS24: E Rols 3C **108**
Box Hedge La. BS36: H'fld 4J **39**
Box Rd. BA1: Bathf 7K **83**
Box Wlk. BS31: Key 6A **78**
Boyce Cl. BA2: Bath 6F **99**
Boyce Dr. BS2: Bris 6C **48**
Boyce's Av. BS8: Clif 2G **61**
Boyd Cl. BS30: Wick 2B **66**
Boyd Rd. BS31: Salt 7H **79**
Brabazon Office Pk. BS34: Fil 4B **36**
Brabazon Rd. BS34: Fil 5D **36**
Bracewell Gdns. BS10: Bren 3J **35**
Bracey Dr. BS16: Fish 2A **50**
Brackenbury Dr. BS34: Stok G 2H **37**
Brackendene BS32: Brad S 5E **26**
Brackenwood Gdns. BS20: P'head 3B **42**
Brackenwood Rd. BS21: Clev 3E **54**

Bracton Dr.—Brockley La.

Bracton Dr. BS14: Whit .6C 76
Bradeston Gro. BS16: B'hll .1J 49
Bradford Cl. BS21: Clev .1C 68
BRADFORD LEIGH .2K 125
BRADFORD-ON-AVON .6H 125
Bradford-on-Avon Mus. .6H 125
Bradford-on-Avon Station (Rail) .6G 125
Bradford-on-Avon Swimming Pool .6G 125
Bradford Pk. BA2: C Down .2C 122
(not continuous)
Bradford Rd. BA1: Bathf, Warl .7K 83
BA2: C Down .3B 122
BA15: W'ley .6B 124
Bradford Wood La. BA15: Brad A .6K 125
Bradhurst St. BS5: Bar H .3D 62
Bradley Av. BS11: Shire .2J 45
BS36: Wint .2C 38
Bradley Ct. BS16: Down .3A 50
Bradley Cres. BS11: Shire .2J 45
BRADLEY CROSS .7F 151
Bradley Cross La. BS27: Ched .7F 151
Bradley Ho. BS1: Bris .4E 4
Bradley Pavilions BS32: Brad S .4E 26
Bradley Rd. BS20: P'bry .3C 44
BS34: Pat .6B 26
BRADLEY STOKE .4E 26
Bradley Stoke Leisure Cen. .5G 27
Bradley Stoke Way BS32: Brad S .4D 26
Bradstone Rd. BS36: Wint .2B 38
Bradville Gdns. BS41: L Ash .2K 73
Bradwell Gro. BS10: S'mead .7J 35
Braemar Av. BS7: Fil .6A 36
Braemar Cres. BS7: Fil .6B 36
Brae Ri. BS25: Wins .5G 131
Brae Rd. BS25: Wins .5G 131
Bragg's La. BS2: Bris .2K 5 (2B 62)
Braikenridge Cl. BS21: Clev .1C 68
Braikenridge Rd. BS4: Brisl .5F 63
Brainsfield BS9: W Trym .2F 47
Braithwaite Pl. TA8: Bur S .5C 156
Brake, The BS36: Coal H .2G 39
BS37: Yate .1E 30
Brake Cl. BS15: K'wd .2D 64
BS32: Brad S .7G 27
Brakewell Gdns. BS14: Whit .6C 76
Bramble Dr. BS9: Stok B .5C 46
TA8: Berr .2B 156
Bramble La. BS9: Stok B .5C 46
Brambles, The BS13: Hart .6J 75
BS22: St Geo .2H 107
BS31: Key .7B 78
(not continuous)
Brambles Rd. TA8: Bur S .6C 156
Bramble Way BA2: C Down .2D 122
Bramblewood BS49: Yat .2H 87
Bramblewood Rd. BS22: Wor .1C 106
Brambling La. BS20: P'head .2J 43
Brambling Wlk. BS16: B'hll .2H 49
(not continuous)
Bramley Cl. BA2: Pea J .6D 142
BS20: Pill .4G 45
BS24: Lock .1E 128
BS25: Sandf .1G 131
BS35: Olv .2C 18
BS49: Yat .4H 87
Bramley Copse BS41: L Ash .2J 73
Bramley Ct. BS30: Bar C .5D 64
Bramley Dr. BS48: Back .5J 71
Bramleys, The BS20: P'head .4H 43
BS48: Nail .2D 70
Bramley Sq. BS49: Cong .1A 110
Brampton Way BS20: P'head .3F 43
Bramshill Dr. BS22: Wor .1D 106
Branche Gro. BS13: Hart .7K 75
Brandash Rd. BS37: Chip S .5J 31
Brandon Hill Nature Pk. .4B 4 (3H 61)
Brandon Ho. BS8: Clif .4A 4 (3H 61)
Brandon Steep BS1: Bris .4C 4 (3J 61)
Brandon Steps BS1: Bris .4C 4 (3J 61)
Brandon St. BS1: Bris .5C 4 (3J 61)
Brangwyn Gro. BS7: L'lze .3D 48
Brangwyn Sq. BS22: Wor .2D 106
Branksome Cres. BS34: Fil .4D 36
Branksome Dr. BS34: Fil .4D 36
BS36: Wint .1C 38
Branksome Rd. BS6: Redl .5H 47
Bransby Way BS24: W'ton V .4E 106
Branscombe Rd. BS9: Stok B .4C 46
Branscombe Wlk. BS20: P'head .5B 42
Branwhite Cl. BS7: L'lze .1D 48
BRASSKNOCKER .2H 123
Brassknocker Hill
BA2: Clav D, Mon C .1H 123
Brassmill Ent. Cen. BA1: Bath .4G 99
Brassmill La. BA1: Bath .3G 99
Brassmill La. Trad. Est. BA1: Bath .4G 99
Bratton Rd. BS4: Know .3K 75
Braunton Rd. BS3: Bedm .6J 61
Braydon Av. BS34: Lit S .6E 26
Brayne Ct. BS30: L Grn .6D 64
Braysbridge BS27: Ched .7E 150
BRAYSDOWN .1D 154
Braysdown Cl. BA2: Pea J .7B 142
Braysdown La. BA2: Pea J .6C 142
(not continuous)
BREACH .6H 117
Breaches, The BS20: Eas .4F 45
Breaches Ga. BS32: Brad S .1H 37
Breaches La. BS31: Key .6E 78
BREACH HILL COMMON .1A 136
Breach Hill La. BS40: Chew S .7B 114
Breach La. BS48: Nail .2B 70
Breach Rd. BS3: Bedm .6G 61
Breachwood Vw. BA2: Odd D .2J 121
Breakneck BS48: Back .6K 71
BREAN .1B 144
Brean Ct. TA8: Brean .3B 144
Brean Down Av. BS9: Henle .3H 47
(not continuous)
BS23: W Mare .1F 127
Brean Down Rd. TA8: Brean .3B 126
Brean Gdns. BS3: Wind H .7A 62
Brean Leisure Pk. .4B 144
Brean Rd. BS24: Lym .5G 145
Brecknock Rd. BS4: Wind H .6C 62
Brecon Cl. BS9: Henle .2H 47
Brecon Ct. BS16: Fren .6F 37
Brecon Rd. BS9: Henle .2G 47
Brecon Vw. BS24: W Mare .4J 127
Bredon BS37: Yate .7D 30
Bredon Cl. BS15: K'wd .2D 64
Bredon Nook Rd. BS10: W Trym .1J 47
Bree Cl. BS22: Wor .7E 84
Brendon Av. BS23: W Mare .3H 105
Brendon Cl. BS30: Old C .5G 65
Brendon Gdns. BS48: Nail .1G 71
Brendon Rd. BS3: Wind H .6K 61
BS20: P'head .3C 42
Brendon Way BS27: Ched .6D 150
Brenner St. BS5: E'tn .6D 48
Brent Broad TA8: Bur S .5D 156
Brent Cl. BS24: W Mare .3K 127
TA9: Bre K .6K 157
BRENT KNOLL .5J 157
Brent Rd. BS7: Hor .3B 48
TA8: Bur S .3C 156
TA9: Bre K .3C 156
TA9: E Brnt .2K 157
BRENTRY .4H 35
Brentry Av. BS5: Bar H .2D 62
Brentry Hill BS9: W Trym .6G 35
Brentry Ho. BS10: Bren .4H 35
Brentry La. BS10: Bren .5G 35
Brentry Rd. BS16: Fish .4G 49
Brent St. TA9: Bre K .4H 157
Brereton Way BS30: C Hth .5F 65
Brewerton Cl. BS10: Bren .4J 35
Brewery Ct. BS3: Ash G .5G 61
Brewery Hill BS30: Upton C .3K 79
Brewhouse, The BS1: Bris .4G 5 (3A 62)
Briar Cl. BA3: Rads .6H 153
BS48: Nail .7J 57
TA8: Bur S .2E 158
Briar Ct. BS20: Pill .5G 45
Briarfield Av. BS15: Han .4K 63
Briarlands Office Pk. BS35: Rudg .2J 19
Briarleaze BS35: Rudg .3H 19
Briar Mead BS49: Yat .2G 87
Briar Rd. BS24: Hut .2C 128
Briars, The BS48: Back .3H 71
Briars Ct. BA2: Bath .7G 99
Briarside Rd. BS10: Bren .4J 35
Briar Wlk. BS16: Fish .5A 50
Briar Way BS16: Fish .4K 49
Briarwood BS9: W Trym .2F 47
Briary Rd. BS20: P'head .3E 42
Briavels Gro. BS6: Bris .6B 48
Brick La. BS39: High L .4B 140
Brick St. BS2: Bris .2K 5 (2B 62)
Bridewell La. BA1: Bath .4F 7 (5B 100)
BS24: Ban, Hut .5F 129
Bridewell St. BS1: Bris .2F 5 (2K 61)
Bridge Cl. BS14: Whit .6E 76
Bridge Farm Cl. BS14: Whit .7C 76
Bridge Farm Sq. BS49: Cong .7K 87
Bridge Farm Wlk. BS16: Mang .5F 51
Bridge Gdns. BA2: F'boro .6E 118
Bridgeleap Rd. BS16: Down .7D 38
Bridge Pl. Rd. BA2: Cam .5J 141
Bridge Rd. BA2: Bath .7A 6 (6J 99)
BS5: Eastv .5D 48
BS8: L Wds .3D 60
BS15: Soun .5D 50
BS16: Short .4G 51
BS23: W Mare .6H 105
BS24: B'don .7K 127
BS37: Yate .4A 30
Bridge Rd. Ind. Est. BS15: Soun .5E 50
Bridges Ct. BS16: Fish .4K 49
Bridges Dr. BS16: Fish .2A 50
Bridge St. BA2: Bath .4G 7 (5C 100)
BA15: Brad A .6H 125
BS1: Bris .4F 5 (3A 62)
BS5: Eastv .6F 49
Bridge Valley Rd. BS8: Clif .1E 60
Bridge Vw. BS35: Aust .4G 9
Bridge Vw. Cl. BS5: E'tn .7E 48
Bridge Wlk. BS7: Hor .7C 36
Bridge Way BS36: Fram C .6F 29
BRIDGEYATE .2H 65
Bridgman Gro. BS34: Fil .4D 36
Bridgwater Ct. BS24: W Mare .2J 127
Bridgwater Rd. BS13: Bis .3E 74
BS23: W Mare, B'don .2G 127
BS24: Lym .1A 146
BS25: Wins .1G 149
BS26: Axb, Cross .5E 148
BS40: F'tn .3E 90
BS41: Dun .1G 91
BS48: Bar G .1G 91
Bridle Way BS35: Alv .1H 19
Bridleway Cl. BA3: Mid N .6C 152
Briercliffe Rd. BS9: Stok B .1D 46
Brierly Furlong BS34: Stok G .4F 37
Briery Leaze Rd. BS14: Whit .5C 76
Brighton Cres. BS3: Bedm .7H 61
Brighton M. BS8: Clif .1H 61
Brighton Pk. BS5: E'tn .1D 62
Brighton Pl. BS15: K'wd .7B 50
Brighton Rd. BS6: Redl .7J 47
BS23: W Mare .6G 105
BS34: Pat .6B 26
Brighton St. BS2: Bris .7A 48
Brighton Ter. BS3: Bedm .7H 61
Brightstowe Rd. TA8: Bur S .5C 156
Bright St. BS5: Bar H .2D 62
BS15: K'wd .1B 64
Brigstocke Rd. BS2: Bris .7A 48
Brigstowe St. BS1: Bris .2H 5 (2A 62)
Brimbles, The BS7: Hor .5D 36
Brimbleworth La. BS22: St Geo .1G 107
Brimridge Rd. BS25: Wins .5G 131
Brimsham Pk. Shop. Cen.
BS37: Yate .2E 30
Brinkmarsh La. GL12: Fal .1H 13
Brinkworthy Rd. BS16: Stap .2F 49
Brinmead Wlk. BS13: Withy .7F 75
Brins Cl. BS34: Stok G .3H 37
Brinscombe La. BA2: Shos, Ston L .7F 143
BRINSEA .4A 110
Brinsea Batch BS49: Cong .3A 110
Brinsea La. BS49: Cong .4A 110
Brinsea Rd. BS49: Cong .1K 109
Brinsham La. BS37: Yate .7G 23
Brinsmead Cres. *BS20: Pill* .4H 45
(off Heywood Rd.)
Briscoes Av. BS13: Hart .6J 75
BRISLINGTON .7G 63
Brislington Hill BS4: Brisl .7G 63
Brislington Retail Pk. BS4: Brisl .1G 77
Brislington Trad. Est. BS4: Brisl .7H 63
(not continuous)
BRISTOL .3E 4 (2K 61)
Bristol & Anchor Ho. *BS5: W'hall* .1F 63
(off Park Cres.)
Bristol & Exeter M. BS1: Bris .6J 5 (4B 62)
Bristol Bri. Ho. BS1: Bris .4F 5 (3A 62)
Bristol Bus. Pk. BS16: Fren .6H 37
Bristol Cathedral .5D 4 (3J 61)
Bristol City FC .6F 61
Bristol Distribution Pk. BS32: Brad S .3F 27
Bristol Ga. BS8: Clif .4F 61
Bristol Harbour Railway .6C 4 (4J 61)
Bristol Hill BS4: Brisl .7F 63
Bristol Hippodrome .4D 4 (3K 61)
Bristol Ho. BS1: Bris .4G 5
Bristol Ice Rink .3D 4 (2J 61)
Bristol Indoor Bowls Club .1E 74
BRISTOL INTERNATIONAL AIRPORT .4D 90
Bristol Megabowl .5F 61
Bristol North Swimming Pool .5A 48
Bristol Outdoor Pursuits .3C 118
Bristol Parkway Nth. BS34: Stok G .2J 37
Bristol Parkway Station (Rail) .3G 37
Bristol Rd. BA2: Cor, New L .3B 98
BA3: Rads .2K 153
BS14: Whit .5E 76
BS16: Fren, Ham .7J 37
BS16: Ham .4B 38
BS20: P'head .4F 43
BS22: St Geo, Wor .2F 107
BS24: W Wick .2F 107
BS25: C'hll .1B 132
BS25: Row, Star, Wins .6H 131
BS31: Key .4B 78
BS35: T'bry .5K 11
BS36: Fram C, Wint .7C 28
BS37: Iron A .3G 29
BS39: Far G, Hall .7H 139
BS39: Paul .7C 140
BS39: Pens, Pub .5F 95
BS40: But, Redh .7E 90
BS40: Chew S .4D 114
BS40: L'frd .1B 132
BS48: Wrax .6J 57
BS49: Cong .7K 87
GL12: Crom .2B 14
TA9: Bre K, Edith, High .4G 159
Bristol Rd. Lwr. BS23: W Mare .4F 105
Bristol Rovers FC .2B 48
Bristol RUFC .2B 48
Bristol Southend BS3: Wind H .7K 61
Bristol South Swimming Pool .5J 61
Bristol Sports Cen. .1E 62
Bristol Temple Meads Station (Rail)
.6K 5 (4B 62)
Bristol Va. Cen. for Industry
BS3: Bedm .1H 75
Bristol Va. Trad. Est. BS3: Bedm .2J 75
Bristol Vw. BA2: Odd D .4J 121
Bristol Zoo Gdns. .7F 47
Bristow B'way. BS11: A'mth .6G 33
Bristowe Ho. BS16: Fish .3K 49
Britannia Cl. BS16: Down .6E 38
Britannia Cres. BS34: Stok G .2F 37
Britannia Ho. BS34: Fil .5B 36
Britannia Rd. BS5: E'tn .7D 48
BS15: K'wd .1A 64
BS34: Pat .6K 25
Britannia Way BS21: Clev .1C 68
British, The BS37: Yate .2B 30
British Rd. BS3: Bedm .6H 61
Brittan Pl. BS20: P'bry .5C 44
Britten Ct. BS30: L Grn .5D 64
BRITTENS .7D 140
Brittens BS39: Paul .7D 140
Britten's Cl. BS39: Paul .7D 140
Britten's Hill BS39: Paul .7D 140
Britton Gdns. BS15: K'wd .7A 50
Britton Ho. BS15: Warm .1F 65
Brixham Rd. BS3: Wind H .7J 61
Brixton Rd. BS5: E'tn .1D 62
Brixton Rd. M. BS5: E'tn .1D 62
Broadbury Rd. BS4: Know .2K 75
Broad Cft. BS32: Brad S .4E 26
Broadcroft BS40: Chew M .1F 115
Broadcroft Av. BS49: Clav .2B 88
Broadcroft Cl. BS49: Clav .2B 88
Broadfield Av. BS15: K'wd .1A 64
Broadfield Rd. BS4: Know .2C 76
Broadhurst Gdns. TA8: Bur S .3D 158
Broadlands BS21: Clev .6F 55
Broadlands Av. BS31: Key .4B 78
Broadlands Dr. BS11: Law W .7A 34
Broad La. BS36: Coal H .2H 39
BS37: W'lgh .3A 40
BS37: Yate .2B 30
(not continuous)
Broadleas BS13: Bis .3J 75
Broadleaze BS11: Shire .1H 45
Broadleaze Way BS25: Wins .3F 131
Broadleys Av. BS9: Henle .1J 47
BROAD MEAD .3D 36
BROADMEAD .3G 5 (2A 62)
Broadmead BS1: Bris .2G 5 (2A 62)
Broad Mead La. BS40: Regil .1K 113
Broadmead La. BS31: Key .5F 79
Broadmead La. Ind. Est. BS31: Key .3F 79
Broadmoor La. BA1: W'ton .6F 81
Broadmoor Pk. BA1: W'ton .1H 99
Broadmoor Va. BA1: W'ton .7G 81
Broadoak Hill BS41: Dun .1F 93
Broad Oak Rd. BS13: Withy .6F 75
Broadoak Rd. BS23: W Mare .2F 127
BS40: L'frd .7C 110
Broad Oaks BS8: L Wds .3E 60
Broadoak Wlk. BS16: Fish .4K 49
Broad Plain BS2: Bris .4J 5 (2B 62)
Broad Quay BA1: Bath .6F 7 (6B 100)
BS1: Bris .4E 4 (3K 61)
Broad Quay Ho. BS1: Bris .5E 4
Broad Rd. BS15: K'wd .7A 50
BS40: Blag .5B 134
Broadstone La. BS21: Kings S .1K 85
Broadstones BA15: Mon F .4C 102
Broadstone Wlk. BS13: Hart .5K 75
Broad St. BA1: Bath .3G 7 (4C 100)
BS1: Bris .3F 5 (2K 61)
BS16: Stap H .4B 50
BS37: Chip S .5H 31
BS40: Wrin .2F 111
BS49: Cong .7K 87
Broad St. Pl.
BA1: Bath .3G 7 (4C 100)
Broad Wlk. BS4: Know .7B 62
BS20: P'head .1G 43
Broadwalk Shop. Cen. BS4: Know .7D 62
Broadway BA2: Bath .5J 7 (5D 100)
BS24: Lock .1H 129
BS24: W Mare .3H 127
BS25: S'ham, Star .4K 131
BS31: Salt .7H 79
BS37: Yate .4F 31
Broadway Av. BS9: Henle .2K 47
Broadway Ct.
BA2: Bath .6H 7 (6C 100)
Broadway Ho. Holiday Touring Cvn. Pk.
BS27: Ched .4B 150
Broadway La. BA3: Rads .7F 141
Broadway Rd. BS7: B'stn .5K 47
BS13: Withy .5F 75
Broadways Dr. BS16: B'hll .1H 49
Broad Weir BS1: Bris .3H 5 (2A 62)
Brock End BS20: P'head .5B 42
Brockhurst Gdns. BS15: K'wd .1J 63
Brockhurst Rd. BS15: K'wd .1J 63
BROCKLEY .1F 89
Brockley Cl. BS24: W Mare .4H 127
BS34: Lit S .7E 26
BS48: Nail .1F 71
Brockley Combe Rd.
BS48: Back, B'ley .1G 89
Brockley Cres. BS24: W Mare .4H 127
Brockley La. BS48: B'ley, C'vey .5F 71

168 A-Z Bristol, Bath & North Somerset Atlas

Brockley Rd.—Cambridge Pk.

Brockley Rd. BS31: Salt 7H 79
Brockley Wlk. BS13: Bis 2G 75
Brockley Way BS48: B'ley 7C 70
BS49: Clav, C've 1B 88
(not continuous)
Brockridge La. BS36: Fram C 7G 29
Brocks La. BS41: L Ash 1K 73
Brocks Rd. BS13: Hart 7J 75
Brock St. BA1: Bath 2E 6 (4B 100)
Brockway BS48: Nail 7H 57
Brockwood BA15: W'ley 5D 124
Brockworth BS37: Yate 1C 40
Brockworth Cres. BS16: B'hll 2H 49
Bromfield Wlk. BS16: Emer G 1F 51
Bromley Dr. BS16: Down 7B 38
Bromley Farm BS16: Down 6B 38
BROMLEY HEATH 7C 38
Bromley Heath Av. BS16: Down 7B 38
Bromley Heath Rd.
BS16: Down 1B 50
BS16: Ham 5B 38
Bromley Rd. BS7: Hor 3B 48
BS39: Stan D 2B 116
Brompton Cl. BS15: K'wd 1D 64
Brompton Ho. BA2: Bath 1H 7 (4C 100)
Brompton Rd. BS24: W Mare 3J 127
Broncksea Rd. BS7: Fil 6B 36
Bronte Cl. BS23: W Mare 1J 127
Bronte Wlk. BS7: Hor 7C 36
Brook Cl. BS41: L Ash 1B 74
Brookcote Dr. BS34: Lit S 1F 37
Brookdale Rd. BS13: Bis 4H 75
Brooke Rd. TA8: Berr 3B 156
Brookfield Av. BS7: B'stn 5K 47
Brookfield Cl. BS37: Chip S 4J 31
Brookfield La. BS6: Cot 6K 47
Brookfield Pk. BA1: W'ton 1H 99
Brookfield Rd. BS6: Cot 6K 47
BS34: Pat 6D 26
Brookfield Wlk. BS21: Clev 6F 55
BS30: Old C 6G 65
Brookgate BS3: Ash V 1E 74
Brook Hill BS6: Bris 7B 48
Brook Ho. BS34: Lit S 6E 26
Brookland Rd. BS6: Henle 3K 47
BS22: W Mare 5K 105
Brooklands BA2: Dunk 2D 142
Brook La. BS6: Bris 7B 48
BS16: B'hll 2G 49
Brooklea BS30: Old C 5F 65
Brookleaze BS9: Sea M 3C 46
Brookleaze Bldgs. BA1: Bath 1D 100
Brook Lintons BS4: Brisl 6F 63
Brook Lodge Touring Cvn. & Camping Pk.
BS40: Redh 3K 111
Brooklyn BS40: Wrin 2F 111
Brooklyn Rd. BA1: Bath 1E 100
BS13: Bis 2H 75
Brookmead BS35: T'bry 5B 12
Brook Office Pk. BS16: Emer G 5F 39
Brookridge Ho. BS10: Hen 4F 35
Brook Rd. BA2: Bath 4A 6 (5K 99)
BS3: Bedm 5K 61
BS5: S'wll 7G 49
BS6: Bris 7B 48
BS15: K'wd, Warm 1E 64
(not continuous)
BS15: Warm 1F 65
BS16: Fish 4J 49
(not continuous)
BS16: Mang 2D 50
Brookside BS20: Pill 5G 45
BS39: Paul 7C 140
BS40: Winf 4K 91
Brookside Cl. BA1: Bathe 5H 83
BS39: Paul 7C 140
Brookside Dr. BA2: F'boro 6D 118
BS36: Fram C 6F 29
Brookside Ho. BA1: W'ton 2H 99
Brookside Rd. BS4: Brisl 7G 63
Brook St. BS5: Redf 2E 62
BS37: Chip S 5G 31
Brookthorpe BS37: Yate 6D 30
Brookthorpe Av. BS11: Law W 6A 34
Brookthorpe Ct. BS37: Yate 6D 30
Brook Vw. BS10: Hen 4F 35
Brookview Wlk. BS13: Bis 3H 75
Brook Way BS32: Brad S 5E 26
Broom Farm Cl. BS48: Nail 2G 71
Broomground BA15: W'ley 5C 124
BROOM HILL 5H 63
BROOMHILL 2H 49
Broom Hill BS16: B'hll 2G 49
Broom Hill La. BS39: High L 5C 140
Broomhill La. BS39: Clut 2G 139
Broomhill Rd. BS4: Brisl 6H 63
Brooms, The BS16: Emer G 5E 38
Brotherswood Ct. BS32: Brad S 3F 27
Brougham Hayes BA2: Bath 6B 6 (5K 99)
Brougham Pl. BA1: Bath 1E 100
(off St Saviours Rd.)
Broughton Ho. BS1: Bris 7H 5 (4A 62)
Brow, The BA2: Bath 6H 99
BA2: C Down 3E 122
Brow Hill BA1: Bathe 6H 83
Brow Hill Vs. BA1: Bathe 6H 83
Browne Ct. BS8: Clif 3F 61
(off Cumberland Pl.)
Browning Ct. BS7: Hor 7D 36
Brownlow Rd. BS23: W Mare 1G 127
Brown's Folly Nature Reserve 2B 102
Broxholme Wlk. BS11: Law W 7K 33
Bruce Av. BS5: E'tn 7E 48
Bruce Rd. BS5: E'tn 7E 48
Brue Cl. BS23: W Mare 7J 105
Brue Cres. TA8: Bur S 3D 158
Brue Way TA9: High 6H 159
Brummel Way BS39: Paul 7A 140
Brunel Cl. BS24: W Mare 5H 127
BS30: Warm 2G 65
Brunel Ct. BS20: P'head 2F 43
BS37: Yate 4C 30
Brunel Gro. BS14: H'gro 3C 76
Brunel Ho. BA2: Bath 5G 99
BS1: Bris 4C 4 (3J 61)
Brunel Lock Rd. BS1: Bris 4F 61
Brunel Rd. BS13: Bis 2F 75
BS48: Nail 1D 70
Brunel's SS Great Britain 6B 4 (4H 61)
Brunel's Way TA9: High 3G 159
Brunel Way BS1: Bris 4F 61
BS3: Ash G, Bwr A 5F 61
BS35: T'bry 5K 11
BS49: Yat 2F 87
Brunswick Ct. BS2: Bris 1G 5
Brunswick Pl. BA1: Bath 2F 7 (4B 100)
BS1: Bris 4F 61
Brunswick Sq. BS2: Bris 1G 5 (1A 62)
Brunswick St. BA1: Bath 2D 100
BS2: Bris 1A 62
BS5: Redf 2E 62
Bruton BS24: W Mare 3J 127
Bruton Av. BA2: Bath 7E 6 (7B 100)
BS20: P'head 3C 42
Bruton Cl. BS5: St G 1H 63
BS48: Nail 2G 71
Bruton Pl. BS8: Clif 3A 4 (2H 61)
Bryanson's Cl. BS16: Stap 2F 49
Bryant Av. BA3: Rads 5H 153
Bryant Gdns. BS21: Clev 1C 68
Bryants Cl. BS16: Fren 6A 38
Bryants Hill BS5: St G 3K 63
Brynland Av. BS7: B'stn 4A 48
Buchanans Wharf Nth. BS1: Bris 5F 5
Buchanans Wharf Sth. BS1: Bris 5F 5
Buckingham Dr. BS34: Stok G 3F 37
Buckingham Gdns. BS16: Down 2C 50
Buckingham Ho. BS34: Fil 5B 36
Buckingham Pde. BS35: T'bry 3K 11
Buckingham Pl. BS8: Clif 2A 4 (2G 61)
BS16: Down 2C 50
Buckingham Rd. BS4: Brisl 4F 63
BS24: W Mare 3K 127
Buckingham St. BS3: Bedm 7J 61
Buckingham Va. BS8: Clif 1G 61
Buckland Cl. TA8: Bur S 7E 156
Buckland Grn. BS22: Wor 6E 84
Bucklands Batch BS48: Nail 2H 71
Bucklands Dr. BS48: Nail 2H 71
Bucklands End BS48: Nail 2H 71
Bucklands Gro. BS48: Nail 2H 71
Bucklands La. BS48: Nail 2H 71
Bucklands Vw. BS48: Nail 2J 71
Bucklewell Cl. BS11: Shire 2K 45
BUCKOVER 3E 12
Budbury Circ. BA15: Brad A 5G 125
Budbury Cl. BA15: Brad A 5G 125
Budbury Pl. BA15: Brad A 5G 125
(not continuous)
Budbury Ridge BA15: Brad A 5G 125
Budbury Tyning BA15: Brad A 5F 125
Bude Av. BS5: St G 1J 63
Bude Cl. BS48: Nail 1J 71
Bude Rd. BS34: Fil 4D 36
Budgetts Mead BS27: Ched 6C 150
Building of Bath Mus. 2F 7 (4C 100)
Bullens Cl. BS32: Brad S 4F 27
Buller Rd. BS4: Know 7E 62
Bullhouse La. BS40: Wrin 1F 111
(not continuous)
Bull La. BS5: St G 3H 63
BS20: Pill 4G 45
Bullocks La. BS21: Kings S 6C 68
Bull Pit BA15: Brad A 6H 125
Bull Wharf BS1: Bris 4G 5 (3K 61)
Bully La. BS37: Yate 4D 22
BULWARK 1A 8
Bumper's Batch BA2: S'ske 4C 122
Bungay's Hill BA2: High L, Tim 4B 140
BS39: High L 4B 140
Bunker Underground Military Mus., The 5F 159
Bunting Ct. BS22: Wor 3C 106
Burbank Cl. BS30: L Grn 6E 64
Burbarrow La. BS37: Cod, W'lgh 4D 40
Burchells Av. BS15: K'wd 7K 49
BURCHELLS GREEN 1K 63
Burchells Grn. Cl. BS15: K'wd 7K 49
Burchells Grn. Rd. BS15: K'wd 7K 49
Burchill Cl. BS39: Clut 2H 139
Burcombe Cl. BS36: Coal H 7H 29
Burcott Rd. BS11: A'mth 2G 33
Burden Cl. BS32: Brad S 1H 37
Burfoote Gdns. BS14: Stoc 6G 77
Burfoote Rd. BS14: Stoc 6G 77
Burford Av. BS34: Pat 6E 26
Burford Cl. BA2: Bath 1H 121
BS20: P'head 4G 43
Burford Gro. BS11: Shire 3K 45
Burgage Cl. BS37: Chip S 6H 31
Burgess Grn. Cl. BS4: St Ap 2G 63
Burghill Rd. BS10: W Trym 6G 35
Burghley Ct. BS36: Wint 2C 38
Burghley Rd. BS6: Bris 6A 48
Burgis Rd. BS14: Stoc 4F 77
Burleigh Gdns. BA1: Bath 3G 99
Burleigh Way GL12: Wickw 7H 15
(not continuous)
Burley Av. BS16: Mang 3D 50
Burley Crest BS16: Mang 2D 50
Burley Gro. BS16: Mang 2D 50
Burlington Ct. BS6: Redl 6H 47
BS20: P'head 2G 43
Burlington Pl. BA1: Bath 2E 6
Burlington Rd. BA3: Mid N 4G 153
BS6: Redl 6H 47
BS20: P'head 1G 43
Burlington St. BA1: Bath 1E 6 (3B 100)
BS23: W Mare 4G 105
Burltons, The GL12: Crom 2B 14
Burnbush Cl. BS14: Stoc 4G 77
Burnell Dr. BS2: Bris 1B 62
BURNETT 4F 97
Burnett Bus. Pk. BS31: Key 2F 97
Burnett Cl. TA8: Bur S 1E 158
Burnett Hill BS31: Burn, Key 2E 96
Burnett Ind. Est. BS40: Wrin 3G 111
Burney Way BS30: L Grn 6E 64
Burnham Cl. BS15: K'wd 7D 50
BS24: W Mare 4H 127
Burnham Dr. BS15: K'wd 7D 50
BS24: W Mare 4H 127
Burnham Golf Range 2J 159
Burnham Moor La. TA9: Edith, W'fld 2J 159
BURNHAM-ON-SEA 1C 158
Burnham-on-Sea Holiday Village
TA8: Bur S 3D 158
Burnham Rd. BA2: Bath 5J 99
BS11: Shire 2H 45
TA8: Bur S 3E 158
TA9: High 3E 158
Burnham Touring Pk. TA8: Bur S 6E 156
Burnside Cl. BS10: S'mead 5J 35
Burnt Ho. Cotts. BA2: Odd D 4J 121
Burnthouse Ct. BA2: Odd D 4J 121
Burnt Ho. Rd. BA2: Odd D 4K 121
BURRINGTON 2H 133
Burrington Av. BS24: W Mare 4H 127
Burrington Cl. BS24: W Mare 4H 127
BS48: Nail 1G 71
Burrington Combe 4H 133
Burrington Combe BS40: Blag 4K 133
Burrington La. BS40: Burr 2J 133
Burrington Wlk. BS13: Bis 2G 75
Burrough Way BS36: Wint 2C 38
Burrows, The BS22: St Geo 1H 107
Burton Cl. BS1: Bris 7G 5 (4A 62)
Burton Ct. BS8: Clif 3A 4 (2H 61)
Burton Row TA9: Bre K 3H 157
Burton St. BA1: Bath 4G 7 (5C 100)
Burwalls Rd. BS8: L Wds 3F 60
Bury, The BS24: Elbgh, Lock 2E 128
Bury Ct. Cl. BS11: Law W 6A 34
Bury Hill BS16: Ham 5C 38
BS36: Wint D 5C 38
Buryhill La. BS37: Yate 6F 23
Bury Hill Vw. BS16: Down 6C 38
Bury La. BS30: Doy, Wick 3E 66
Bush Av. BS34: Lit S 1E 36
Bush Ct. BS4: Wind H 6B 62
BS35: Alv 7H 11
Bush Ind. Est. BS5: St G 1F 63
Bush La. BS3: Bris 5H 61
Bushy Coombe BA3: Mid N 3D 152
Bushy Ho. BS4: Wind H 6B 62
Bushy Pk. BS4: Wind H 6B 62
Bushythorn Rd. BS40: Chew S 4E 114
BUTCOMBE 4E 112
Butcombe BS24: W Mare 3J 127
Butcombe La. BS40: But, Nem T 5F 113
Butcombe Wlk. BS14: Whit 5D 76
Butham La. BS40: Chew M 7G 93
Buthay, The GL12: Wickw 7G 15
Butlass Cl. BS39: High L 4B 140
Butler Ho. BS5: St G 1H 63
Butlers Cl. BS5: St G 3H 63
Butlers Wlk. BS5: St G 3H 63
Buttercliffe Ri. BS41: L Ash 6C 60
Buttercup Cres. BS22: Wor 7E 84
Butterfield Cl. BS10: Hor 1A 48
BS36: Fram C 1F 39
Butterfield Pk. BS21: Clev 1C 68
Butterfield Rd. BS10: Hor 1A 48
Buttermere Rd. BS23: W Mare 1J 127
Butterworth Ct. BS4: Know 3K 75
Butt La. BS35: T'bry 1A 12
Button Cl. BS14: Whit 4C 76
BUTTS BATCH 3F 111
Butts Batch BS26: Comp B 3B 148
BS40: Wrin 3F 111
Butt's La. BA15: Mon F 5D 102
BS39: Hall 7A 140
Butts Orchard BS40: Wrin 3F 111
Buxton Wlk. BS7: Hor 7C 36
Byefields BS21: Clev 2C 68
Bye Mead BS16: Emer G 7E 38
Byeways La. BS25: Sandf 1J 131
Byfield BA2: C Down 3D 122
Byfield Bldgs. BA2: C Down 3D 122
(off Byfield Pl.)
Byfield Pl. BA2: C Down 3D 122
Byron Cl. BS24: Lock 1E 128
Byron Ct. BS23: W Mare 4H 105
Byron Pl. BS8: Clif 3B 4 (2H 61)
BS16: Stap H 4C 50
Byron Rd. BA2: Bath 7F 7 (7B 100)
BS23: W Mare 1J 127
BS24: Lock 1E 128
Byron St. BS2: Bris 7C 48
BS5: Redf 2E 62
Byways Pk. BS21: Clev 1C 68
Byzantine Ct. BS1: Bris 7E 4

C

Cabot Cir. BS1: Bris 2H 5
Cabot Cl. BS15: K'wd 2A 64
BS31: Salt 1H 97
BS37: Yate 5F 31
Cabot Ct. BS7: Fil 6B 36
Cabot Grn. BS5: Bar H 2D 62
Cabot Ho. BS35: T'bry 4A 12
Cabot Ri. BS20: P'head 3C 42
Cabot Tower 4B 4 (3H 61)
Cabot Way BS8: Clif 4F 61
BS20: Pill 5H 45
BS22: Wor 1E 106
Cabstand BS20: P'head 2F 43
Cadbury Camp 4C 56
Cadbury Camp La. BS20: Clap G 3D 56
BS21: Tic 3D 56
Cadbury Camp La. W. BS21: Tic 5J 55
Cadbury Cl. TA8: Bur S 6E 156
Cadbury Farm Rd. BS49: Yat 4H 87
Cadbury Gdns. BS30: C Hth 3F 65
Cadbury Halt BS20: Wes 7B 42
CADBURY HEATH 3F 65
Cadbury Heath Rd. BS30: C Hth 4E 64
Cadbury La. BS20: Wes 7B 42
Cadbury Rd. BS20: P'head 4F 43
BS31: Key 1E 96
Cadbury Sq. BS49: Cong 1K 109
Cadby Ho. BA2: Bath 5G 99
Caddick Cl. BS15: K'wd 6D 50
Cade Cl. BS15: K'wd 3D 64
BS34: Stok G 2G 37
Cadogan Gro. BS48: Back 4K 71
Cadogan Rd. BS14: H'gro 2C 76
Caen Rd. BS3: Wind H 6K 61
Caernarvon Rd. BS31: Key 6A 78
Caernarvon Way TA8: Bur S 6D 156
Caern Well Pl. BA1: Bath 1G 7
Caine Rd. BS7: Hor 1B 48
Cains Cl. BS15: K'wd 3C 64
Cairn Cl. BS48: Nail 1J 71
Cairn Gdns. BS36: Wint D 3C 38
Cairns Ct. BS6: Redl 4J 47
Cairns Cres. BS2: Bris 7B 48
Cairns Rd. BS6: Henle, Redl 3H 47
Caister Cl. BS23: W Mare 7H 105
Cala Trad. Est. BS3: Ash V 6F 61
Calcott Rd. BS4: Know 7C 62
Caldbeck Cl. BS10: S'mead 5K 35
Calder Cl. BS31: Key 6E 78
Caldicot Cl. BS11: Law W 5C 34
BS30: Will 7F 65
Caledonia M. BS8: Clif 3F 61
Caledonian Rd. BA2: Bath 5A 6 (5K 99)
BS1: Bris 6B 4 (4H 61)
Caledonia Pl. BS8: Clif 3F 61
California Rd. BS30: L Grn 6E 64
Callard Ho. BS16: Fish 4H 49
Callicroft Rd. BS34: Pat 7C 26
Callington Rd. BS4: Brisl 1D 76
BS14: H'gro 1D 76
Callow Drove BS25: Wins 1J 149
Callowhill Ct. BS1: Bris 2G 5 (2A 62)
Calluna Cl. BS22: Wick L 6E 84
Calton Gdns. BA2: Bath 7F 7 (6B 100)
Calton Rd. BA2: Bath 7G 7 (6C 100)
Calton Wlk. BA2: Bath 7F 7 (6B 100)
Camberley Dr. BS36: Fram C 6D 28
Camberley Rd. BS4: Know 2J 75
(not continuous)
Camberley Wlk.
BS22: W Mare 4C 106
Camborne Rd. BS7: Hor 1C 48
Cambrian Dr. BS37: Yate 3D 30
CAMBRIDGE BATCH 2G 73
Cambridge Ct. BS40: Wrin 2F 111
Cambridge Cres. BS9: W Trym 1G 47
Cambridge Gro. BS21: Clev 4D 54
Cambridge Pk. BS6: Redl 5H 47

Cambridge Pl.—Chardyke Dr.

Cambridge Pl. BA2: Bath 7J 7 (6D 100)
BS23: W Mare 4F 105
Cambridge Rd. BS7: B'stn 4K 47
BS21: Clev 4D 54
Cambridge St. BS3: Wind H 5B 62
BS5: Redf 2E 62
Cambridge Ter. BA2: Bath 7J 7 (6D 100)
Cam Brook Cl. BA2: Cam 5H 141
Camden Ct. BA1: Bath 1F 7 (3B 100)
Camden Cres. BA1: Bath 1F 7 (3B 100)
Camden Rd. BA1: Bath 3C 100
BS3: Bris 7B 4
Camden Row BA1: Bath 1F 7 (3B 100)
(not continuous)
Camden Ter. BA1: Bath 3C 100
(off Camden Rd.)
BS8: Clif 3G 61
BS23: W Mare 5G 105
CAMELEY 5E 138
Cameley Cl. BS39: Temp C 5G 139
Cameley Grn. BA2: Bath 5F 99
Cameley Rd.
BS39: Came, Hin B, Temp C 6B 138
Camelford Rd. BS5: E'tn 7F 49
Camellia Dr. BS32: Alm 1F 27
Cameron Wlk. BS7: L'lze 2E 48
Cameroons Cl. BS31: Key 6C 78
CAMERTON .5J 141
Camerton Cl. BS31: Salt 7J 79
Camerton Hill BA2: Cam 5J 141
Camerton Rd. BA2: Cam 3J 141
BS5: E'tn 7F 49
Camomile Wlk. BS20: P'head 3H 43
Campbells Farm Dr. BS11: Law W 6K 33
Campbell St. BS2: Bris 7A 48
Campian Wlk. BS4: Know 4K 75
Campion Cl. BS22: W Mare 5B 106
BS35: T'bry .2B 12
Campion Dr. BS32: Brad S 4F 27
Camplins BS21: Clev 1C 68
Camp Rd. BS8: Clif 2F 61
BS23: W Mare 3D 104
Camp Rd. Nth. BS23: W Mare 3D 104
Camp Vw. BS36: Wint D 3C 38
BS48: Nail .7F 57
Camvale BA2: Pea J 5B 142
Camview BS39: Paul 7B 140
Camwal Ind. Est. BS2: Bris 4C 62
Camwal Rd. BS2: Bris 4C 62
Canada Coombe BS24: Hut 3D 128
Canada Way BS1: Bris 7A 4 (4G 61)
Canal Path BA2: B'ptn 1J 101
Canal Ter. BA2: B'ptn 2H 101
Canal Vw. BA2: Cam 5J 141
Canberra Cres. BS24: Lock 6F 107
Canberra Gro. BS34: Fil 3D 36
Canberra Rd. BS23: W Mare 2H 127
Canford Crematorium BS9: W Trym 1E 46
Canford La. BS9: W Trym 1D 46
Canford Rd. BS9: W Trym 7F 35
Cannans Cl. BS36: Wint 7C 28
Cann La. BS30: B'yte, Old C 3H 65
Cannons Ga. BS21: Clev 2C 68
Cannon St. BS1: Bris 1F 5 (1K 61)
BS3: Bedm .5J 61
Canons Cl. BA2: Bath 2H 121
Canons Ho. BS1: Bris 6D 4 (4J 61)
CANON'S MARSH 5C 4 (3J 61)
Canon's Rd. BS1: Bris 5D 4 (3J 61)
(Anchor Sq., not continuous)
BS1: Bris 6B 4 (4H 61)
(Lime Kiln Rd.)
Canon St. BS5: Redf 1E 62
Canon's Wlk. BS15: Soun 6C 50
BS22: Wor 2B 106
Canons Way BS1: Bris 5C 4 (3J 61)
Canowie Rd. BS6: Redl 5H 47
Canteen La. BA2: Wel 4K 143
Cantell Gro. BS14: Stoc 5H 77
Canterbury Cl. BS22: Wor 7E 84
BS37: Yate .3E 30
Canterbury Rd. BA2: Bath 6B 6 (6K 99)
Canterbury St. BS5: Bar H 3D 62
Canters Leaze GL12: Wickw 1H 23
Cantock's Cl. BS8: Clif 3C 4 (2J 61)
Canton Pl. BA1: Bath 1H 7
Canvey Cl. BS10: Hor 1A 48
Canynge Ho. BS1: Bris 7G 5 (4A 62)
Canynge Rd. BS8: Clif 1F 61
Canynge Sq. BS8: Clif 1F 61
Canynge St. BS1: Bris 5G 5 (3A 62)
Capel Cl. BS15: Warm 1F 65
Capell Cl. BS22: W Mare 4K 105
Capel Rd. BS11: Law W 6B 34
Capenor Cl. BS20: P'head 4E 42
Capgrave Cl. BS4: Brisl 6J 63
Capgrave Cres. BS4: Brisl 6J 63
Capital Edge BS8: Clif 5A 4 (4H 61)
Caple La. BS40: Chew S 7B 114
Cappards Rd. BS39: Bis S 1K 137
Capricorn Quay BS8: Clif 5B 4 (3H 61)
Caraway Gdns. BS5: Eastv 6E 48
Carberry Vw. BS24: W'ton V 5E 106
Cardigan Cres. BS22: W Mare 4A 106
Cardigan La. BS9: Henle 2H 47
Cardigan M. BS9: Henle 3H 47
Cardigan Rd. BS9: Henle 2H 47
Cardill Cl. BS13: Bis 2G 75
Cardinal Cl. BA2: Odd D 4K 121
Carditch Drove BS49: Cong 4H 109
Carey's Cl. BS21: Clev 5F 55
Careys Way BS24: W'ton V 5C 106
Carfax Ct. BS6: Redl 5G 47
Carice Gdns. BS21: Clev 2D 68
Carisbrooke Rd. BS4: Know 2K 75
CARLINGCOTT 4A 142
Carlingford Ter. BA3: Rads 4A 154
Carlingford Ter. Rd. BA3: Rads 4A 154
Carlow Rd. BS4: Know 2A 76
Carlton Cl. BS39: Clut 3H 139
Carlton Ct. BS9: W Trym 1G 47
Carlton Mans. Nth. BS23: W Mare 5F 105
(off Beach Rd.)
Carlton Mans. Sth.
BS23: W Mare 5F 105
(off Beach Rd.)
Carlton Pk. BS5: Redf 1E 62
Carlton St. BS23: W Mare 5F 105
Carlyle Rd. BS5: E'tn 7E 48
Carmarthen Cl. BS37: Yate 2F 31
Carmarthen Gro. BS30: Will 1F 79
Carmarthen Rd. BS9: Henle 2G 47
Carnarvon Rd. BS6: Redl 6J 47
Carolina Ho. BS2: Bris 1F 5 (1K 61)
Caroline Bldgs. BA2: Bath 6J 7 (6D 100)
Caroline Cl. BS31: Key 6A 78
BS37: Chip S 4H 31
Caroline Pl. BA1: Bath 1F 7 (3B 100)
BS48: Back .5J 71
Carousel La. BS24: W'ton V 5C 106
Carpenter Cl. BS23: W Mare 5J 105
Carpenters La. BS31: Key 5C 78
Carpenters Pl. BS4: Know 1A 76
(off Leinster Av.)
Carpenters Shop La. BS16: Down 2C 50
Carpenters Way BA3: Mid N 6F 153
Carre Gdns. BS22: Wor 7D 84
Carr Ho. BA2: Bath 5G 99
BS2: Bris 7B 48
Carriage Ct. BA1: Bath 2E 6
Carriage Dr. BS10: Bren 5H 35
Carrick Ho. BS8: Clif 3F 61
(off Hotwell Rd.)
Carrington Rd. BS3: Ash G 5G 61
Carroll Ct. BS16: Fren 6G 37
Carrs Cl. BA2: Bath 5G 99
Carsons Rd. BS16: Mang, Sis 5F 51
Carter Rd. BS39: Paul 1B 152
Carter Wlk. BS32: Brad S 6F 27
Cart La. BS1: Bris 5H 5 (3A 62)
Cartledge Rd. BS5: E'tn 7E 48
Cashmore Ho. BS5: Bar H 2D 62
Caslon Ct. BS1: Bris 7H 5 (4A 62)
Cassell Rd. BS16: Down, Fish 3A 50
Cassey Bottom La. BS5: St G 2J 63
Cassis Cl. TA8: Bur S 3E 158
Casson Dr. BS16: Stap 7G 37
Castle Cl. BS10: Hen 5D 34
BS48: Flax B 3D 72
Castle Coombe BS35: T'bry 3A 12
Castle Ct. BS34: Stok G 3J 37
BS35: T'bry .3K 11
Castle Farm La. BS41: Dun 1B 92
Castle Farm Rd. BS15: Han 7K 63
Castle Gdns. BA2: Bath 1A 122
Castlegate Ho. BS4: Brisl 7G 63
Castle Hill BS29: Ban 3C 130
Castle Ho. GL12: Wickw 7H 15
Castlemead Shop. Cen. BS22: Wor 6E 84
Castle M. GL12: Wickw 7H 15
Castle Rd. BS15: K'wd 6B 50
BS16: Puck .2C 52
BS21: Clev .3D 54
BS22: Wor 1C 106
BS30: Old C 6G 65
Castle St. BS1: Bris 3H 5 (2A 62)
BS35: T'bry .2J 11
Castle Vw. BS24: W'ton V 4D 106
Castle Vw. Rd. BS21: Clev 4D 54
Castlewood Cl. BS21: Clev 4D 54
Caswell Hill BS20: Clap G 1J 57
Caswell La. BS20: Clap G, P'bry 7H 43
CATBRAIN 1H 35
Catbrain Hill BS10: Pat 1H 35
Catbrain La. BS10: Pat 1H 35
Catemead BS21: Clev 2C 68
Cater Rd. BS13: Bis 4G 75
Catharine Pl. BA1: Bath 2E 6 (4B 100)
Cathay BS1: Bris 7G 5
Cathay La. BS27: Ched 7D 150
Cathcart Ho. BA1: Bath 2C 100
Cathedral, The BS8: Clif 3A 4 (2H 61)
Cathedral Sq. BS1: Bris 5D 4 (3J 61)
Cathedral Wlk. BS1: Bris 6C 4 (4J 61)
Catherine Ct. BS6: Bris 7A 48
(off Backfields La.)
Catherine Hill BS35: Olv 3B 18
Catherine Mead St. BS3: Bedm 5J 61
Catherine St. BS11: A'mth 7G 33
TA9: E Hunt 7J 159
Catherine Way BA1: Bathe 6H 83
Catley Gro. BS41: L Ash 1B 74
Cato St. BS5: E'tn 6D 48
Catsley Pl. BA1: Swa 7E 82
Cattistock Dr. BS5: St G 3J 63
Cattle Mkt. Rd. BS1: Bris 6J 5 (4B 62)
Cattybrook Rd. BS16: Short 3H 51
Cattybrook Rd. Nth. BS16: Short 3H 51
Cattybrook St. BS5: E'tn 1D 62
Caulfield Rd. BS22: Wor 7E 84
Causeway BS21: Nail, Tic 6D 56
BS48: Nail 7D 56
Causeway, The BS20: Clap G 7G 43
BS36: Coal H 7G 29
BS49: Cong .7K 87
BS49: Yat 4J 87
Causeway Vw. BS48: Nail 7E 56
Causley Dr. BS30: Bar C 4D 64
Cautletts Cl. BA3: Mid N 6D 152
Cavan Wlk. BS4: Know 1K 75
Cave Cl. BS16: Down 2B 50
Cave Ct. BS2: Bris 1H 5 (1A 62)
Cave Dr. BS16: Fish 2B 50
Cave Gro. BS16: Emer G 1F 51
Cavell Ct. BS21: Clev 1C 68
Cavendish Cl. BS31: Salt 1H 97
Cavendish Cres. BA1: Bath 3A 100
Cavendish Gdns. BS9: Stok B 4C 46
Cavendish Lodge BA1: Bath 3A 100
Cavendish Pl. BA1: Bath 1D 6 (3A 100)
Cavendish Rd. BA1: Bath 1D 6 (3A 100)
BS9: Henle .3G 47
BS34: Pat 6B 26
Caveners Ct. BS22: W Mare 3K 105
Caversham Dr. BS48: Nail 7J 57
Cave St. BS2: Bris 1H 5 (1A 62)
Caxton Ct. BA2: Bath 3G 7 (4C 100)
Caxton Ga. BS1: Bris 7H 5 (4A 62)
Cecil Av. BS5: S'wll 7H 49
Cecil Rd. BS8: Clif 1F 61
BS15: K'wd .1B 64
BS23: W Mare 3G 105
Cedar Av. BS22: W Mare 3A 106
Cedar Cl. BS30: Old C 5F 65
BS34: Pat 7B 26
BS41: L Ash .1K 73
TA9: Bre K 5K 157
Cedar Ct. BA15: Brad A 4H 125
BS9: Stok B .4C 46
BS16: Down .2C 50
Cedar Dr. BS31: Key 6B 78
Cedar Gro. BA2: Bath 1K 121
BS9: Stok B .3D 46
Cedar Hall BS16: Fren 7A 38
Cedar Hill Ct. BS16: Stap H 4B 50
Cedarhurst Rd. BS20: P'head 5A 42
Cedarn Ct. BS22: Kew 1K 105
Cedar Pk. BS9: Stok B 3D 46
Cedar Row BS11: Shire 2K 45
Cedars, The BS9: Stok B 5D 46
BS40: Chew S 4D 114
Cedars Way BS36: Wint 2B 38
Cedar Ter. BA3: Rads 5H 153
Cedar Vs. BA2: Bath 7D 6 (6A 100)
Cedar Wlk. BA2: Bath 6D 6 (6A 100)
(not continuous)
Cedar Way BA2: Bath 6D 6 (6A 100)
BS16: Puck .3B 52
BS20: P'head 4E 42
BS48: Nail 7J 57
Cedern Av. BS24: Elbgh 2G 129
Cedric Cl. BA1: Bath 4J 99
Cedric Rd. BA1: Bath 4J 99
Celandine Cl. BS35: T'bry 2B 12
Celestine Rd. BS37: Yate 3C 30
Celia Ter. BS4: St Ap 3H 63
Celtic Way BS24: B'don 5K 127
Cemetery La. BA15: Brad A 5J 125
Cemetery Rd. BS4: Wind H 6C 62
Cennick Av. BS15: K'wd 7C 50
Centaurus Rd. BS34: Pat 7J 25
Centenary Way BS27: Ched 7C 150
Central Av. BS10: H'len 3A 24
BS15: Han 4A 64
Central Pk. BS14: H'gro 2D 76
Central Trad. Est. BS4: Bris 5D 62
Central Way BS10: S'mead 7A 36
BS21: Clev .1D 68
Centre, The BS23: W Mare 5G 105
BS31: Key 5C 78
Centre Dr. BS29: Ban 1J 129
Centre for Sport 5G 37
Centre for Sport, Exercise and Health
. . . . .1C 4 (1J 61)
Centre Ho. BS23: W Mare 4E 104
Centre Quay BS20: P'head 1G 43
Centro BS1: Bris 1F 5
Centrum BS5: E'tn 1K 5 (1B 62)
Ceres Cl. BS30: L Grn 7D 64
Cerimon Ga. BS34: Stok G 2G 37
Cerney Gdns. BS48: Nail 7J 57
Cerney La. BS11: Shire 3J 45
Cesson Cl. BS37: Chip S 6J 31
Chadleigh Gro. BS4: Know 3K 75
Chaffinch Dr. BA3: Mid N 6F 153
Chaffins, The BS21: Clev 7E 54
Chaingate La. BS37: Iron A 7K 21
Chakeshill Cl. BS10: Bren 4J 35
Chakeshill Dr. BS10: Bren 4J 35
Chalcombe Cl. BS34: Lit S 6E 26
Chalcroft Ho. BS3: Bris 5G 61
Chalcroft Wlk. BS13: Withy 6E 74
Chalet, The BS10: Hen 4F 35
Chalfield Cl. BS31: Key 1E 96
Chalfont Rd. BS22: W Mare 4A 106
Chalford Cl. BS37: Yate 6D 30
Chalk Farm Cl. BS39: Nor M 4C 94
Chalks, The BS40: Chew M 1H 115
Chalks Rd. BS5: St G 1F 63
Challender Av. BS10: Hen 5F 35
Challoner Ct. BS1: Bris 6E 4 (4K 61)
Challow Dr. BS22: W Mare 2K 105
Champion Rd. BS15: K'wd 6D 50
Champneys Av. BS10: Hen 4F 35
Champs Sur Marne BS32: Brad S 6G 27
Chancel Cl. BS9: Stok B 5D 46
BS48: Nail 2F 71
Chancery St. BS5: Bar H 2D 62
Chandag Rd. BS31: Key 6D 78
Chandler Cl. BA1: Bath 2H 99
Chandos BS6: Redl 6J 47
Chandos Bldgs. BA1: Bath 5F 7
(off Westgate Bldgs.)
Chandos Rd. BS6: Redl 7H 47
BS31: Key 3C 78
Chandos Trad. Est. BS2: Bris 4C 62
Channel Ct. TA8: Bur S 3D 158
Channel Hgts. BS24: W Mare 4H 127
Channells Hill BS9: W Trym 7G 35
Channel Rd. BS21: Clev 3D 54
Channel Vw. Cvn. Pk. TA8: Brean 6B 126
Channel Vw. Cres. BS20: P'head 3D 42
Channel Vw. Rd. BS20: P'head 3D 42
Channing Cl. TA8: Bur S 3D 158
Channon's Hill BS16: Fish 4H 49
Chanterelle Pk. BA15: Brad A 7G 125
Chantry Cl. BS11: Law W 5C 34
BS48: Nail 1E 70
Chantry Ct. BS1: Bris 4D 4
(off Denmark St.)
Chantry Dr. BS22: Wor 7D 84
Chantry La. BS16: Down 6D 38
Chantry Mead Rd. BA2: Bath 1A 122
Chantry Rd. BS8: Clif 7H 47
BS35: T'bry 2K 11
Chapel Barton BS3: Bedm 7H 61
BS39: High L 4B 140
BS48: Nail 7E 56
Chapel Cl. BS15: Warm 1F 65
BS40: Chew S 4E 114
BS40: Winf 5A 92
BS48: Nail 7G 57
Chapel Ct. BA1: Bath 5F 7
(off Westgate Bldgs.)
BA3: Clan .2J 153
BS4: Brisl 7F 63
Chapel Fld. BA2: Pea J 5E 142
Chapel Gdns. BS10: W Trym 6G 35
Chapel Grn. La. BS6: Redl 6H 47
Chapel Hill BS21: Clev 6D 54
BS40: Nem T 7G 113
BS40: Wrin .1F 111
Chapel Ho. BS1: Bris 3E 4
Chapel La. BS5: S'wll 6G 49
BS11: Law W 5B 34
BS15: Warm .1F 65
BS16: Fren 1A 50
BS40: Chew S 4D 114
BS40: Winf 5A 92
BS48: Back .2B 72
BS49: Clav .2B 88
BS49: C've .4D 88
GL12: Buck .3E 12
SN14: Hin 3J 53
Chapel Lawns BA3: Clan 2J 153
Chapel Orchard BS37: Yate 4B 30
Chapel Pill La. BS20: Pill 4J 45
Chapel Rd. BA3: Clan 2J 153
BS5: E'tn 7D 48
BS13: Bis 4G 75
BS15: Han 4A 64
Chapel Row BA1: Bath 4E 6 (5B 100)
BA1: Bathf 1A 102
BA2: B'ptn 2H 101
BS20: Pill 4G 45
Chapel St. BS2: Bris 4C 62
BS35: T'bry 4K 11
TA8: Bur S 1C 158
Chapel Wlk. BA2: Tim 3G 141
Chapel Way BS4: St Ap 3G 63
Chaplains Wood BS20: P'head 3A 42
Chaplin Rd. BS5: E'tn 7D 48
Chapter St. BS2: Bris 1A 62
Chapter Wlk. BS6: Redl 5H 47
Charbon Ga. BS34: Stok G 2H 37
Charborough Ct. BS34: Fil 5B 36
Charborough Rd. BS34: Fil 5B 36
Charbury Wlk. BS11: Shire 3J 45
Chard Cl. BS48: Nail 2H 71
Chard Ct. BS14: H'gro 4D 76
Chardel Pl. BS26: Cross 4F 149
Chard Rd. BS21: Clev 1D 68
Chardstock Av. BS9: C Din 7C 34
Chardyke Dr. BS39: Temp C 4G 139

Church Path Rd.—Cobley Cft.

Church Path Rd. BS20: Pill 4G 45
Church Path Steps BS8: Clif 6A 4 (4G 61)
Church Pl. BS20: Pill 4G 45
Church Ri. BS40: Winf 4A 92
Church Rd. BA1: W'ton 2J 99
BA2: C Down 3D 122
BA2: Pea J 5B 142
BS3: Bedm 5J 61
BS5: Redf, St G 2E 62
BS7: Hor 2A 48
BS8: Abb L 1A 60
BS8: L Wds 3D 60
BS9: Stok B 5D 46
BS9: W Trym 1G 47
BS13: Bis 5F 75
BS14: Whit 6D 76
BS15: Han 4K 63
BS15: K'wd 1C 64
BS16: Fren 1K 49
BS16: Soun 5B 50
BS20: Eas 4E 44
BS20: P'bry 4C 44
BS22: Wor 2B 106
BS24: Lym 5K 145
BS25: Wins 7E 130
BS30: Bit 2J 79
BS30: Doy 7G 53
BS30: Wick 3B 66
BS32: Alm 1C 26
BS34: Fil 4C 36
BS34: Stok G 3G 37
BS35: C'hill 1D 10
BS35: E Comp 5G 25
BS35: E Grn, Rudg 3H 19
BS35: Sev B 7A 16
(not continuous)
BS35: T'bry 2K 11
BS36: Fram C 5E 28
BS36: Wint D 3C 38
BS37: Yate 3E 30
(not continuous)
BS39: Nor M 4C 94
BS40: Redh 1B 112
BS40: Winf 4A 92
BS41: Dun 1D 92
BS49: Yat 4J 87
TA8: Brean 2B 144
TA9: W Hunt 7D 158
Church Rd. Nth. BS20: P'head 3F 43
Church Rd. Sth. BS20: P'head 4F 43
Church Sq. BA3: Mid N 5E 152
BS39: Clut 3G 139
Church St. *BA1: Bath 5G 7*
(off York St.)
BA1: Bathf 1K 101
BA1: W'ly 4B 82
BA1: W'ton 2H 99
BA2: Bath 7K 7 (7D 100)
BA3: Rads 4K 153
BA15: Brad A 6G 125
BS1: Bris 5H 5 (3A 62)
BS5: Bar H 3D 62
BS5: E'tn 7D 48
BS27: Ched 7D 150
BS29: Ban 2B 130
BS39: Paul 7B 140
BS39: Pens 7F 95
BS40: Blag 3C 134
TA9: High 5F 159
CHURCH TOWN 5A 72
Church Town BS48: Back 5A 72
Church Vw. *BS15: K'wd 1C 64*
(off High St.)
BS16: Down 3B 50
BS32: Alm 2B 26
BS34: Fil 4C 36
BS48: Wrax 7K 57
TA8: Berr 2B 156
Church Wlk. BS20: Pill 4G 45
BS40: Wrin 2F 111
BS48: Flax B 3D 72
Churchward Cl. BS15: Han 4J 63
Churchward Rd. BS22: Wor 1F 107
BS37: Yate 3B 30
Churchway BA3: Faul 5K 155
Churchways BS14: Whit 6E 76
Churchways Av. BS7: Hor 2A 48
Churchways Cres. BS7: Hor 2A 48
Churston Cl. BS14: Whit 7C 76
Cinder Path, The BA2: Shos 1E 154
Cinema De Lux 2H 5
Cineworld Cinema
Whitchurch 4A 76
Circle, The BA2: Bath 1H 121
Circuit 32 BS5: E'tn 1D 62
Circular Rd. BS9: Stok B 6D 46
Circus, The BA1: Bath 2F 7 (4B 100)
Circus M. BA1: Bath 2E 6 (4B 100)
Circus Pl. BA1: Bath 2E 6 (4B 100)
(not continuous)
Circus,The BS1: Bris 2H 5
City Academy, The *1E 62*
(within Bristol Sports Cen.)
City Bus. Pk. BS5: E'tn 2C 62
City Mus. & Art Gallery 2C 4 (2J 61)
City of Bristol Gymnastics Cen. 6A 76
City Rd. BS2: Bris 1A 62
City Vw. BA1: Bath 1G 7
City Vw. Apartments *BS5: Bar H 2D 62*
(off Chancery St.)
Clamp, The BS30: Old C 6G 65
Clanage Rd. BS3: Bwr A 5E 60
Clanders Batch BS40: Blag 2B 134
CLANDOWN 2J 153
Clandown Rd. BS39: Paul 2D 152
Clan Ho. BA2: Bath 2K 7 (4D 100)
CLAPTON 7A 152
Clapton Drove BS20: Clap G 1E 56
CLAPTON IN GORDANO 7G 43
Clapton La. BS20: Clap G, P'head 5F 43
Clapton Rd. BA3: C'tn, Mid N 6A 152
Clapton Wlk. BS9: Sea M 3C 46
CLAPTON WICK 3A 56
Clara Cross La. BA2: Odd D 3A 122
Clare Av. BS7: B'stn 5J 47
Claredge Ho. BS21: Clev 6D 54
Clare Gdns. BA2: Odd D 3K 121
Claremont Av. BS7: B'stn 5J 47
Claremont Bldgs. BA1: Bath 2C 100
Claremont Ct. BS9: Henle 3J 47
BS21: Clev 5E 54
Claremont Cres. BS23: W Mare 3D 104
Claremont Gdns. BS21: Clev 1E 68
BS39: Hall 6K 139
BS48: Nail 1F 71
Claremont Pk. TA8: Berr 1B 156
Claremont Rd. BA1: Bath 2D 100
BS7: B'stn 5K 47
Claremont St. BS5: E'tn 7C 48
Claremont Ter. *BA1: Bath 2D 100*
(off Camden Rd.)
BS5: St G 2F 63
Claremont Vs. *BA1: Bath 2C 100*
(off Camden Rd.)
Claremont Wlk. BA1: Bath 2C 100
Clarence Av. BS16: Stap H 3C 50
Clarence Ct. *BS15: K'wd 7K 49*
(off Clarence Rd.)
Clarence Gdns. BS16: Stap H 3C 50
Clarence Gro. Rd. BS23: W Mare 7G 105
Clarence Ho. *BS15: K'wd 7K 49*
(off Clarence Rd.)
Clarence Pl. BA1: Bath 4H 99
BS2: Bris 1D 4 (1J 61)
BS23: W Mare 7F 105
Clarence Rd. BS1: Bris 7G 5 (4A 62)
BS2: Bris 2C 62
BS15: K'wd 7K 49
BS16: Down 3B 50
Clarence Rd. E. BS23: W Mare 7G 105
Clarence Rd. Nth. BS23: W Mare 7F 105
Clarence Rd. Sth. BS23: W Mare 7F 105
Clarence St. BA1: Bath 1G 7 (3C 100)
Clarence Ter. BA2: Clav D 7F 101
Clarendon M. BS16: Fren 7K 37
Clarendon Rd. BA2: Bath 7J 7 (6D 100)
BS6: Redl 6J 47
BS23: W Mare 4H 105
Clarendon Vs. BA2: Bath 7J 7 (6D 100)
Clare Rd. BS5: Eastv 6D 48
BS6: Cot 7K 47
BS15: K'wd 6A 50
Clare St. BS1: Bris 4E 4 (3K 61)
BS5: Redf 1E 62
Clare Wlk. BS35: T'bry 2K 11
Clark Cl. BS48: Wrax 7J 57
Clarke Dr. BS16: B'hll 1H 49
Clarken Cl. BS48: Nail 1G 71
Clarken Coombe BS41: L Ash 6K 59
Clarke St. BS3: Bedm 5K 61
Clarkson Av. BS22: W Mare 3A 106
Clark St. BS3: Bedm 5K 61
BS5: E'tn 1C 62
Clarks Way BA2: Odd D 2J 121
Clatworthy Dr. BS14: H'gro 3C 76
Claude Av. BA2: Bath 7A 6 (6J 99)
Claude Ter. BA2: Bath 6J 99
Claude Va. BA2: Bath 6J 99
Clavell Rd. BS10: Hen 5F 35
CLAVERHAM 2B 88
Claverham Cl. BS49: Yat 3K 87
Claverham Drove BS49: Clav 6H 69
Claverham Pk. BS49: Clav 2B 88
Claverham Rd. BS16: Fish 3J 49
BS49: Clav, Yat 4K 87
CLAVERTON 6K 101
Claverton Bldgs. BA2: Bath 7H 7
Claverton Ct. BA2: Clav D 7G 101
CLAVERTON DOWN 1H 123
Claverton Down Rd.
BA2: Clav D, C Down 6G 101
Claverton Dr. BA2: Clav D 1H 123
Claverton Hill BA2: C'ton, Clav D 6H 101
Claverton Manor 6J 101
Claverton Pumping Station 6A 102
Claverton Rd. BS31: Salt 7H 79
Claverton Rd. W. BS31: Salt 7H 79
Claverton St. BA2: Bath 6G 7 (6C 100)
CLAY BOTTOM 6F 49
Clay Bottom BS5: Eastv 6F 49
Claydon Grn. BS14: Whit 7B 76
Clayfield BS37: Yate 1E 30
Clayfield Rd. BS4: Brisl 6G 63
CLAY HILL 6G 49
Clay Hill BS5: S'wll 6G 49
Clay La. BS30: Bit 2H 79
BS34: Lit S 7D 26
BS35: T'bry 3C 12
Claymore Cres. BS15: K'wd 7K 49
Claypiece Rd. BS13: Withy 6F 75
Claypit Hill BS37: Chip S 7H 31
Clay Pit Rd. BS6: Henle 5G 47
Claypool Rd. BS15: K'wd 2B 64
CLAYS END 6D 98
Clayton Cl. BS20: P'head 4G 43
Clayton St. BS5: E'tn 1D 62
BS11: A'mth 6E 32
Cleave St. BS2: Bris 6C 48
CLEEVE 3C 88
Cleeve Av. BS16: Down 1C 50
Cleeve Ct. BS16: Down 1B 50
Cleevedale Rd. BA2: C Down 3C 122
Cleeve Dr. BS49: C've 3C 88
Cleeve Gdns. BS16: Down 1B 50
Cleeve Grn. BA2: Bath 5F 99
Cleeve Gro. BS31: Key 5B 78
Cleeve Hill BS16: Down 1B 50
BS40: Ubl 5J 135
Cleeve Hill Extension BS16: Down 2C 50
Cleeve Hill Rd. BS40: Wrin 4F 89
BS49: C've 3D 88
Cleeve La. BS30: Wick 7D 52
Cleeve Lawns BS16: Down 1B 50
Cleeve Lodge Cl. BS16: Down 2C 50
Cleeve Lodge Rd. BS16: Down 1C 50
Cleeve Pk. Rd. BS16: Down 1B 50
Cleeve Pl. BS48: Nail 1J 71
Cleeve Rd. BS4: Know 6D 62
BS16: Down 2C 50
BS16: Fren 7A 38
BS37: Yate 5E 30
Cleeves Ct. BS30: L Grn 7D 64
Cleeve Wood Pk. BS16: Down 7A 38
Cleeve Wood Rd. BS16: Down 7A 38
(not continuous)
Clement St. BS2: Bris 1J 5 (1B 62)
Clermont Cl. BS34: Pat 6B 26
Cleve Ct. *BS8: Clif 3F 61*
(off Cumberland Pl.)
BS34: Fil 3D 36
Clevedale BS16: Down 1B 50
Clevedale Ct. BS16: Down 1B 50
CLEVEDON 6D 54
Clevedon Court 5G 55
Clevedon Hall Est. BS21: Clev 6C 54
Clevedon Heritage Cen. 5C 54
Clevedon La. BS20: Clap G 4K 55
BS21: Clev 4K 55
Clevedon Miniature Railway 6B 54
Clevedon Pier 4C 54
Clevedon Rd. BA3: Mid N 4E 152
BS7: B'stn 4K 47
BS8: Fail 5F 59
BS20: P'head 6E 42
BS21: Tic 5J 55
BS23: W Mare 6F 105
BS41: L Ash 5F 59
BS48: Flax B, Wrax 7C 58
BS48: Nail 5D 56
BS48: Wrax 3J 57
(Cuckoo La.)
BS48: Wrax 4H 57
(Tower Ho. La.)
Clevedon Ter. BS6: Bris 1E 4 (1K 61)
Clevedon Town Football Club 2F 69
Clevedon Triangle Cen. BS21: Clev 6D 54
Clevedon Wlk. BS48: Nail 7G 57
Cleveland Cl. BS35: T'bry 4C 12
Cleveland Cotts. BA1: Bath 1G 7 (3C 100)
Cleveland Ct. BA2: Bath 5E 100
Cleveland Pl. BA1: Bath 1H 7 (3C 100)
Cleveland Pl. E. BA1: Bath 1H 7
Cleveland Pl. W. BA1: Bath 1H 7
Cleveland Reach BA1: Bath 1H 7
Cleveland Row BA2: Bath 1K 7 (3D 100)
Cleveland Ter. *BA1: Bath 1G 7*
(off London Rd.)
Cleveland Wlk. BA2: Bath 5E 100
Cleve Rd. BS34: Fil 3C 36
Cleweson Ri. BS14: Whit 7B 76
Cliff Ct. Dr. BS16: Fren 1K 49
Cliffe Dr. BA2: Lim S 6J 123
Clifford Dr. BS39: Paul 7B 140
Clifford Gdns. BS11: Shire 2J 45
Clifford Rd. BS16: Fish 4A 50
Cliff Rd. BA5: Ched 5J 151
BS22: W Mare 1J 105
BS27: Ched 5F 151
Cliffs, The BS27: Ched 6E 150
Cliff St. BS27: Ched 7E 150
Clift Ho. Rd. BS3: Ash G 5F 61
Clift Ho. Spur BS3: Ash G 5F 61
CLIFTON 1G 61
Clifton Arc. *BS8: Clif 2G 61*
(off Boyce's Av.)
Clifton Av. BS23: W Mare 7G 105
Clifton Cl. BS8: Clif 2F 61
Clifton College Sports Ground 2B 60
Clifton Ct. BS21: Clev 7C 54
Clifton Down BS8: Clif 1F 61
Clifton Down Rd. BS8: Clif 2F 61
Clifton Down Shop. Cen. BS8: Clif 7H 47
Clifton Down Station (Rail) 7H 47
Clifton Hgts. BS8: Clif 2B 4 (2H 61)
Clifton High Gro. BS9: Stok B 3E 46
Clifton Hill BS8: Clif 3G 61
Clifton Hill Ho. BS8: Clif 4A 4 (3H 61)
Clifton Observatory and Camera Obscura 2F 61
Clifton Pk. BS8: Clif 2G 61
Clifton Pk. Rd. BS8: Clif 1F 61
Clifton Pl. BS5: E'tn 1C 62
Clifton Rd. BS8: Clif 3A 4 (2G 61)
BS23: W Mare 6F 105
Clifton Roman Catholic Cathedral 1G 61
Clifton St. BS3: Bedm 6J 61
BS20: P'head 6E 42
Clifton Suspension Bridge 2E 60
Clifton Suspension Bridge (Toll) 2E 60
Clifton Suspension Bridge Vis. Cen. 2F 61
Clifton Va. BS8: Clif 3G 61
Clifton Va. Cl. BS8: Clif 3G 61
Clifton Vw. BS3: Wind H 5B 62
BS13: Bis 1G 75
CLIFTON WOOD 5A 4 (3G 61)
Clifton Wood Ct. BS8: Clif 5A 4 (3H 61)
Clifton Wood Cres. BS8: Clif 5A 4 (3H 61)
Clifton Wood Rd. BS8: Clif 4A 4 (3H 61)
Cliftonwood Ter. BS8: Clif 5A 4 (3G 61)
Clift Pl. BS1: Bris 6F 5 (4K 61)
Clift Rd. BS3: Ash G 5G 61
Clinton Rd. BS3: Bedm 7J 61
Clive Rd. BS14: H'gro 2E 76
Clockhouse M. BS20: P'head 2F 43
Clocktower Yd. BS1: Bris 6J 5 (4B 62)
Cloisters Ct. BS36: Wint 1C 38
Cloisters Cft. TA8: Bur S 2D 158
Cloisters Rd. BS36: Wint 1D 38
Clonmel Rd. BS4: Know 1K 75
Close, The BS10: Hen 2F 35
BS16: Fren 6H 37
BS16: Soun 5B 50
BS20: Wes 7B 42
BS34: Lit S 1E 36
BS34: Pat 5E 26
BS35: T'bry 4K 11
BS36: Coal H 1G 39
Closemead BS21: Clev 1D 68
Clothier Rd. BS4: Brisl 7H 63
Cloud Hill Ind. Est. BS39: Temp C 5J 139
Clouds Hill Av. BS5: St G 1G 63
Clouds Hill Rd. BS5: St G 1H 63
Clovelly Cl. BS5: St G 1H 63
Clovelly Rd. BS5: St G 1H 63
BS22: Wor 2E 106
Clover Cl. BS21: Clev 6F 55
BS39: Paul 2D 152
Clover Ct. BS22: W Mare 5B 106
Cloverdale Dr. BS30: L Grn 6E 64
Cloverdown BS4: Know 1A 76
Clover Ground BS9: W Trym 7H 35
Cloverlea Bus. Cen. BS36: H'fld 4G 39
Cloverlea Rd. BS30: Old C 5G 65
Clover Leaze BS32: Brad S 1F 37
Clover Rd. BS22: Wick L 5E 84
Clover Way TA9: High 4G 159
CLUTTON 2G 139
CLUTTON HILL 1K 139
Clutton Hill BS39: Clut 2H 139
Clyce Rd. TA9: High 5E 158
Clyde Av. BS31: Key 6D 78
Clyde Gdns. BA2: Bath 5H 99
BS5: St G 3K 63
Clyde Gro. BS34: Fil 5B 36
Clyde La. BS6: Redl 6H 47
Clyde M. BS6: Redl 6J 47
Clyde Pk. BS6: Redl 6H 47
Clyde Rd. BS4: Know 6C 62
BS6: Redl 6H 47
BS36: Fram C 6F 29
Clydesdale Cl. BS14: H'gro 4C 76
Clyde Ter. BS3: Bedm 6J 61
BS4: Know 6C 62
Clynder Gro. BS21: Clev 3E 54
Coach Ho. La. *BS5: St G 1G 63*
(off Beaconsfield Rd.)
Coach Rd. BA15: Brad A 6G 125
Coalbridge Cl. BS22: Wor 2D 106
Coaley Rd. BS11: Shire 3H 45
COALPIT HEATH 1G 39
Coalpit Rd. BA1: Bathe 6J 83
Coalsack La. BS36: H'fld 4F 39
Coalville Rd. BS36: Coal H 7H 29
Coape Rd. BS14: Stoc 5H 77
Coast Rd. TA8: Berr 2A 156
Coates Gro. BS48: Nail 7J 57
Coates Wlk. BS4: Know 4K 75
Cobblestone M. BS8: Clif 2G 61
Cob Ct. BS34: Stok G 4E 36
Cobden Cen., The BS16: Emer G 5E 38
Cobden St. BS5: Redf 2D 62
Coberley BS15: K'wd 3A 64
Cobhorn Dr. BS13: Withy 6F 75
Cobley Cft. BS21: Clev 2C 68

Cobourg Rd.—Cottisford Rd.

Cobourg Rd. BS6: Bris 7B 48
Cobthorn Way BS49: Cong 6A 88
Coburg Vs. BA1: Bath 2C 100
Cock and Yew Tree Hill
BS40: Regil 2A 114
Cockers Hill BS39: Comp D 7K 95
Cock La. SN14: Hin 3J 53
Cock Rd. BS15: K'wd 3C 64
COCKSHOT HILL 6C 50
CODRINGTON 4H 41
Codrington Pl. BS8: Clif 2G 61
Codrington Rd. BS7: B'stn 5K 47
BS37: W'lgh 4D 40
Cody Ct. BS15: Han 4K 63
Cogan Rd. BS16: Soun 5C 50
Cogmill La. BS36: Fram C 2D 28
BS37: Iron A 2D 28
Cogsall Rd. BS14: Stoc 4H 77
Coity Pl. BS21: Clev 5C 54
Coker Rd. BS22: Wor 2F 107
Colbourne Rd. BA2: Odd D 3K 121
Colchester Cres. BS4: Know 3K 75
Coldbath BA2: F'boro 6D 118
Coldharbour La. BS16: Fren, Stap 6G 37
BS23: W Mare 2F 127
Coldharbour Rd. BS6: Redl 5H 47
Coldpark Gdns. BS13: Withy 5E 74
Coldpark Rd. BS13: Withy 5E 74
Coldrick Cl. BS14: Whit 7B 76
Colebrook Rd. BS15: K'wd 1A 64
Coleford Rd. BS10: S'mead 7K 35
Colehouse Farm Cvn. Pk.
BS21: Clev 3D 68
Colehouse La. BS21: Clev 2B 68
Cole Mead BS13: Bis 5H 75
Coleridge Gdns. TA8: Bur S 5D 156
Coleridge Rd. BS5: Eastv 5E 48
BS21: Clev 6C 54
BS23: W Mare 2H 127
Coleridge Va. Rd. E. BS21: Clev 6D 54
Coleridge Va. Rd. Nth. BS21: Clev 7C 54
Coleridge Va. Rd. Sth. BS21: Clev 7C 54
Coleridge Va. Rd. W. BS21: Clev 7C 54
Cole Rd. BS2: Bris 3D 62
Colesborne Cl. BS37: Yate 6D 30
Coleshill Dr. BS13: Hart 5H 75
Coley Rd. BS40: E Harp 6K 137
Colin Cl. BS35: T'bry 3K 11
College Av. BS16: Fish 3J 49
College Ct. BS8: Clif 1G 61
BS16: Fish 3J 49
TA8: Bur S 1C 158
College Flds. BS8: Clif 1F 61
College Grn. BS1: Bris 4D 4 (3J 61)
College Ho. *BS1: Bris* *4D 4*
(off Orchard St.)
College La. BS1: Bris 4D 4
College Pk. Dr. BS10: Hen 6F 35
College Rd. BA1: L'dwn, Bath 1A 100
BS8: Clif 1F 61
BS9: W Trym 1G 47
BS16: Fish 3J 49
College Sq. BS1: Bris 5C 4 (3J 61)
College St. BS1: Bris 5C 4 (3J 61)
TA8: Bur S 1C 158
College Vw. BA1: Bath 2C 100
College Way BS34: Fil 3C 36
Collett Cl. BS15: Han 4K 63
BS22: Wor 7G 85
Collett Way BS37: Yate 3C 30
Collier Cl. BA2: Cam 5H 141
Colliers Break BS16: Emer G 3F 51
Colliers Gdns. BS16: Fish 3K 49
Collier's La. BA1: Charl 6A 82
BS40: C'hse 2H 151
Collier's Pl. BS16: Soun 6B 50
Colliers Ri. BA3: Rads 3A 154
Colliers Wlk. BS48: Nail 7G 57
Colliers Way BA3: Hay 6K 153
Collingwood Av. BS15: K'wd 7C 50
Collingwood Cl. BS22: Wor 7C 84
BS31: Salt 1J 97
Collingwood Rd. BS6: Redl 7H 47
Collin Rd. BS4: Brisl 5F 63
Collins Av. BS34: Lit S 1E 36
Collins Bldgs. BS31: Salt 7J 79
Collins Dr. BS35: Sev B 3C 24
Collinson Rd. BS13: Hart 5H 75
Collins St. BS11: A'mth 7F 33
Colliter Cres. BS3: Bedm 7G 61
Collum La. BS22: Kew 4B 84
Colne Grn. BS31: Key 6E 78
Coln Sq. BS35: T'bry 4A 12
Colombo Cres. BS23: W Mare 2G 127
Colonnades, The BA1: Bath 5F 7
Colony, The TA8: Bur S 6C 156
Colston Av. BS1: Bris 4E 4 (3K 61)
Colston Cen. *BS1: Bris* *3E 4*
(off Colston St.)
Colston Cl. BS16: Soun 5B 50
BS36: Wint D 3C 38
Colston Ct. BS7: B'stn 5K 47
Colston Dale BS16: Stap 4G 49
Colston Fort *BS6: Bris* *1E 4*
(off Montague Pl.)
Colston Hall 3E 4 (2K 61)
Colston Hill BS16: Stap 4F 49
Colston M. BS6: Bris 7A 48
Colston Pde. BS1: Bris 7G 5 (4A 62)
Colston Pl. BS1: Bris 5H 5 (3A 62)
Colston Rd. BS5: E'tn 7E 48
Colston's Almshouses BS2: Bris 2D 4
Colston St. BS1: Bris 3E 4 (2K 61)
BS16: Soun 5B 50
Colston Twr. *BS1: Bris* *3E 4*
(off Colston Av.)
Colston Yd. *BS2: Bris* *2E 4*
(off Colston St.)
Colthurst Dr. BS15: Han 4C 64
COLT'S GREEN 6K 31
Colwyn Rd. BS5: E'tn 7E 48
Combe, The BA3: Writ 4D 154
BS40: Burr 2H 133
Combe Av. BS20: P'head 2E 42
COMBE DOWN 3D 122
Combe Flds. BS20: P'head 2E 42
Combe Gro. BA1: Bath 3H 99
COMBE HAY 7J 121
Combe Hay La. BA2: C Hay, Odd D 6H 121
Combe La. BS39: Hall 7K 139
Combe Pk. BA1: Bath 4J 99
Combermere BS35: T'bry 4B 12
Combe Rd. BA2: C Down 3D 122
BS20: P'head 3F 43
Combe Rd. Cl. BA2: C Down 3D 122
Combe Royal Cres. BA2: Clav D 6F 101
Combeside BA2: Bath 1C 122
BS48: Back 3J 71
Combfactory La. BS5: E'tn 1D 62
Comb Paddock BS9: W Trym 1H 47
Comer Rd. BS27: Ched 7C 150
Comfortable Pl. BA1: Bath 3C 6 (4A 100)
Commerce Way TA9: High 6H 159
Commercial Rd. BS1: Bris 7E 4 (4K 61)
Commercial Way BS22: Wor 2F 107
Common, The BS16: Fren 1K 49
BS34: Pat 5D 26
BS35: Olv 2B 18
Common E., The BS34: Brad S 5E 26
Commonfield Rd. BS11: Law W 6B 34
Common La. BS8: Fail 5F 45
BS20: Eas 5F 45
BS25: C'hll 6H 109
BS35: Aust 7G 9
Common Mead La. BS16: Ham 6J 37
Common Rd. BS15: Han 6K 63
BS36: Wint 7D 28
Como Ct. *BS20: P'head* *2E 42*
(off Kilkenny Pl.)
Compass Ct. BA1: Bath 2E 6
COMPTON BISHOP 3B 148
COMPTON COMMON 7A 96
COMPTON DANDO 5A 96
Compton Dr. BS9: Sea M 1C 46
BS24: W'ton V 5C 106
COMPTON GREEN 6C 96
Compton Grn. BS31: Key 6C 78
COMPTON GREENFIELD 6F 25
Compton La. BS26: Axb 4H 149
Compton Lodge *BS6: Redl* *7H 47*
(off Hampton Rd.)
COMPTON MARTIN 6A 136
Compton Martin Rd. BS40: W Har 7C 136
Compton Mead BS48: Bar G 6H 73
Compton St. BS5: Redf 2E 62
Comrade Av. BS25: S'ham 5A 132
Comyn Wlk. BS16: Fish 3J 49
Concorde Dr. BS10: S'mead 6H 35
BS21: Clev 1B 68
Concorde Ho. BS34: Fil 5B 36
Concorde Rd. BS34: Pat 7A 26
Concorde St. BS1: Bris 2H 5 (2A 62)
Concourse, The BS4: Brisl 7G 63
Condor Cl. BS22: W Mare 4B 106
Condor Ho. BS7: L'lze 1E 48
Condover Rd. BS4: Brisl 6H 63
Conduit Pl. BS2: Bris 7C 48
Conduit Rd. BS2: Bris 7C 48
Coneygree BS13: Bis 5F 75
Conference Av. BS20: P'head 3G 43
Conference Cl. BS20: P'head 4H 43
Congleton Rd. BS5: W'hall 7F 49
CONGRESBURY 7K 87
CONHAM 4H 63
Conham Hill BS15: Han 4J 63
Conham Rd. BS5: St G 4H 63
BS15: Han, St G 4H 63
Conham Va. BS15: St G 4H 63
(not continuous)
Conifer Cl. BS16: Fish 2B 50
BS36: Fram C 5E 28
Conifer Way BS24: Lock 7C 106
Conigre Hill BA15: Brad A 5G 125
Coniston Av. BS9: W Trym 2E 46
Coniston Cl. BS30: Old C 3H 65
Coniston Cres. BS23: W Mare 1H 127
Coniston Rd. BS34: Pat 6A 26
CONKWELL 3A 124
Connaught Pl. BS23: W Mare 4F 105
Connaught Rd. BS4: Know 2A 76
Connection Rd. BA2: Bath 5G 99
Constable Cl. BS31: Key 4D 78
Constable Dr. BS22: Wor 1D 106
Constable Rd. BS7: L'lze 2D 48
Constantine Av. BS34: Stok G 2G 37
Constitution Hill BS8: Clif 4A 4 (3G 61)
Contemporis *BS8: Clif* *2G 61*
(off Merchants Rd.)
Convent Cl. BS10: Hen 4D 34
Convocation Av. BA2: Clav D 6H 101
Conway Cres. TA8: Bur S 6D 156
Conway Grn. BS31: Key 7E 78
Conway Rd. BS4: Brisl 5E 62
Conygar Cl. BS21: Clev 4F 55
Conygre Grn. BA2: Tim 3F 141
Conygre Gro. BS34: Fil 3D 36
Conygre Ri. BA2: F'boro 6D 118
Conygre Rd. BS34: Fil 4C 36
Cook Cl. BS30: Old C 5G 65
Cooke's Dr. BS35: E Comp 5G 25
Cooks Bridle Path
BS48: Back 4B 90
Cooks Cl. BS32: Brad S 3E 26
Cooks Folly Rd. BS9: Stok B 5D 46
Cooks Gdns. BS48: Wrax 7K 57
Cook's Hill BS39: Clut 2G 139
Cooks La. BS21: Clev 7G 55
BS29: Ban 1A 130
BS36: H'fld 4H 39
Cooksley Rd. BS5: Redf 1E 62
Cookson Cl. TA8: Bur S 3E 158
Cook St. BS11: A'mth 7F 33
Cookworthy Cl. BS5: Bar H 3D 62
Coombe, The BS40: Blag, R'frd 2K 133
BS40: Comp M 7A 136
Coombe Av. BS35: T'bry 2K 11
Coombe Bri. Av. BS9: Stok B 2D 46
Coombe Brook Cl. BS15: K'wd 7K 49
Coombe Brook La. BS5: Eastv 6G 49
Coombe Cl. BS10: Hen 4D 34
BS20: P'head 3F 43
Coombe Dale BS9: Sea M 2C 46
BS48: Back 3E 90
COOMBE DINGLE 1D 46
Coombe Dingle Sports Complex 1E 46
Coombe Gdns. BS9: Stok B 2E 46
Coombe La. BS8: Fail 7D 44
BS9: Stok B, W Trym 1D 46
BS20: Eas 6E 44
BS26: Comp B 2B 148
BS40: E Harp 7J 137
Coombend BA3: Clan, Rads 2J 153
Coombe Orchard *BA3: Rads* *3K 153*
(off Bath New Rd.)
Coombe Rd. BS5: Eastv 6E 48
BS23: W Mare 4G 105
BS48: Nail 1F 71
Coombe Rocke BS9: Stok B 1D 46
Coombe Side TA9: Bre K 5K 157
Coombes Way BS26: Bidd 6J 147
BS30: Old C 5H 65
Coombe Way BS10: Hen 6F 35
Cooperage La. BS3: Bris 7A 4 (4H 61)
Cooperage Rd. BS5: Redf 2F 63
Co-operation Rd. BS5: E'tn 7E 48
Cooper Rd. BS9: W Trym 1F 47
BS35: T'bry 5K 11
Coopers Dr. BS37: Yate 1F 31
Coots, The BS14: Stoc 4G 77
Copeland Dr. BS14: Whit 5D 76
Cope Pk. BS32: Alm 1E 26
Copford La. BS41: L Ash 1B 74
Cophills La. BS35: L Sev 2A 10
Copley Ct. BS15: Han 4C 64
Copley Gdns. BS7: L'lze 2D 48
BS22: Wor 2D 106
Copper Cl. BS27: Ched 6C 150
Copperfield Dr. BS22: Wor 7D 84
Coppice, The BS13: Withy 6E 74
BS32: Brad S 7G 27
Coppice Hill BA15: Brad A 5H 125
Coppice M. BS21: Clev 5C 54
Copse, The BS22: St Geo 2H 107
Copse Cl. BS24: W Mare 4J 127
Copse Cnr. BS24: Lym 4A 146
Copse End BS25: Wins 3F 131
Copseland BA2: Clav D 6F 101
Copse Rd. BS4: Know 6D 62
BS21: Clev 5C 54
BS31: Salt 6G 79
Copthorne Cl. BS14: H'gro 5D 76
Copthorn La. BS40: Burr, L'frd 7H 111
Coralberry Dr. BS22: Wor 3D 106
Corbet Cl. BS11: Law W 5B 34
Corbett Cl. BS37: Yate 2F 31
Corbett Ho. BS5: Bar H 2E 62
Cordwell Wlk. BS10: Hor 1K 47
Corey Cl. BS2: Bris 7B 48
Corfe Cl. BS48: Nail 1F 71
Corfe Cres. BS31: Key 6C 78
Corfe Pl. BS30: Will 1F 79
Corfe Rd. BS4: Know 3K 75
Coriander Dr. BS32: Brad S 1J 37
Coriander Wlk. BS5: Eastv 6E 48
Corinthian Ct. BS1: Bris 6H 5 (4A 62)
Corinum Cl. BS16: Emer G 2G 51
Corkers Hill BS5: St G 3H 63
Cork Pl. BA1: Bath 3A 6
Cork St. BA1: Bath 2A 6 (4K 99)
Cork Ter. BA1: Bath 2A 6 (4K 99)
Cormorant Cl. BS22: Wor 3D 106
Corner Cft. BS21: Clev 1D 68
Cornfield Cl. BS32: Brad S 5E 26
Cornfields, The BS22: Wor 6D 84
Cornhill Dr. BS14: H'gro 3C 76
Cornish Gro. BS14: Stoc 4G 77
Cornish Rd. BS14: Stoc 4G 77
Cornish Wlk. BS14: Stoc 4G 77
Cornleaze BS13: Bis 5G 75
Corn St. BA1: Bath 5F 7 (5B 100)
BS1: Bris 4F 5 (3K 61)
Cornwall Cres. BS37: Yate 3F 31
Cornwallis Av. BS8: Clif 3G 61
BS22: Wor 7C 84
Cornwallis Cres. BS8: Clif 3F 61
Cornwallis Gro. BS8: Clif 3F 61
Cornwallis Ho. BS8: Clif 3G 61
Cornwall Rd. BS7: B'stn 4K 47
Coromandel Hgts. BA1: Bath 1F 7
Coronation Av. BA2: Bath 1J 121
BA15: Brad A 5J 125
BS16: Fish 4J 49
BS31: Key 6B 78
Coronation Cl. BS30: C Hth 4E 64
Coronation Cotts. BA1: Bathe 7H 83
Coronation Est. BS23: W Mare 2H 127
Coronation Pl. BS1: Bris 4F 5 (3K 61)
Coronation Rd. BA1: Bath 2A 6 (4K 99)
BS3: Ash G, Bris 7A 4 (5G 61)
BS15: K'wd 2D 64
BS16: Down 3C 50
BS22: Wor 2C 106
BS24: B'don 7A 128
BS29: Ban 2A 130
BS30: C Hth 4E 64
TA9: High 4F 159
Coronation Vs. BA3: Rads 3A 154
Corondale Rd. BS22: W Mare 4B 106
Corridor, The BA1: Bath 4G 7 (5C 100)
Corsham Dr. TA8: Bur S 7E 156
Corsley Wlk. BS4: Know 2B 76
CORSTON 4B 98
Corston BS24: W Mare 3J 127
Corston Dr. BA2: New L 5B 98
CORSTON FIELDS 5G 97
Corston La. BA2: Cor 4A 98
Corston Vw. BA2: Odd D 2J 121
Corston Wlk. BS11: Shire 1H 45
Corum Office Pk. BS30: Warm 2G 65
Coryton BS22: Wor 2E 106
Cossham Cl. BS35: T'bry 2A 12
Cossham Rd. BS5: St G 1F 63
BS16: Puck 4C 52
Cossham St. BS16: Emer G, Mang 3E 50
Cossham Wlk. BS5: St G 7J 49
Cossington Rd. BS4: Know 1B 76
Cossins Rd. BS6: Redl 5H 47
Costers Cl. BS35: Alv 7J 11
Costiland Dr. BS13: Bis 4F 75
Cote Bank Ho. BS9: W Trym 1H 47
Cote Dr. BS9: W Trym 4G 47
Cote Ho. La. BS9: W Trym 3G 47
Cote La. BS9: W Trym 3G 47
BS35: L Sev 1K 9
Cote Lea Pk. BS9: W Trym 1G 47
Cote Paddock BS9: W Trym 4F 47
Cote Pk. BS9: W Trym 2E 46
Cote Rd. BS9: W Trym 3G 47
COTHAM 7J 47
Cotham Brow BS6: Cot 7K 47
Cotham Gdns. BS6: Cot 7H 47
Cotham Gro. BS6: Cot 7K 47
Cotham Hill BS6: Cot 7H 47
Cotham Lawn Apartments *BS6: Cot* *1J 61*
(off Cotham Lawn Rd.)
Cotham Lawn Rd. BS6: Cot 1J 61
Cotham Pk. BS6: Cot 7J 47
Cotham Pk. Nth. BS6: Cot 7J 47
Cotham Pl. BS6: Cot 7J 47
Cotham Rd. BS6: Cot 1J 61
Cotham Rd. Sth. BS6: Bris 1K 61
Cotham Side BS6: Cot 7K 47
Cotham Va. BS6: Cot 7J 47
Cotman Wlk. BS7: L'lze 2D 48
BS22: Wor 2D 106
Cotrith Gro. BS10: Hen 4E 34
Cotswold Cl. BS20: P'head 4G 43
Cotswold Ct. BS16: Fren 6G 37
BS37: Chip S 5H 31
Cotswold Rd. BA2: Bath 7K 99
BS3: Wind H 6K 61
BS37: Chip S 6H 31
Cotswold Vw. BA2: Bath 6H 99
BS15: K'wd 6B 50
BS34: Fil 4C 36
GL12: Wickw 6H 15
Cottage Gdns. BS5: St G 2J 63
Cottage Pl. BA1: Bath 1E 100
BS2: Bris 1E 4 (1K 61)
Cottage Row TA8: Bur S 2C 158
Cottages, The BS40: Wrin 2F 111
BS48: Bar G 4K 73
Cottington Ct. BS15: Han 4C 64
Cottisford Rd. BS5: Eastv 4D 48

Daventry Rd.—Dundonald Rd.

Daventry Rd. BS4: Know 1A 76
Davey St. BS2: Bris 7B 48
David Lloyd Leisure
Bristol 6E 60
David's Cl. BS35: Alv 1J 19
David's La. BS35: Alv 1J 19
David's Rd. BS14: H'gro 3E 76
David St. BS2: Bris 3J 5 (2B 62)
David Thomas Ho. BS6: Bris 6A 48
Davies Dr. BS4: St Ap 4H 63
Davin Cres. BS20: Pill 5G 45
Davis Cl. BS30: Bar C 4D 64
Davis Ct. BS35: T'bry 2A 12
Davis La. BS21: Clev 2D 68
Davis St. BS11: A'mth 7F 33
Dawes Cl. BS21: Clev 1D 68
Dawes Ct. *BS8: Clif 3F 61*
(off Cumberland Pl.)
Dawley Cl. BS36: Wint 7C 28
Dawlish Rd. BS3: Wind H 7K 61
Dawn Ri. BS15: K'wd 7D 50
Daws Ct. BS16: Fish 4K 49
Day Cres. BA2: Bath 5F 99
Days La. BS2: Bris 2C 62
Day's Rd. BS2: Bris 3C 62
BS5: Bar H 3C 62
Days Rd. Commercial Cen.
BS2: Bris 3C 62
Deacon Cl. BS36: Wint 2C 38
Deacons Cl. BS22: Wor 2C 106
Deacon Way TA8: Bur S 2D 158
Deadmill La. BA1: Swa 7E 82
Dean Av. BS35: T'bry 2A 12
Dean Cl. BS15: Han 4J 63
BS22: Wor 1F 107
Dean Ct. BS37: Yate 3B 30
Dean Cres. BS3: Bedm 5J 61
(not continuous)
Deanery Rd. BS1: Bris 5C 4 (3J 61)
BS15: Warm 1E 64
Deanery Wlk. BA2: Lim S 6A 124
DEAN HILL 1F 99
Deanhill La. BA1: W'ton 1F 99
Dean La. BS3: Bedm 7D 4 (5J 61)
Deanna Ct. BS16: Down 2C 50
Dean Rd. BS11: A'mth 2G 33
BS37: Yate 3C 30
Deans, The BS20: P'head 4D 42
Dean's Ct. BS1: Bris 4C 4 (3J 61)
Deans Dr. BS5: S'wll 6J 49
Deans Mead BS11: Law W 7A 34
Dean St. BS2: Bris 1H 5 (1A 62)
BS3: Bedm 5J 61
Debeccas La. BS20: Eas 4F 45
De Clifford Rd. BS11: Law W 5C 34
Decoypool Drove BS49: Clav 5J 69
Deep Coombe Rd. BS3: Bedm 7G 61
Deep Pit Rd. BS5: S'wll 3K 49
Deep St. BS1: Bris 2F 5 (2K 61)
Deerhurst BS15: K'wd 6C 50
BS37: Yate 6C 30
Deering Cl. BS11: Law W 6B 34
Deerleap BS25: S'ham 5B 132
Deer Mead BS21: Clev 1B 68
Deerswood BS15: Soun 6E 50
Delabere Av. BS16: Fish 3K 49
Delapre Rd. BS23: W Mare 2F 127
De La Warre Ct. BS4: St Ap 3H 63
Delhorn La. BS24: E'wth 7A 146
Delius Gro. BS4: Know 3K 75
Dell, The BS9: W Trym 3F 47
BS22: Wor 7C 84
BS30: Old C 4G 65
BS32: Brad S 7G 27
BS48: Nail 7F 57
Delvin Rd. BS10: W Trym 7J 35
De Montalt Pl. BA2: C Down 3D 122
Denbigh Dr. NP16: Bulw 1A 8
Denbigh St. BS2: Bris 7B 48
Dene Cl. BS31: Key 7D 78
Dene Rd. BS14: Whit 6E 76
Denleigh Cl. BS14: Whit 6C 76
Denmark Av. BS1: Bris 4D 4 (3J 61)
Denmark Pl. BS7: B'stn 5A 48
Denmark Rd. BA2: Bath 5A 6 (5K 99)
Denmark St. BS1: Bris 4D 4 (3J 61)
Denning Ct. BS22: Wor 7F 85
Dennisworth BS16: Puck 3B 52
Dennor Pk. BS14: H'gro 3D 76
Denny Cl. BS20: P'head 3C 42
Denny Isle Dr. BS35: Sev B 7A 16
Denny La. BS40: Chew M 4G 115
Denny Vw. BS20: P'head 3B 42
Dennyview Rd. BS8: Abb L 1K 59
Denston Dr. BS20: P'head 4G 43
Denston Wlk. BS13: Bis 3G 75
Denton Patch BS16: Emer G 1F 51
Dentwood Gro. BS9: C Din 1B 46
Denys Ct. BS35: Olv 2B 18
Derby Rd. BS7: B'stn 5A 48
Derby St. BS5: St G 1F 63
Derham Cl. BS49: Yat 3H 87
Derham Pk. BS49: Yat 3H 87
Derham Rd. BS13: Bis 5G 75
Dermot St. BS2: Bris 7B 48
Derricke Rd. BS14: Stoc 4H 77
Derrick Rd. BS15: K'wd 1B 64
Derry Rd. BS3: Bedm 7H 61
Derwent Cl. BS34: Pat 6D 26
Derwent Ct. BS35: T'bry 4B 12
Derwent Gro. BS31: Key 5E 78
Derwent Rd. BS5: S'wll 7H 49
BS23: W Mare 1J 127
Devaney Cl. BS4: St Ap 4H 63
Deverell Cl. BA15: Brad A 7J 125
Deveron Gro. BS31: Key 6E 78
Deverose Ct. BS15: Han 5C 64
Devil's La. GL12: Char 2F 15
Devon Gro. BS5: E'tn 1E 62
Devon Rd. BS5: E'tn 7E 48
Devonshire Bldgs. BA2: Bath 7B 100
(not continuous)
Devonshire Dr. BS20: P'head 3B 42
Devonshire M. *BA1: Bath 5C 100*
(off St James's Pde.)
BA2: Bath 1B 122
(off Devonshire Bldgs.)
Devonshire Pl. BA2: Bath 7B 100
Devonshire Rd. BA2: B'ptn 2G 101
BS6: Henle 4H 47
BS23: W Mare 2G 127
Devonshire Vs. BA2: Bath 1B 122
Dewar Cl. TA8: Bur S 1E 158
Dewfalls Dr. BS32: Brad S 5F 27
Dial Hill Rd. BS21: Clev 4C 54
Dial La. BS16: Down 2B 50
BS40: F'tn 2G 91
Diamond Batch BS24: W'ton V 3F 107
Diamond Farm Cvn. & Touring Pk.
TA8: Brean 1D 144
Diamond Rd. BS5: St G 2H 63
Diamond St. BS3: Bedm 6J 61
Diana Gdns. BS32: Brad S 6G 27
Dibden Cl. BS16: Down 7E 38
Dibden Ct. BS16: Emer G 1F 51
Dibden La. BS16: Emer G 1E 50
Dibden Rd. BS16: Down 7E 38
Dickens Cl. BS7: Hor 7C 36
Dickenson Rd. BS23: W Mare 6G 105
Dickensons Gro. BS49: Cong 1A 110
Dickinsons Fld. BS3: Wind H 7K 61
Didsbury Cl. BS10: Hen 6F 35
Dighton Ct. BS2: Bris 1F 5
Dighton Ga. BS34: Stok G 2G 37
Dighton St. BS2: Bris 1F 5 (1K 61)
Dillon Ct. BS5: St G 2F 63
Dinder Cl. BS48: Nail 1G 71
DINGHURST 1A 132
Dinghurst Rd. BS25: C'hll 1K 131
Dingle, The BS9: C Din 1D 46
BS36: Wint D 3C 38
BS37: Yate 2F 31
Dingle Cl. BS9: Sea M 2C 46
Dingle Rd. BS9: C Din 1D 46
Dingle Vw. BS9: Sea M 1C 46
Dinglewood Cl. BS9: C Din 1D 46
DINGS, THE 4C 62
Dings Wlk. BS2: Bris 4K 5 (3C 62)
Dipland Gro. BS40: Blag 3D 134
Dirac Rd. BS7: B'stn 4B 48
District Cen. Rdbt. BS32: Brad S 6G 27
Dixon Gdns. BA1: Bath 2B 100
Dixon Rd. BS4: Brisl 7H 63
Dock Ga. La. BS8: Clif 4G 61
Doctor White's Cl. BS1: Bris 7G 5 (4A 62)
Dodington La. BS37: Dod 1H 41
Dodington Rd. BS37: Chip S 7H 31
Dodisham Wlk. BS16: Fish 2K 49
Dodmore Crossing BS37: W'lgh 3B 40
Dodsmoor La. BS35: Alv 1A 20
Dog La. BS10: H'len 3C 34
Dogwood Rd. BS32: Alm 1F 27
Doleberrow BS25: C'hll 2B 132
Dolebury Warren Hill Fort 2B 132
Dolebury Warren Nature Reserve 2B 132
Dolemoor La. BS49: Cong 7G 87
(Old Weston Rd.)
BS49: Cong 1G 109
(The Causeway)
Dolman Cl. BS10: Hen 4E 34
Dolphin Sq. BS23: W Mare 5F 105
Dominion Rd. BA2: Bath 5G 99
BS16: Fish 5H 49
Donald Rd. BS13: Bis 3F 75
Donal Early Way BS7: Hor 7A 36
Doncaster Rd. BS10: S'mead 6H 35
Donegal Rd. BS4: Know 1K 75
Dongola Av. BS7: B'stn 4A 48
Dongola Rd. BS7: B'stn 4A 48
Donnington Wlk. BS31: Key 6B 78
Donstan Rd. TA9: High 3F 159
Doone Rd. BS7: Hor 7B 36
Dorcas Av. BS34: Stok G 2H 37
Dorchester Cl. BS48: Nail 2F 71
Dorchester Rd. BS7: Hor 1C 48
Dorchester St. BA1: Bath 6G 7 (6C 100)
Dorester Cl. BS10: Bren 3J 35
Dorian Cl. BS7: Hor 1A 48
Dorian Rd. BS7: Hor 1A 48
Dorian Way BS7: Hor 7A 36
Dormeads Vw. BS24: W'ton V 5D 106
Dormer Cl. BS36: Coal H 1H 39
Dormer Rd. BS5: Eastv 5D 48
Dorset Cl. BA2: Bath 5B 6 (5K 99)
TA9: High 6G 159
Dorset Cotts. BA2: C Down 3E 122
Dorset Gro. BS2: Bris 6C 48
Dorset Ho. BA2: Bath 1K 121
Dorset Rd. BS9: W Trym 2H 47
BS15: K'wd 7B 50
Dorset St. BA2: Bath 5A 6 (5K 99)
BS3: Bedm 6H 61
Dorset Way BS37: Yate 3G 31
DOUBLE HILL 6F 143
Doudney Ct. BS3: Bedm 7G 5 (5A 62)
Douglas Ct. BS23: W Mare 7H 105
Douglas Rd. BS7: Hor 1B 48
BS15: K'wd 2B 64
BS23: W Mare 7H 105
Douglas Rd. Ind. Pk. BS15: K'wd 2B 64
Doulton Way BS14: Whit 5D 76
Dovecote BS37: Yate 6E 30
Dovedale BS35: T'bry 5B 12
Dove La. BS2: Bris 1J 5 (1B 62)
BS5: Redf 2E 62
Dovercourt Rd. BS7: Hor 3C 48
Dover Ho. BA1: Bath 3C 100
Dover Pl. BA1: Bath 3C 100
BS8: Clif 3A 4 (2H 61)
Dover Pl. Cotts. BS8: Clif 3A 4 (2H 61)
Dovers La. BA1: Bathf 1A 102
Dovers Pk. BA1: Bathf 1A 102
Dover Ter. *BA1: Bath 3D 100*
(off London Rd.)
Dove St. BS2: Bris 1F 5 (1K 61)
Dove St. Sth. BS2: Bris 1F 5 (1K 61)
Doveswell Gro. BS13: Withy 6G 75
Dovetail Dr. BS23: W Mare 5J 105
Dovey Ct. BS30: Old C 4G 65
Dowdeswell Cl. BS10: Hen 4F 35
Dowding Cl. BS37: Chip S 4J 31
Dowding Rd. BA1: Bath 2D 100
Dowding Vs. BA1: Bath 2D 100
Dower Ho. BS16: Stap 1G 49
(not continuous)
Dowland BS22: Wor 2E 106
Dowland Gro. BS4: Know 4K 75
Dowling Rd. BS13: Hart 7J 75
Down, The BS32: Old D 2F 19
BS35: Alv 7H 11
Down Av. BA2: C Down 3C 122
Downavon BA15: Brad A 7H 125
Down Cl. BS20: P'head 3B 42
DOWNEND 2C 50
Downend Pk. BS7: Hor 3B 48
Downend Pk. Rd. BS16: Down 3B 50
Downend Rd. BS7: Hor 3B 48
BS15: K'wd 7B 50
BS16: Down 3A 50
BS16: Fish 3K 49
Downend Sports Cen. 1D 50
Down Farm Ho. BS36: Wint 1B 38
Downfield BS9: Sea M 1C 46
BS31: Key 5B 78
Downfield Cl. BS35: Alv 7H 11
Downfield Dr. BS36: Fram C 6F 29
Downfield Lodge BS8: Clif 7G 47
Downfield Rd. BS8: Clif 7G 47
Downland Cl. BS48: Nail 1F 71
Down La. BA2: B'ptn 2H 101
Down Leaze BS35: Alv 7J 11
Downleaze BS9: Stok B 5F 47
BS16: Down 7B 38
BS20: P'head 3C 42
Downleaze Dr. BS37: Chip S 6G 31
Downman Rd. BS7: L'lze 3C 48
Down Rd. BS20: P'head 5A 42
BS35: Alv 7H 11
BS36: Wint D 3C 38
Downs, The BA3: Clan 1J 153
BS20: P'head 4D 42
GL12: Wickw 5F 15
Downs Cl. BA15: Brad A 5F 125
BS22: Wor 3D 106
BS35: Alv 7J 11
Downs Cote Av. BS9: W Trym 2F 47
Downs Cote Dr. BS9: W Trym 2F 47
Downs Cote Gdns. BS9: W Trym 2G 47
Downs Cote Pk. BS9: W Trym 2G 47
Downs Cote Vw. BS9: W Trym 2G 47
DOWNSIDE 2B 90
Downside BS20: P'head 3E 42
Downside Cvn. Pk. BS48: Back 2D 90
Downside Cl. BA2: B'ptn 2H 101
BS30: Bar C 4D 64
Downside Ct. *BS8: Clif 7G 47*
(off Downside Rd.)
Downside Rd. BS8: Clif 7G 47
BS23: W Mare 1H 127
BS48: Back 2A 90
Downs Pk. E. BS6: Henle 3G 47
Downs Pk. W. BS6: Henle 3G 47
Downs Rd. BS9: W Trym 2G 47
(not continuous)
BS41: Dun 1D 92
Downs Vw. BA15: Brad A 5F 125
Downsway BS39: Paul 7B 140
Downton Rd. BS4: Know 1K 75
Down Vw. BA3: Hay 6K 153
BS7: B'stn 5B 48
Dowry Pl. BS8: Clif 4F 61
Dowry Rd. BS8: Clif 3G 61
Dowry Sq. BS8: Clif 3F 61
DOYNTON 7G 53
Doynton La. BS30: Doy 7G 53
SN14: Dyr 7G 53
Dragon Ct. BS5: S'wll 7G 49
Dragonfly Cl. BS15: K'wd 2B 64
Dragon Rd. BS36: Wint 2B 38
Dragons Hill Cl. BS31: Key 5D 78
Dragons Hill Ct. BS31: Key 5D 78
Dragons Hill Gdns. BS31: Key 5D 78
Dragonswell Rd. BS10: Hen 5G 35
Dragon Wlk. BS5: St G 7H 49
Drake Av. BA2: C Down 2B 122
Drake Cl. BS22: Wor 7D 84
BS31: Salt 1H 97
Drake Ho. *BS1: Bris 3F 5*
(off Rupert St.)
Drake Rd. BS3: Ash G 6G 61
Drakes Way BS20: P'head 3C 42
Dram La. BS5: St G 3J 63
Dramway Footpath, The
BS36: Coal H 3H 39
Dransfield Way BA2: Bath 7J 99
Draycot Pl. BS1: Bris 7E 4 (4K 61)
Draycott Ct. BA2: Bath 2H 7 (4C 100)
Draycott Rd. BS7: Hor 3B 48
BS27: Ched 7J 151
Draydon Rd. BS4: Know 2J 75
Drayton BS24: W Mare 3J 127
Drayton Cl. BS14: H'gro 2D 76
Drayton Rd. BS9: C Din 7C 34
Drews Orchard GL12: Crom 2B 14
Dr Fox's BS23: W Mare 4E 104
Drill Hall, The BS2: Bris 3J 5
Dring, The BA3: Rads 4J 153
Drive, The BS9: Henle 2H 47
BS14: H'gro 4E 76
BS23: W Mare 4H 105
BS25: C'hll 1A 132
BS25: S'ham 5A 132
BS31: Key 4C 78
BS39: Stan D 3B 116
TA8: Bur S 5C 156
Drove, The BS20: P'bry 1A 44
Drove Ct. BS48: Nail 6G 57
Drove Rd. BS23: W Mare 7G 105
BS49: Cong 1K 109
Drove Way BS24: Nye 4E 108
Druett's Cl. BS10: Hor 1A 48
Druid Cl. BS9: Stok B 3E 46
Druid Hill BS9: Stok B 3E 46
Druid Rd. BS9: Stok B 4D 46
Druid Stoke Av. BS9: Stok B 3C 46
Druid Woods BS9: Stok B 3C 46
Drumhead Way, The BS25: S'ham 5A 132
Drummond Ct. BS30: L Grn 5D 64
Drummond Rd. BS2: Bris 7A 48
BS16: Fish 5H 49
Drungway BA2: Mon C 3G 123
DRY ARCH 6B 102
Dryleaze BS31: Key 3C 78
BS37: Yate 1E 30
Dryleaze Rd. BS16: B'hll 2H 49
Drysdale Cl. BS22: W Mare 3B 106
Dubber's La. BS5: Eastv 6G 49
Dublin Cres. BS9: Henle 2H 47
Duchess Rd. BS8: Clif 7G 47
Duchess Way BS16: Stap 3F 49
Duchy Cl. BA3: Clan 1J 153
Duchy Rd. BA3: Clan 1J 153
Ducie Cl. GL12: Crom 2B 14
Ducie Rd. BS5: Bar H 2D 62
BS16: Stap H 3C 50
Ducie Rd. Bus. Pk. BS5: Bar H 2D 62
Duck La. BS21: Kenn 3G 69
BS22: Wick L 3E 84
BS40: L'frd 4C 110
Duckmoor Rd. BS3: Ash G, Bedm 5G 61
Duckmoor Rd. Ind. Est. BS3: Ash G 5F 61
Duck St. BS25: C'hll 7J 109
GL12: Tyth 7F 13
Dudley Cl. BS31: Key 6C 78
Dudley Ct. BS30: Bar C 5D 64
Dudley Gro. BS7: Hor 7C 36
Dugar Wlk. BS6: Redl 5J 47
Duicie Ct. BS16: Stap H 4C 50
Duke St. BA2: Bath 5H 7 (5C 100)
Dulhorn Farm Camping Site
BS24: E'wth 7B 146
Dulverton Rd. BS7: B'stn 4K 47
Dumaine Av. BS34: Stok G 2G 37
Dumfries Pl. BS23: W Mare 7G 105
Dumpers La. BS40: Chew M 2G 115
Dunbar Cl. TA9: High 4E 158
Duncan Gdns. BA1: W'ton 7G 81
Duncan M. BS8: Clif 2G 61
Duncombe La. BS15: K'wd 6J 49
Duncombe Rd. BS15: K'wd 7K 49
Dundas Aqueduct 2J 123
Dundas Cl. BS10: Hen 5E 34
Dundee Dr. BS16: Fish 3A 50
Dundonald Rd. BS6: Redl 5H 47

Dundridge Gdns.—Elms, The

Dundridge Gdns. BS5: St G 3J 63
Dundridge La. BS5: St G 3J 63
DUNDRY 1D 92
Dundry Cl. BS15: K'wd 3B 64
Dundry La. BS40: Winf 4A 92
BS41: Dun 6B 74
Dundry Vw. BS4: Know 1C 76
Dunedin Way BS22: St Geo 7G 85
Dunford Rd. BS3: Wind H 6K 61
Dungarvon Rd. BS24: W'ton V 5D 106
Dunkeld Av. BS34: Fil 5B 36
Dunkerry Rd. BS3: Wind H 6K 61
DUNKERTON 2D 142
Dunkerton Hill BA2: Dunk, Pea J 4D 142
Dunkery Cl. BS48: Nail 1G 71
Dunkery Rd. BS23: W Mare 3H 105
Dunkirk Rd. BS16: Fish 5H 49
Dunkite La. BS22: Wor 7D 84
Dunlin Dr. BS20: P'bry, P'head 2H 43
Dunmail Rd. BS10: S'mead 5J 35
Dunmore St. BS4: Wind H 5B 62
Dunsford Pl. BA2: Bath 4K 7 (5D 100)
Dunstan Rd. TA8: Bur S 1D 158
Dunstan Way BS27: Ched 7H 151
Dunster Ct. BS25: Wins 5F 131
Dunster Cres. BS24: W Mare 3H 127
Dunster Gdns. BS30: Will 7F 65
BS48: Nail 1G 71
Dunster Ho. BA2: C Down 2C 122
Dunster Rd. BS4: Know 2B 76
BS31: Key 6B 78
Dunsters Rd. BS49: Clav 2B 88
Durban Rd. BS34: Pat 6B 26
Durban Way BS49: Yat 2H 87
Durbin Pk. Rd. BS21: Clev 4D 54
Durbin Wlk. BS5: E'tn 1C 62
Durcott La. BA2: Cam, Tim 5G 141
Durdham Ct. BS6: Redl 5G 47
Durdham Hall BS9: Stok B 4F 47
Durdham Pk. BS6: Redl 5G 47
Durham Gro. BS31: Key 6B 78
Durham Rd. BS2: Bris 6C 48
Durleigh Cl. BS13: Bis 4G 75
Durley Hill BS31: Key 2K 77
Durley La. BS31: Key 3A 78
Durley Pk. BA2: Bath 7A 100
BS31: Key 3A 78
Durnford Av. BS3: Ash G 5G 61
Durnford St. BS3: Ash G 5G 61
Durnhill BS40: Comp M 6K 135
Dursley Cl. BS37: Yate 5E 30
Dursley Rd. BS11: Shire 3H 45
Durston BS24: W Mare 3J 127
Durville Rd. BS13: Bis 4H 75
Durweston Wlk. BS14: Stoc 2E 76
Dutton Cl. BS14: Stoc 4F 77
Dutton Rd. BS14: Stoc 4F 77
Dutton Wlk. BS14: Stoc 4F 77
Dyers Cl. BS13: Hart 6K 75
Dyer's La. BS37: Iron A 7A 22
Dylan Thomas Ct. BS30: Bar C 4E 64
Dymboro, The BA3: Mid N 5D 152
Dymboro Av. BA3: Mid N 5D 152
Dymboro Cl. BA3: Mid N 5D 152
Dymboro Gdns. BA3: Mid N 5D 152
DYRHAM 4K 53
Dyrham BS16: Fren 6A 38
(off Harford Dr.)
Dyrham Cl. BS9: Henle 2K 47
BS15: K'wd 1D 64
BS35: T'bry 1A 12
TA8: Bur S 1F 159
Dyrham Pde. BS34: Pat 6E 26
Dyrham Pk. 4K 53
Dyrham Rd. BS15: K'wd 1D 64
Dyrham Vw. BS16: Puck 4C 52
Dysons Cl. BS49: Yat 3H 87

E

Eagle Cl. BS22: W Mare 4B 106
Eagle Cotts. BA1: Bathe 5H 83
Eagle Cres. BS16: Puck 4C 52
Eagle Dr. BS34: Pat 6A 26
Eagle Pk. BA1: Bathe 5H 83
Eagle Rd. BA1: Bathe 5H 83
BS4: Brisl 7F 63
Eagles, The BS49: Yat 3H 87
Eagles Wood Bus. Pk.
BS32: Brad S 3E 26
Earlesfield BS48: Nail 1E 70
Earlham Gro. BS23: W Mare 5H 105
Earl Russell Way BS5: E'tn 2D 62
Earls Mead BS16: Stap 4G 49
Earlstone Cl. BS30: C Hth 5E 64
Earlstone Cres. BS30: C Hth 5E 64
Earl St. BS1: Bris 1F 5 (1K 61)
EARTHCOTT GREEN 6C 20
Earthcott Rd. BS35: Alv, E Grn, Itch 5C 20
Easedale Cl. BS10: S'mead 5K 35
East Av. TA9: High 4E 158
Eastbourne Av. BA1: Bath 2D 100
Eastbourne Rd. BS5: E'tn 1D 62
Eastbourne Vs. BA1: Bath 2D 100
Eastbury Cl. BS35: T'bry 3A 12
Eastbury Rd. BS16: Fish 4J 49
BS35: T'bry 3A 12
EAST CLEVEDON 6F 55
E. Clevedon Triangle BS21: Clev 5E 54
Eastcliff BS20: P'head 1G 43
East Cl. BA2: Bath 6G 99
Eastcombe Gdns. BS23: W Mare 3H 105
Eastcombe Rd. BS23: W Mare 3H 105
Eastcote Pk. BS14: Whit 5D 76
East Ct. BS3: Ash V 6F 61
Eastcourt Rd. BS39: Temp C 5G 139
East Cft. BS9: Henle 1J 47
Eastcroft BS40: Blag 3D 134
Eastcroft Cl. BS40: Blag 3D 134
Eastdown Pl. BA3: Clan 1J 153
(off Eastdown Rd.)
Eastdown Rd. BA3: Clan 1J 153
EAST DUNDRY 2G 93
E. Dundry La. BS41: Dun 1F 93
E. Dundry Rd. BS14: Whit 1B 94
EAST END
BS40 3C 134
BS48 1J 71
East End BS26: L Wre 7D 148
EASTER COMPTON 4G 25
Easter Ct. BS37: Yate 5A 30
Eastermead La. BS29: Ban 2C 130
Eastern Drove BS49: Clav 4K 69
Eastern Ho. BS23: W Mare 4G 105
EASTERTOWN 4B 146
Eastertown BS24: Lym 4A 146
EASTFIELD 1J 47
Eastfield BS9: W Trym 1H 47
Eastfield Av. BA1: W'ton 7H 81
Eastfield Dr. BS37: Yate 1E 30
Eastfield Gdns. BS23: W Mare 3H 105
Eastfield La. BS35: N'wick 2D 16
Eastfield Pk. BS23: W Mare 3G 105
Eastfield Rd. BS6: Cot 6K 47
BS9: W Trym 1G 47
BS24: Hut 3C 128
Eastfield Ter. BS9: Henle 2H 47
Eastgate Cen. BS5: Eastv 5D 48
Eastgate Office Cen. BS5: Eastv 5D 48
Eastgate Rd. BS5: Eastv 5D 48
East Gro. BS6: Bris 7B 48
EAST HARPTREE 7K 137
EAST HEWISH 5B 86
Eastlake Cl. BS7: L'lze 1D 48
Eastland Av. BS35: T'bry 2A 12
Eastland Rd. BS35: T'bry 2A 12
Eastlea BS21: Clev 1B 68
E. Lea Rd. BA1: Bath 3G 99
Eastleigh Cl. BS16: Soun 4C 50
TA8: Bur S 7E 156
Eastleigh Rd. BS10: S'mead 6K 35
BS16: Soun 5C 50
Eastlyn Rd. BS13: Bis 2H 75
East Mead BA3: Mid N 4F 153
Eastmead Ct. BS9: Stok B 4E 46
E. Mead Drove BS24: B'don 7H 127
Eastmead La. BS9: Stok B 4E 46
Eastnor Rd. BS14: Whit 7C 76
Easton Bus. Cen. BS5: E'tn 1D 62
Easton Hill Rd. BS35: T'bry 2B 12
Easton Ho. BA1: Bath 2E 100
EASTON-IN-GORDANO 4E 44
Easton Leisure Cen. 1C 62
Easton Rd. BS2: Bris 2C 62
BS5: E'tn 2C 62
BS20: Pill 4G 45
Easton Way BS5: E'tn 7C 48
Eastover Cl. BS9: W Trym 7G 35
Eastover Gro. BA2: Odd D 3J 121
Eastover Rd. BS39: High L 4B 140
East Pde. BS9: Sea M 2C 46
East Pk. BS5: Eastv 6E 48
East Pk. Dr. BS5: Eastv 6E 48
East Pk. Trad. Est.
BS5: E'tn, W'hall 7F 49
E. Priory Cl. BS9: W Trym 1G 47
East Ride TA9: Bre K 6K 157
Eastridge Dr. BS13: Bis 5F 75
EAST ROLSTONE 3B 108
East Shrubbery BS6: Redl 6H 47
East St. BS3: Bedm 6J 61
BS11: A'mth 6E 32
BS29: Ban 2B 130
East St. M. BS3: Bedm 5K 61
(off East St.)
EAST TWERTON 5B 6 (5K 99)
East Vw. BS16: Mang 2D 50
EASTVILLE 5E 48
Eastville BA1: Bath 2D 100
East Wlk. BS37: Yate 5E 30
East Way BA2: Bath 6G 99
Eastway BS48: Nail 6F 57
Eastway Cl. BS48: Nail 7F 57
Eastway Sq. BS48: Nail 6G 57
Eastwell La. BS25: Wins 7E 130
Eastwood BA2: B'ptn 5G 101
Eastwood Cl. BS39: High L 3B 140
Eastwood Cres. BS4: Brisl 5H 63
Eastwood Pl. BS20: P'head 1F 43
Eastwood Rd. BS4: Brisl 5H 63
Eastwoods BA1: Bathf 7K 83
Eaton Cl. BS14: Stoc 5G 77
BS16: Fish 4K 49
Eaton Cres. BS8: Clif 1A 4 (1G 61)
Eaton St. BS3: Bedm 6J 61
Ebden Lodge BS22: Wor 2E 106
EBDON 5E 84
Ebdon Ct. BS22: Wor 2E 106
Ebdon Rd. BS22: Wick L, Wor 6D 84
Ebenezer La. BS9: Stok B 2D 46
(not continuous)
Ebenezer St. BS5: St G 2F 63
Ebenezer Ter. BA2: Bath 6H 7
Eccleston Ho. BS5: Bar H 3D 62
Eckweek Gdns. BA2: Pea J 5D 142
Eckweek La. BA2: Pea J 5D 142
(not continuous)
Eckweek Rd. BA2: Pea J 5D 142
Eclipse Office Pk. BS16: Stap H 4A 50
Eddington Ct. BS23: W Mare 6F 105
Eden Apartments BS23: W Mare 3F 105
Eden Cft. BS24: W'ton V 4C 106
Eden Gro. BS7: Hor 6B 36
Eden Pk. Cl BA1: Bathe 6J 83
Eden Pk. Dr. BA1: Bathe 6J 83
Eden Ter. BA1: Bath 1D 100
Eden Vs. BA1: Bath 1E 100
(off Dafford's Bldgs.)
Edgar Bldgs. BA1: Bath 3F 7
Edgarley Ct. BS21: Clev 4C 54
Edgecombe Av. BS22: W Mare 2B 106
Edgecombe Cl. BS15: K'wd 7D 50
Edgecumbe Rd. BS6: Redl 6K 47
Edgefield Cl. BS14: Whit 7B 76
Edgefield Rd. BS14: Whit 7B 76
Edgehill Rd. BS21: Clev 3D 54
Edgeware Rd. BS3: Bris 5J 61
BS16: Stap H 4B 50
Edgewood Cl. BS14: H'gro 2D 76
BS30: L Grn 6E 64
Edgeworth BS37: Yate 1C 40
Edgeworth Rd. BA2: Bath 2J 121
Edinburgh Pl. BS23: W Mare 4F 105
Edinburgh Rd. BS31: Key 6C 78
Edington Gro. BS10: Hen 5G 35
EDINGWORTH 7D 146
Edingworth Rd. BS24: E'wth 6C 146
Edith Cl. TA8: Bur S 5C 156
EDITHMEAD 1J 159
Edithmead La. TA9: Edith 7G 157
Edithmead Pk. TA9: Edith 2K 159
Edmund Cl. BS16: Down 2B 50
Edmund Ct. BS16: Puck 2B 52
Edmund Rd. BS14: H'gro 3C 76
Edmunds Way BS27: Ched 7E 150
Edna Av. BS4: Brisl 6G 63
Edward Bird Ho. BS7: L'lze 1D 48
Edward Rd. BS4: Bris 5D 62
BS15: K'wd 1C 64
BS21: Clev 4E 54
Edward Rd. Sth. BS21: Clev 4E 54
Edward Rd. W. BS21: Clev 3E 54
Edward St. BA1: Bath 3A 6 (4J 99)
BA2: Bath 3J 7 (4D 100)
BS5: Eastv 6F 49
BS5: Redf 1E 62
Edwin Short Cl. BS30: Bit 2J 79
Effingham Rd. BS6: Bris 6A 48
Egerton Brow BS7: B'stn 4K 47
Egerton Ct. BS7: B'stn 4A 48
(off Gloucester Rd.)
Egerton La. BS7: B'stn 4K 47
Egerton Rd. BA2: Bath 7A 100
BS7: B'stn 4K 47
Eggshill La. BS37: Yate 5D 30
Egg Theatre, The 4F 7
Eglin Cft. BS13: Withy 6H 75
Eighth Av. BS7: Hor 7D 36
BS14: H'gro 3C 76
Eirene Ter. BS20: Pill 4H 45
ELBERTON 7B 10
Elberton BS15: K'wd 1E 64
Elberton Rd. BS9: Sea M 1B 46
BS35: Elbton, Olv 6B 10
ELBOROUGH 2G 129
Elborough Av. BS49: Yat 3H 87
Elborough Gdns. BS24: Elbgh 2G 129
Elbridge Ho. BS2: Bris 2J 5
Elbury Av. BS15: K'wd 6A 50
Elderberry Wlk. BS10: S'mead 5J 35
BS22: Wor 3D 106
(off Silverberry Rd.)
Elderberry Way BS32: Alm 1F 27
Elder Cl. TA9: High 3F 159
Elderwood Dr. BS30: L Grn 6E 64
Elderwood Rd. BS14: H'gro 3D 76
Eldon Pl. BA1: Bath 1D 100
Eldon Ter. BS3: Wind H 6K 61
Eldonwall Trad. Est. BS4: Brisl 4E 62
Eldon Way BS4: Brisl 4E 62
Eldred Cl. BS9: Stok B 3D 46
Eleanor Cl. BA2: Bath 6F 99
Eleventh Av. BS7: Hor 6D 36
Elfin Rd. BS16: Fish 3J 49
Elgar Cl. BS4: Know 4K 75
BS21: Clev 1E 68
Elgin Av. BS7: Fil 6B 36
Elgin Pk. BS6: Redl 6H 47
Elgin Rd. BS16: Fish 6K 49
Eliot Cl. BS7: Hor 6C 36
BS23: W Mare 2J 127
Elizabeth Cl. BS24: Hut 2B 128
BS35: T'bry 4B 12
Elizabeth Ct. BS13: Withy 6F 75
TA8: Bur S 2D 158
Elizabeth Cres. BS34: Stok G 3G 37
Elizabeth's M. BS4: St Ap 3H 63
Elizabeth Way BS16: Mang 5F 51
Elkstone Wlk. BS30: Bit 7G 65
Ella Cl. BS16: Fish 2A 50
Ellacombe Rd. BS30: L Grn 7C 64
Ellan Hay Rd. BS32: Brad S 1J 37
Ellbridge Cl. BS9: Stok B 3D 46
Ellenborough Cres. BS23: W Mare 6G 105
Ellenborough Ho. BS8: Clif 5A 4
Ellenborough Mnr. BS23: W Mare 6G 105
Ellenborough Pk. Nth.
BS23: W Mare 6F 105
Ellenborough Pk. Rd.
BS23: W Mare 6G 105
Ellenborough Pk. Sth.
BS23: W Mare 6F 105
Ellen Ho. BA2: Bath 6G 99
Ellesmere BS35: T'bry 4A 12
Ellesmere Rd. BS4: Brisl 2F 77
BS15: K'wd 1B 64
BS23: Uph 3F 127
Ellfield Cl. BS13: Bis 4F 75
Ellick Rd. BS40: Blag 5A 134
Ellicks Cl. BS32: Brad S 4G 27
Ellicott Rd. BS7: Hor 2B 48
Ellinghurst Cl. BS10: Bren 5G 35
Elliott Av. BS16: Fren 6A 38
Ellis Av. BS13: Bis 2G 75
Ellis Pk. BS22: St Geo 1G 107
Elliston Dr. BA2: Bath 7H 99
Elliston La. BS6: Redl 6J 47
Elliston Rd. BS6: Redl 6J 47
Ellsbridge Cl. BS31: Key 5F 79
Ellsworth Rd. BS10: Hen 5F 35
Elm Av. TA8: Bur S 2D 158
Elm Cl. BS11: Law W 6K 33
BS25: Star 4K 131
BS29: Ban 1J 129
BS34: Lit S 7F 27
BS37: Chip S 5G 31
BS48: Nail 1E 70
BS49: Yat 4H 87
Elm Ct. BS6: Redl 6H 47
BS14: Whit 4C 76
BS31: Key 6A 78
Elmcroft BA1: Bath 1E 100
Elmcroft Cres. BS7: L'lze 4C 48
Elm Cross Bus. Pk. BA15: Brad A 7H 125
(off Moulton Dr.)
Elm Cross Shop. Cen. BA15: Brad A 7H 125
(off Moulton Dr.)
Elmdale Cres. BS35: T'bry 3A 12
Elmdale Gdns. BS16: Fish 4J 49
Elmdale Rd. BS3: Bedm 7H 61
BS8: Clif 1B 4 (1H 61)
Elmfield BA15: Brad A 5G 125
BS15: K'wd 3C 64
Elmfield Cl. BS15: K'wd 3C 64
Elmfield Rd. BS9: S'mead 7G 35
Elm Gro. BA1: Swa 1E 100
BA2: Bath 7J 99
BS24: Lock 1D 128
Elmgrove Av. BS5: E'tn 1D 62
Elmgrove Dr. BS37: Yate 4F 31
Elmgrove Pk. BS6: Cot 7K 47
Elmgrove Rd. BS6: Cot 7K 47
BS16: Fish 5G 49
Elmham Way BS24: W'ton V 3F 107
Elm Hayes BS13: Bis 4F 75
Elm Hayes Vw. BS39: Paul 1C 152
Elmhirst Gdns. BS37: Yate 4G 31
Elmhurst Av. BS5: Eastv 5F 49
Elmhurst Est. BA1: Bathe 6J 83
Elmhurst Gdns. BS41: L Ash 1K 73
Elmhurst Rd. BS24: Hut 3C 128
Elmhyrst Rd. BS23: W Mare 4H 105
Elming Down Cl. BS32: Brad S 1F 37
Elm La. BS6: Redl 6H 47
Elmlea Av. BS9: W Trym 3F 47
Elmleigh Av. BS16: Mang 3F 51
Elmleigh Cl. BS16: Mang 3F 51
Elmleigh Rd. BS16: Mang 3E 50
Elm Lodge Rd. BS48: Wrax 6J 57
Elmore BS15: Soun 6D 50
BS37: Yate 6D 30
Elmore Rd. BS7: Hor 2C 48
BS34: Pat 5B 26
Elm Pk. BS34: Fil 5C 36
Elm Pl. BA2: Bath 7B 100
Elm Rd. BS7: Hor 3A 48
BS15: K'wd 3C 64
BS39: Paul 1C 152
Elms, The BA1: Bath 1E 100
BA2: Tim 3F 141
BA15: Brad A 4F 125
BS16: Fren 6A 38
BS16: Stap H 5B 50

Gt. Ann St.—Hanham Green

Gt. Ann St. BS2: Bris 2K **5** (2B **62**)
GREAT ASHLEY 3E **124**
Gt. Bedford St. BA1: Bath 1E **6** (3B **100**)
Great Brockeridge BS9: W Trym 2F **47**
Great Dowles BS30: C Hth 5E **64**
Gt. George St. BS1: Bris 4C **4** (3J **61**)
BS2: Bris 2J **5** (2B **62**)
Gt. Hayles Rd. BS14: H'gro 3B **76**
Great Leaze BS30: C Hth 5E **64**
Great Mdw. Rd. BS32: Brad S 7H **27**
Great Pk. Rd. BS32: Brad S 3E **26**
Gt. Pulteney St. BA2: Bath 3H **7** (4C **100**)
Gt. Stanhope St. BA1: Bath 4D **6** (5A **100**)
GREAT STOKE 2H **37**
Gt. Stoke Way BS34: Stok G 5F **37**
(Filton Rd.)
BS34: Stok G 2J **37**
(Winterbourne Rd.)
Greatstone La. BS40: Winf 7K **91**
Gt. Swanmoor Cl. BS34: Stok G 4E **36**
Gt. Western Bus. Pk. BS37: Yate 3B **30**
(not continuous)
Gt. Western Ct. BS34: Stok G 3H **37**
Gt. Western La. BS5: Bar H 3E **62**
Gt. Western Rd. BS21: Clev 6D **54**
Great Weston Train Experience 6G **105**
Gt. Wood Cl. BS13: Hart 6J **75**
Green, The BA2: Odd D 3K **121**
BA3: Faul 4K **155**
BS11: Shire 2J **45**
BS15: Soun 6C **50**
BS20: Pill 4H **45**
(not continuous)
BS24: Lock 1E **128**
BS25: Wins 5F **131**
BS30: Wick 4B **66**
BS34: Stok G 3G **37**
BS35: Olv 3C **18**
BS39: Comp D 6B **96**
BS48: Back 5H **71**
GL12: Crom 4B **14**
Greenacre BS22: W Mare 2K **105**
Greenacre Pl. Cvn. Pk. TA9: Edith 2J **159**
Green Acre Rd. BS14: Whit 7C **76**
Greenacres BA1: W'ton 7H **81**
BA3: Mid N 5C **152**
BS9: W Trym 1E **46**
Green Acres Cvn. Site BS35: Aust 5G **9**
Greenacres Pk. BS36: Coal H 2H **39**
Greenbank Av. E. BS5: E'tn 7E **48**
Greenbank Av. W. BS5: E'tn 7D **48**
Greenbank Gdns. BA1: W'ton 2H **99**
Greenbank Rd. BS3: Bris 7A **4** (4G **61**)
BS5: E'tn 7E **48**
BS15: Han 5B **64**
Greenbank Vw. BS5: Eastv 6E **48**
BS15: K'wd 2C **64**
Green Cl. BS7: Hor 7C **36**
BS39: Paul 7C **140**
Green Cotts. BA2: C Down 3E **122**
Green Ct. BS35: Olv 3C **18**
Green Cft. BS5: S'wll 7J **49**
Greendale Rd. BS3: Wind H 6A **62**
BS6: Redl 4H **47**
Green Dell Cl. BS10: Hen 4D **34**
Greenditch Av. BS13: Hart 5J **75**
Green Ditch La. BA3: C'tn 7A **152**
Greenditch St. BS35: Olv, Toc 4A **18**
BS35: Piln, Toc 4J **17**
Greendown BS5: St G 2J **63**
Greendown Pl. BA2: C Down 3C **122**
Green Dragon Rd. BS36: Wint 2B **38**
Green Farm Bus. Pk.
BS37: Iron A 1E **28**
Greenfield Av. BS10: S'mead 7K **35**
Greenfield Cres. BS48: Nail 6G **57**
Greenfield Pk. BS20: P'head 5E **42**
Greenfield Pl. BS23: W Mare 4E **104**
Greenfield Rd. BS10: S'mead 6K **35**
Greenfields Av. BS29: Ban 2A **130**
Greenfield Wlk. BA3: Mid N 3E **152**
Greenfinch Lodge BS16: B'hll 2H **49**
Greengage Cl. BS22: W Mare 4C **106**
Green Hayes BS37: Chip S 6J **31**
Greenhayes BS27: Ched 6D **150**
Greenhill BS35: Alv 1J **19**
Greenhill Cl. BS22: Wor 1E **106**
BS48: Nail 7F **57**
Greenhill Cft. BS25: Sandf 1H **131**
Greenhill Down BS35: Alv 1J **19**
Greenhill Gdns. BS35: Alv 1J **19**
Greenhill Gro. BS3: Bedm 7G **61**
Greenhill La. BS11: Law W 6C **34**
BS25: Sandf 1H **131**
BS35: Alv 2H **19**
Greenhill Pde. BS35: Alv 7J **11**
Greenhill Pl. BA3: Mid N 3E **152**
Greenhill Rd. BA3: Mid N 3E **152**
BS25: Sandf 1G **131**
BS35: Alv 7J **11**
Greenland Mills BA15: Brad A 6J **125**
Greenland Rd. BS22: W Mare 3B **106**
Greenlands Rd. BA2: Pea J 5C **142**
BS10: Hen 3E **34**
Greenlands Way BS10: Hen 4E **34**
Greenland Vw. BA15: Brad A 6J **125**
Green La. BA15: Tur 6D **124**
BS8: Fail 5G **59**
BS11: A'mth 7F **33**
BS35: Redw, Sev B 6A **16**
BS36: Wint 1A **38**
BS39: Far G, Hall 7G **139**
(not continuous)
BS40: Blag, Comp M 6F **135**
BS40: But 5E **112**
BS40: Redh, Winf 7E **90**
GL12: Bag 3A **22**
GL12: Buck 3F **13**
TA8: Berr 6C **144**
Greenleaze BS4: Know 1D **76**
Greenleaze Av. BS16: Down 6B **38**
Greenleaze Cl. BS16: Down 6B **38**
Greenmore Rd. BS4: Know 7D **62**
Greenore BS15: K'wd 2A **64**
Green Pk. BA1: Bath 5D **6**
BS30: Old C 3H **65**
Green Pk. Ho. BA1: Bath 5E **6**
Green Pk. M. BA1: Bath 5D **6** (5A **100**)
Green Pk. Rd. BA1: Bath 5E **6** (5B **100**)
Greenpark Rd. BS10: S'mead 6A **36**
Green Pk. Sta. BA1: Bath 4E **6** (5A **100**)
GREEN PARLOUR 5D **154**
Green Parlour Rd. BA3: Writ 5D **154**
Green Pastures Rd. BS48: Wrax 6J **57**
Greenridge BS39: Clut 2H **139**
Greenridge Cl. BS13: Withy 6E **74**
GREENSBROOK 2H **139**
Greens Hill BS16: Fish 5G **49**
Greenside BS16: Mang 2E **50**
Greenside Cl. BS10: Hen 4D **34**
Greenslade Gdns. BS48: Nail 6F **57**
Green St. BA1: Bath 4F **7** (5B **100**)
BA2: Shos 1D **154**
BS3: Wind H 5B **62**
Green Tree Rd. BA3: Mid N 3F **153**
GREENVALE 4F **141**
Greenvale Cl. BA2: Tim 4F **141**
Greenvale Dr. BA2: Tim 4F **141**
Greenvale Rd. BS39: Paul 1B **152**
Greenview BS30: L Grn 7E **64**
Green Wlk. BS4: Know 1C **76**
GREENWAY 7B **138**
Greenway BA3: Faul 5J **155**
Greenway, The BS16: Fish 5A **50**
Greenway Bush La. BS3: Bris 7A **4** (5G **61**)
Greenway Ct. BA2: Bath 7B **100**
Greenway Dr. BS10: S'mead 4B **36**
Greenway La. BA1: C Ash 5K **67**
BA2: Bath 1B **122**
BS10: S'mead 6K **35**
Greenway Pk. BS10: S'mead 7K **35**
BS21: Clev 6F **55**
Greenway Rd. BS6: Redl 6H **47**
Greenways BS15: K'wd 7E **50**
Greenways Rd. BS37: Yate 3D **30**
Greenwell La. BS40: L'frd 5E **110**
Greenwood Cl. BS7: Hor 1A **48**
TA9: W Hunt 7E **158**
Greenwood Dr. BS35: Alv 1H **19**
Greenwood Rd. BS4: Know 7C **62**
BS22: Wor 2C **106**
Gregory Ct. BS30: C Hth 3J **64**
Gregory Mead BS49: Yat 2G **87**
Gregorys Gro. BA2: Odd D 4K **121**
Gregory's Tyning BS39: Paul 7C **140**
Greinton BS24: W Mare 3J **127**
Grenville Av. BS24: Lock 1E **128**
Grenville Cl. BS5: St G 1H **63**
Grenville Pl. *BS1: Bris* *4F 61*
(off Brunel Lock Rd.)
Grenville Rd. BS6: Bris 5A **48**
TA8: Bur S 1E **158**
Greve Ct. BS30: Bar C 5D **64**
Greville M. BS3: Bris 5H **61**
Greville Rd. BS3: Bris 5H **61**
Greville St. BS3: Bedm 5J **61**
GREYFIELD 3A **140**
Greyfield Comn. BS39: High L 3A **140**
Greyfield Rd. BS39: High L 3A **140**
Greyfield Vw. BS39: Temp C 4H **139**
Greyfriars BS1: Bris 2E **4** (2K **61**)
Grey Hollow BS40: E Harp 7K **137**
Greylands Rd. BS13: Bis 3F **75**
Greystoke BS10: W Trym 6G **35**
Greystoke Av. BS10: S'mead 7G **35**
Greystoke Gdns. BS10: S'mead 7H **35**
(not continuous)
Greystones BS16: Down 6C **38**
Grib La. BS40: Blag 3D **134**
Griffen Rd. BS24: W'ton V 5C **106**
Griffin Cl. BS22: Wor 2E **106**
Griffin Ct. BA1: Bath 5E **6**
Griffin Rd. BS21: Clev 6D **54**
Griggfield Wlk. BS14: H'gro 3B **76**
Grimsbury Rd. BS15: K'wd 1E **64**
Grindell Rd. BS5: St G 2F **63**
Grinfield Av. BS13: Hart 6J **75**
Grittleton Rd. BS7: Hor 7A **36**
Grosvenor Bri. Rd. BA1: Bath 2E **100**
Grosvenor Pk. BA1: Bath 2E **100**
Grosvenor Pl. BA1: Bath 2E **100**
Grosvenor Rd. BS2: Bris 7B **48**
Grosvenor Ter. BA1: Bath 1E **100**
Grosvenor Vs. BA1: Bath 2D **100**
Grove, The BA1: W'ton 2J **99**
BS1: Bris 6E **4** (4K **61**)
BS21: Clev 1B **68**
BS25: Wins 4F **131**
BS30: C Hth 5E **64**
BS34: Pat 7D **26**
BS37: Rang 5A **22**
BS39: Hall 6K **139**
BS40: Blag 3C **134**
BS48: Wrax 6A **58**
TA8: Bur S 6D **156**
Grove Av. BS1: Bris 6F **5** (4K **61**)
BS9: C Din 1C **46**
BS16: Fish 4H **49**
Grove Bank BS16: Fren 6A **38**
Grove Dr. BS22: W Mare 3A **106**
Grove Ho. *BS8: Clif* *3G 61*
(off Cornwallis Gro.)
Grove Ind. Est., The BS34: Pat 6D **26**
Grove La. BA3: Faul 4J **155**
BS23: W Mare 4F **105**
SN14: Hin 2J **53**
Grove Leaze BA15: Brad A 6F **125**
BS11: Shire 2G **45**
Grove M., The BS36: Wint 7C **28**
Grove Orchard BS40: Blag 3C **134**
Grove Pk. BS4: Brisl 7F **63**
BS6: Redl 6J **47**
BS23: W Mare 4F **105**
Grove Pk. Av. BS4: Brisl 7F **63**
Grove Pk. Ct. BS4: Brisl 7F **63**
Grove Pk. Rd. BS4: Brisl 7F **63**
BS23: W Mare 3F **105**
Grove Pk. Ter. BS16: Fish 4H **49**
Grove Rd. BS6: Redl 6G **47**
BS9: C Din 7C **34**
BS16: Fish, Stap 4G **49**
BS22: W Mare 3A **106**
BS23: W Mare 4F **105**
BS29: Ban 1J **129**
TA8: Bur S 7C **156**
Groves, The BS13: Hart 6K **75**
GROVESEND 5C **12**
Grovesend Rd. BS35: Grov, T'bry 4A **12**
BS35: T'bry 3K **11**
Grove Sports Cen. 2F **71**
Grove St. BA2: Bath 3G **7** (4C **100**)
Grove Vw. BS16: Ham 4A **38**
BS16: Stap 2G **49**
Grove Wood Rd. BA3: Hay 6J **153**
Guernsey Av. BS4: Brisl 5H **63**
Guest Av. BS16: Emer G 1F **51**
Gug, The BS39: High L 3A **140**
Guild Ct. BS1: Bris 6G **5** (3A **62**)
Guildford Rd. BS4: St Ap 4G **63**
Guildhall Market *4G 7*
(off High St.)
Guillemot Rd. BS20: P'head 2H **43**
Guinea La. BA1: Bath 2F **7** (4B **100**)
BS16: Fish 3J **49**
(not continuous)
Guinea St. BS1: Bris 7F **5** (4K **61**)
Gullen BA2: Shos, Ston L 1F **155**
Gulliford Cl. TA9: High 4F **159**
Gulliford's Bank BS21: Clev 7E **54**
Gullimore Gdns. BS13: Hart 6H **75**
Gullivers Pl. BS37: Chip S 6G **31**
Gullock Tyning BA3: Mid N 5F **153**
Gullons Cl. BS13: Bis 4G **75**
Gullon Wlk. BS13: Withy 5F **75**
Gully, The BS36: Wint 7D **28**
Gullybrook La. BS5: Bar H 3D **62**
Gumhurn La. BS35: Piln 5E **16**
Gunning Cl. BS15: K'wd 3B **64**
Gunter's Hill BS5: St G 3J **63**
Guthrie Rd. BS8: Clif 1F **61**
Gwilliam St. BS3: Wind H 6K **61**
Gwyn St. BS2: Bris 7A **48**
Gypsy La. BS16: Puck 5J **39**
BS31: Key 3E **96**
BS36: H'fld 5J **39**

H

Haberfield Hill BS8: Abb L 6J **45**
Haberfield Ho. *BS8: Clif* *3F 61*
(off Hotwell Rd.)
HACKET, THE 3C **12**
Hacket BS35: T'bry 3C **12**
Hacket Hill BS35: T'bry 4D **12**
Hacket La. BS35: Grov 5D **12**
BS35: T'bry 3B **12**
(not continuous)
Haddrell Ct. BS35: Alv 7H **11**
Hadley Ct. BS30: C Hth 3F **65**
Hadley Rd. BA2: C Down 2D **122**
Hadrian Cl. BS9: Stok B 4C **46**
Hadrians Wlk. BS16: Emer G 2G **51**
Ha Ha, The BA2: Tim 3E **140**
Haig Cl. BS9: Sea M 1B **46**
Halbrow Cres. BS16: Fish 3A **50**
Haldon Cl. BS3: Wind H 1K **75**
Hale Cl. BS15: Han 5B **64**
HALE COOMBE 7H **131**
Hales Horn Cl. BS32: Brad S 1F **37**
Halfacre Cl. BS14: Whit 7C **76**
Halfacre La. BS14: Whit 7D **76**
Half Yd. BS40: L'frd 5E **110**
Halifax Rd. BS37: Yate 2D **30**
Hallam Rd. BS21: Clev 5C **54**
Hallards Cl. BS11: Law W 7K **33**
HALLATROW 6K **139**
Hallatrow Bus. Pk. BS39: Hall 7J **139**
Hallatrow Rd. BS39: Hall, Paul 6K **139**
HALLEN 3C **34**
Hallen Cl. BS10: Hen 4D **34**
BS16: Emer G 2G **51**
HALL END 3D **22**
Hall End La. BS37: H End 4C **22**
GL12: H End 4C **22**
Hallen Dr. BS9: Sea M 1C **46**
Hallen Ind. Est. BS10: H'len 7A **24**
Hallen Rd. BS10: H'len, Hen 3C **34**
Halletts Way BS20: P'head 3F **43**
Halliwell Rd. BS20: P'head 4A **42**
Hall La. BA1: L Ham, Tad 7H **67**
Halls Gdn. BS34: Stok G 3J **37**
Halls Rd. BS15: K'wd 1B **64**
Hall St. BS3: Bedm 7H **61**
Hall Ter. TA8: Bur S 7C **156**
Halsbury Rd. BS6: Henle, Redl 4H **47**
Halstock Av. BS16: Fish 5H **49**
Halston Dr. BS2: Bris 1B **62**
Halswell Gdns. BS13: Hart 6H **75**
Halswell Rd. BS21: Clev 1D **68**
Halt End BS14: Whit 7E **76**
Halwyn Cl. BS9: Stok B 3D **46**
HAM
BS39 1D **152**
TA9 3G **157**
Hamble Cl. BS35: T'bry 4A **12**
Hambledon Rd. BS22: St Geo 7G **85**
HAMBROOK 5A **38**
Hambrook La. BS16: Ham 4H **37**
BS34: Stok G 4H **37**
Ham Cl. BS39: Temp C 4H **139**
Ham Farm La. BS16: Emer G 2F **51**
Ham Gdns. BA1: Bath 5G **7** (5C **100**)
BA3: Mid N 5F **153**
HAM GREEN 5H **45**
Ham Grn. BS20: Pill 4H **45**
Ham Gro. BS39: Paul 1C **152**
Ham Hill BA3: Rads 3K **153**
Hamilton Ct. BS1: Bris 1F **5**
Hamilton Ho. BA1: L'dwn 7K **81**
Hamilton Rd. BA1: Bath 1A **100**
BS3: Bris 5H **61**
BS5: E'tn 1D **62**
BS23: W Mare 3E **104**
Hamilton Ter. BA2: Shos 1F **155**
Ham La. BS16: B'hll 2G **49**
(not continuous)
BS21: Kings S 1J **85**
BS30: Doy 7E **52**
BS39: Bis S 7J **115**
BS39: Paul 1C **152**
BS41: Dun 7D **74**
BS48: Wrax 5J **57**
BS49: Yat 7F **69**
TA8: Bur S 2D **158**
Hamlet, The BS48: Nail 6J **57**
Hamlet's Yd. BS31: Key 5C **78**
Ham Link BS40: Burr 2H **133**
Hammersmith Rd. BS5: St G 1F **63**
Hammond Cl. BS4: Brisl 1F **77**
Hammond Gdns. BS9: W Trym 1E **46**
Hampden Cl. BS37: Yate 2D **30**
Hampden Rd. BS4: Know 6D **62**
BS22: Wor 2C **106**
Hampshire Way BS37: Yate 2F **31**
Hampstead Rd. BS4: Brisl 6E **62**
Hampton Cl. BS30: C Hth 4E **64**
Hampton Cnr. BS11: Shire 2J **45**
Hampton Ct. BS6: Redl 7H **47**
Hampton Ho. BA1: Bath 2E **100**
Hampton La. BS6: Cot 7H **47**
Hampton Pk. BS6: Redl 7H **47**
Hampton Rd. BS6: Cot, Redl 6H **47**
Hampton Row BA2: Bath 1K **7** (3D **100**)
Hampton St. BS15: K'wd 7B **50**
Hampton Vw. BA1: Bath 2D **100**
Ham Rd. TA8: Berr 2D **144**
TA9: Bre K 3F **157**
Hams La. BS26: Lox 3G **147**
Hamwood Cl. BS24: W Mare 3K **127**
Hanbury Cl. BS15: Han 4B **64**
Hanbury Ct. BS8: Clif 1G **61**
Hanbury Rd. BS8: Clif 1A **4** (1G **61**)
Handel Av. BS5: St G 2F **63**
Handel Cossham Ct. BS15: K'wd 7A **50**
Handel Rd. BS31: Key 5B **78**
Handford Way BS30: L Grn 6F **65**
Hand Stadium 2F **69**
Hanford Ct. BS14: Stoc 3F **77**
Hang Hill BA2: Shos, Ston L 7E **142**
Hangstone Wlk. BS21: Clev 6C **54**
HANHAM 4A **64**
Hanham Bus. Pk. BS15: Han 5K **63**
HANHAM GREEN 6K **63**

Hanham La.—Hensley Gdns.

Hanham La. BS39: Paul 6D 140
Hanham Mt. BS15: K'wd 3B 64
Hanham Rd. BS15: K'wd 3B 64
Hanham Way BS48: Nail 7D 56
Hanna Cl. BA2: Bath 5G 99
Hannah More Cl. BS27: Ched 7D 150
BS40: Wrin 2G 111
Hannah More Ct. BS27: Ched 6D 150
Hannah More Rd. BS48: Nail 1E 70
Hannay Rd. BS27: Ched 5C 150
Hanny's La. BS40: Chew M 1J 115
Hanover Cl. BS22: Wor 7E 84
Hanover Ct. BA1: Bath 2D 100
BA3: Writ 4B 154
BS1: Bris 2H 5 (1A 62)
BS34: Fil 4C 36
Hanover Ho. BS2: Bris 2C 62
Hanover Pl. *BA1: Bath 3D 100*
(off London Rd.)
BS1: Bris 7B 4 (4H 61)
Hanover Quay BS1: Bris 6C 4
Hanover St. BA1: Bath 2D 100
BS1: Bris 4E 4
BS5: Redf 2E 62
Hanover Ter. *BA1: Bath 2D 100*
(off Gillingham Ter.)
Hansford Cl. BA2: C Down 3A 122
Hansford M. BA2: C Down 3B 122
Hansford Sq. BA2: C Down 3A 122
Hansons Way BS21: Clev 7C 54
Hans Price Cl. BS23: W Mare 4G 105
Hantone Hill BA2: B'ptn 3H 101
Hapgood St. BS5: Bar H 2D 62
Hapgood St. Sth. BS5: Bar H 2D 62
Happerton La. BS20: Eas 6G 45
Happy La. BS7: B'stn, Bris 5B 48
Hapsburg Cl. BS22: Wor 7E 84
Harbour Cres. BS20: P'head 3G 43
Harbour Ho. *BS8: Clif 6A 4*
(off Hotwell Rd.)
Harbourne Cl. TA8: Bur S 7E 156
Harbour Rd. BS20: P'head 2F 43
Harbour Rd. Trad. Est. BS20: P'head 3G 43
Harbourside Wlk. BS1: Bris 6B 4
Harbour Wlk. BS1: Bris 7C 4
Harbour Wall BS9: Sea M 4C 46
Harbour Way BS1: Bris 6C 4 (4J 61)
Harbury Rd. BS9: Henle 1J 47
Harbutts BA2: B'ptn 2H 101
Harcombe Hill BS36: Wint D 3C 38
Harcombe Rd. BS36: Wint 2B 38
Harcourt Av. BS5: St G 3J 63
Harcourt Cl. BS31: Salt 1J 97
Harcourt Gdns. BA1: W'ton 1H 99
Harcourt Hill BS6: Redl 5J 47
Harcourt Rd. BS6: Redl 4H 47
Hardenhuish Rd. BS4: Brisl 4F 63
Harden Rd. BS14: Stoc 5G 77
Harding Pl. BS31: Key 5F 79
Hardings Ter. *BS5: St G 1H 63*
(off Clovelly Rd.)
Hardington Dr. BS31: Key 1E 96
Hardwick BS37: Yate 7C 30
Hardwick Cl. BS4: Brisl 6G 63
BS30: Old C 4H 65
Hardwick Rd. BS20: Pill 3G 45
Hardy Av. BS3: Ash G 5G 61
Hardy Ct. BS30: Bar C 4D 64
Hardy La. BS32: Toc 5B 18
Hardy Rd. BS3: Bedm 7H 61
Hareclive Rd. BS13: Hart 5H 75
Harefield Cl. BS15: Han 7A 64
Hare Knapp BA15: Brad A 6F 125
Harescombe BS37: Yate 7E 30
Harewood Rd. BS5: S'wll 7J 49
Harford Cl. BS9: C Din 1C 46
Harford Dr. BS16: Fren 6A 38
Harford Sq. BS40: Chew M 1H 115
Harington Ct. BA2: New L 6B 98
Harington Pl. BA1: Bath 4F 7 (5B 100)
Harlech Way BS30: Will 7F 65
Harleston St. BS5: E'tn 1K 5 (1C 62)
Harley Ct. BS8: Clif 2F 61
Harley La. BS21: Clev 3J 55
Harley M. BS8: Clif 2F 61
Harley Pl. BS8: Clif 2F 61
Harley St. BA1: Bath 1E 6 (3B 100)
Harmer Cl. BS10: Hen 4F 35
Harmony Dr. BS20: P'head 4B 42
Harnhill Cl. BS13: Hart 6H 75
Harolds Way BS15: K'wd 3A 64
Harp Rd. TA9: Bre K 7K 157
Harptree BS24: W Mare 3J 127
Harptree Cl. BS48: Nail 2F 71
Harptree Ct. BS30: Bar C 5E 64
Harptree Gro. BS3: Bedm 7H 61
Harptree Hill BS40: W Har 7B 136
Harratz Pl. BS1: Bris 5J 5 (3B 62)
Harrier Path BS22: Wor 4C 106
Harriet Brook BS10: Bren 5H 35
Harrington Av. BS14: Stoc 4G 77
Harrington Cl. BS30: Bit 2J 79
Harrington Gro. BS14: Stoc 4G 77
Harrington Rd. BS14: Stoc 5F 77
Harrington Wlk. BS14: Stoc 4G 77
Harris Barton BS36: Fram C 7F 29
Harris Ct. BS30: L Grn 5D 64
Harris Gro. BS13: Hart 7H 75
Harris La. BS8: Abb L 1K 59
Harrison Cl. BS16: Emer G 2F 51
Harrowdene Rd. BS4: Know 6D 62
Harrow Rd. BS4: Brisl 6F 63
HARRY STOKE 5G 37
Harry Stoke Rd. BS34: Stok G 5G 37
HARTCLIFFE 6J 75
Hartcliffe Rd. BS4: Know 2A 76
Hartcliffe Wlk. BS4: Know 2B 76
Hartcliffe Way BS3: Bedm 1J 75
BS13: Bis 1J 75
BS13: Hart 5K 75
Hart Cl. BS20: Pill 4J 45
Hartfield Av. BS6: Cot 7J 47
Hartgill Cl. BS13: Hart 7H 75
Hartington Pk. BS6: Redl 6H 47
Hartland BS22: Wor 2E 106
HARTLEY 4C 124
Hartley Cl. BS37: Chip S 5J 31
Harts Cft. BS37: Yate 2F 31
Hart's La. BS39: Hall 6J 139
Harts Paddock BA3: Mid N 3D 152
Harvest Cl. BS32: Brad S 5F 27
Harvest La. BS22: W Wick 4F 107
Harvest Way BS22: Wor 6E 84
Harvey Cl. BS22: Wor 7E 84
Harvey's La. BS5: St G 1H 63
Harwood Grn. BS22: Kew 1C 106
Harwood Ho. BS5: Bar H 2D 62
Harwood Sq. BS7: Hor 3A 48
Haselbury Gro. BS31: Salt 1J 97
Haskins Ct. BS30: Bar C 5E 64
Haslands BS48: Nail 2F 71
Haslemere Ind. Est. BS11: A'mth 5G 33
Hassage Hill BA2: Wel 5K 143
Hassell Dr. BS2: Bris 2C 62
Hastings Cl. BS3: Bedm 1J 75
Hastings Rd. BS3: Bedm 1J 75
Hatcher Cl. TA8: Bur S 3F 159
Hatches La. BS24: E Rols 2A 108
BS24: Lym 3F 145
Hatchet La. BS34: Stok G 3G 37
Hatchet Rd. BS34: Stok G 2F 37
Hatchmere BS35: T'bry 4B 12
Hatfield Bldgs. BA2: Bath 7J 7 (6D 100)
Hatfield Rd. BA2: Bath 1A 122
BS23: W Mare 4J 105
Hathaway Ho. *BS2: Bris 1K 61*
(off Dove St. Sth.)
Hatherley BS37: Yate 7E 30
Hatherley Rd. BS7: B'stn 4A 48
Hathway Wlk. BS5: E'tn 1C 62
Hatters Cl. BS36: Wint 7C 28
Hatters La. BS37: Chip S 5H 31
Havage Cl. TA9: High 3G 159
Havage Drove BS24: E Rols 4C 108
Haven, The BS15: K'wd 7C 50
Haversham Cl. BS22: W Mare 3B 106
Haverstock Rd. BS4: Wind H 6C 62
Haviland Gro. BA1: W'ton 7G 81
Haviland Ho. BS2: Bris 2K 5
Haviland Pk. BA1: W'ton 1H 99
Havory BA1: Bath 2E 100
Havyatt Bus. Pk. BS40: Wrin 3G 111
HAVYATT GREEN 6G 111
Havyatt Rd. BS40: L'frd, Wrin 4G 111
Hawarden Ter. BA1: Bath 2D 100
Hawburn Cl. BS4: Brisl 7F 63
Haweswater BS10: S'mead 5H 35
Haweswater Cl. BS30: Old C 3H 65
Hawke Rd. BS22: Kew 7C 84
Hawkesbury Rd. BS16: Fish 5G 49
Hawkesley Dr. BS34: Lit S 1F 37
(not continuous)
Hawkesworth Rd. BS37: Yate 3C 30
Hawkfield Bus. Pk. BS14: Hart 5K 75
Hawkfield Cl. BS14: Hart 5K 75
Hawkfield Rd. BS13: Hart 5K 75
Hawkfield Way BS14: Hart 5K 75
Hawkins Cl. BS30: Old C 5G 65
TA8: Bur S 1E 158
Hawkins Cres. BS32: Brad S 6F 27
Hawkins St. BS2: Bris 3J 5 (2B 62)
Hawkley Dr. BS32: Brad S 3F 27
Hawkridge Dr. BS16: Puck 3C 52
Hawksmoor Cl. BS14: H'gro 4C 76
Hawksmoor La. BS16: Stap 7G 37
Hawksworth Dr. BS15: Han 4K 63
BS22: Wor 7G 85
Haw La. BS32: Old D 3C 18
BS35: Olv 3C 18
Hawleys La. GL12: Crom 3C 14
Hawley Way TA8: Bur S 1E 158
Hawthorn Av. BS15: Han 4K 63
Hawthorn Cl. BS16: Puck 3C 52
BS20: P'head 3B 42
BS34: Pat 6A 26
Hawthorn Coombe BS22: Wor 1B 106
Hawthorn Cres. BS35: T'bry 2A 12
BS49: Yat 2G 87
Hawthorne Gdns. BS16: Stap H 4D 50
Hawthorne Ri. BS10: Bren 4J 35
Hawthornes, The BS16: Stap H 4D 50
Hawthorne St. BS4: Wind H 6C 62
Hawthorn Gdns. BS22: Wor 2B 106
Hawthorn Gro. BA2: C Down 3B 122
Hawthorn Hgts. BS22: Wor 1B 106
Hawthorn Hill BS22: Wor 2B 106
Hawthorn Pk. BS22: Wor 1C 106
Hawthorn Rd. BA3: Rads 4B 154
Hawthorns BS31: Key 5C 78
Hawthorns, The BS8: Clif 1C 4 (1J 61)
BS21: Clev 6C 54
Hawthorns La. BS31: Key 5C 78
Hawthorn Way BS34: Stok G 2G 37
BS48: Nail 7H 57
Hayboro Way BS39: Paul 2C 152
Haycombe BS14: H'gro 4B 76
Haycombe Crematorium BA2: Bath 7F 99
Haycombe Dr. BA2: Bath 6G 99
Haycombe La. BA2: Eng 1F 121
Haycroft Rd. BS34: Fil 4B 36
Hayden Cl. BA2: Bath 7D 6 (6A 100)
Haydock Cl. BS16: Down 6D 38
HAYDON 6K 153
Haydon Gdns. BS7: L'lze 3D 48
Haydon Ga. BA3: Hay 6K 153
Haydon Hill BA3: Hay 6K 153
Haydon Ind. Est. BA3: Hay 6K 153
Hayeley Dr. BS32: Brad S 1G 37
Hayes, The BS27: Ched 7D 150
Hayes Cl. BS2: Bris 2C 62
Hayes Ct. BS34: Pat 7D 26
Hayesfield Pk. BA2: Bath 7D 6 (6B 100)
HAYES PARK 4D 152
Hayes Pk. Rd. BA3: Mid N 4D 152
Hayes Pl. BA2: Bath 7E 6 (6B 100)
Hayes Rd. BA3: Mid N 4D 152
Hayeswood Rd. BA2: Tim 1B 140
Haygarth Ct. BA1: Bath 1F 7 (3B 100)
Hay Hill BA1: Bath 2F 7 (4B 100)
Hay La. BS40: Winf 5H 91
Hay Leaze BS37: Yate 2D 30
Hayleigh Ho. BS3: Bedm 5H 61
BS13: Hart 6J 75
Haymans Ct. *BS15: K'wd 6A 50*
(off Cherrytree Cres.)
Haymarket, The BS1: Bris 2F 5 (2K 61)
Haymarket Wlk. BS1: Bris 1F 5
Haynes La. BS16: Stap H 3B 50
Haythorne Ct. BS16: Stap H 3D 50
Haytor Pk. BS9: Stok B 2D 46
Hayward Cl. BS21: Clev 1C 68
Hayward Ind. Est. BS16: Soun 5B 50
Hayward Rd. BS5: Redf 2E 62
BS16: Stap H 4B 50
Haywood Cl. BS24: W Mare 4J 127
Haywood Gdns. BS24: W Mare 4J 127
Hazel Av. BS6: Redl 6H 47
Hazel Barrow BS40: Comp M 6A 136
Hazelbury Cl. BS48: Nail 7G 57
Hazelbury Dr. BS30: Old C 4G 65
Hazelbury Rd. BS14: H'gro 2E 76
BS48: Nail 1F 71
Hazel Cote Rd. BS14: Whit 6D 76
Hazel Cres. BS35: T'bry 3B 12
Hazeldene Rd. BS23: W Mare 4J 105
BS34: Pat 7C 26
Hazel Gdns. BS35: Alv 1H 19
Hazel Gro. BA2: Bath 7K 99
BA3: Mid N 6F 153
BS7: Hor 7C 36
Hazelgrove BS36: Wint 2B 38
Hazel La. BS35: Alv, Rudg 2F 19
Hazell Ct. BS21: Clev 1E 68
Hazel Ter. BA3: Mid N 6F 153
Hazelton Rd. BS7: B'stn 5K 47
Hazel Way BA2: Odd D 4K 121
Hazelwood Cl. BS16: Stap H 3D 50
Hazelwood Ct. BS9: Stok B 5D 46
Hazelwood Rd. BS9: Stok B 5D 46
Hazleton Gdns. BA2: Clav D 1H 123
Head Cft. BS48: Flax B 2F 73
Headford Av. BS5: St G 2K 63
Headford Rd. BS4: Know 1K 75
Headington Cl. BS15: Han 5B 64
Headland, The NP16: Bulw 1A 8
Headley Ct. BS13: Bis 4H 75
Headley La. BS13: Bis 4G 75
HEADLEY PARK 3H 75
Headley Pk. Av. BS13: Bis 4H 75
Headley Pk. Rd. BS13: Bis 3G 75
Headley Rd. BS13: Bis 4G 75
Headley Wlk. BS13: Bis 3H 75
Heal Cl. TA8: Bur S 3F 159
Healey Dr. SN14: Hin 2J 53
Heart Meers BS14: H'gro 5D 76
Heath Cl. BS36: Wint 1C 38
Heathcote Dr. BS36: Coal H 7H 29
Heathcote La. *BS36: Coal H 7H 29*
(off Boundary Rd.)
Heathcote Rd. BS16: Fish 6K 49
BS16: Stap H 3C 50
Heathcote Wlk. BS16: Fish 6A 50
Heath Ct. BS16: Down 1B 50
HEATH END 4B 14
Heather Av. BS36: Fram C 1F 39
Heather Cl. BS15: K'wd 1K 63
Heatherdene BS14: H'gro 3B 76
Heather Dr. BA2: Odd D 4K 121
Heathfield Cl. BA1: W'ton 7G 81
BS31: Key 5A 78
Heathfield Cres. BS14: Whit 6C 76
Heathfield Rd. BS48: Nail 7G 57
Heathfields BS16: Down 7B 38
Heathfield Way BS48: Nail 7G 57
Heath Gdns. BS16: Down 7B 38
BS36: Coal H 1G 39
Heathgate BS49: Yat 3H 87
Heath Gates *BS48: Nail 7H 57*
(off Heath Rd.)
Heathgates BS23: W Mare 1F 127
Heath Ho. La. BS16: Stap 4D 48
Heath Ridge BS41: L Ash 7A 60
Heath Ri. BS30: C Hth 4F 65
Heath Rd. BS5: Eastv 5D 48
BS15: Han 5K 63
BS16: Down 1B 50
BS48: Nail 6H 57
(not continuous)
Heath St. BS5: Eastv 5E 48
Heath Wlk. BS16: Down 1B 50
Heber St. BS5: Redf 2E 62
Hebron Rd. BS3: Bedm 6J 61
Hedge Cl. BS22: W Wick 3F 107
Hedgemead Cl. BS16: Stap 3F 49
Hedgemead Ct. *BA1: Bath 1G 7*
(off Margaret's Hill)
Hedgemead Vw. BS16: Stap 3G 49
Hedgerows, The BS32: Brad S 5F 27
Hedgers Cl. BS3: Bedm 7G 61
Hedges, The BS22: St Geo 2G 107
Hedges Cl. BS21: Clev 1B 68
Hedwick Av. BS5: St G 2G 63
Hedwick St. BS5: St G 2G 63
Heggard Cl. BS13: Bis 5G 75
Helens Rd. BS25: Sandf 1H 131
Helicopter Mus., The 7C 106
Heligan Wlk. BS24: W'ton V 5C 106
Hellier Wlk. BS13: Hart 7J 75
Helston Rd. BS48: Nail 1J 71
HEMINGTON 7H 155
Hemmings Pde. BS5: Bar H 2D 62
Hemming Way BS24: Hut 2C 128
Hemplow Cl. BS14: Stoc 3F 77
Hempton La. BS32: Alm 4C 26
Henacre Rd. BS11: Law W 7K 33
HENBURY 5E 34
Henbury Ct. BS10: Hen 4E 34
Henbury Gdns. BS10: Hen 5E 34
Henbury Hill BS9: W Trym 7F 35
Henbury Leisure Cen. 4E 34
Henbury Rd. BS9: W Trym 7F 35
BS10: Hen 5E 34
BS15: Han 4K 63
Hencliffe Rd. BS14: Stoc 3F 77
Hencliffe Way BS15: Han 6K 63
Hencliffe Wood 7K 63
Henderson Rd. BS15: Han 4K 63
Hendon Cl. TA9: High 3G 159
Hendre Rd. BS3: Bedm 7G 61
HENFIELD 4H 39
Henfield Bus. Pk. BS36: H'fld 5H 39
Henfield Cres. BS30: Old C 5F 65
Henfield Rd. BS36: Coal H, H'fld 3G 39
Hengaston St. BS3: Bedm 7H 61
HENGROVE 4D 76
Hengrove Av. BS14: H'gro 2D 76
Hengrove La. BS14: H'gro 2C 76
Hengrove Leisure Pk. BS14: H'gro 4A 76
Hengrove Rd. BS4: Know 7C 62
Hengrove Way BS13: Bis 4H 75
BS14: H'gro 4K 75
HENLEAZE 2H 47
Henleaze Av. BS9: Henle 3G 47
Henleaze Gdns. BS9: Henle 3G 47
Henleaze Pk. BS9: Henle 3J 47
Henleaze Pk. Dr. BS9: Henle 2H 47
Henleaze Rd. BS9: Henle 3G 47
Henleaze Ter. BS9: Henle 1H 47
Henley Gro. BS9: Henle 3H 47
Henley La. BS49: Yat 4K 87
SN13: Kings 1F 103
Henley Lodge BS49: Yat 4K 87
Henley Pk. BS49: Yat 4J 87
Henley Vw. BA2: Wel 4K 143
Hennessy Cl. BS14: Whit 7B 76
Henrietta Ct. BA2: Bath 1H 7 (3C 100)
Henrietta Gdns. BA2: Bath 2H 7 (4C 100)
Henrietta M. BA2: Bath 3H 7 (4C 100)
Henrietta Pl. BA2: Bath 3G 7 (4C 100)
Henrietta Rd. BA2: Bath 2H 7 (4C 100)
Henrietta St. BA2: Bath 3H 7 (4C 100)
BS2: Bris 1D 4 (1J 61)
BS5: E'tn 7D 48
Henrietta Vs. BA2: Bath 2H 7 (4C 100)
Henry Butt Ho. *BS23: W Mare 4G 105*
(off Boulevard)
Henry Ho. BS13: Withy 6F 75
Henry St. BA1: Bath 5G 7 (5C 100)
BS3: Wind H 5B 62
Henry Williamson Ct. BS30: Bar C 4D 64
Henshaw Cl. BS15: K'wd 6A 50
Henshaw Rd. BS15: K'wd 6A 50
Henshaw Wlk. BS15: K'wd 6A 50
Hensley Gdns. BA2: Bath 7A 100

Hensley Rd.—Hollowpit La.

Hensley Rd. BA2: Bath 7A **100**
Hensman's Hill BS8: Clif 3G **61**
Hepburn Rd. BS2: Bris 1A **62**
Herald Cl. BS9: Stok B 3D **46**
Herapath St. BS5: Bar H 3E **62**
Herbert Cres. BS5: Eastv 5F **49**
Herbert Rd. BA2: Bath 7A **6** (6K **99**)
BS21: Clev 5D **54**
TA8: Bur S 7C **156**
Herbert St. BS3: Bedm 5J **61**
(not continuous)
BS5: W'hall 1E **62**
Hercules Cl. BS34: Lit S 1F **37**
Hereford Rd. BS2: Bris 6C **48**
Hereford St. BS3: Bedm 6K **61**
Heritage, The BA2: Cam 5J **141**
Heritage Cl. BA2: Pea J 5D **142**
Herkomer Cl. BS7: L'lze 1D **48**
Herluin Way BS22: W Mare 5B **106**
BS23: W Mare 6J **105**
Hermes Cl. BS31: Salt 1H **97**
Hermitage Cl. BS11: Shire 1J **45**
Hermitage Rd. BA1: Bath 2A **100**
BS16: Stap H 3B **50**
Hern La. BS48: Bar G 5J **73**
Heron Cl. BS22: W Mare 3C **106**
Heron Gdns. BS20: P'head 4G **43**
Heron Pk. TA8: Berr 7A **144**
Heron Rd. BS5: E'tn 7D **48**
HERONS GREEN 2C **136**
Heron Way BS37: Chip S 7F **31**
Herridge Cl. BS13: Hart 6H **75**
Herridge Rd. BS13: Hart 6H **75**
Herschel Mus. of Astronomy, The 4E **6** (5B **100**)
Herschel Pl. BA2: Bath 2J **7** (4C **100**)
Hersey Gdns. BS13: Withy 7E **74**
Hesding Cl. BS15: Han 6A **64**
Hestercombe Cl. BS24: W'ton V 5C **106**
Hestercombe Rd. BS13: Bis 4H **75**
Hester Wood BS37: Yate 2F **31**
Hetling Ct. BA1: Bath 5F **7** (5B **100**)
HEWISH 6B **86**
Hewlands Ct. BS11: Law W 5C **34**
Hexagon, The BA2: Odd D 3A **122**
Heyford Av. BS5: Eastv 4D **48**
Heyron Wlk. BS13: Hart 6H **75**
Heywood Rd. BS20: Pill 4G **45**
Heywood Ter. BS20: Pill 4G **45**
Hiatt Baker Hall BS9: Stok B 4F **47**
Hicking Ct. BS15: K'wd 7B **50**
Hickory La. BS32: Alm 1F **27**
Hicks Av. BS16: Emer G 7F **39**
Hick's Barton BS5: St G 1H **63**
HICKS COMMON 1D **38**
Hicks Comn. Rd. BS36: Wint 3C **38**
Hicks Ct. BS5: St G 1H **63**
BS30: L Grn 5D **64**
HICKS GATE 2K **77**
Hicks Ga. Ho. BS31: Key 2K **77**
Hidcote M. BS24: W'ton V 5C **106**
Hide Mkt. BS2: Bris 3K **5** (2B **62**)
High Acre BS39: Paul 2D **152**
Higham St. BS4: Wind H 5B **62**
High Bannerdown BA1: Bathe 6K **83**
HIGHBRIDGE 5F **159**
Highbridge & Burnham Station (Rail) 5G **159**
Highbridge Quay TA9: High 5F **159**
Highbridge Rd. TA8: Bur S 2D **158**
Highburn Cl. TA8: Bur S 4E **158**
Highbury Farm Bus. Pk.
BS39: Hall 5J **139**
Highbury Pde. BS23: W Mare 3E **104**
Highbury Pl. BA1: Bath 2C **100**
Highbury Rd. BS3: Bedm 1J **75**
BS7: Hor 1B **48**
BS23: W Mare 3E **104**
BS39: Hall 5K **139**
Highbury Ter. BA1: Bath 2C **100**
Highbury Vs. *BA1: Bath* *2C* ***100***
(off Highbury Pl.)
BS2: Bris 1C **4** (1J **61**)
High Cnr. BS10: Hen 6F **35**
High Cft. BS30: Old C 3G **65**
Highdale Av. BS21: Clev 6D **54**
Highdale Cl. BS14: Whit 6D **76**
Highdale Rd. BS21: Clev 6D **54**
High Elm BS15: K'wd 3C **64**
Highett Dr. BS5: E'tn 7C **48**
Highfield Av. BS15: Han 4B **64**
Highfield Cl. BA2: Bath 6H **99**
Highfield Dr. BS20: P'head 5A **42**
Highfield Gdns. BS30: Bit 7G **65**
Highfield Gro. BS7: Hor 3K **47**
Highfield La. BS40: Comp M 7A **136**
Highfield Rd. BA2: Pea J 5C **142**
BA15: Brad A 5H **125**
BS24: W Mare 4J **127**
BS31: Key 1D **96**
BS37: Chip S 5G **31**
Highfields BA3: Rads 4H **153**
BS39: Stan D 3B **116**
Highfields Cl. BS34: Stok G 4H **37**
High Gro. BS9: Sea M 2B **46**
Highgrove St. BS4: Wind H 5C **62**
Highgrove Wlk. BS24: W'ton V 4E **106**
High Kingsdown BS2: Bris 1D **4** (1J **61**)
Highland Cl. BS22: W Mare 2K **105**
Highland Cres. BS8: Clif 6G **47**
Highland Pl. BS8: Clif 6G **47**
Highland Rd. BA2: Bath 6H **99**
Highlands La. BS24: W'ton V 4E **106**
Highland Sq. BS8: Clif 6G **47**
Highlands Rd. BS20: P'head 3D **42**
BS41: L Ash 7A **60**
Highland Ter. BA2: Bath 5A **6** (5K **99**)
High La. BS36: Wint 6A **28**
(not continuous)
Highleaze Rd. BS30: Old C 5G **65**
HIGH LITTLETON 4B **140**
Highmead Gdns. BS13: Withy 6E **74**
BS39: Bis S 2K **137**
High Mdws. BA3: Mid N 5D **152**
Highmore Ct. BS7: L'lze 1D **48**
Highmore Gdns. BS7: L'lze 1E **48**
Highnam Cl. BS34: Pat 5D **26**
High Pk. BS14: H'gro 1D **76**
BS39: Paul 7B **140**
Highpoint Ho. *BS15: K'wd* *7A* ***50***
(off Lodge Rd.)
HIGHRIDGE 5E **74**
Highridge Ct. BS13: Bis 3F **75**
Highridge Cres. BS13: Bis 5F **75**
Highridge Grn. BS13: Bis 3E **74**
Highridge Pk. BS13: Bis 4F **75**
Highridge Rd. BS3: Bedm 7H **61**
BS13: Bis, Withy 6E **74**
BS41: Dun 7C **74**
Highridge Wlk. BS13: Bis 3E **74**
High St. BA1: Bath 4G **7** (5C **100**)
BA1: Bathe 7H **83**
BA1: Bathf 1A **102**
BA1: W'ly 4B **82**
BA1: W'ton 1G **99**
BA2: Bath 5G **99**
BA2: B'ptn 2H **101**
BA2: F'frd 7K **123**
BA2: Tim 3F **141**
BA2: Wel 4K **143**
BA3: Mid N 5E **152**
BS1: Bris 3F **5** (2K **61**)
BS5: E'tn 7D **48**
BS8: Clif 6G **47**
BS9: W Trym 1G **47**
BS11: Shire 1H **45**
BS15: Han 4A **64**
BS15: K'wd 1C **64**
BS15: Warm 1F **65**
BS16: Stap H 4A **50**
BS20: P'bry 5B **44**
BS20: P'head 4F **43**
BS22: Wor 3C **106**
BS23: W Mare 4F **105**
(not continuous)
BS26: Axb 4H **149**
BS29: Ban 3J **129**
BS30: Bit 2J **79**
BS30: Doy 7F **53**
BS30: Old C 6G **65**
BS30: Wick 3C **66**
BS31: Key 4C **78**
BS31: Salt 7J **79**
BS35: T'bry 4K **11**
BS36: Wint 1B **38**
BS37: Chip S 5H **31**
BS37: Iron A 2H **29**
BS39: High L 4A **140**
BS39: Paul 7C **140**
(not continuous)
BS39: Pens 7F **95**
BS40: Blag 2B **134**
BS40: Chew M 1G **115**
BS40: E Harp 6K **137**
BS40: Winf 4K **91**
BS40: Wrin 1F **111**
BS48: Nail 7G **57**
BS49: Clav 2B **88**
BS49: Cong 7K **87**
BS49: Yat 2H **87**
GL12: Wickw 6G **15**
TA8: Bur S 2C **158**
High Vw. BA2: Bath 7D **6** (6A **100**)
BS20: P'head 4C **42**
Highview Rd. BS15: Soun 6C **50**
Highwall La. BS31: Q Char 2H **95**
Highway BS37: Yate 4F **31**
Highwood La. BS34: Pat 7H **25**
Highwood Pk. BS34: Pat 1A **36**
Highwood Rd. BS34: Pat 1A **36**
Highworth Cres. BS37: Yate 6D **30**
Highworth Rd. BS4: St Ap 4F **63**
Hilcot Gro. BS22: W Mare 3K **105**
Hildesheim Bri.
BS23: W Mare 5G **105**
Hildesheim Cl. BS23: W Mare 5H **105**
Hill, The BA2: F'frd 7A **124**
BS32: Alm 2D **26**
Hill Av. BA2: C Down 3B **122**
BS3: Wind H 6A **62**
Hillbrook Rd. BS35: T'bry 4B **12**
Hill Burn BS9: Henle 2J **47**
Hillburn Rd. BS5: St G 2J **63**
Hill Cl. BS16: Emer G 7F **39**
Hillcote BS24: W Mare 5K **127**
Hill Ct. BS39: Paul 7C **140**
HILLCREST 1F **117**
Hill Crest BS4: Know 1D **76**
BS49: Cong 6A **88**
Hillcrest BA2: Pea J 5C **142**
BS35: T'bry 3K **11**
BS39: Pens 1G **117**
Hillcrest Cl. BS48: Nail 1G **71**
Hillcrest Dr. BA2: Bath 7H **99**
Hillcrest Flats
BA15: Brad A 5J **125**
Hillcrest Rd. BS20: P'head 4A **42**
BS48: Nail 1G **71**
Hillcroft Cl. BS15: Han 5C **64**
BS22: W Mare 2J **105**
Hilldale Rd. BS48: Back 5K **71**
Hill Dr. BS8: Fail 6G **59**
HILLEND 3H **129**
Hill End BS22: Wor 1C **106**
Hill End Dr. BS10: Hen 4D **34**
HILLFIELD 7C **150**
Hillfield BS27: Ched 7D **150**
HILLFIELDS 5K **49**
Hillfields Av. BS16: Fish 6A **50**
Hill Gay Cl. BS20: P'head 4B **42**
Hill Gro. BS9: Henle 2J **47**
Hillgrove St. BS2: Bris 1A **62**
Hillgrove St. Nth. BS2: Bris 1K **61**
Hillgrove Ter. BS23: Uph 4F **127**
Hillhouse BS9: Sea M 2C **46**
BS16: Stap H 4D **50**
Hill Ho. Rd. BS16: Stap H 2D **50**
Hillier's La. BS25: C'hll 1K **131**
Hill La. BS20: Wes 7B **42**
BS21: Tic 5J **55**
BS25: Row 4C **132**
TA9: Bre K, E Brnt 5J **157**
Hill Lawn BS4: Brisl 6F **63**
Hill Lea Gdns. BS27: Ched 6D **150**
Hillmead BS40: L'frd 7C **110**
Hillmer Ri. BS29: Ban 2K **129**
Hill Moor BS21: Clev 7E **54**
Hill Pk. BS49: Cong 6A **88**
Hill Path BS29: Ban 3B **130**
Hill Rd. BS21: Clev 5C **54**
BS22: Wor 2C **106**
BS23: W Mare 4H **105**
BS25: Sandf 2F **131**
BS41: Dun 1D **92**
Hill Rd. E. BS22: Wor 2C **106**
Hills Barton BS13: Bis 1G **75**
Hillsborough Flats BS8: Clif 3G **61**
Hillsborough Gdns. TA8: Bur S 6D **156**
Hillsborough Ho. BS23: W Mare 1J **127**
Hillsborough Rd. BS4: Brisl 5E **62**
Hills Cl. BS31: Key 5E **78**
Hillsdon Rd. BS9: W Trym 7F **35**
HILLSIDE
BA3 6C **152**
BS26 4J **149**
Hillside BS6: Cot 1J **61**
BS8: Clif 4A **4** (3H **61**)
BS16: Mang 3D **50**
BS20: P'bry 5B **44**
BS26: Axb 4J **149**
Hillside Av. BA3: Mid N 6C **152**
BS15: K'wd 1A **64**
Hillside Cl. BS36: Fram C 7G **29**
BS39: Paul 7D **140**
Hillside Cotts. BA2: Mid 6D **122**
Hillside Ct. BS5: St G 2K **63**
Hillside Cres. BA3: Mid N 6C **152**
Hillside Gdns. BS22: W Mare 3K **105**
BS39: Bis S 2J **137**
Hillside La. BS36: Fram C 7G **29**
Hillside Rd. BA2: Bath 7K **99**
BA3: Mid N 6D **152**
BS5: St G 2J **63**
BS20: P'head 4A **42**
BS21: Clev 6D **54**
BS24: B'don 5K **127**
BS41: L Ash 7B **60**
BS48: Back 5J **71**
Hillside St. BS4: Wind H 5C **62**
Hillside Vw. BA2: Pea J 5C **142**
BA3: Mid N 4E **152**
Hillside W. BS24: Hut 2D **128**
Hill St. BS1: Bris 3C **4** (2J **61**)
BS3: Wind H 5B **62**
BS5: St G 1H **63**
BS15: K'wd 1D **64**
Hilltop BS20: P'head 4C **42**
Hilltop Gdns. BS5: St G 2J **63**
BS16: Soun 6B **50**
(not continuous)
Hilltop Rd. BS16: Soun 6B **50**
Hilltop Vw. BS5: St G 2J **63**
Hill Vw. BA2: Mark 3F **119**
BS8: Clif 4A **4** (3H **61**)
BS9: Henle 2J **47**
BS16: Emer G 7E **38**
BS16: Soun 6B **50**
BS34: Fil 4C **36**
Hillview BA2: Tim 4F **141**
BA3: Mid N 7C **152**
TA8: Brean 4A **144**
Hillview Av. BS21: Clev 7D **54**
Hill Vw. Cvn. Pk. BS40: F'tn 2F **91**
Hill Vw. Cl. BS30: Old C 5G **65**
Hill Vw. Ct. BS22: W Mare 4B **106**
Hillview Gdns. BS40: F'tn 3G **91**
Hill Vw. Ho. *BS15: K'wd* *7A* ***50***
(off Lodge Rd.)
Hillview Pk. Homes
BS22: W Mare 4B **106**
Hill Vw. Rd. BA1: Bath 1D **100**
BS13: Bis 2G **75**
BS23: W Mare 5J **105**
Hillview Rd. BS16: Puck 3C **52**
BS26: Lox 2G **147**
Hillyfield Rd. BS13: Bis 4G **75**
Hillyfields BS25: Wins 5H **131**
Hillyfields Way BS25: Wins 5G **131**
Hilton Ct. BS5: E'tn 1D **62**
Hinckley Cl. BS22: St Geo 1G **107**
Hind Pitts BS25: S'ham 6A **132**
HINTON 2J **53**
Hinton BS24: W Mare 3J **127**
HINTON BLEWETT 7A **138**
Hinton Cl. BA2: Bath 5F **99**
BS31: Salt 7J **79**
Hinton Dr. BS30: Old C 3G **65**
Hinton La. BS8: Clif 3F **61**
Hinton Rd. BS5: E'tn 7E **48**
BS16: Fish 4J **49**
BS16: Puck 2D **52**
Hippisley Dr. BS26: Axb 4K **149**
Hiscocks Ct. BA2: New L 5B **98**
Hiscocks Dr. BA2: Bath 7A **100**
Hither Bath Bri. BS4: Brisl 2E **76**
Hither Grn. BS21: Clev 7F **55**
Hither Grn. Ind. Est. BS21: Clev 7F **55**
Hither Mead BS36: Fram C 1F **39**
Hi-Ways Cvn. Pk. BS10: H'len 3B **34**
HMP Bristol BS7: B'stn 4K **47**
Hobart Rd. BS23: W Mare 2H **127**
Hobbiton Rd. BS22: Wor 6E **84**
Hobbs Ct. BS48: Nail 7H **57**
Hobbs La. BS1: Bris 4D **4** (3J **61**)
BS30: Sis 7F **51**
BS48: Bar G 6J **73**
HOBB'S WALL 7C **118**
Hobb's Wall BA2: F'boro 7C **118**
Hobhouse Cl. BA15: Brad A 7J **125**
BS9: Henle 1J **47**
Hobwell La. BS41: L Ash 7C **60**
Hockey's La. BS16: Fish 4J **49**
Hockley Ct. BA1: W'ton 2K **99**
Hodden La. BS16: Puck 3C **52**
Hodshill BA2: S'ske 6B **122**
Hogarth M. BS22: Wor 1E **106**
Hogarth Wlk. BS7: L'lze 7D **36**
BS22: Wor 1E **106**
Hogues Wlk. BS13: Hart 6H **75**
Holbeach Way BS14: Whit 7C **76**
Holbrook BS39: Stan D 2C **116**
HOLBROOK COMMON 1B **66**
Holbrook Cres. BS13: Hart 6K **75**
Holbrook La. BS30: Wick 2A **66**
Holburne Mus. of Art 2J **7** (4D **100**)
Holcombe BS14: H'gro 5C **76**
Holcombe Cl. BA2: B'ptn 2H **101**
Holcombe Grn. BA1: W'ton 1H **99**
(not continuous)
Holcombe Gro. BS31: Key 5B **78**
Holcombe La. BA2: B'ptn 2H **101**
Holcombe Va. BA2: B'ptn 2H **101**
Holdenhurst Rd. BS15: K'wd 7A **50**
Holders Wlk. BS41: L Ash 2K **73**
Holford Cl. BS48: Nail 1G **71**
Holford Ct. BS14: Whit 5D **76**
Holiday Resort Unity at Unity Farm
TA8: Berr 6B **144**
Holland Rd. BA1: Bath 2D **100**
BS21: Clev 1B **68**
Holland St. BS23: W Mare 4J **105**
Hollidge Gdns. BS3: Bedm 5K **61**
Hollies, The BA3: Mid N 5E **152**
BS15: K'wd 3C **64**
BS16: Stap 3G **49**
Hollies La. BA1: Bathe 3H **83**
Hollis Av. BS20: P'head 5E **42**
Hollis Cl. BS41: L Ash 1A **74**
Hollis Cres. BS20: P'head 5E **42**
Hollister's Dr. BS13: Hart 7K **75**
Hollow, The BA2: Bath 7G **99**
BA2: Dunk 7D **120**
Holloway BA2: Bath 7E **6** (6B **100**)
Holloway La.
BS25: Row, S'ham 5C **132**
Holloway Rd. BS35: Sev B 2C **24**
HOLLOW BROOK 6J **115**
Hollowbrook La. BS39: Bis S 6J **115**
BS40: Chew M 6J **115**
Hollow La. BS22: Wor 1D **106**
Hollow Marsh La. BS39: Hin B 7B **138**
Hollowmead BS49: Clav 3A **88**
Hollowmead Cl. BS49: Clav 3B **88**
Hollowpit La. BA3: Hem 7G **155**

Ivy Ter.—Kingsley Pl.

Ivy Ter. BA15: Brad A 5H 125
BS37: W'lgh 3B 40
Ivy Vs. BA2: Bath 7J 99
Ivy Wlk. BA3: Mid N 6F 153
BS29: Ban 1J 129
Ivywell Rd. BS9: Stok B 5E 46
IWOOD 1C 110
Iwood La. BS40: Iwood 3C 110

J

Jack Knight Ho. BS7: Hor 3B 48
Jack Price Cl. BS13: Hart 7J 75
Jackson Cl. BS35: Piln 6D 16
Jacob Bldg., The BS8: Clif 3A 4 (2H 61)
Jacob Ct. BS2: Bris 3K 5 (2B 62)
Jacobs Ct. BS1: Bris 5C 4
Jacob's Ladder 6E 150
Jacob's Mdw. BS20: P'head 4H 43
Jacob's Tower 6E 150
Jacob St. BS2: Bris 3J 5 (2B 62)
(Hawkins St.)
BS2: Bris 3H 5 (2A 62)
(Tower Hill)
Jacob's Wells Rd. BS8: Clif 4A 4 (3H 61)
Jamaica St. BS2: Bris 1F 5 (1A 62)
James Cl. BS16: Soun 4C 50
James Rd. BS16: Soun 5C 50
James St. BS2: Bris 6C 48
BS5: E'tn 1K 5 (1B 62)
James St. W. BA1: Bath 4D 6 (5A 100)
Jane Austen Cen. 3F 7
Jane St. BS5: E'tn 2D 62
Jarratts Rd. BS10: S'mead 5K 35
Jarvis St. BS5: Bar H 3D 62
Jasmine Cl. BS22: Wor 3E 106
TA9: High 4F 159
Jasmine Gro. BS11: Law W 5C 34
Jasmine La. BS49: Clav 7B 70
Jasmine Way BS24: W'ton V 3E 106
Jasper St. BS3: Bedm 6H 61
Jaycroft Rd. TA8: Bur S 2D 158
Jays, The GL12: Tyth 6F 13
Jays Cl. BS15: K'wd 3B 64
Jay Vw. BS23: W Mare 7J 105
Jean Rd. BS4: Brisl 7G 63
Jeffery Ct. BS30: C Hth 3F 65
JEFFRIES HILL 4K 63
Jeffries Hill Bottom BS15: St G 4K 63
Jekyll Cl. BS16: Stap 7G 37
Jellicoe Av. BS16: Stap 7G 37
Jellicoe Ct. BS22: Wor 7C 84
Jena Ct. BS31: Salt 7H 79
Jenner Cl. BS37: Chip S 6K 31
Jennings Ct. BS3: Bris 7A 4
Jenny La. BS10: S'mead 5K 35
Jersey Av. BS4: Brisl 5H 63
Jesmond Rd. BS21: Clev 6C 54
BS22: St Geo 7G 85
Jesse Hughes Ct. BA1: Bath 1E 100
Jessop Ct. BS1: Bris 5G 5 (3A 62)
Jessop Cres. BS10: W Trym 6G 35
Jessop Underpass BS3: Ash G 5F 61
Jews La. BA2: Bath 5J 99
BS25: C'hll 1B 132
Jill's Garden 4F 105
Jim O'Neil Ho. BS11: Shire 1H 45
Jinty La. BS16: Sis 6F 51
Jobbins Cl. BS37: Chip S 6G 31
Jocelin Dr. BS22: Wor 7D 84
Jocelyn Rd. BS7: Hor 1B 48
Jockey La. BS5: St G 2J 63
John Cabot Ct. BS1: Bris 6A 4 (4G 61)
John Carr's Ter. BS8: Clif 4B 4 (3H 61)
John Cozens Ho. BS2: Bris 2K 5
John James Ct. BS7: L'lze 1D 48
Johnny Ball La. BS2: Bris 2E 4 (2K 61)
John Rennie Cl. *BA15: Brad A 7H 125*
(off Moulton Dr.)
John Repton Gdns. BS10: Bren 5H 35
John Slessor Ct. BA1: Bath 1F 7 (3B 100)
Johnson Dr. BS30: Bar C 4D 64
Johnson Rd. BS16: Emer G 2G 51
Johnsons La. BS5: W'hall 7F 49
Johnsons Rd. BS5: W'hall 7E 48
Johnstone St. BA2: Bath 4H 7 (5C 100)
John St. BA1: Bath 3F 7 (4B 100)
BS1: Bris 3F 5 (2K 61)
BS2: Bris 6C 48
BS15: K'wd 1A 64
TA8: Bur S 1C 158
TA9: High 5F 159
John Wesley Rd. BS5: St G 3K 63
BS15: St G 3K 63
John Wesley's Chapel 2G 5 (2A 62)
Jones Cl. BS49: Yat 2F 87
Jones Hill BA15: Brad A 7F 125
Jordan Wlk. BS32: Brad S 6F 27
Jorrocks Ind. Est. BS37: W'lgh 3C 40
Joyce Cl. BS7: Hor 7C 36
Joy Hill BS8: Clif 3F 61
Jubilee Cotts. BS13: Bis 2F 75
Jubilee Cres. BS16: Mang 1E 50
Jubilee Dr. BS8: Fail 5F 59
BS35: T'bry 3B 12
Jubilee Gdns. BS37: Yate 4G 31
Jubilee Ho. BS34: Lit S 6E 26
Jubilee La. BS40: L'frd 6C 110
GL12: Crom 5A 14
Jubilee Path BS22: W Mare 3A 106
Jubilee Pl. BS1: Bris 6F 5 (4K 61)
BS15: K'wd 2E 64
BS21: Clev 1D 68
Jubilee Rd. BA3: Rads 5H 153
BS2: Bris 7C 48
BS4: Know 7E 62
BS5: St G 2H 63
BS15: Soun 5C 50
BS23: W Mare 5G 105
BS26: Axb 4J 149
Jubilee Row *BS2: Bris 7C 48*
(off Ashley St.)
Jubilee St. BS2: Bris 4K 5 (3B 62)
TA8: Bur S 2D 158
Jubilee Swimming Pool 7D 62
Jubilee Ter. BS39: Paul 7C 140
Jubilee Way BS11: A'mth 5F 33
BS22: St Geo 1G 107
Julian Cl. BS9: Stok B 5E 46
Julian Cotts. BA2: Mon C 3G 123
Julian Ct. BS9: Stok B 5E 46
Julian Rd. BA1: Bath 1E 6 (3B 100)
BS9: Stok B 5E 46
Julian's Acres TA8: Berr 2B 156
Julier Ho. BA1: Bath 1G 7
Julius Cl. BS16: Emer G 2G 51
Julius Rd. BS7: B'stn 5K 47
Junction Av. BA2: Bath 7C 6 (6A 100)
Junction Rd. BA2: Bath 6C 6 (6A 100)
BA15: Brad A 6H 125
Junction Way BS16: Soun 5E 50
Juniper Ct. BS5: Eastv 6E 48
Juniper Pl. BS22: Wor 7D 84
Juniper Way BS32: Brad S 7H 27
Jupiter Rd. BS34: Pat 7K 25
Justice Av. BS31: Salt 7J 79
Justice Rd. BS16: Fish 5H 49
Jutland Rd. BS11: A'mth 6F 33

K

Karen Cl. BS48: Back 6J 71
Karen Dr. BS48: Back 5J 71
Kathdene Gdns. BS7: Bris 5B 48
Kaynton Mead BA1: Bath 5H 99
Keats Cl. BS7: Hor 7C 36
Keats Rd. BA3: Rads 6F 153
Keble Av. BS13: Withy 6F 75
Keed's La. BS41: L Ash 7J 59
Keedwell Hill BS41: L Ash 1K 73
Keel Cl. BS5: St G 3H 63
Keel's Hill BA2: Pea J 5C 142
Keene's Way BS21: Clev 7C 54
Keen's Gro. BS35: Piln 6C 16
Keep, The BS22: Wor 1E 106
BS30: Old C 4H 65
Keepers La. BS7: Bris 5B 48
Keg Store, The BS1: Bris 4G 5 (3A 62)
Keinton Wlk. BS10: Hen 5G 35
Kelbra Cres. BS36: Fram C 1F 39
Kellaway Av. BS6: B'stn, Hor 3J 47
BS7: Hor 3J 47
Kellaway Cres. BS9: Henle 2K 47
Kellways BS48: Back 6J 71
Kelso Pl. BA1: Bath 3A 6 (4K 99)
KELSTON 7C 80
Kelston Cl. BS31: Salt 7H 79
BS37: Yate 7D 30
Kelston Gdns. BS10: W Trym 7K 35
BS22: Wor 6F 85
Kelston Gro. BS15: Han 3C 64
Kelston M. BS10: W Trym 7K 35
Kelston Rd. BA1: Bath 2E 98
BS10: W Trym 7K 35
BS22: Wor 7F 85
BS31: Key 5B 78
Kelston Vw. BA2: Bath 6F 99
BS31: Salt 7H 79
Kelston Wlk. BS16: Fish 4A 50
Kelting Gro. BS21: Clev 7F 55
Kemble Cl. BS15: K'wd 3C 64
BS48: Nail 1J 71
Kemble Gdns. BS11: Shire 3J 45
Kemm Cl. BS27: Ched 7H 151
Kemperleye Way BS32: Brad S 7F 27
Kempes Cl. BS41: L Ash 7A 60
Kempe Way BS24: W'ton V 5C 106
Kempthorne La. BA2: Odd D 3A 122
Kempton Cl. BS16: Down 6D 38
BS35: T'bry 1K 11
Kencot Wlk. BS13: Withy 7H 75
Kendall Cl. BS37: Yate 5B 30
Kendall Gdns. BS16: Stap H 4B 50
Kendall Rd. BS16: Stap H 4B 50
Kendal Rd. BS7: Hor 1C 48
KENDLESHIRE 4E 38
Kendon Dr. BS10: Hor 1K 47
Kendon Way BS10: S'mead 7K 35
Kenilworth BS37: Yate 6F 31
Kenilworth Cl. BS31: Key 6B 78
Kenilworth Ct. *BA1: Bath 3D 100*
(off Longacre Ho.)
Kenilworth Dr. BS30: Will 7F 65
Kenilworth Rd. BS6: Cot 7J 47
Kenmare Rd. BS4: Know 1A 76
Kenmeade Cl. BS25: S'ham 5A 132
Kenmore Cres. BS7: Hor 6A 36
Kenmore Dr. BS7: Hor 6A 36
Kenmore Gro. BS7: Hor 6A 36
KENN 3F 69
Kennard Cl. BS15: K'wd 2A 64
Kennard Ri. BS15: K'wd 1A 64
Kennard Rd. BS15: K'wd 1A 64
Kennaway Path BS21: Clev 7E 54
Kennaway Rd. BS21: Clev 7D 54
Kenn Bus. Pk. BS21: Clev 2E 68
Kenn Cl. BS23: W Mare 7J 105
Kenn Ct. BS4: Know 3A 76
Kennedy Cl. TA9: High 4G 159
Kennedy Ho. BS37: Yate 5F 31
Kennedy Way BS37: Chip S, Yate 5E 30
Kennel La. BS26: Webb 3J 147
Kennel Lodge Rd. BS3: Bwr A 5E 60
BS41: L Ash 5D 60
Kenn Est. BS21: Kenn 5E 68
Kennet Gdns. BA15: Brad A 7H 125
Kenneth Rd. BS4: Brisl 7F 63
Kennet Pk. BA2: B'ptn 2G 101
Kennet Rd. BS31: Key 6E 78
Kennet Way BS35: T'bry 4B 12
Kennford BS22: Wor 2D 106
Kennington Av. BS7: B'stn 4A 48
BS15: K'wd 7B 50
Kennington Rd. BA1: Bath 4H 99
Kennion Rd. BS5: St G 2J 63
Kennmoor Cl. BS30: C Hth 3E 64
Kenn Moor Dr. BS21: Clev 1E 68
Kenn Moor Rd. BS49: Yat 2H 87
Kennmoor Rd. BS21: Clev, Kenn 3G 69
Kenn Rd. BS5: St G 2J 63
BS21: Clev, Kenn 1D 68
Kenn St. BS21: Kenn 4F 69
Kensal Av. BS3: Wind H 6A 62
Kensal Rd. BS3: Wind H 6A 62
Kensington Cl. BS35: T'bry 2K 11
Kensington Ct. BA1: Bath 2D 100
BS8: Clif 2G 61
Kensington Gdns. BA1: Bath 2D 100
KENSINGTON HILL 7F 63
KENSINGTON PARK 6E 62
Kensington Pk. BS5: E'tn 7C 48
Kensington Pk. Rd. BS4: Brisl 7E 62
Kensington Pl. BA1: Bath 3D 100
BS8: Clif 2G 61
Kensington Rd. BS5: St G 1J 63
BS6: Redl 7J 47
BS16: Stap H 4B 50
BS23: W Mare 7H 105
Kent Av. BS24: W Wick 4G 107
BS37: Yate 3F 31
Kent Cl. BS34: Stok G 3F 37
Kent La. BA1: Up Swa 4D 82
Kent M. BS16: Stap 1G 49
Kenton M. BS9: Henle 3J 47
Kent Rd. BS7: B'stn 5A 48
BS49: Cong 6K 87
Kents Grn. BS15: K'wd 6C 50
Kentshare La. BS40: Winf 5A 92
Kent St. BS3: Bedm 6J 61
BS27: Ched 5D 150
Kent Way BS22: Wor 7F 85
Kenwood Cl. BS15: K'wd 7D 50
Keppel Cl. BS31: Salt 1H 97
Kerry Rd. BS4: Know 1A 76
Kersteman Rd. BS6: Redl 6J 47
Kestrel Cl. BS34: Pat 6A 26
BS35: T'bry 2B 12
BS37: Chip S 6F 31
Kestrel Ct. BS20: P'head 2G 43
Kestrel Dr. BS16: Puck 4C 52
BS22: W Mare 3C 106
Kestrel Pl. BA3: Mid N 6F 153
Keswick Wlk. BS10: S'mead 5J 35
Ketch Rd. BS3: Wind H 6B 62
Kew Rd. BS23: W Mare 3G 105
Kewside BS22: Kew 1K 105
KEWSTOKE 1K 105
Kewstoke Rd. BA2: C Down 2C 122
BS9: Stok B 4E 46
BS22: Kew 1H 105
BS23: W Mare 3D 104
Kew Wlk. BS4: Brisl 2E 76
Keyes Path BS22: Wor 7D 84
KEYNSHAM 4C 78
Keynsham By-Pass BS31: Key 2A 78
Keynsham Leisure Cen. 5D 78
Keynsham Rd. BS30: Will 4D 78
BS31: Key 4D 78
Keynsham Station (Rail) 4D 78
Key Point BS32: Brad S 2F 27
Keys Av. BS7: Hor 1B 48
Kidscove 6K 105
Kielder Dr. BS22: Wor 1D 106
Kilbirnie Rd. BS14: Whit 7C 76
Kilburn St. BS5: E'tn 1D 62
Kildare Rd. BS4: Know 1K 75
Kilkenny La. BA2: Eng, Ing 5E 120
Kilkenny Pl. BS20: P'head 2E 42
Kilkenny St. BS2: Bris 4K 5 (3B 62)
Killarney Av. TA8: Bur S 2D 158
Kilmersdon Rd. BA3: Hay, Kil, Rads 6J 153
BS13: Hart 6H 75
Kilminster Cl. BS34: Lit S 1F 37
Kilminster Rd. BS11: Shire 1H 45
Kiln Cl. BS15: K'wd 6K 49
Kiln Dr. TA9: High 5F 159
Kilnhurst Cl. BS30: L Grn 7D 64
Kiln Pk. BS23: W Mare 6J 105
Kilve BS24: W Mare 3H 127
Kilvert Cl. BS4: Brisl 4F 63
Kimber Cl. TA9: High 5F 159
Kimberley Av. BS16: Fish 3A 50
Kimberley Cl. BS16: Down 1D 50
Kimberley Cres. BS16: Fish 3A 50
Kimberley Rd. BS15: K'wd 7B 50
BS16: Fish 3A 50
(not continuous)
BS21: Clev 7C 54
Kinber Cl. BA1: W'ton 7G 81
Kinema Ho. *BS4: Brisl 5E 62*
(off Belmont Rd.)
King Alfred Sports Cen. 3E 158
King Alfred Way BA15: W'ley 5B 124
Kingcott Mill Farm Caravans
BS48: Flax B 2F 73
King Dick's La. BS5: St G 1H 63
KINGDOWN 6H 91
Kingdown La. BS40: Winf 5G 91
Kingdown Rd. BS40: Redh, Winf 7E 90
King Edward Cl. BS14: H'gro 4C 76
(not continuous)
King Edward Rd. BA2: Bath 7B 6 (6K 99)
Kingfisher Cl. BS10: Bren 3H 35
BS32: Brad S 4G 27
BS35: T'bry 2B 12
Kingfisher Ct. BA2: Lim S 6A 124
Kingfisher Dr. BA3: Mid N 6F 153
BS16: B'hll 2G 49
Kingfisher Rd. BS20: P'bry, P'head 1H 43
BS22: Wor 4D 106
BS37: Chip S 6G 31
King George V Pl. BS1: Bris 5E 4 (3K 61)
King Georges Rd. BA2: Bath 6J 99
BS13: Bis 5F 75
King John's Rd. BS15: K'wd 6K 49
King La. BS39: Clut 7H 117
King Rd. BS4: Know 1E 76
BS25: C'hll 6K 109
King Rd. Av. BS11: A'mth 5E 32
Kingrove Cres. BS37: Chip S 6J 31
Kingrove La. BS37: Chip S 7J 31
Kings Av. BS7: B'stn 4J 47
BS15: Han 5K 63
Kings Bus. Pk. BS2: Bris 3E 62
King's Chase Shop. Cen. BS15: K'wd 1B 64
Kingscote BS37: Yate 1D 40
Kingscote Pk. BS5: St G 3K 63
Kings Ct. BS2: Bris 1F 5 (1A 62)
BS13: Withy 6F 75
BS34: Lit S 1E 36
Kingscourt Cl. BS14: Whit 5C 76
Kings Cft. BS41: L Ash 1J 73
KINGSDOWN
BS2 1D 4 (1J 61)
SN13 1D 102
Kingsdown Gro. SN13: Kings 1D 102
Kingsdown Pde. BS6: Bris 1E 4 (1K 61)
Kingsdown Sports Cen. 1J 61
Kingsdown Vw. BA1: Bath 2C 100
Kings Dr. BS7: B'stn 3J 47
BS15: Han 5K 63
BS34: Stok G 3J 37
Kings Fld. BS37: Rang 5A 22
Kingsfield BA2: Bath 1J 121
BA15: Brad A 5H 125
Kingsfield Cl. BA15: Brad A 5H 125
Kingsfield Grange Rd. BA15: Brad A 5J 125
Kingsfield La. BS15: Han 4C 64
(not continuous)
BS30: L Grn 5C 64
Kings Head La. BS13: Bis 3E 74
KING'S HILL 7E 56
Kingshill BS48: Nail 7E 56
Kingshill Gdns. BS48: Nail 7E 56
Kingshill La. BS40: Chew S 7B 114
Kingshill Rd. BS4: Know 1D 76
Kingsholme Ct. BS23: W Mare 3G 105
Kingsholme Rd. BS15: K'wd 7B 50
Kingsholm Rd. BS10: S'mead 7K 35
Kingsland Cl. BS2: Bris 4K 5 (3C 62)
Kingsland Rd. BS2: Bris 3C 62
Kingsland Rd. Bri. BS2: Bris 4K 5 (3C 62)
Kingsland Trad. Est.
BS2: Bris 3K 5 (2B 62)
Kings La. BS16: Puck 3K 51
BS23: W Mare 4G 105
Kingsleigh Ct. BS15: K'wd 2D 64
Kingsleigh Gdns. BS15: K'wd 2D 64
Kingsleigh Pk. BS15: K'wd 2D 64
Kingsley Ho. BS2: Bris 4K 5 (3B 62)
Kingsley Pl. *BS3: Bris 5J 61*
(off Beauley Rd.)

Kingsley Rd.—Lawfords Ga.

Kingsley Rd. BA3: Rads 5G 153
BS5: E'tn 7E 48
BS6: Cot 6K 47
BS21: Clev 7D 54
BS23: W Mare 2H 127
Kingsmarsh Ho. BS5: E'tn 2D 62
Kingsmead BS48: Nail 7E 56
Kingsmead Ct. *BA1: Bath 5E 6*
(off Kingsmead Nth.)
Kingsmead E. BA1: Bath 5E 6 (5B 100)
Kingsmead Ho. BA1: Bath 4E 6
Kingsmead Nth. BA1: Bath 5E 6 (5B 100)
Kingsmead Rd. BS5: S'wll 7J 49
Kingsmead Sq. BA1: Bath 5F 7 (5B 100)
Kingsmead St. BA1: Bath 4F 7 (5B 100)
Kingsmead Ter. BA1: Bath 5F 7
Kingsmead Wlk. BS5: S'wll 7J 49
Kingsmead W. BA1: Bath 5E 6 (5B 100)
Kings M. BS6: Bris 1K 61
Kingsmill BS9: Stok B 3D 46
Kings Oak Mdw. BS39: Clut 3G 139
Kings of Wessex Leisure Cen. 7D 150
Kings Pde. Av. BS8: Clif 7H 47
Kings Pde. M. BS8: Clif 7G 47
Kings Pk. Av. BS2: Bris 3E 62
King Sq. BS2: Bris 1F 5 (1K 61)
(not continuous)
King Sq. Av. BS2: Bris 1F 5 (1K 61)
Kings Quarter Apartments BS1: Bris 1F 5
Kings Rd. BS4: Brisl 6E 62
BS8: Clif 2G 61
BS20: P'head 4B 42
BS21: Clev 4C 54
BS40: Wrin 3F 111
Kings Sq. BS30: Bit 2H 79
Kingston Av. BA15: Brad A 7J 125
BS21: Clev 6E 54
BS31: Salt 1G 97
Kingston Bldgs. *BA1: Bath 5G 7*
(off York St.)
Kingston Cl. BS16: Mang 1E 50
Kingston Dr. BS16: Mang 1E 50
BS48: Nail 2E 70
Kingston La. BS40: Winf 4J 91
Kingston Mead *BS40: Winf 4K 91*
(off Felton La.)
Kingston Pde. *BA1: Bath 5G 7*
(off York St.)
Kingston Rd. BA1: Bath 5G 7 (5C 100)
BA15: Brad A 6H 125
BS3: Bedm 5J 61
BS48: Nail 2E 70
KINGSTON SEYMOUR 1C 86
Kingston Way BS48: Nail 2E 70
Kingstree St. BS4: Wind H 5C 62
King St. BS1: Bris 5E 4 (3K 61)
BS5: E'tn 7E 48
BS11: A'mth 6E 32
BS15: K'wd 1K 63
TA9: High 5F 159
King's Wlk. BS13: Bis 3E 74
Kingsway BA2: Bath 1J 121
BS5: St G 2K 63
BS15: K'wd 1K 63
BS20: P'head 4B 42
BS34: Lit S 1E 36
Kingsway Av. BS5: St G 1K 63
BS15: K'wd 1K 63
Kingsway Cvn. Pk. BS20: P'head 2F 43
Kingsway Cres. BS15: K'wd 1A 64
Kingsway Pk. BS30: Warm 3F 65
Kingsway Rd. TA8: Bur S 1D 158
Kingsway Shop. Pct. BS5: St G 3K 63
Kingswear BS22: Wor 2E 106
Kingswear Rd. BS3: Know 1K 75
Kings Weston Av. BS11: Shire 1H 45
Kingsweston Down Nature Reserve . . . 6C 34
Kings Weston La.
BS11: A'mth, Law W 3G 33
Kings Weston Rd. BS10: Hen 1A 46
BS11: Law W 1A 46
KINGSWOOD 1B 64
Kingswood Douglas Est.
BS15: K'wd 2B 64
Kingswood Fountain Est.
BS15: K'wd 1A 64
Kingswood Hgts. BS15: K'wd 7B 50
Kingswood Heritage Mus. 3F 65
Kingswood Ind. Est.
BS30: L Grn 5D 64
Kingswood Leisure Cen. 5B 50
Kingswood Theatre 1A 100
Kingswood Trad. Est.
BS15: K'wd 7B 50
KINGTON 3G 11
Kington La. BS35: King, T'bry 3G 11
Kington Rd. BS35: King 1G 11
Kingwell Vw. BS39: High L 3B 140
King William Av.
BS1: Bris 5F 5 (3K 61)
King William St. BS3: Bedm 5H 61
Kinsale Rd. BS14: H'gro 3E 76
Kinsale Wlk. BS4: Know 1A 76
Kinvara Rd. BS4: Know 2A 76
Kinver Ter. TA8: Bur S 1C 158
Kipling Av. BA2: Bath 7B 100
Kipling Rd. BA3: Rads 5G 153
BS7: Hor 6D 36
BS23: W Mare 2J 127
Kirkby Rd. BS11: Law W 6A 34
Kirkstone Gdns. BS10: S'mead 5J 35
Kirtlington Rd. BS5: Eastv 5D 48
Kite Hay Cl. BS16: Stap 3G 49
Kites Cl. BS32: Brad S 4E 26
Kite Wlk. BS22: Wor 4C 106
Kitland La. BS40: L'frd 5D 110
Kitley Hill BA3: Mid N 2G 153
Knapp, The BS37: Yate 1F 31
Knapp La. GL12: Crom 1B 14
Knapp Rd. BS35: T'bry 4A 12
Knapps Cl. BS25: Wins 5F 131
Knapps Dr. BS25: Wins 5F 131
Knapps La. BS5: S'wll 6G 49
Kneller Cl. BS11: Law W 7A 34
Knight Cl. BS22: Wor 6E 84
KNIGHTCOTT 2J 129
Knightcott Gdns. BS29: Ban 2K 129
Knightcott Ind. Est. BS29: Ban 2J 129
Knightcott Pk. BS29: Ban 2A 130
Knightcott Rd. BS8: Abb L 1K 59
BS29: Ban 2J 129
Knighton Rd. BS10: S'mead 6A 36
Knights Acres BS29: Ban 2K 129
Knightsbridge Pk. BS13: Hart 6A 76
Knights Cl. BS9: Henle 2H 47
Knightstone C'way. BS23: W Mare 4E 104
Knightstone Cl. BA2: Pea J 5B 142
BS26: Axb 5J 149
Knightstone Ct. BS21: Clev 1D 68
BS23: W Mare 3F 105
TA8: Bur S 3D 158
Knightstone Gdns. BS23: W Mare 7F 105
Knightstone Ho. BS2: Bris 1D 4
BS23: W Mare 4F 105
(off Bristol Rd. Lwr.)
BS40: Chew M 1H 115
(off Bristol Rd. Lwr.)
Knightstone Lodge *BS6: Cot 7K 47*
(off Archfield Rd.)
Knightstone Mt. *BS5: St G 3J 63*
(off Nicholas La.)
Knightstone Pl. BA1: W'ton 2H 99
BS15: Han 6K 63
BS22: Wor 2D 106
Knightstone Ri. *BS5: St G 1H 63*
(off Summerhill Rd.)
Knightstone Rd. BS23: W Mare 4E 104
Knightstone Sq. BS14: H'gro 4E 76
Knightswood BS48: Nail 6F 57
Knightwood Rd. BS34: Stok G 2H 37
Knobsbury Hill BA3: Rads 7D 154
Knobsbury La. BA3: Writ 5C 154
Knole Cl. BS32: Alm 2B 26
Knole La. BS10: Bren 4G 35
Knole Pk. BS32: Alm 3B 26
Knoll, The BS20: P'head 1F 43
Knoll Ct. BS9: Stok B 5D 46
Knoll Hill BS9: Stok B 5D 46
Knoll Pk. TA8: Brean 4B 144
Knoll Vw. TA8: Bur S 7E 156
Knovill Cl. BS11: Law W 5B 34
KNOWLE 7D 62
KNOWLE HILL 5J 115
KNOWLE PARK 1D 76
Knowle Rd. BS4: Wind H 6B 62
Knowles Rd. BS21: Clev 7C 54
Knowsley Rd. BS16: Fish 5G 49
Kyght Cl. BS15: Warm 1E 64
Kylross Av. BS14: H'gro 5D 76
Kynges Mill Cl. BS16: B'hll 1J 49
Kyrle Gdns. BA1: Bathe 7H 83

L

Labbott, The BS31: Key 5C 78
Labourham Drove BS27: Ched 7H 151
Labourham Way BS27: Ched 7H 151
Laburnum Cl. BA3: Mid N 6D 152
Laburnum Ct. BS23: W Mare 5K 105
Laburnum Gro. BA3: Mid N 6D 152
BS16: Fish 4K 49
Laburnum Rd. BS15: Han 4A 64
BS23: W Mare 5J 105
Laburnum Ter. BA1: Bathe 7H 83
Laburnum Wlk. BS31: Key 7A 78
Lacey Rd. BS14: Stoc 4G 77
Lacock Dr. BS30: Bar C 4D 64
Ladd Cl. BS15: K'wd 2D 64
TA9: High 5F 159
Ladden Ct. BS35: T'bry 4A 12
Laddon Mead BS37: Yate 2D 30
Ladies Mile BS9: Stok B 7F 47
Ladman Gro. BS14: Stoc 4G 77
Ladman Rd. BS14: Stoc 4G 77
Ladycroft BS21: Clev 2A 68
Ladye Bay BS21: Clev 2D 54
Ladye Wake BS22: Wor 7D 84
Ladymead BS20: P'head 3H 43
Ladymeade BS48: Back 3J 71
Ladymead La. BS25: C'hll 1B 132
BS40: L'frd 1B 132
Ladysmith Rd. BS6: Henle 4H 47
Ladywell BS40: Wrin 2F 111
Laggan Gdns. BA1: Bath 2A 100
Lake La. GL12: Crom 3C 14
Lakemead Gdns. BS13: Withy 6F 75
Lakemead Gro. BS13: Bis 4F 75
Lake Rd. BS10: W Trym 1J 47
BS20: P'head 2E 42
Lake Shore BS13: Bis 4J 75
Lakeshore Dr. BS13: Bis 4J 75
Lakeside BS16: Fish 5G 49
TA9: High 4G 159
Lakeside Cl. BS40: Nem T 7G 113
Lakeside Ct. BS24: W'ton V 3F 107
Lake Vw. BS16: Fish 5H 49
Lakeview Cres. TA9: High 5G 159
Lake Vw. Rd. BS5: St G 1F 63
Lakewood Cres. BS10: W Trym 7H 35
Lakewood Rd. BS10: W Trym 7H 35
Lambert Pl. BS4: Know 4K 75
Lamb Hill BS5: St G 2H 63
Lambley Rd. BS5: St G 1G 63
Lambourn Cl. BS3: Wind H 6K 61
Lambourne Way BS20: P'head 4H 43
Lambourn Rd. BS31: Key 6E 78
LAMBRIDGE 2E 100
Lambridge Bldgs. BA1: Bath 1D 100
Lambridge Bldgs. M.
BA1: Bath 2E 100
(off St Saviours Rd.)
Lambridge Grange BA1: Bath 1E 100
Lambridge M. BA1: Bath 2E 100
Lambridge Pl. BA1: Bath 2E 100
Lambridge St. BA1: Bath 1E 100
(not continuous)
Lambrook Rd. BS16: Fish 4J 49
Lamb St. BS2: Bris 2K 5 (2B 62)
Lamington Cl. BS13: Bis 4F 75
Lamont Ho. BA1: Bath 1E 100
Lamord Ga. BS34: Stok G 2G 37
Lampards Bldgs.
BA1: Bath 1F 7 (3B 100)
Lampeter Rd. BS9: W Trym 1F 47
Lampley Rd. BS21: Kenn, Kings S 1C 86
Lampton Av. BS13: Hart 7A 76
Lampton Gro. BS13: Hart 7A 76
Lampton Rd. BS41: L Ash 1K 73
Lanaway Rd. BS16: Fish 2K 49
Lancashire Rd. BS7: B'stn 5A 48
Lancaster Cl. BS34: Stok G 3F 37
Lancaster Rd. BS2: Bris 6C 48
BS37: Yate 3E 30
Lancaster St. BS5: Redf 2E 62
Lancelot Rd. BS16: Stap 7G 37
Land, The BS36: Coal H 7G 29
Landemann Cir. BS23: W Mare 4G 105
Landemann Path BS23: W Mare 4G 105
Land La. BS49: Yat 4J 87
Landmark Ct. BS1: Bris 7C 4
Landrail Wlk. BS16: B'hll 2H 49
Landseer Av. BS7: L'lze 2D 48
Landseer Cl. BS22: Wor 1D 106
Landseer Rd. BA2: Bath 5H 99
Lane, The BS35: E Comp 4F 25
Lanercost Rd. BS10: S'mead 5J 35
Lanesborough Ri. BS14: Stoc 3F 77
Lanes End BS4: Brisl 1E 76
Laneys Drove BS24: Lock 7C 106
Langdale Ct. BS34: Pat 6C 26
Langdale Rd. BS16: Fish 4H 49
Langdon Rd. BA2: Bath 7H 99
Langdown Ct. BS14: Stoc 5G 77
Langfield Cl. BS10: Hen 4E 34
LANGFORD GREEN 2G 133
Langford La. BS40: Burr, L'frd 7G 111
Langford Pl. Gdns. BS40: L'frd 6F 111
Langford Rd. BS13: Bis 2F 75
BS23: W Mare 6J 105
BS40: L'frd 7D 110
Langford's La. BS39: High L 5A 140
Langford Way BS15: K'wd 2C 64
Langham Rd. BS4: Know 7E 62
Langhill Av. BS4: Know 3J 75
Langlands La. TA9: W Hunt 7D 158
Langley Cres. BS3: Ash V 1E 74
Langley Down La. BA3: Mid N 4A 152
Langley Mow BS16: Emer G 1F 51
Langley's La. BA3: C'tn, Mid N 6A 152
BS39: Paul 6A 152
Langport Gdns. BS48: Nail 2G 71
Langport Rd. BS23: W Mare 6G 105
LANGRIDGE 2A 82
Langridge La.
BA1: L'rdge, L'dwn 3H 81
Langthorn Cl. BS36: Fram C 7G 29
Langton Ct. BA2: New L 6B 98
Langton Ct. Rd. BS4: St Ap 4F 63
Langton Ho. BS2: Bris 2J 5
Langton Pk. BS3: Bedm 5J 61
Langton Rd. BS4: St Ap 4F 63
Langton Way BS4: St Ap 3H 63
LANSDOWN 4H 81
Lansdown BS37: Yate 6E 30
Lansdown (Park & Ride) 5J 81
Lansdown Cl. BA1: Bath 2A 100
BS15: K'wd 6B 50
Lansdown Cres. BA1: Bath 2B 100
BA2: Tim 3G 141
Lansdowne *BS16: Fren 6A 38*
(off Avon Ring Rd.)
Lansdowne Ct. BS5: E'tn 1C 62
Lansdown Gdns. BS22: Wor 6F 85
Lansdown Gro. BA1: Bath 1F 7 (3B 100)
Lansdown Gro. Ct. *BA1: Bath 3B 100*
(off Lansdown Gro.)
Lansdown Hgts. BA1: Bath 1B 100
Lansdown Ho. BS16: Soun 6B 50
Lansdown La. BA1: L'dwn, W'ton 1H 99
BS30: Upton C 1B 80
Lansdown Lawn Tennis &
Squash Racquets Club 2B 100
Lansdown M. BA1: Bath 3F 7 (4B 100)
Lansdown Pk. BA1: L'dwn 7A 82
Lansdown Pl. BS8: Clif 2G 61
BS16: Emer G 1F 51
BS39: High L 4A 140
Lansdown Pl. E. BA1: Bath 3B 100
Lansdown Pl. W. BA1: Bath 2B 100
Lansdown Rd.
BA1: Bath 1F 7 (3B 100)
BA1: L'dwn 4H 81
BS5: E'tn 7C 48
BS6: Redl 7J 47
BS8: Clif 2G 61
BS15: K'wd 6B 50
BS16: Puck 2C 52
BS31: Salt 7J 79
Lansdown Ter. *BA1: Bath 1F 7*
(off Lansdown Rd.)
BA1: W'ton 2J 99
BS6: Henle 3K 47
Lansdown Vw. BA2: Bath 5J 99
BA2: Tim 3G 141
BS15: K'wd 1C 64
Lanthony Cl. BS24: W'ton V 4E 106
Laphams Ct. BS30: L Grn 5D 64
Lapwing Cl. BS20: P'bry, P'head 2H 43
BS32: Brad S 4F 27
Lapwing Gdns. BS16: B'hll 2H 49
BS22: Wor 3D 106
Larch Cl. BS40: L'frd 7C 110
BS48: Nail 7J 57
Larch Ct. BA3: Rads 6H 153
Larches, The BS22: Wor 1E 106
Larchgrove Cres. BS22: Wor 3D 106
Larchgrove Wlk. *BS22: Wor 3E 106*
(off Chestnut Av.)
Larch Rd. BS15: Soun 5C 50
Larch Way BS34: Pat 7A 26
Lark Cl. BA3: Mid N 6F 153
Larkfield BS36: Coal H 7H 29
LARKHALL 1D 100
Larkhall Bldgs. *BA1: Bath 1E 100*
(off Larkhall Ter.)
Larkhall Ter. BA1: Bath 1E 100
Larkhill Pl. BA1: Bath 1E 100
Larkhill Rd. BS24: Lock 6F 107
Larkin Pl. BS7: Hor 6C 36
Lark Pl. BA1: Bath 3A 6
Lark Ri. BS37: Yate 2E 30
Lark Rd. BS22: Wor 3D 106
Larks Fld. BS16: Stap 3G 49
Lark's La. BS37: Iron A 6F 21
Larksleaze Rd. BS30: L Grn 7C 64
Larkspur Cl. BS35: T'bry 3B 12
Lasbury Gro. BS13: Hart 5J 75
Latchmoor Ho. BS13: Bis 2G 75
Late Broads BA15: W'ley 5B 124
Latimer Cl. BS4: Brisl 5G 63
LATTERIDGE 7E 20
Latteridge La. BS35: Alv, Itch 3D 20
BS37: Iron A 3D 20
Latteridge Rd. BS37: Iron A 7E 20
Latton Rd. BS7: Hor 7B 36
Launceston Av. BS15: Han 4K 63
Launceston Rd. BS15: K'wd 7K 49
Laura Pl. BA2: Bath 3H 7 (4C 100)
Laurel Av. TA9: Bre K 5J 157
Laurel Dr. BS23: Uph 3G 127
BS39: Paul 1B 152
BS48: Nail 7H 57
Laurel Gdns. BA2: Tim 4F 141
BS49: Yat 2H 87
Laurels, The BA2: Mid 7E 122
BS10: Hen 1G 35
BS16: Mang 2E 50
BS25: C'hll 2B 132
Laurel St. BS15: K'wd 1B 64
Laurel Ter. BS49: Yat 2H 87
Laurie Cres. BS9: Henle 2K 47
Laurie Lee Ct. BS30: Bar C 4E 64
Lavender Cl. BS22: Wick L 6E 84
BS35: T'bry 3B 12
Lavender Ct. BS5: S'wll 7H 49
Lavender Way BS32: Brad S 7H 27
Lavenham Rd. BS37: Yate 4B 30
Lavers Cl. BS15: K'wd 3C 64
Lavington Cl. BS21: Clev 1A 68
Lavington Rd. BS5: St G 3K 63
Lawford Av. BS34: Lit S 1E 36
Lawford M. BS2: Bris 3K 5 (2B 62)
Lawfords Ga. BS5: E'tn 2K 5 (2B 62)

Manor Gdns. Ho.—Mendip Cres.

Manor Gdns. Ho. BS16: Fish .3H 49
Manor Grange BS24: B'don .6K 127
Manor Gro. BS16: Mang .4E 50
BS34: Pat .4D 26
Manor Hall BS8: Clif .3A 4 (2H 61)
Manor Ho. La. BS14: H'gro .5E 76
Manor La. BS8: Abb L .1K 59
BS36: Wint .7D 28
Manor Pk. BA1: Bath .3H 99
BA3: Writ .4C 154
BS6: Redl .5H 47
BS32: Toc .3D 18
Manor Pk. Cl. BA3: Writ .4C 154
Manor Pl. BS16: Fren .6A 38
BS34: Stok G .3J 37
Manor Ride TA9: Bre K .5K 157
Manor Rd. BA1: W'ton .2J 99
BA3: Writ .4C 154
BS7: B'stn .4A 48
BS8: Abb L .3K 59
BS13: Bis .4F 75
BS16: Fish .3H 49
BS16: Mang .4E 50
BS23: W Mare .3H 105
BS30: Wick .3C 66
BS31: Key, Salt .7D 78
BS37: Rang, Yate .6A 22
TA8: Bur S .1D 158
Manor Ter. BA3: Writ .4C 154
Manor Valley BS23: W Mare .3J 105
Manor Vs. BA1: W'ton .2J 99
Manor Wlk. BS35: T'bry .1K 11
Manor Way BS8: Fail .6G 59
BS37: Chip S .5J 31
TA8: Berr .1B 156
Mansbrook Ho. BA3: Mid N .5E 152
Mansel Cl. BS31: Salt .7G 79
Mansfield Av. BS23: W Mare .4K 105
Mansfield Cl. BS23: W Mare .4K 105
Mansfield St. BS3: Bedm .7H 61
Manston Cl. BS14: Stoc .3E 76
Mantle Cl. BS21: Clev .7E 54
Manvers St. BA1: Bath .5H 7 (5C 100)
Manworthy Rd. BS4: Brisl .6F 63
Manx Rd. BS7: Hor .1B 48
Maple Av. BS16: Fish .5A 50
BS35: T'bry .3A 12
Maple Cl. BS14: Stoc .5F 77
BS23: W Mare .4J 105
BS30: Old C .5F 65
BS34: Lit S .7E 26
Maple Ct. BS15: K'wd .7B 50
BS23: W Mare .3E 104
Maple Dr. BA3: Rads .5J 153
TA8: Bur S .2D 158
Maple Gdns. BA2: Bath .7A 100
Maple Grange BS9: W Trym .2H 47
Maple Gro. BA2: Bath .7A 100
TA8: Berr .2B 156
Maple Ho. BS2: Bris .1F 5
Maple Leaf Ct. BS8: Clif .3A 4 (2H 61)
Mapleleaze BS4: Brisl .6F 63
Maplemeade BS7: B'stn .4J 47
Mapleridge La. BS37: Hort, Yate .5H 23
Maple Ri. BA3: Rads .4B 154
Maple Rd. BS4: St Ap .4F 63
BS7: Hor .3K 47
Maples, The BS48: Nail .1E 70
Maplestone Rd. BS14: Whit .7C 76
Mapleton La. BS25: Star .3K 131
Maple Wlk. BS16: Puck .3C 52
BS31: Key .6B 78
Mapstone Cl. BS16: Ham .4K 37
Marbeck Rd. BS10: S'mead .6H 35
Marchfields Way BS23: W Mare .6H 105
Marconi Cl. BS23: W Mare .5K 105
Marconi Rd. BS20: P'head .3B 42
Mardale Cl. BS10: S'mead .5J 35
Marden Rd. BS31: Key .6E 78
Mardon Rd. BS4: St Ap .3F 63
Mardyke Ferry Rd. BS1: Bris .6A 4 (4H 61)
Margaret Cres. TA8: Bur S .3C 158
Margaret Rd. BS13: Withy .6F 75
Margaret's Bldgs. BA1: Bath .2E 6 (4B 100)
Margaret's Hill BA1: Bath .1G 7 (3C 100)
Margate St. BS3: Wind H .6B 62
Marguerite Rd. BS13: Bis .3F 75
Marigold Wlk. BS3: Bedm .7G 61
Marina Gdns. BS16: Fish .5G 49
Marindin Dr. BS22: Wor .7F 85
Marine Dr. TA8: Bur S .2D 158
Marine Hill BS21: Clev .4C 54
Marine Pde. BS20: Pill .3G 45
BS21: Clev .5C 54
BS23: W Mare .7F 105
(Beach Rd.)
BS23: W Mare .3D 104
(Claremont Cres.)
Mariners Cl. BS22: W Mare .3B 106
BS48: Back .4J 71
Mariners Dr. BS9: Stok B .4D 46
BS48: Back .4J 71
Mariners Path BS9: Stok B .4D 46
BS20: P'head .3A 42
Mariners Way BS20: Pill .3G 45
Marion Rd. BS15: Han .6K 63
Marion Wlk. BS5: St G .2J 63
Marissal Cl. BS10: Hen .4E 34
Marissal Rd. BS10: Hen .4D 34
Mariston Way BS30: Old C .3G 65
Maritime Heritage Cen. .6B 4 (4H 61)
Marjoram Pl. BS32: Brad S .7H 27
Marjoram Way BS20: P'head .3H 43
Marjorie Whimster Ho. BA2: Bath .5H 99
Market Av. BS22: St Geo .1G 107
Marketgate BS1: Bris .2J 5
Market Ind. Est. BS49: Yat .2H 87
Market La. BS23: W Mare .4F 105
Market Pl. BA3: Rads .3K 153
BS40: Winf .4K 91
Marketside BS2: Bris .5C 62
Market Sq. BS16: Fish .5A 50
BS35: T'bry .4K 11
Market St. BA15: Brad A .5H 125
TA9: High .5G 159
Market Ter. TA9: High .5G 159
Markham Cl. BS11: Shire .1G 45
Marklands BS9: Stok B .5E 46
Mark La. BS1: Bris .4D 4 (3J 61)
Mark Rd. TA9: High, W'fld .5H 159
MARKSBURY .3F 119
Marksbury Ga. BA2: Cor .7F 97
Marksbury Rd. BS3: Bedm, Wind H .7J 61
Marlborough Av. BS16: Fish .5G 49
Marlborough Bldgs.
BA1: Bath .2D 6 (4A 100)
Marlborough Ct. BA2: Clav D .5G 101
TA8: Bur S .6D 156
Marlborough Dr. BS16: Fren .6K 37
BS22: Wor .2E 106
Marlborough Flats BS2: Bris .1E 4
Marlborough Hill BS2: Bris .1E 4 (1K 61)
Marlborough Hill Pl. BS2: Bris .1E 4 (1K 61)
Marlborough La. BA1: Bath .3D 6 (4A 100)
Marlborough St. BA1: Bath .1D 6 (3A 100)
BS1: Bris .1F 5 (1K 61)
BS2: Bris .1F 5 (1K 61)
BS5: Eastv .5G 49
Marlepit Gro. BS13: Bis .4E 74
Marle Pits BS48: Back .4H 71
Marlfield Wlk. BS13: Bis .3E 74
Marling Rd. BS5: St G .1H 63
Marlwood Dr. BS10: Bren .4G 35
Marmaduke St. BS3: Wind H .6B 62
Marmalade La. BS4: Brisl .1E 76
Marmion Cres. BS10: Hen .4E 34
Marne Cl. BS14: Stoc .5F 77
Marron Cl. BS26: Axb .4J 149
Marsden Rd. BA2: Bath .1H 121
Marshacre La. BS35: Elbton .5B 10
Marshall Ho. BS16: Fish .4H 49
Marshall Wlk. BS4: Know .3K 75
Marsham Way BS30: Bar C, L Grn .4C 64
Marsh Cl. BS36: Wint .3C 38
MARSH COMMON .2E 24
Marsh Comn. Rd.
BS35: E Comp, Piln .7D 16
Marshfield La. BS30: Upton C .2A 80
Marshfield Pk. BS16: Down .7A 38
Marshfield Rd. BS16: Fish .4K 49
Marshfield Way BA1: Bath .2C 100
Marsh La. BS3: Bedm .7G 61
BS5: Redf .3E 62
BS20: Eas .1C 44
BS39: Clut, Hall .3H 139
Marsh La. Ind. Est. BS20: Eas .2C 44
Marsh Rd. BS3: Ash G .6F 61
BS49: Yat .4H 87
Marsh St. BS1: Bris .5E 4 (3K 61)
BS11: A'mth .7G 33
Marshwall La. BS32: Alm .7A 18
Marson Rd. BS21: Clev .6D 54
Marston Rd. BS4: Know .7D 62
Martcombe Rd. BS20: Eas .5E 44
Martha's Orchard BS13: Bis .3E 74
Martin Cl. BS34: Pat .6A 26
Martindale Ct. BS22: W Mare .4B 106
Martindale Rd. BS22: W Mare .4B 106
Martingale Rd. BS4: Brisl .5F 63
Martingale Way BS20: P'head .2G 43
Martins, The BS20: P'head .2J 43
Martin's Cl. TA8: Bur S .4C 156
Martins Gro. BS22: Wor .2C 106
Martin's Rd. BS15: Han .4A 64
Martin St. BS3: Bedm .6H 61
Martock BS24: W Mare .3H 127
Martock Cres. BS3: Bedm .1J 75
Martock Rd. BS3: Bedm .1J 75
BS31: Key .7E 78
Marwood Cl. TA8: Bur S .7E 156
Marwood Rd. BS4: Know .2A 76
Marybush La. BS2: Bris .3H 5 (2A 62)
Mary Carpenter Pl. BS2: Bris .7B 48
Mary Ct. BS5: Redf .1F 63
(off Alfred St.)
Marygold Leaze BS30: C Hth .5E 64
Mary Seacole Ct. BS2: Bris .6C 48
(off Mercia Dr.)
Mary St. BS5: Redf .1F 63
Mascall's Wood Nature Reserve .6F 151
Mascot Rd. BS3: Wind H .6K 61
Masefield Way BS7: Hor .2C 48
Maskelyne Av. BS10: Hor .1K 47
Masonpit Pool La. BS36: Wint .6A 28
Masons La. BA15: Brad A .5H 125
Masons Vw. BS36: Wint .1D 38
Mason's Way BS27: Ched .7E 150
Matchells Cl. BS4: St Ap .3G 63
Materman Rd. BS14: Stoc .5G 77
Matford Cl. BS10: Bren .3K 35
BS36: Wint .2C 38
Matthews Cl. BS14: Stoc .4H 77
Matthews Rd. BS5: Redf .2E 62
Maules La. BS16: Ham .5H 37
Maunsell Rd. BS11: Law W .5B 34
BS24: W'ton V .5C 106
Maurice Rd. BS6: Bris .6A 48
Mautravers Cl. BS32: Brad S .7F 27
Mawdeley Ho. BS3: Bedm .5J 61
(off Catherine Mead St.)
Max Mill La.
BS25: Ban, Wins .4B 130
Maxse Rd. BS4: Know .6D 62
Maybank Rd. BS37: Yate .5D 30
Maybec Gdns. BS5: St G .3J 63
Maybourne BS4: Brisl .7J 63
Maybrick Rd. BA2: Bath .7A 6 (6K 99)
Maycliffe Pk. BS6: Bris .7A 48
Mayfair Av. BS48: Nail .1G 71
Mayfield Av. BS16: Fish .6J 49
BS22: Wor .3C 106
MAYFIELD PARK .6J 49
Mayfield Pk. BS16: Fish .6J 49
Mayfield Pk. Nth. BS16: Fish .6J 49
Mayfield Pk. Sth. BS16: Fish .6J 49
Mayfield Rd. BA2: Bath .7A 6 (6K 99)
Mayfields BS31: Key .5C 78
Mayflower Ct. BS16: Stap H .3C 50
TA9: High .4G 159
Mayflower Gdns. BS48: Nail .7J 57
May La. BA1: Bath .3H 99
Maynard Cl. BS13: Hart .5J 75
BS21: Clev .6F 55
Maynard Rd. BS13: Hart .5J 75
Maynard Ter. BS39: Clut .2H 139
Mayors Bldgs. BS16: Fish .3K 49
Maypole Cl. BS39: Clut .2G 139
Maypole Sq. BS15: Han .4A 64
Mays Cl. BS36: Coal H .7H 29
Maysfield Cl. BS20: P'head .5F 43
MAY'S GREEN .7B 86
Maysgreen La. BS24: Hew .7B 86
MAYSHILL .5J 29
Mays Hill BS36: Fram C .5J 29
May's La. BS24: Hew, Pux .1B 108
(not continuous)
Maysmead La. BS40: L'frd .6E 110
May St. BS15: K'wd .7A 50
Maytree Av. BS13: Bis .3H 75
May Tree Cl. BS48: Nail .1E 70
Maytree Cl. BS13: Bis .3H 75
May Tree Rd. BA3: Rads .5J 153
Maytrees BS5: Eastv .6E 48
May Tree Wlk. BS31: Key .7A 78
Mayville Av. BS34: Fil .4C 36
Maywood Av. BS16: Fish .4K 49
Maywood Cres. BS16: Fish .4K 49
Maywood Rd. BS16: Fish .4A 50
Maze St. BS5: Bar H .3D 62
Mead, The BA2: F'boro .6E 118
BA2: Tim .2G 141
BA15: W'ley .5C 124
BS25: S'ham .5A 132
BS34: Fil .3D 36
BS35: Alv .7J 11
BS39: Clut .2G 139
(not continuous)
BS39: Paul .1B 152
BS41: Dun .1D 92
Mead Cl. BA2: Bath .1A 122
BS11: Shire .2J 45
BS27: Ched .7H 151
Mead Ct. BS36: Wint .1C 38
Mead Ct. Bus. Pk.
BS35: T'bry .5K 11
Meade Ho. BA2: Bath .6G 99
Meadgate BS16: Emer G .1F 51
MEADGATE EAST .3J 141
MEADGATE WEST .3H 141
Meadlands BA2: Cor .4B 98
Mead La. BS24: Nye, Sandf .7D 108
BS25: Sandf .1E 130
BS31: Salt .6K 79
BS32: Brad S .1G 37
BS35: Olv .3K 17
(not continuous)
BS40: Blag .2C 134
(off High St.)
Meadowbank BS22: Wor .1D 106
Meadow Cl. BS16: Down .1D 50
BS48: Back .4K 71
BS48: Nail .6G 57
TA9: High .4F 159
Meadow Ct. BA1: Bath .4G 99
Meadow Ct. Dr. BS30: Old C .6G 65
Meadow Cft. BS24: W Mare .3K 127
Meadowcroft BS16: Down .7E 38
Meadowcroft Dr. TA8: Bur S .7E 156
Meadow Dr. BA2: Odd D .4K 121
BS20: Wes .7B 42
BS24: Lock .1F 129
Meadowfield BA15: Brad A .6F 125
Meadow Gdns. BA1: Bath .2G 99
Meadow Gro. BS11: Shire .1H 45
Meadowland BS49: Yat .2G 87
Meadowland Rd. BS10: Hen .3E 34
Meadowlands BS22: St Geo .2G 107
Meadow La. BA2: B'ptn .2F 101
Meadow Lea BS39: Hall .7J 139
Meadow Mead BS36: Fram C .6F 29
BS37: Yate .1E 30
Meadow Pk. BA1: Bathf .7K 83
Meadow Pl. BS22: St Geo .1H 107
Meadow Rd. BS21: Clev .6E 54
BS37: Chip S .5G 31
BS39: Paul .2D 152
GL12: Ley .1B 14
Meadows, The BS15: Han .5B 64
Meadows Cl. BS20: P'head .3B 42
Meadows End BS25: C'hll .1K 131
Meadow Side BS37: Iron A .2H 29
Meadowside BS35: T'bry .4B 12
Meadowside Dr. BS14: Whit .7C 76
Meadow St. BS11: A'mth .6E 32
BS23: W Mare .5G 105
BS26: Axb .5J 149
Meadowsweet Av. BS34: Fil .4D 36
Meadowsweet Ct. BS16: Stap .3G 49
(off Foxglove Cl.)
Meadow Va. BS5: St G .7J 49
Meadow Vw. BA3: Rads .5A 154
BS36: Fram C .7G 29
Meadow Vw. Cl. BA1: Bath .3G 99
Meadow Vs. BS23: W Mare .4G 105
(off Prospect Pl.)
Meadow Way BS32: Brad S .7G 27
Mead Ri. BS3: Bris .7J 5 (5B 62)
Mead Rd. BS20: P'head .6E 42
BS34: Stok G .1G 37
BS37: Chip S .6J 31
Meads, The BS16: Down .1D 50
(not continuous)
Mead St. BS3: Bris .7J 5 (5B 62)
Mead Va. BS22: W Mare, Wor .3C 106
Mead Way BS9: Sea M .2C 46
BS35: T'bry .5K 11
Meadway BA2: F'boro .6E 118
BS39: Temp C .4G 139
Meadway Av. BS48: Nail .7F 57
Mearcombe La. BS24: B'don .1D 146
Meardon Rd. BS14: Stoc .4G 77
Meare BS24: W Mare .3H 127
Meare Rd. BA2: C Down .2B 122
MEARNS .3C 140
Mecca Bingo
Bristol .2D 62
Mede Cl. BS1: Bris .7G 5 (4A 62)
Media Ho. BS8: Clif .3A 4
Medical Av. BS2: Bris .3D 4 (2J 61)
Medina Cl. BS35: T'bry .5A 12
Medway Cl. BS31: Key .7E 78
Medway Ct. BS7: B'stn .3K 47
BS35: T'bry .4B 12
Medway Dr. BS31: Key .7E 78
BS36: Fram C .7F 29
Meere Bank BS11: Law W .6B 34
Meer Wall BS24: Cong .1F 109
BS25: Cong .1F 109
Meeting Ho. La. BS49: Clav, C've .1C 88
Meg Thatchers Gdns. BS5: St G .2K 63
Meg Thatcher's Grn. BS5: St G .2K 63
Melbourne Dr. BS37: Chip S .5H 31
Melbourne Rd. BS7: B'stn .4K 47
Melbourne Ter. BS21: Clev .7D 54
Melbury Rd. BS4: Know .7B 62
Melcombe Ct. BA2: Bath .7A 6 (7K 99)
Melcombe Rd. BA2: Bath .7A 6 (6K 99)
Melita Rd. BS6: Bris .5A 48
Mellent Av. BS13: Hart .7J 75
Mells Cl. BS31: Key .1E 96
Mells La. BA3: Rads .4B 154
Melrose Av. BS8: Clif .1H 61
BS37: Yate .4F 31
Melrose Cl. BS37: Yate .4G 31
Melrose Gro. BA2: Bath .1H 121
Melrose Pl. BS8: Clif .1H 61
Melrose Ter. BA1: Bath .1C 100
Melton Cres. BS7: Hor .7C 36
Melville Rd. BS6: Redl .7H 47
Melville Ter. BS3: Bedm .6J 61
Melvin Sq. BS4: Know .1A 76
Memorial Cl. BS15: Han .5K 63
Memorial Cotts. BA1: W'ton .2J 99
Memorial Rd. BS15: Han .4K 63
BS40: Wrin .2G 111
Memorial Stadium .2B 48
Mendip Av. BS22: Wor .2C 106
Mendip Cl. BS26: Axb .4J 149
BS31: Key .5B 78
BS39: Paul .2C 152
BS48: Nail .1G 71
BS49: Yat .4H 87
Mendip Ct. BS16: Fren .6G 37
Mendip Cres. BS16: Down .1E 50

Morpeth Rd.—Northend Av.

Morpeth Rd. BS4: Know 2K **75**
Morris Cl. BA1: Bathf 7K **83**
Morris La. BA1: Bathf 7K **83**
Morris Rd. BS7: L'lze 3C **48**
Morse Rd. BS5: Redf 2E **62**
Morston Ct. BS22: W Mare 5A **106**
Mortimer Cl. BA1: W'ton 1H **99**
Mortimer Rd. BS8: Clif 2G **61**
BS34: Fil 6D **36**
MORTON 2B **12**
Morton St. BS5: Bar H 2D **62**
Morton Way BS35: T'bry 1B **12**
Moseley Gro. BS23: Uph 3G **127**
Motion Media Cen. BS35: Aust 4F **9**
Motorway Distribution Cen.
BS11: A'mth 5G **33**
Moulton Dr. BA15: Brad A 7H **125**
Mountain Ash BA1: W'ton 2K **99**
Mountain M. BS5: St G 2J **63**
Mountain's La. BA2: F'boro 5B **118**
Mountain Wood BA1: Bathf 1A **102**
Mountbatten Cl. BS22: Kew 7C **84**
BS37: Yate 3D **30**
TA8: Bur S 6C **156**
Mount Beacon BA1: Bath 2C **100**
Mt. Beacon Pl. BA1: Bath 2B **100**
Mt. Beacon Row BA1: Bath 2C **100**
Mount Cl. BS36: Fram C 6D **28**
Mount Cres. BS36: Wint 2C **38**
Mounteney's La. GL12: Wickw 6K **15**
Mount Gdns. BS15: K'wd 3B **64**
Mount Gro. BA2: Bath 1H **121**
MOUNT HILL 3C **64**
Mount Hill Rd. BS15: Han, K'wd 3A **64**
Mt. Pleasant BA2: Mon C 3F **123**
BA3: Rads 4B **154**
BA15: Brad A 5H **125**
BS10: H'len 3C **34**
BS20: Pill 4H **45**
Mt. Pleasant Ter. BS3: Bedm 5J **61**
Mount Rd. BA1: Bath 3B **100**
BA2: Bath 7G **99**
Mount Vw. *BA1: Bath* *2C* ***100***
(off Beacon Rd.)
BA2: Bath 1H **121**
Mow Barton BS13: Bis 4F **75**
BS37: Yate 4D **30**
Mowbray Rd. BS14: H'gro 3E **76**
Mowcroft Rd. BS13: Hart 6J **75**
Moxham Dr. BS13: Hart 6H **75**
Muddy La. BS22: Wick L 2E **84**
Mud La. BS49: Clav 1K **87**
Muirfield BS30: Warm 3E **64**
BS37: Yate 6E **30**
Mulberry Av. BS20: P'head 3G **43**
Mulberry Cl. BS15: K'wd 1C **64**
BS20: P'head 3H **43**
BS22: Wor 3D **106**
BS48: Back 4J **71**
Mulberry Dr. BS15: K'wd 7D **50**
Mulberry Gdns. BS16: Soun 5B **50**
Mulberry La. BS24: B'don 7A **128**
Mulberry Rd. BS49: Cong 1A **110**
Mulberry Wlk. BS9: C Din 7C **34**
Muller Av. BS7: B'stn 4B **48**
Muller Ho. BS7: B'stn 4B **48**
Muller Rd. BS5: Eastv 5E **48**
(not continuous)
BS7: Hor 2B **48**
Mulready Cl. BS7: L'lze 2E **48**
Mumbleys La. BS35: T'bry 6G **11**
Murdoch Sq. BS7: Hor 7B **36**
Murford Av. BS13: Hart 5H **75**
Murford Wlk. BS13: Hart 6H **75**
MURHILL 6A **124**
Murray St. BS3: Bedm 5J **61**
Mus. of Bath at Work 1F **7** (3B **100**)
Mus. of Costume, The 2F **7** (4B **100**)
Mus. of East Asian Art 2E **6** (4B **100**)
Musgrove Cl. BS11: Law W 5C **34**
Musthay Flds. BS32: Toc 3D **18**
Myrtleberry Mead BS22: Wick L 6E **84**
Myrtle Ct. *BS3: Bedm* *5H* ***61***
(off Exmoor St.)
Myrtle Dr. BS11: Shire 3J **45**
TA8: Bur S 1C **158**
Myrtle Gdns. BS49: Yat 3J **87**
Myrtle Hill BS20: Pill 4G **45**
Myrtle Rd. BS2: Bris 1D **4** (1J **61**)
Myrtles, The BS24: Hut 3B **128**
Myrtle St. BS3: Bedm 5H **61**
Mythern Mdw. BA15: Brad A 7J **125**

N

Nags Head Hill BS5: St G 2J **63**
NAILSEA 7G **57**
Nailsea & Backwell Station (Rail) 3H **71**
Nailsea Cl. BS13: Bis 3G **75**
Nailsea Moor La. BS48: Nail 3B **70**
Nailsea Pk. BS48: Nail 7H **57**
Nailsea Pk. Cl. BS48: Nail 6H **57**
Nailsea Wall BS21: Clev 2G **69**
BS48: Nail 2G **69**
Nailsea Wall La. BS48: Nail 3A **70**
Nailsworth Av. BS37: Yate 5E **30**
NAILWELL 6D **120**
Naishcombe Hill BS30: Wick 3C **66**
Naishes Av. BA2: Pea J 5D **142**
Naish Hill BS20: Clap G 7H **43**
Naish Ho. BA2: Bath 5G **99**
Naish La. BS48: Bar G 7G **73**
Naish Rd. TA8: Bur S 4C **156**
Nanny Hurn's La. BS39: Came, Clut 3C **138**
Napier Ct. BS1: Bris 7A **4** (4H **61**)
Napier Miles Rd. BS11: Law W 7A **34**
Napier Rd. BA1: W'ton 7G **81**
BS5: Eastv 6D **48**
BS6: Redl 6H **47**
BS11: A'mth 6F **33**
Napier Sq. BS11: A'mth 6E **32**
Napier St. BS5: Bar H 3D **62**
Narroways Rd. BS2: Bris 5C **48**
Narrow La. BS16: Soun 5C **50**
Narrow Lewins Mead BS1: Bris 3E **4**
Narrow Plain BS2: Bris 4H **5** (3A **62**)
Narrow Quay BS1: Bris 6E **4** (4K **61**)
(not continuous)
Narrow Quay Ho. BS1: Bris 5E **4**
Naseby Wlk. BS5: S'wll 7H **49**
Nash Cl. BS31: Key 5E **78**
Nash Dr. BS7: L'lze 1E **48**
Nates La. BS40: Wrin 3H **111**
Naunton Way BS22: W Mare 2K **105**
Neads Dr. BS30: Old C 4G **65**
Neale La. BS11: A'mth 6G **33**
Neate Ct. BS34: Pat 6E **26**
Neath Rd. BS5: W'hall 1F **63**
Nelson Bldgs. BA1: Bath 1H **7** (3C **100**)
Nelson Ct. BS22: Wor 7C **84**
Nelson Ho. BA1: Bath 3D **6** (4A **100**)
BS1: Bris *3F* ***5***
(off Rupert St.)
BS16: Stap H 3B **50**
Nelson Pde. BS3: Bedm 7F **5** (5K **61**)
Nelson Pl. E. BA1: Bath 1G **7** (3C **100**)
Nelson Pl. W. BA1: Bath 4D **6** (5A **100**)
Nelson Rd. BS16: Stap H 3B **50**
(not continuous)
Nelson St. BS1: Bris 3F **5** (2K **61**)
BS3: Bedm 7G **61**
Nelson Vs. BA1: Bath 4C **6** (5A **100**)
Nempnett St. BS40: Nem T 6G **113**
NEMPNETT THRUBWELL 7H **113**
Neston Wlk. BS4: Know 2B **76**
NETHAM 3F **63**
Netham Ct. *BS5: Redf* *2F* ***63***
(off Netham Rd.)
Netham Gdns. BS5: Redf 2F **63**
Netham Ind. Pk. BS5: Redf 2F **63**
Netham Pk. Ind. Est. BS5: Redf 3F **63**
Netham Rd. BS5: Redf 2F **63**
Netherton Wood La. BS48: Nail 4B **70**
Netherways BS21: Clev 1B **68**
Nettlefrith La. TA8: Berr 6D **144**
Nettlestone Cl. BS10: Hen 3E **34**
Nevalan Dr. BS5: St G 3J **63**
Neva Rd. BS23: W Mare 6G **105**
Nevill Ct. BA2: New L 6B **98**
Neville Rd. BS15: K'wd 6C **50**
Nevil Rd. BS7: B'stn 4A **48**
New Bond St. BA1: Bath 4F **7** (5B **100**)
New Bond St. Bldgs. *BA1: Bath* *4F* ***7***
(off New Bond St.)
New Bond St. Pl. BA1: Bath 4G **7**
Newbourne Rd. BS22: W Mare 5A **106**
Newbrick Rd. BS34: Stok G 2J **37**
NEWBRIDGE 3G **99**
Newbridge (Park & Ride) 3F **99**
Newbridge Cl. BS4: St Ap 3F **63**
Newbridge Ct. BA1: Bath 4H **99**
Newbridge Drove TA9: E Hunt 7H **159**
Newbridge Gdns. BA1: Bath 3G **99**
Newbridge Hill BA1: Bath 3G **99**
Newbridge La. TA9: E Hunt 7H **159**
(not continuous)
Newbridge Rd. BA1: Bath 3F **99**
BA2: Bath 3F **99**
BS4: St Ap 3F **63**
Newbridge Trad. Est. BS4: St Ap 4F **63**
New Bristol Rd. BS22: Wor 3C **106**
New Brunswick Av. BS5: St G 2K **63**
NEW BUILDINGS 6A **142**
New Bldgs. BS16: Fish 4H **49**
Newbury Rd. BS7: Hor 1C **48**
New Charlotte St. BS3: Bedm 7F **5** (5K **61**)
New Charlton Way BS10: Pat 1G **35**
NEW CHELTENHAM 7C **50**
New Cheltenham Rd. BS15: K'wd 7B **50**
New Church Rd. BS23: Uph 3F **127**
Newclose La. BS40: Comp M 4D **136**
Newcombe Dr. BS9: Stok B 4C **46**
Newcombe La. BS25: Wins 6H **131**
Newcombe Rd. BS9: W Trym 1F **47**
New Cut Bow BS21: Kings S 5A **68**
Newditch La. BS40: F'tn 2G **91**
Newdown La. BS41: Dun 2H **93**
New Ear La. BS24: Hew 7J **85**
New Engine Rank BS36: H'fld 4H **39**
Newent Av. BS15: K'wd 2K **63**
Newfields BS40: Blag 4A **134**
New Fosseway Rd. BS14: H'gro 4D **76**
Newfoundland Cir. BS2: Bris 1J **5** (1B **62**)
Newfoundland Rd. BS2: Bris 1J **5** (1B **62**)
Newfoundland St. BS2: Bris 1J **5** (1B **62**)
Newfoundland Way BS2: Bris 1J **5** (1B **62**)
BS20: P'head 2G **43**
Newgate BS1: Bris 3G **5** (2A **62**)
New Grove BS16: Fish 4H **49**
Newhaven Pl. BS20: P'head 4A **42**
Newhaven Rd. BS20: P'head 5A **42**
New John St. BS3: Bedm 6J **61**
New Kings Ct. BS7: B'stn 4J **47**
New Kingsley Rd. BS2: Bris 4J **5** (3B **62**)
New King St. BA1: Bath 4D **6** (5B **100**)
Newland Dr. BS13: Withy 6G **75**
Newland Rd. BS13: Withy 6G **75**
BS23: W Mare 6H **105**
Newlands, The BS16: Fren 1K **49**
Newlands Av. BS36: Coal H 7G **29**
Newlands Cl. BS20: P'head 3E **42**
Newlands Grn. BS21: Clev 1E **68**
Newlands Hgts. *BS7: Bris* *6B* ***48***
(off Hurlingham Rd.)
Newlands Hill BS20: P'head 4E **42**
Newlands Rd. BS31: Key 6B **78**
Newland Wlk. BS13: Withy 7G **75**
New La. BS35: Alv 7A **12**
BS40: Regil, Winf 6H **91**
NEWLEAZE 5D **36**
New Leaze BS32: Brad S 3E **26**
Newleaze Ho. BS34: Fil 5D **36**
Newlyn Av. BS9: Stok B 3D **46**
Newlyn Wlk. BS4: Know 1D **76**
Newlyn Way BS37: Yate 4F **31**
Newman Cl. BS37: W'lgh 3B **40**
Newmans La. BA2: Tim 3F **141**
TA9: E Hunt 7K **159**
Newmarket Av. BS1: Bris 3F **5** (2K **61**)
Newmarket Row *BA2: Bath* *4G* ***7***
(off Grand Pde.)
New Mdws. BS14: H'gro 4C **76**
Newnham Cl. BS14: Stoc 3F **77**
Newnham Pl. BS34: Pat 5B **26**
New Orchard St. BA1: Bath 5G **7** (5C **100**)
NEW PASSAGE 4A **16**
New Passage Rd. BS35: Redw 4A **16**
New Pit BS39: Paul 7D **140**
New Pit La. BS30: Bit 6J **65**
Newport Cl. BS20: P'head 4B **42**
BS21: Clev 7C **54**
Newport Rd. BS20: Pill 3G **45**
Newport St. BS3: Wind H 6A **62**
Newquay Rd. BS4: Know 1B **76**
New Queen St. BS3: Bedm 5A **62**
BS15: K'wd 7K **49**
New Rd. BA1: Bathf 1B **102**
BA2: F'frd 7K **123**
BA2: Tim 3A **140**
BA15: Brad A 5H **125**
BS20: Pill 4G **45**
BS21: Clev 7D **54**
BS25: C'hll 2B **132**
BS25: Row, S'ham 5A **132**
BS29: Ban 1J **129**
BS34: Fil 4B **36**
BS34: Fil, Stok G 5E **36**
BS35: Olv 3C **18**
BS37: Rang 5A **22**
(not continuous)
BS39: High L 3A **140**
BS39: Pens 1F **117**
BS40: Redh 7D **90**
GL12: Tyth 7F **13**
TA9: E Hunt, W Hunt 7E **158**
New Rd. Ct. BA15: Brad A 5J **125**
Newry Wlk. BS4: Know 1A **76**
Newsome Av. BS20: Pill 4G **45**
New Stadium Rd. BS5: Eastv 6D **48**
New Station Rd. BS16: Fish 4J **49**
New Station Way BS16: Fish 4J **49**
New St. BA1: Bath 5F **7** (5B **100**)
BS2: Bris 2J **5** (2B **62**)
New St. Flats BS2: Bris 2J **5**
New Thomas St. BS2: Bris 3J **5** (3B **62**)
NEWTON 4F **159**
Newton Cl. BS15: K'wd 7E **50**
BS40: W Har 7E **136**
TA8: Bur S 5C **156**
Newton Dr. BS30: C Hth 4E **64**
Newton Grn. BS48: Nail 2E **70**
Newton Mill Camping & Cvn. Pk.
BA2: New L 5E **98**
Newton Rd. BA2: Bath 6F **99**
BS23: W Mare 7G **105**
BS30: C Hth 4E **64**
NEWTON ST LOE 5D **98**
Newtons Rd. BS22: Kew, Wor 7C **84**
(not continuous)
Newton St. BS5: E'tn 1K **5** (1C **62**)
NEWTOWN
BS2 2C **62**
BS40 5K **115**
Newtown BA15: Brad A 6G **125**
BS39: Paul 1B **152**
Newtown Rd. TA9: High 5F **159**
(not continuous)
New Tyning Ter. *BA1: Bath* *2D* ***100***
(off Fairfield Rd.)
New Villas BA2: Bath 7C **100**
New Wlk. BS15: Han 4K **63**
New Walls BS4: Wind H 5B **62**
Next Generation Club
Westbury-on-Trym 7H **35**
Niblett Cl. BS15: K'wd 3D **64**
Niblett's Hill BS5: St G 3H **63**
NIBLEY 5A **30**
Nibley Bus. Pk. BS37: Yate 5A **30**
Nibley La. BS37: Iron A, Yate 3J **29**
BS37: W'lgh, Yate 5A **30**
Nibley Rd. BS11: Shire 3H **45**
Nicholas La. BS5: St G 3J **63**
Nicholas Rd. BS5: E'tn 7D **48**
Nicholas St. BS3: Bedm 5A **62**
Nicholettes BS30: Old C 4H **65**
Nicholls Ct. BS36: Wint 1C **38**
Nicholls La. BS36: Wint 7C **28**
Nicholl's Pl. *BA1: Bath* *2F* ***7***
(off Lansdown Rd.)
Nichol's Rd. BS20: P'head 2B **42**
Nigel Pk. BS11: Shire 1J **45**
Nightingale Cl. BS4: St Ap 3G **63**
BS22: Wor 3C **106**
BS35: T'bry 2B **12**
BS36: Fram C 1E **38**
TA8: Bur S 6D **156**
Nightingale Ct. BS22: Wor 3C **106**
Nightingale Gdns. BS48: Nail 7E **56**
Nightingale La. BS36: Wint 6E **28**
Nightingale Ri. BS20: P'head 5B **42**
Nightingale Valley BS4: St Ap 4G **63**
Nightingale Way BA3: Mid N 6F **153**
Nile St. BA1: Bath 4D **6** (5A **100**)
NINE ELMS 4G **137**
Nine Tree Hill BS1: Bris 7A **48**
Ninth Av. BS7: Hor 6D **36**
Nippors Way BS25: Wins 5F **131**
Nithsdale Rd. BS23: W Mare 1G **127**
Noble Av. BS30: Old C 5G **65**
Noel Coward Cl. TA8: Bur S 2E **158**
Nomis Pk. BS49: Cong 2A **110**
Nordrach La. BS40: Comp M 7H **135**
Nore Gdns. BS20: P'head 2E **42**
Nore Pk. Dr. BS20: P'head 2B **42**
Nore Rd. BS20: P'head 4A **42**
Norewood Gro. BS20: P'head 3B **42**
Norfolk Av. BS2: Bris 1H **5** (1A **62**)
BS6: Bris 6A **48**
Norfolk Bldgs. BA1: Bath 4D **6** (5A **100**)
Norfolk Cres. BA1: Bath 4D **6** (5A **100**)
Norfolk Gro. BS31: Key 6A **78**
Norfolk Hgts. *BS2: Bris* *1H* ***5***
(off Norfolk Av.)
Norfolk Pl. BS3: Bedm 6J **61**
Norfolk Rd. BS20: P'head 4G **43**
BS23: W Mare 7H **105**
Norland Rd. BS8: Clif 1F **61**
Norley Rd. BS7: Hor 1B **48**
Normanby Rd. BS5: E'tn 7D **48**
Norman Gro. BS15: K'wd 6B **50**
Norman Rd. BS2: Bris 6C **48**
BS30: Warm 7F **51**
BS31: Salt 7H **79**
Normans, The BA2: B'ptn 2H **101**
Normans Way BS20: Eas 1C **44**
Normanton Rd. BS8: Clif 6G **47**
Norrisville Rd. BS6: Bris 7A **48**
Northam Farm Cvn. & Touring Pk.
TA8: Brean 3C **144**
Northampton Bldgs.
BA1: Bath 1E **6** (3B **100**)
Northampton St. BA1: Bath 1E **6** (3B **100**)
Northanger Ct. *BA2: Bath* *3G* ***7***
(off Grove St.)
North Av. TA9: High 4E **158**
Northavon Bus. Cen. BS37: Yate 3B **30**
Nth. Bristol Pk. BS34: Lit S 2D **36**
Nth. Chew Ter. BS40: Chew M 1H **115**
NORTH COMMON 3H **65**
North Contemporis *BS8: Clif* *2G* ***61***
(off Merchants Rd.)
NORTH CORNER 5D **28**
North Cnr. *BS3: Bedm* *6H* ***61***
(off North St.)
Northcote Rd. BS5: St G 1G **63**
BS8: Clif 7F **47**
BS16: Down, Mang 2D **50**
Northcote St. BS5: E'tn 7D **48**
North Ct. BS32: Brad S 3F **27**
North Cft. BS30: Old C 5H **65**
Nth. Devon Rd. BS16: Fish 3J **49**
Nth. Down Cl. BS25: S'ham 5B **132**
Nth. Down La. BS25: S'ham 5B **132**
Northdown Rd. BA3: Clan 1J **153**
North Drove BS48: Nail 1K **69**
Nth. East Rd. BS35: T'bry 2A **12**
NORTH END
BA1 5H **83**
BS39 7G **117**
BS49 7F **69**
North End BS49: Yat 7F **69**
Northend BA3: Mid N 4F **153**
Northend Av. BS15: K'wd 6B **50**

Patchway Trad. Est.—Poplar Pl.

Patchway Trad. Est. BS34: Pat 6A 26
(Britannia Rd.)
BS34: Pat 7K 25
(Olympus Rd.)
Patricia Cl. TA8: Bur S 5C 156
Patterson Ho. BS1: Bris 7G 5
Paulman Gdns. BS41: L Ash 2K 73
Paulmont Ri. BS39: Temp C 4G 139
Paul's C'way. BS49: Cong 7K 87
Paul St. BS2: Bris 1D 4 (1J 61)
Paulto Hill BS39: Paul 7D 140
PAULTON 7C 140
Paulton Dr. BS7: B'stn 4J 47
Paulton La. BA2: Cam 6H 141
Paulton Rd. BA3: Mid N 5D 152
BS39: Far G 2A 152
Paulton Swimming Pool 1C 152
Paultow Av. BS3: Wind H 6A 62
Paultow Rd. BS3: Wind H 6A 62
Paulwood Rd. BS39: Temp C 4G 139
Pavey Cl. BS13: Hart 6J 75
Pavey Rd. BS13: Hart 6J 75
Pavilion, The 5J 7 (5C 100)
Pavilion, The BS23: W Mare 4E 104
Pavilion Rd. NP16: B'ly 2C 8
Pavilions, The BS4: Brisl 1E 76
Pawlett BS24: W Mare 3J 127
Pawlett Rd. BS13: Hart 7H 75
Pawlett Wlk. BS13: Hart 7J 75
Paxton BS16: Stap 7G 37
Paybridge Rd. BS13: Withy 6F 75
Payne Dr. BS5: E'tn 2D 62
Payne Rd. BS24: Hut 3B 128
Paynes Orchard Cvn. Pk.
BS10: Bren 3K 35
Peache Ct. BS16: Down 2C 50
Peache Rd. BS16: Down 2C 50
Peacocks La. BS15: K'wd 1A 64
Pearce Dr. TA9: High 4F 159
Pearces Hill BS16: Fren 1K 49
Pearl St. BS3: Bedm 6H 61
Pearsall Rd. BS30: L Grn 7C 64
Pearse Cl. BS22: Wor 6F 85
Peart Cl. BS13: Withy 5E 74
Peart Dr. BS13: Withy 6E 74
Pear Tree Av. BS41: L Ash 2J 73
Peartree Cl. BS13: Hart 6H 75
Pear Tree Est. BS40: L'frd 1E 132
Peartree Fld. BS20: P'head 3H 43
Peartree Gdns. BS24: B'don 6K 127
Pear Tree Hey BS37: Yate 1E 30
Pear Tree La. BS5: St G 3K 63
Peartree La. BS15: Soun 6D 50
Pear Tree Rd. BS32: Brad S 4E 26
PEASEDOWN ST JOHN 6C 142
Peasedown St John By-Pass
BA2: Pea J 7B 142
Peats Hill BS39: Pub 6G 95
Pedder Rd. BS21: Clev 1D 68
Peel St. BS5: E'tn 1B 62
Pegasus Ct. BS20: P'head 3F 43
BS23: W Mare 7F 105
BS48: Nail 7G 57
Pegasus Pk. BS34: Lit S 1D 36
Pegasus Rd. BS34: Pat 7K 25
Peg Hill BS37: Yate 2F 31
Peg La. BS16: Puck 1A 52
Pelican Cl. BS22: Wor 4D 106
Pemberton Ct. BS16: Fish 3K 49
Pembery Rd. BS3: Bedm 6H 61
Pembroke Av. BS11: Shire 2J 45
Pembroke Cl. TA8: Bur S 6D 156
Pembroke Ct. BA1: W'ton 2J 99
BS21: Clev 5C 54
Pembroke Gro. BS8: Clif 2G 61
Pembroke Pl. BS8: Clif 4G 61
Pembroke Rd. BS3: Bris 5J 61
BS8: Clif 7G 47
BS11: Shire 2J 45
BS15: K'wd 5C 50
BS20: P'head 5A 42
BS23: W Mare 7H 105
Pembroke St. BS2: Bris 1H 5 (1A 62)
Pembroke Va. BS8: Clif 2A 4 (1G 61)
Penard Way BS15: K'wd 2D 64
Penarth Dr. BS24: W Mare 4J 127
Pendennis Av. BS16: Stap H 3B 50
Pendennis Ho. BS16: Stap H 3B 50
Pendennis Pk. BS4: Brisl 7F 63
BS16: Stap H 4B 50
Pendennis Rd. BS16: Stap H 3B 50
Pendlesham Gdns. BS23: W Mare 3J 105
Pendock Cl. BS30: Bit 1G 79
Pendock Ct. BS16: Emer G 1F 51
Pendock Rd. BS16: Fish 2K 49
BS36: Wint 2C 38
Penfield Ct. BS2: Bris 6C 48
Penfield Rd. BS2: Bris 6C 48
Penlea Ct. BS11: Shire 1H 45
Penmoor Pl. TA8: Berr 2B 156
Penmoor Rd. TA8: Berr 2B 156
Pennant Pl. BS20: P'head 1H 43
Pennard BS24: W Mare 3J 127
Pennard Ct. BS14: Whit 5D 76
Pennard Grn. BA2: Bath 5G 99
Penn Cl. BS27: Ched 7E 150
Penn Dr. BS16: Fren 6A 38
Penn Gdns. BA1: Bath 3G 99
Penngrove BS30: L Grn 6E 64
Penn Hill Rd. BA1: Bath, W'ton 3G 99
Pennine Gdns. BS23: W Mare 3J 105
Pennine Rd. BS30: Old C 5G 65
Penns, The BS21: Clev 7E 54
Pennlea BS13: Bis 3J 75
Penn Lea Ct. BA1: Bath 3H 99
(not continuous)
Penn Lea Rd. BA1: Bath 2G 99
Penn Rd. BS27: Ched 7E 150
Penns, The BS21: Clev 7E 54
Penn St. BS1: Bris 2H 5 (2A 62)
Penn Way BS26: Axb 5J 149
Pennycress BS22: W Mare 5B 106
Penny La. BS15: Soun 5D 50
Pennyquick BA2: New L 4C 98
Pennyquick Vw. BA2: Bath 5F 99
Pennyroyal Gro. BS16: Stap 3G 49
Pennywell Ct. BS5: E'tn 1K 5
Pennywell Rd. BS5: E'tn 1K 5 (1B 62)
Pen Pk. Rd. BS10: S'mead 4J 35
Pen Pk. Sports Pavilion 5K 35
Penpole Av. BS11: Shire 2J 45
Penpole Cl. BS11: Shire 1H 45
Penpole La. BS11: Shire 1H 45
Penpole Pk. BS11: Shire 1J 45
Penpole Pl. BS11: Shire 2J 45
Penrice Cl. BS22: W Mare 2A 106
Penrith Gdns. BS10: S'mead 6K 35
(not continuous)
Penrose BS14: H'gro 3B 76
Penrose Dr. BS32: Brad S 7F 27
Pensfield Pk. BS10: Bren 3K 35
PENSFORD 7F 95
Pensford Ct. BS14: Stoc 5F 77
Pensford Hill BS39: Pens 6F 95
Pensford La. BS39: Stan D 2C 116
Pensford Lock Up 7G 95
Pensford Old Rd. BS39: Pens 1G 117
Pentagon, The BS9: Sea M 2B 46
Penthouse Hill BA1: Bathe 7H 83
Pentire Av. BS13: Bis 4G 75
Pentland Av. BS35: T'bry 4C 12
Pepperall Rd. TA9: High 4F 159
Peppershells La. BS39: Comp D 5A 96
Pepys Cl. BS31: Salt 1H 97
Pera Pl. BA1: Bath 3C 100
Pera Rd. BA1: Bath 1G 7 (3C 100)
Percival Ct. BS8: Clif 1F 61
Percival Rd. BS8: Clif 1F 61
Percy Pl. BA1: Bath 2D 100
Percy St. BS3: Bedm 5K 61
Percy Walker Ct. BS16: Down 2A 50
Peregrine Cl. BS22: Wor 3D 106
Perfect Vw. BA1: Bath 2C 100
Pero's Bridge 6E 4 (3K 61)
Perrett Ho. *BS2: Bris* 2J 5
(off Redcross St.)
Perretts Ct. BS1: Bris 7D 4 (4J 61)
Perrett Way BS20: Pill 4J 45
Perrin Cl. BS39: Temp C 5G 139
Perrings, The BS48: Nail 1G 71
Perrinpit Rd. BS36: Fram C, Wint 2B 28
Perrott Rd. BS15: K'wd 7E 50
Perry Cl. BS36: Wint 2B 38
Perrycroft Av. BS13: Bis 4G 75
Perrycroft Rd. BS13: Bis 4G 75
Perrymans Cl. BS16: Fish 2J 49
BS30: Doy 1G 67
PERRYMEAD 1D 122
Perrymead BA2: Bath 7D 100
BS22: Wor 6F 85
Perrymead Pl. BA2: Bath 7D 100
Perry Rd. BS1: Bris 3D 4 (2J 61)
BS41: L Ash 1K 73
Perry's Cl. BS27: Ched 7C 150
Perrys Lea BS32: Brad S 4F 27
Perry St. BS5: E'tn 1C 62
Pesley Cl. BS13: Withy 6G 75
Petercole Dr. BS13: Bis 4G 75
Peterside BS39: Temp C 6G 139
Peterson Sq. BS13: Hart 7J 75
(not continuous)
Peter's Ter. BS5: Bar H 2D 62
Petersway Gdns. BS5: St G 3J 63
Petherbridge Way BS7: Hor 3C 48
Petherton Cl. BS15: K'wd 2C 64
Petherton Gdns. BS14: H'gro 3D 76
Petherton Rd. BS14: H'gro 2D 76
Petticoat La. BS1: Bris 4H 5 (3A 62)
Pettigrove Gdns. BS15: K'wd 2C 64
Pettigrove Rd. BS15: K'wd 3C 64
Pevensey Wlk. BS4: Know 3K 75
Peverell Cl. BS10: Hen 4F 35
Peverell Dr. BS10: Hen 4F 35
Philfare La. BS25: Row 4B 132
Philidelphia St. BS1: Bris 2G 5
Philippa Cl. BS14: H'gro 3C 76
Philips Ho. *BS2: Bris* 1A 62
(off Dove St. Sth.)
Philip St. BS2: Bris 4D 62
BS3: Bedm 5K 61
Phillips Rd. BS23: W Mare 6J 105
Phillis Hill BA3: Mid N 2D 152
BS39: Paul 2D 152
Phippen St. BS1: Bris 6G 5 (4A 62)
Phipps Barton BS15: K'wd 1K 63
Phipps St. BS3: Bris 7A 4 (5H 61)
Phoenix Bus. Pk. BS3: Bedm 7G 61
Phoenix Ct. BS2: Bris 2J 5
Phoenix Gro. BS6: Henle 3J 47
Phoenix Ho. BA1: Bath 1E 6
BS1: Bris 6F 5 (4K 61)
BS5: Bar H 3D 62
Phoenix St. BS5: Bar H 3D 62
Phoenix Ter. TA8: Bur S 2D 158
Phoenix Way BS20: P'bry, P'head 1H 43
Piccadilly Pl. BA1: Bath 2D 100
Pickwick Rd. BA1: Bath 1C 100
Picton La. BS6: Bris 7A 48
Picton M. BS6: Bris 7A 48
Picton St. BS6: Bris 7A 48
Pier Cl. BS20: P'head 1G 43
Pierrepont Pl. BA1: Bath 5G 7 (5C 100)
Pierrepont St. BA1: Bath 5G 7 (5C 100)
Pier Rd. BS20: P'head 1F 43
Pier St. TA8: Bur S 2C 158
Pigeon Ho. Dr. BS13: Hart 6K 75
Pigeon La. BS40: Redh 3B 112
Pigott Av. BS13: Withy 6G 75
PILE MARSH 2F 63
Pilemarsh BS5: St G 2F 63
Pilgrims Way BS11: Shire 1G 45
BS16: Down 7B 38
BS22: Wor 2C 106
BS40: Chew S 4D 114
Pilgrims Wharf BS4: St Ap 2G 63
Pilkington Cl. BS34: Fil 5E 36
PILL 4G 45
Pillengers Pl. *BS8: Clif* 5A 4
(off Hotwell Rd.)
Pillingers Gdns. BS6: Redl 6H 47
Pillingers Rd. BS15: K'wd 2A 64
Pillmore La. TA9: W'fld 4K 159
Pill Rd. BS8: Abb L 6J 45
BS20: Pill 5H 45
Pill St. BS20: Pill 4G 45
Pill Way BS21: Clev 7B 54
PILNING 6D 16
Pilning Station (Rail) 1F 25
Pilning St. BS32: Piln, Toc 7F 17
BS35: Piln 7F 17
Pimm's La. BS22: W Mare 1K 105
(not continuous)
Pimpernel Mead BS32: Brad S 7G 27
PINCKNEY GREEN 6C 102
Pincots La. GL12: Wickw 2G 23
Pine Cl. BS22: Wor 2B 106
BS35: T'bry 3A 12
Pine Ct. BA3: Rads 4A 154
BS31: Key 6A 78
BS40: Chew M 1H 115
Pinecroft BS14: H'gro 3B 76
BS20: P'head 2B 42
Pine Gro. BS7: Fil 6C 36
Pine Gro. Pl. BS7: B'stn 5K 47
Pine Hill BS22: Wor 2B 106
Pine Lea BS24: B'don 6K 127
Pine Ridge Cl. BS9: Stok B 4C 46
Pine Rd. BS10: Bren 4H 35
Pines, The BS9: Stok B 5D 46
BS16: Soun 6E 50
Pines La. BS32: Old D 2F 19
Pines Rd. BS30: Bit 1G 79
Pines Way BA2: Bath 5C 6 (5A 100)
BA3: Rads 4A 154
Pines Way Ind. Est. BA2: Bath 5D 6
Pinetree Rd. BS24: Lock 1H 129
Pine Wlk. BA3: Rads 5J 153
Pinewood BS15: K'wd 7D 50
Pinewood Av. BA3: Mid N 5D 152
Pinewood Cl. BS9: W Trym 1H 47
Pinewood Gro. BA3: Mid N 5D 152
Pinewood Rd. BA3: Mid N 5D 152
Pinewood Way TA8: Brean 3B 144
Pinghay La. BS40: Regil, Winf 6A 92
Pinhay Rd. BS13: Bis 4H 75
Pinkers Mead BS16: Emer G 2G 51
Pinkhams Twist BS14: Whit 5C 76
Pinnell Gro. BS16: Emer G 1G 51
Pinnockscroft TA8: Berr 2B 156
Pinter Cl. TA8: Bur S 2E 158
Pioneer Av. BA2: C Down 3B 122
Pioneer Pk. BS4: Brisl 4E 62
PIPEHOUSE 7H 123
Pipehouse La. BA2: F'frd 7G 123
Pipe La. BS1: Bris 4D 4 (3J 61)
Piper Rd. BS37: Yate 3E 30
Pipers Cl. BS26: Weare 7E 148
Piplar Ground BA15: Brad A 7H 125
Pippin Cl. BA2: Pea J 6D 142
Pippin Ct. BS30: Bar C 5D 64
Pippins, The BS20: P'head 3H 43
Pitch & Pay La. BS9: Stok B 5E 46
Pitch & Pay Pk. BS9: Stok B 5E 46
Pitchcombe BS37: Yate 7C 30
Pitchcombe Gdns. BS9: C Din 1D 46
Pitch La. BS6: Cot 7K 47
Pithay, The BS1: Bris 3F 5 (2K 61)
BS39: Paul 7C 140
Pithay Ct. BS1: Bris 3F 5 (2K 61)
Pit La. BS40: Nem T 1J 135
BS40: Nem T, Up Str 6J 113
BS48: Back 6J 71
Pitlochry Cl. BS7: Hor 6B 36
Pitman Ct. BA1: Bath 1E 100
Pitman Ho. BA2: Bath 1K 121
Pitman Rd. BS23: W Mare 6G 105
Pitmoor La. TA9: High 3J 159
Pit Rd. BA3: Mid N 5F 153
Pitt Rd. BS7: Hor 3A 48
Pitt's La. BS40: Chew M 3H 115
Pittville Cl. BS35: T'bry 1A 12
Pittville Pl. BS6: Cot 1H 61
Pixash Bus. Cen. BS31: Key 5F 79
Pixash La. BS31: Key 5F 79
Pizey Av. BS21: Clev 7B 54
TA8: Bur S 6C 156
Pizey Av. Ind. Est. BS21: Clev 7B 54
Pizey Cl. BS21: Clev 7B 54
Plain, The BS35: T'bry 1A 12
Planetarium, The 6D 4 (3J 61)
PLASTER'S GREEN 6K 113
Player Av. BS35: Sev B 3C 24
Players Cl. BS16: Ham 3K 37
Player's La. TA8: Bur S 6C 156
Playford Gdns. BS11: Law W 7J 33
Playhouse Theatre
Weston-Super-Mare 4F 105
Plaza, The BS2: Bris 4K 5
Pleasant Ho. BS16: Stap H 3B 50
Pleasant Pl. BA1: Bathf 1B 102
Pleasant Rd. BS16: Stap H 3B 50
Pleshey Cl. BS22: Wor 2B 106
Plimsoll Ho. BS1: Bris 7G 5
Ploughed Paddock BS48: Nail 1F 71
Plover Cl. BS22: Wor 3D 106
BS37: Yate 4C 30
Plovers Ri. BA3: Rads 3A 154
Plowright Ho. BS15: Han 4K 63
Plumers Cl. BS21: Clev 1E 68
Plumley Ct. BS23: W Mare 7F 105
Plumley Cres. BS24: Lock 1E 128
PLUMMER'S HILL 7B 140
Plummer's Hill
BS5: S'wll, St G 1G 63
Plumpton Ct. BS16: Down 6D 38
Plumptre Cl. BS39: Paul 1C 152
Plumptre Rd. BS39: Paul 1B 152
Plum Tree Cl. BS25: Wins 4G 131
Plum Tree Rd.
BS22: W Mare 4C 106
Plunder St. BS49: C've 4D 88
Podgers Dr. BA1: W'ton 1H 99
Podium, The BA1: Bath 3G 7 (5C 100)
Poet's Cl. BS5: W'hall 1F 63
Poets Cnr. BA3: Rads 6G 153
Poet's Wlk. BS21: Clev 7A 54
Polden Cl. BS48: Nail 1G 71
Polden Ho. BS3: Wind H 6K 61
Polden Rd. BS20: P'head 3D 42
(not continuous)
BS23: W Mare 4H 105
Polestar Way BS24: W'ton V 4E 106
Pollard Rd. BS24: W'ton V 4D 106
Polly Barnes Cl. BS15: Han 4K 63
Polly Barnes Hill BS15: Han 4K 63
Polygon, The *BS8: Clif* 3F 61
(off Polygon Rd.)
BS11: A'mth 6H 33
Polygon La. BS8: Clif 3F 61
Polygon La. Sth. *BS8: Clif* 3F 61
(off Polygon Rd.)
Polygon Rd. BS8: Clif 3F 61
Pomfrett Gdns. BS14: Stoc 5G 77
POMPHREY 3F 51
Pomphrey Hill
BS16: Emer G 3F 51
Pond Cl. BS34: Pat 5D 26
Pond Head Ct. *BS20: Pill* 4H 45
(off Eirene Ter.)
Ponsford Rd. BS4: Know 2D 76
Ponting Cl. BS5: S'wll 7J 49
Poolbarton BS31: Key 4C 78
Pool Cnr. BS32: Toc 3D 18
Poole Ct. BS37: Yate 4E 30
Poole Ct. Dr. BS37: Yate 4E 30
Poole Ho. BA2: Bath 6F 99
Poolemead Rd. BA2: Bath 6F 99
Poole St. BS11: A'mth 7F 33
Pooles Wharf BS8: Clif 4G 61
Pooles Wharf Ct. BS8: Clif 4G 61
Pool Ho. BS34: Pat 6C 26
Pool La. BS40: Regil 2A 114
Pool Rd. BS15: Soun 5C 50
Poor Hill BA2: F'boro 6D 118
Pope Ct. BA2: New L 6B 98
Popes Wlk. BA2: Bath 1D 122
Poplar Av. BS9: Stok B 2D 46
Poplar Cl. BA2: Bath 7K 99
BS30: Old C 3G 65
Poplar Dr. BS16: Puck 3B 52
Poplar Est. TA9: High 5F 159
Poplar Flds. BS30: Old C 3H 65
Poplar La. GL12: Wickw 1H 23
Poplar Pl. BS16: Fish 5J 49
BS23: W Mare 4G 105

Poplar Rd.—Queen St.

Poplar Rd. BA2: Odd D 4K 121
BS5: S'wll 7H 49
BS13: Bis 3F 75
BS15: St G 4J 63
BS30: Old C 4G 65
TA8: Bur S 7C 156
Poplar Rdbt. BS11: A'mth 2J 33
Poplars, The BS20: Eas 4F 45
BS22: Wor 3D 106
Poplar Ter. BS15: K'wd 1D 64
Poplar Wlk. BS24: Lock 7C 106
Poplar Way E. BS11: A'mth 2J 33
Poplar Way W. BS11: A'mth 1H 33
Poples Bow TA9: High 3G 159
Pople Wlk. BS7: B'stn 5B 48
Poppy Cl. BS22: Wick L 6E 84
Poppy Mead BS32: Brad S 7G 27
Porlock Cl. BS21: Clev 1E 68
BS23: W Mare 3H 127
Porlock Gdns. BS48: Nail 1G 71
Porlock Rd. BA2: C Down 3C 122
BS3: Wind H 6K 61
Portal Rd. BS24: Lock 1H 129
PORTBURY 5B 44
Portbury Comn. BS20: P'head 4G 43
Portbury Gro. BS11: Shire 2H 45
Portbury Hundred, The
BS20: P'bry 4H 43
Portbury La. BS20: P'bry 6C 44
Portbury Wlk. BS11: Shire 2H 45
Portbury Way BS20: P'bry 3B 44
PORTBURY WHARF 2J 43
PORTISHEAD 3F 43
Portishead Bus. Pk. BS20: P'head 3F 43
Portishead Rd. BS22: Wor 7F 85
Portishead Swimming Pool 1E 42
Portishead Way BS3: Ash V, Bwr A 6E 60
Portland Cl. BS48: Nail 1F 71
Portland Ct. BS1: Bris 6A 4 (4G 61)
BS16: Soun 5B 50
Portland Dr. BS20: P'head 4G 43
Portland Lofts *BS2: Bris* *1H 5*
(off Wilson St.)
Portland Mans. *BS2: Bris* *1H 5*
(off Portland Sq.)
Portland Pl. BA1: Bath 1E 6 (3B 100)
BS16: Stap H 5B 50
TA9: Bre K 6K 157
Portland Rd. BA1: Bath 1E 6
Portland Sq. BS2: Bris 1H 5 (1A 62)
Portland St. BS2: Bris 1D 4 (1J 61)
BS8: Clif 2F 61
BS16: Soun, Stap H 5B 50
Portland Ter. *BA1: Bath* *1E 6*
(off Harley St.)
Portmeade Drove BS26: Axb 5J 149
Portmeirion Cl. BS14: Whit 5D 76
Port Side Cl. BS5: St G 3H 63
Port Vw. BS20: Pill 3G 45
Portview Ho. *BS11: A'mth* *6F 33*
(off Portview Rd.)
Portview Rd. BS11: A'mth 6F 33
Portwall La. BS1: Bris 6G 5 (4A 62)
Portwall La. E.
BS1: Bris 6H 5 (4A 62)
Portway BS9: Sea M, Stok B 3B 46
BS11: Shire 7G 33
Portway (Park & Ride) 1G 45
Portway La. BS37: Chip S 4J 31
Portway Rdbt. BS11: Shire 7G 33
Postal Mus. 3F 7 (4C 100)
Post Office La. BS5: St G 1G 63
BS40: Blag 2B 134
BS48: Flax B 3C 72
Post Office Rd. BS23: W Mare 4F 105
BS24: Lock 7F 107
Poston Way BA15: W'ley 5C 124
POTTERS HILL 2F 91
POTTERSWOOD 2K 63
Potterswood Cl. BS15: K'wd 2B 64
Pottery Cl. BS23: W Mare 6J 105
Pottery Farm Cl. BS13: Hart 6J 75
Potts Cl. BA1: Bathe 6H 83
Poulton BA15: Brad A 7H 125
Poulton La. BA15: Brad A 7J 125
(not continuous)
Pound, The BS32: Alm 1C 26
BS40: Redh 1B 112
Pound Dr. BS16: Fish 3H 49
Pound La. BA15: Brad A 6G 125
BS16: Fish 4H 49
BS48: Nail 7E 56
Pound Mead BS40: F'tn 3G 91
Pound Rd. BS15: K'wd, Soun 6D 50
Pountney Dr. BS5: E'tn 1D 62
Powell Ct. BS30: Doy 7E 52
Powells Acres BS21: Clev 6E 54
Powis Cl. BS22: W Mare 2A 106
Powlett Ct. BA2: Bath 2J 7 (4D 100)
Powlett Rd. BA2: Bath 1J 7 (3D 100)
Pow's Hill BA3: Clan 2H 153
Pow's Orchard BA3: Mid N 5E 152
Pow's Rd. BS15: K'wd 2B 64
Poyntz Ct. BS30: L Grn 6D 64
Poyntz Rd. BS4: Know 2B 76
Praedium, The BS6: Redl 6H 47
Prattens La. BS16: Stap H 4B 50
Preacher Cl. BS5: St G 3K 63
Preanes Grn. BS22: Wor 2E 106
Precinct, The BS20: P'head 3F 43
Preddy's La. BS5: St G 3J 63
Prescot Cl. BS22: W Mare 2K 105
Prescott BS37: Yate 6D 30
Press Moor Dr. BS30: Bar C 5D 64
Prestbury BS37: Yate 6D 30
Preston Wlk. BS4: Know 1C 76
Prestwick Cl. BS4: Brisl 1F 77
Pretoria Rd. BS34: Pat 6B 26
Prewett St. BS1: Bris 7G 5 (4A 62)
Priddy Cl. BA2: Bath 6H 99
(not continuous)
Priddy Ct. BS14: Whit 5D 76
Priddy Dr. BS14: Whit 5D 76
PRIEST DOWN 5H 95
Priestley Way TA8: Bur S 3E 158
Priest Path BS31: Q Char 7J 77
Priests Way BS22: Wor 3B 106
Priestwood Cl. BS10: Hen 4G 35
Primrose Cl. BS15: K'wd 1A 64
BS32: Brad S 4F 27
Primrose Dr. BS35: T'bry 2B 12
PRIMROSE HILL 2K 99
Primrose Hill BA1: W'ton 2K 99
Primrose La. BA3: Mid N 5F 153
BS15: K'wd 7A 50
Primrose Ter. BA3: Mid N 5F 153
BS15: K'wd 7A 50
Princes Bldgs. *BA1: Bath* *3F 7*
(off George St.)
BA2: Bath 6J 7 (6D 100)
BS8: Clif 3F 61
Princes Ct. BS30: L Grn 5D 64
Prince's La. BS8: Clif 3F 61
Prince's Pl. BS7: B'stn 5A 48
Prince's Rd. BS21: Clev 6D 54
Princess Cl. BS31: Key 6C 78
Princess Gdns. BS16: Stap 2F 49
Princess Row BS2: Bris 1F 5
Princess Royal Gdns.
BS5: Redf 1E 62
Princess St. BS2: Bris 3C 62
BS3: Bedm 5A 62
TA8: Bur S 1D 158
Princes St. BA1: Bath 4F 7 (5B 100)
BA3: Clan 1J 153
BS2: Bris 1B 62
Princess Victoria St. BS8: Clif 3F 61
Prince St. BS1: Bris 6E 4 (4K 61)
Prinknash Ct. BS37: Yate 7D 30
Prior Pk. Bldgs. BA2: Bath 7J 7 (6D 100)
Prior Pk. Cotts. BA2: Bath 7J 7 (6C 100)
Prior Pk. Gdns. BA2: Bath 7J 7 (6D 100)
Prior Pk. Landscape Garden 1E 122
Prior Pk. Rd. BA2: Bath 7J 7 (6D 100)
Priors Hill BA2: Tim 4D 140
Prior's Hill Flats BS6: Bris 7K 47
Priors Lea BS37: Yate 5D 30
Priory Acre BS22: Wor 2B 106
Priory Av. BS9: W Trym 1G 47
Priory Cl. BA2: C Down 1D 122
BA3: Mid N 5E 152
BA15: Brad A 5G 125
Priory Ct. BS15: Han 6A 64
Priory Ct. Rd. BS9: W Trym 1G 47
Priory Dene BS9: W Trym 1G 47
Priory Farm Trad. Est.
BS20: P'bry 5B 44
Priory Gdns. BS7: Hor 7B 36
BS11: Shire 1H 45
BS20: Eas 4F 45
TA8: Bur S 2D 158
Priory M. BS23: W Mare 5K 105
Priory Pk. BA15: Brad A 5H 125
Priory Rd. BS4: Know 7D 62
BS8: Clif 1B 4 (1H 61)
BS11: Shire 2H 45
BS20: Eas 4F 45
BS20: P'bry 5B 44
BS23: W Mare 5J 105
BS31: Key 3C 78
Priory Wlk. BS20: P'bry 5B 44
PRISTON 7A 120
Priston Cl. BS22: Wor 6F 85
Priston La. BA2: Pris 1K 141
Priston Mill 4B 120
Priston Rd. BA2: Ing 6C 120
Pritchard St. BS2: Bris 1H 5 (1A 62)
Privet Dr. BS13: Hart 5J 75
Probyn Cl. BS16: B'hll 1J 49
Pro-Cathedral La. BS8: Clif 3B 4 (2H 61)
Proctor Cl. BS4: Brisl 1F 77
Proctor Ho. BS1: Bris 7H 5 (4A 62)
Promenade, The BS7: B'stn 6K 47
BS8: Clif 1F 61
Prospect Av. BS2: Bris 1E 4 (1K 61)
BS15: K'wd 7K 49
Prospect Bldgs. BA1: Bathe 5H 83
Prospect Cl. BS35: E Comp 4F 25
BS36: Fram C 6D 28
BS36: Wint D 3C 38
Prospect Cres. BS15: Soun 6D 50
Prospect Gdns. BA1: Bathe 5H 83
Prospect La. BS36: Fram C 6D 28
Prospect Pl. *BA1: Bath* *2C 100*
(off Camden Rd.)
BA1: Bathf 1B 102
BA1: W'ton 1J 99
BA2: Bath 7E 6 (6B 100)
BA2: C Down *3D 122*
(off Combe Rd.)
BS3: Bedm *6J 61*
(off British Rd.)
BS5: W'hall 1E 62
BS6: Cot 6K 47
BS23: W Mare 4G 105
Prospect Rd. BA2: Bath 7E 100
BS35: Sev B 1A 24
Prospect Ter. BS3: Bedm 6J 61
PROUD CROSS 7J 137
PROVIDENCE 7K 59
Providence La. BS41: L Ash 6K 59
PROVIDENCE PLACE 5D 152
Providence Pl. BS2: Bris 4J 5 (3B 62)
BS3: Bedm 6K 61
BS5: Redf 2E 62
BS40: Chew S 4D 114
Providence Ri. BS41: L Ash 7K 59
Providence Vw. BS41: L Ash 1A 74
Prowse Cl. BS35: T'bry 3A 12
Prowse's La. BS26: Axb 6G 149
Prudham St. BS5: E'tn 7E 48
PUBLOW 6G 95
Publow La. BS39: Pens, Pub 7F 95
PUCKLECHURCH 3B 52
Pucklechurch Trad. Est.
BS16: Puck 4B 52
Pudding Pie Cl. BS40: L'frd 6C 110
Pudding Pie La. BS40: L'frd 6C 110
Puffin Cl. BS22: Wor 4D 106
Pullin Ct. BS30: Old C 5H 65
Pullins Grn. BS35: T'bry 3K 11
Pulteney Av. BA2: Bath 5J 7 (5D 100)
Pulteney Bridge 4G 7 (5C 100)
Pulteney Bri. BA2: Bath 4G 7 (5C 100)
Pulteney Ct. BA2: Bath 6J 7 (6D 100)
Pulteney Gdns. BA2: Bath 5J 7 (5D 100)
Pulteney Gro. BA2: Bath 6J 7 (6D 100)
Pulteney M. BA2: Bath 4H 7 (4C 100)
Pulteney Rd. BA2: Bath 6J 7 (6D 100)
Pulteney Ter. *BA2: Bath* *5J 7*
(off Pulteney Av.)
Pump Ho., The BS4: St Ap 4H 63
Pump Ho. La. BS4: St Ap 4H 63
Pump La. BA1: Bathf 2K 101
BS1: Bris 6G 5 (4A 62)
BS32: Old D 1F 19
BS40: Redh 2B 112
Pump Room 4F 7 (5C 100)
Pump Sq. BS20: Pill 3H 45
Punnet Cl. BS27: Ched 7D 150
Purcell Wlk. BS4: Know 3K 75
Purdie Cl. BS27: Ched 6D 150
Purdown Rd. BS7: Hor 3B 48
Purdue Cl. BS22: Wor 1F 107
Purdy Ct. BS16: Fish 4J 49
Purlewent Dr. BA1: W'ton 1J 99
PURN 6J 127
Purnell Way BS39: Paul 7B 140
Purn Holiday Pk. BS24: B'don 7J 127
Purn La. BS24: B'don, W Mare 5J 127
Purn Rd. BS24: W Mare 5H 127
Purn Way BS24: B'don 6J 127
Pursey Dr. BS32: Brad S 1H 37
Purton Cl. BS15: K'wd 3C 64
Purton Rd. BS7: B'stn 6K 47
Purving Row BS24: Lym 5A 146
Purving Row La. BS24: Lym 6A 146
Puttingthorpe Dr. BS22: W Mare 5A 106
Puxley Cl. BS14: Stoc 4G 77
PUXTON 1D 108
Puxton La. BS24: E Rols, Hew, Pux 7D 86
Puxton Pk. 2B 108
Puxton Rd. BS24: E Rols, Pux 4B 108
PYE CORNER 4B 38
Pye Cft. BS32: Brad S 3G 27
Pyecroft Av. BS9: Henle 1H 47
Pylewell La. BS25: Star 3K 131
Pylle Hill Cres. BS3: Wind H 5B 62
Pyne Point BS21: Clev 6C 54
Pynne Cl. BS14: Stoc 4H 77
Pynne Rd. BS14: Stoc 5G 77
Pyracantha Wlk. BS14: H'gro 4C 76

Q

QEH Theatre 3B 4 (2H 61)
Quadrangle, The BS37: W'lgh 3C 40
Quadrant BS32: Brad S 3D 26
Quadrant, The BS2: Bris 4K 5
BS6: Redl 5H 47
BS32: Alm 3C 26
Quadrant E. BS16: Fish 5A 50
Quadrant W. BS16: Fish 5A 50
Quadrilles, The *BS35: Sev B* *7A 16*
(off Ableton La.)
Quaker Ct. *BS35: T'bry* *3K 11*
(off Quaker La.)
Quaker La. BS35: T'bry 3K 11
Quakers Cl. BS16: Down 7B 38
Quakers' Friars BS1: Bris 2G 5 (2A 62)
Quakers Rd. BS16: Down 6B 38
Quantock Cl. BS30: Old C 4G 65
TA8: Bur S 1D 158
Quantock Ct. BS16: Fren 6G 37
TA8: Bur S 3C 158
Quantock Rd. BS3: Wind H 6K 61
BS20: P'head 3D 42
BS23: W Mare 1F 127
Quantocks BA2: C Down 3C 122
Quarries, The BS32: Alm 1D 26
Quarrington Rd. BS7: Hor 3A 48
Quarry Barton BS16: Ham 3A 38
Quarry Cl. BA2: C Down 3B 122
BA2: Lim S 6B 124
BA15: W'ley 6B 124
Quarry Hay BS40: Chew S 4D 114
Quarry La. BS11: Law W 6C 34
BS36: Wint D 3C 38
Quarrymans Ct. BA2: C Down 3D 122
Quarry Mead BS35: Alv 7H 11
Quarry Ri. BS24: W Mare 5H 127
Quarry Rd. BA2: Clav D 6F 101
BS8: Clif 6G 47
BS15: K'wd 3B 64
BS16: Fren 1K 49
BS20: P'head 4E 42
BS25: Sandf 3G 131
BS35: Alv 7H 11
BS37: Chip S 5G 31
Quarry Rock Gdns. Cvn. Pk.
BA2: Clav D 7G 101
Quarry Steps BS8: Clif 6G 47
Quarry Va. BA2: C Down 3D 122
Quarry Way BS16: Emer G 6E 38
BS16: Stap 3G 49
BS48: Nail 7F 57
Quarter Mile All. BS15: K'wd 7B 50
Quays, The BS1: Bris 7D 4 (4J 61)
Quays Av. BS20: P'head 3G 43
Quayside BS1: Bris 4H 5 (3A 62)
BS8: Clif 5A 4 (3H 61)
Quayside La. BS5: St G 3H 63
Quayside Wlk. *BS1: Bris* *5F 5*
(off Redcliff Backs)
Quays Office Pk. BS20: P'head 3G 43
Quay St. BS1: Bris 3E 4 (2K 61)
Quebec BA2: Bath 5G 99
Quedgeley BS37: Yate 6C 30
Queen Ann Rd. BS5: Bar H 3D 62
Queen Charlotte St. BS1: Bris 4F 5 (3K 61)
QUEEN CHARLTON 7J 77
Queen Charlton La. BS14: Whit 7F 77
BS31: Q Char 7F 77
Queen Quay BS1: Bris 5F 5 (3K 61)
Queens Apartments BS8: Clif 3C 4
Queens Av. BS8: Clif 2B 4 (2H 61)
BS20: P'head 3E 42
Queenscote BS20: P'head 3H 43
Queen's Ct. BS8: Clif 2A 4 (2H 61)
Queensdale Cres. BS4: Know 1C 76
Queensdown Gdns. BS4: Brisl 6E 62
Queens Dr. BA2: C Down 3C 122
BS7: B'stn 4J 47
BS15: Han 5K 63
Queens Ga. BS9: Stok B 3D 46
Queenshill Rd. BS4: Know 1C 76
Queensholm Av. BS16: Down 6C 38
Queensholm Cl. BS16: Down 6C 38
Queensholm Cres. BS16: Down 6B 38
Queensholm Dr. BS16: Down 6C 38
Queens Pde.
BA1: Bath 3E 6 (4B 100)
BS1: Bris 5B 4 (3H 61)
Queens Pde. Pl. BA1: Bath 3F 7 (4B 100)
Queens Pl. BA2: Bath 6J 7 (6D 100)
Queen Sq. BA1: Bath 3F 7 (4B 100)
BS1: Bris 5E 4 (3K 61)
BS31: Salt 7K 79
Queen Sq. Apartments BS1: Bris 5F 5
Queen Sq. Av. BS1: Bris 5F 5 (3K 61)
Queen Sq. Pl. BA1: Bath 3E 6 (4B 100)
Queens Rd. BA3: Rads 4B 154
BS4: Know 1E 76
BS5: St G 1H 63
BS7: B'stn 4B 48
BS8: Clif 3A 4 (2G 61)
BS13: Bis, Withy 7F 75
BS16: Puck 3B 52
BS20: P'head 4A 42
BS21: Clev 6D 54
BS23: W Mare 3F 105
BS29: Ban 2A 130
BS30: C Hth 5E 64
BS31: Key 6B 78
BS48: Nail 1E 70
Queens Sq. *BS21: Clev* *6D 54*
(off Station Rd.)
TA9: High 4E 158
Queen St. BA1: Bath 4F 7 (5B 100)
BS2: Bris 3H 5 (2A 62)
BS5: Eastv 5F 49
BS11: A'mth 6E 32
BS15: K'wd 2K 63

Robertson Dr.—St Ann's Way

Robertson Dr. BS4: St Ap ...3H 63
Robertson Rd. BS5: E'tn ...6D 48
Robert St. BS5: Bar H ...2D 62
BS5: Eastv ...6D 48
Robin Cl. BA3: Mid N ...6F 153
BS10: Bren ...5H 35
BS14: Stoc ...4F 77
BS22: W Mare ...4C 106
Robin Cousins Sports Cen. ...7G 33
Robin Dr. BS24: Hut ...3C 128
Robin Hood La. BS2: Bris ...2D 4 (2J 61)
Robinia Wlk. BS14: H'gro ...3B 76
Robin La. BS21: Clev ...4D 54
Robinson Cl. BS48: Back ...5J 71
Robinson Dr. BS5: E'tn ...1C 62
Robinson Way BS48: Back ...5J 71
Robin Way BS37: Chip S ...7F 31
Rob-Lynne Ct. BS25: Wins ...5F 131
Rochester Cl. BS24: W Mare ...4J 127
Rochester Rd. BS4: St Ap ...4G 63
Rochfort Ct. BA2: Bath ...1J 7 (3D 100)
Rochfort Pl. BA2: Bath ...1H 7 (3C 100)
Rock, The BS4: Brisl ...6G 63
Rock Av. BS48: Nail ...7E 56
Rock Cl. BS4: Brisl ...7G 63
Rock Cotts. BA2: C Down ...3D 122
Rockeries Dr. BS25: Wins ...5F 131
Rockfield Cotts. BS22: W Mare ...3K 105
Rock Hall Cotts. BA2: C Down ...3D 122
Rock Hall La. BA2: C Down ...3D 122
Rockhill Est. BS31: Key ...6D 78
Rock Ho. BS10: Bren ...4J 35
Rockingham Gdns.
BS11: Law W ...7A 34
Rockingham Gro. BS23: W Mare ...3J 105
Rockingham Rdbt. BS11: A'mth ...1G 33
Rockland Gro. BS16: Stap ...2F 49
Rockland Rd. BS16: Down ...1A 50
Rock La. BA2: C Down ...3D 122
BS34: Stok G ...2H 37
Rockleaze BS9: Stok B ...6E 46
Rockleaze Av. BS9: Stok B ...5E 46
Rockleaze Ct. BS9: Stok B ...5E 46
Rockleaze Rd. BS9: Stok B ...5E 46
Rockliffe Av. BA2: Bath ...1K 7 (3D 100)
Rockliffe Rd. BA2: Bath ...1J 7 (3D 100)
Rock of Ages ...3H 133
Rock Rd. BA3: Mid N ...4F 153
BS30: Wick ...2C 66
BS31: Key ...5C 78
BS49: Yat ...4J 87
ROCKS, THE ...2F 31
Rockside Av. BS16: Down ...7D 38
Rockside Dr. BS9: Henle ...2H 47
Rockside Gdns. BS16: Down ...7D 38
BS36: Fram C ...6G 29
Rocks La. BS40: F'tn, Winf ...2H 91
Rockstowes Way BS10: Bren ...4K 35
Rock St. BS35: T'bry ...4K 11
Rockwell Av. BS11: Law W ...6B 34
Rockwood Ho. BS37: Yate ...2G 31
Rocky La. BS29: Ban ...3B 130
Rodborough BS37: Yate ...7C 30
Rodborough Way BS15: K'wd ...2E 64
Rodbourne Rd. BS10: Hor ...1K 47
RODFORD ...7D 30
Rodfords Mead BS14: H'gro ...3C 76
Rodford Way BS37: Yate ...7C 30
Rodmead Wlk. BS13: Withy ...6G 75
Rodmoor Rd. BS20: P'head ...2F 43
Rodney BS24: W Mare ...3J 127
Rodney Av. BS15: K'wd ...1J 63
Rodney Cres. BS34: Fil ...3C 36
Rodney Ho. BA2: Bath ...5G 99
BS8: Clif ...2G 61
(off Clifton Down Rd.)
Rodney Pl. BS8: Clif ...2G 61
Rodney Rd. BS15: K'wd ...7J 49
BS31: Salt ...1J 97
BS48: Back ...4J 71
Rodney Wlk. BS15: K'wd ...7J 49
Rodway Ct. BS16: Mang ...2E 50
RODWAY HILL ...4E 50
Rodway Hill BS16: Mang ...4E 50
Rodway Hill Rd. BS16: Mang ...3E 50
Rodway Rd. BS16: Mang ...3E 50
BS34: Pat ...7B 26
Rodway Vw. BS15: Soun ...5D 50
Roebuck Cl. BS22: Wor ...7E 84
Roegate Dr. BS4: St Ap ...3G 63
Roegate Ho. BS5: S'wll ...7H 49
Rogers Cl. BS30: C Hth ...4F 65
BS39: Clut ...2F 139
Rogers Ct. BS37: Chip S ...5J 31
Rogers Wlk. BS30: B'yte ...2H 65
Rokeby Av. BS6: Cot ...7J 47
ROLSTONE ...2K 107
Roman Baths ...5G 7 (5C 100)
Roman Farm Ct. BS11: Law W ...5C 34
Roman Farm Rd. BS4: Know ...3A 76
Roman Rd. BA2: Eng, Odd D ...4J 121
BS5: E'tn ...7D 48
BS24: B'don, W Mare ...5J 127
BS25: Sandf ...1F 131
Roman Wlk. BS4: Brisl ...6E 62
BS34: Stok G ...2G 37
Roman Way BA2: Pea J ...6E 142
BS9: Stok B ...4C 46
BS39: Paul ...7A 140
Romney Av. BS7: L'lze ...3D 48
Romney Gdns. *BS7: L'lze ...3C 48*
(off Romney Av.)
Romo Ct. BS16: Stap H ...4A 50
Ronald Rd. BS16: B'hll ...2H 49
Ronaldson BS30: Bit ...7G 65
Ronayne Wlk. BS16: Fish ...2A 50
Rondo Theatre, The ...2E 100
Rookery Cl. BS21: Kings S ...1C 86
BS22: Wor ...1C 106
BS26: Rook ...7E 146
Rookery La. BS30: Doy ...2F 53
BS35: Piln ...7G 17
SN14: Hin ...2F 53
Rookery Rd. BS4: Know ...7B 62
Rookery Way BS14: Whit ...6B 76
Rooksbridge Rd. BS26: Rook ...7E 146
Rooksbridge Wlk. BA2: Bath ...5J 99
Roper's La. BS40: Wrin ...1F 111
Rope Wlk. BS1: Bris ...4J 5 (3B 62)
BS48: Back ...5J 71
Ropewalk, The BA15: Brad A ...6G 125
Rope Wlk. Ho. BS2: Bris ...2J 5
Rosa Parks La. BS6: Bris ...7B 48
Rosary Rdbt., The BS16: Emer G ...1H 51
Rose Acre BS10: Bren ...4G 35
Rosebay Mead BS16: Stap ...4G 49
Roseberry Pk. BS5: St G ...1F 63
Roseberry Pl. BA2: Bath ...4A 6 (5K 99)
Roseberry Rd. BA2: Bath ...4A 6 (5J 99)
BS5: Redf ...2E 62
Rosebery Av. BS2: Bris ...7C 48
Rosebery Ct. BS2: Bris ...7C 48
Rosebery Ter. BS8: Clif ...4B 4 (3H 61)
Rose Cl. BS36: Wint D ...3C 38
Rose Cotts. BA2: Odd D ...4J 121
BA2: S'ske ...5B 122
Rose Ct. BS15: K'wd ...3B 64
Rosedale Av. BS23: W Mare ...5J 105
Rosedale Rd. BS16: Fish ...5K 49
Rose Gdns. BS22: Wor ...7F 85
ROSE GREEN ...7G 49
Rose Grn. BS5: Eastv ...6F 49
Rose Green Cen. ...7F 49
Rose Grn. Cl. BS5: S'wll ...6G 49
Rose Grn. Rd. BS5: S'wll ...6F 49
Rose Hill BA1: Bath, Swa ...1D 100
(not continuous)
Roseland Cl. BA1: Swa ...7E 82
Roseland Gdns. BS15: Warm ...1F 65
Rose La. BS36: Coal H ...1H 39
Roselarge Gdns. BS10: Bren ...5G 35
Rosemary Cl. BS32: Brad S ...1H 37
Rosemary Cres. BS20: P'head ...3H 43
Rosemary La. BS5: Eastv ...6E 48
Rosemary Wlk. *BA15: Brad A ...6G 125*
(off Newtown)
Rosemead BS7: Hor ...1C 48
Rose Mdw. Vw. BS3: Ash V ...1E 74
Rosemeare Gdns. BS13: Bis ...3E 74
Rosemont Ter. BS8: Clif ...3G 61
Rosemount Ct. BS15: K'wd ...2A 64
Rosemount La. BA2: Bath ...7D 100
Rosemount Rd. BS48: Flax B ...2F 73
Roseneath Av. TA8: Berr ...3B 156
Rose Oak Dr. BS36: Coal H ...7H 29
Rose Oak La. BS36: Coal H ...7H 29
Rose Rd. BS5: St G ...2G 63
Rosery, The BS16: Fish ...5A 50
Rosery Cl. BS9: W Trym ...7G 35
Rose Ter. BA2: C Down ...2E 122
Rosetree Paddock TA8: Berr ...3B 156
Rosevear BS2: Bris ...2C 62
Roseville Av. BS30: L Grn ...7E 64
Rose Wlk. BS16: Fish ...5A 50
Rosewarn Cl. BA2: Bath ...7G 99
Rosewell Ct. BA1: Bath ...4E 6 (5B 100)
Rosewood Av. BS35: Alv ...7H 11
TA8: Bur S ...2E 158
Rosewood Cl. TA8: Bur S ...1D 158
Rosewood Dr. TA8: Bur S ...2E 158
Rosling Rd. BS7: Hor ...2A 48
Roslyn Av. BS22: W Mare ...3A 106
Roslyn Rd. BS6: Redl ...7J 47
Rossall Av. BS34: Lit S ...1E 36
Rossall Rd. BS4: Brisl ...6F 63
Ross Cl. BS37: Chip S ...5H 31
Rossendale Cl. BS22: Wor ...1D 106
Rossiter Grange BS13: Withy ...6F 75
Rossiter Rd. BA2: Bath ...6H 7 (6C 100)
Rossiter's La. BS5: St G ...3J 63
Rossiter Wood Ct. BS11: Law W ...5B 34
Rosslyn Cl. BA1: Bath ...4H 99
Rosslyn Rd. BA1: Bath ...4H 99
Rosslyn Way BS35: T'bry ...1A 12
ROTCOMBE ...3B 140
Rotcombe La. BS39: High L ...4B 140
Rotcombe Va. BS39: High L ...3B 140
Rougemont Gro. NP16: Bulw ...1A 8
Rounceval St. BS37: Chip S ...5G 31
ROUND HILL ...2A 154
Roundhill Gro. BA2: Bath ...1H 121
Roundhill Pk. BA2: Bath ...7G 99
Roundmoor Cl. BS31: Salt ...7H 79
Roundmoor Gdns. BS14: Stoc ...4F 77
Round Oak Gro. BS27: Ched ...6C 150
Round Oak Rd. BS27: Ched ...6C 150
Roundways BS36: Coal H ...1G 39
Rousham Rd. BS5: Eastv ...5C 48
Row, The BS35: Aust ...5G 9
Rowacres BA2: Bath ...1H 121
BS14: H'gro ...4B 76
Rowan Cl. BS16: Fish ...6J 49
BS48: Nail ...7J 57
Rowan Ct. BA3: Rads ...5H 153
BS5: Bar H ...2D 62
BS37: Yate ...3C 30
Rowan Ho. BS13: Hart ...6K 75
Rowan Pl. BS24: W'ton V ...3F 107
Rowans, The BS16: Fren ...6K 37
BS20: P'head ...4D 42
Rowan Wlk. BS31: Key ...6A 78
Rowan Way BS15: Han ...6K 63
BS40: L'frd ...7C 110
TA8: Berr ...1B 156
ROWBERROW ...4C 132
Rowberrow BS14: H'gro ...3B 76
ROWBERROW BOTTOM ...5D 132
Rowberrow La. BS25: Row, S'ham ...3B 132
Rowberrow Way BS48: Nail ...1G 71
Rowland Av. BS16: Stap ...4F 49
Rowlands Cl. BA1: Bathf ...1A 102
Rowlandson Gdns. BS7: L'lze ...2D 48
Rowley St. BS3: Bedm ...6J 61
Rownham Cl. BS3: Bwr A ...5E 60
Rownham Ct. BS8: Clif ...4G 61
Rownham Hill BS8: L Wds ...3D 60
Rownham Mead BS8: Clif ...4G 61
Row of Ashes La. BS40: Redh ...7C 90
Rows, The BS22: Wor ...2C 106
Royal Albert Rd. BS6: Henle ...4G 47
Royal Av. BA1: Bath ...2D 6 (4A 100)
Royal Cl. BS10: Hen ...4D 34
Royal Ct. *BS23: W Mare ...1F 127*
(off Royal Sands)
Royal Crescent ...2D 6 (4A 100)
Royal Cres. BA1: Bath ...2D 6 (4A 100)
BS23: W Mare ...4F 105
Royal Fort Rd. BS2: Bris ...2D 4 (2J 61)
Royal Oak Av. BS1: Bris ...6E 4 (3K 61)
Royal Pde. BS8: Clif ...2B 4 (2H 61)
BS23: W Mare ...4F 105
Royal Pk. BS8: Clif ...2G 61
Royal Pk. M. BS8: Clif ...2G 61
Royal Photographic Society, The
...7D 6 (7A 100)
Royal Portbury Dock ...7C 32
Royal Portbury Dock Rd. BS20: P'bry ...2C 44
Royal Rd. BS16: Mang ...2E 50
Royal Sands BS23: W Mare ...1F 127
(not continuous)
Royal Victoria Pk. BS10: Bren ...5H 35
Royal York Cres. BS8: Clif ...3F 61
Royal York M. BS8: Clif ...3G 61
Royal York Vs. BS8: Clif ...3G 61
Royate Hill BS5: Eastv ...6F 49
Roycroft Rd. BS34: Fil ...5D 36
Roy King Gdns. BS30: C Hth ...3G 65
Roynon Way BS27: Ched ...7E 150
Royston Wlk. BS10: S'mead ...5K 35
Rozel Rd. BS7: Hor ...3A 48
Rubens Cl. BS31: Key ...5E 78
Rubens Ct. BS22: Wor ...1D 106
Ruby St. BS3: Bedm ...6H 61
RUCKLEY FORD ...4G 155
Ruddymead BS21: Clev ...7D 54
Rudford Cl. BS34: Pat ...5D 26
Rudge Cl. BS15: Soun ...6D 50
RUDGEWAY ...4H 19
Rudgeway Pk. BS35: Rudg ...4G 19
Rudgeway Rd. BS39: Paul ...1C 152
Rudgewood Cl. BS13: Hart ...6K 75
Rudgleigh Av. BS20: Pill ...4G 45
Rudgleigh Rd. BS20: Pill ...4G 45
Rudhall Grn. BS22: Wor ...1F 107
Rudhall Gro. BS10: Hor ...1A 48
Rudmore Pk. BA1: Bath ...4G 99
Rudthorpe Rd. BS7: Hor ...3A 48
Ruett La. BS39: Far G ...2A 152
Ruffet Rd. BS36: Coal H ...4E 38
Rugby Rd. BS4: Brisl ...6F 63
Rugosa Dr. TA8: Berr ...3B 156
Runnymead Av. BS4: Brisl ...1F 77
Runnymede BS15: K'wd ...7C 50
Runswick Rd. BS4: Brisl ...6E 62
Rupert St. BS1: Bris ...3E 4 (2K 61)
BS5: Redf ...3E 62
Rush Cl. BS32: Brad S ...4F 27
Rushen La. BS35: L Sev ...3K 9
Rushey La. BA15: Brad L, L Wrax ...7K 103
Rushgrove Gdns. BS39: Bis S ...1J 137
RUSH HILL ...2J 121
Rush Hill BA2: Bath ...2H 121
Rushmead La. BA15: L Wrax ...6J 103
Rushmoor BS21: Clev ...1A 68
Rushmoor Gro. BS48: Back ...5J 71
Rushmoor La. BS48: Back ...5J 71
Rushton Dr. BS36: Coal H ...7H 29
Rushway BS40: Burr ...1H 133
Rushy BS30: C Hth ...5E 64
Rushy Way BS16: Emer G ...6E 38
Ruskin Gro. BS7: Hor ...7C 36
Ruskin Rd. BA3: Rads ...5G 153
Russell Av. BS15: K'wd ...2C 64
Russell Cl. BS40: Winf ...5A 92
Russell Gro. BS6: Henle ...3J 47
Russell Rd. BS6: Henle ...4H 47
BS16: Fish ...6K 49
BS21: Clev ...6C 54
BS24: Lock ...6F 107
Russell St. BA1: Bath ...2F 7 (4B 100)
RUSSELL TOWN ...2D 62
Russell Town Av. BS5: E'tn ...1D 62
Russell Town Av. Ind. Cen. *BS5: Redf ...2E 62*
(off Russell Town Av.)
Russel M. BS37: Chip S ...5H 31
Russet Cl. BS35: Olv ...2C 18
Russets, The BS20: P'head ...4H 43
Russett Cl. BS48: Back ...4K 71
Russett Gro. BS48: Nail ...2E 70
Russet Way BA2: Pea J ...6D 142
Russ La. BS21: Kenn ...4E 68
Russ St. BS2: Bris ...4K 5 (3B 62)
Rustic Pk. Cvn. Site BS35: Sev B ...7A 16
Rutherford Cl. BS30: L Grn ...6E 64
Ruthven Rd. BS4: Know ...2A 76
Rutland Av. BS30: Will ...7E 64
Rutland Cl. BS22: W Mare ...4A 106
Rutland Rd. BS7: B'stn ...5A 48
Rydal Av. BS24: Lock ...1D 128
Rydal Rd. BS23: W Mare ...1H 127
Ryde Rd. BS4: Know ...7D 62
Rye Cl. BS13: Bis ...4E 74
Ryecroft Av. BS22: Wor ...2C 106
Ryecroft Ri. BS41: L Ash ...1B 74
Ryecroft Rd. BS36: Fram C ...6G 29
Ryedown La. BS30: Bit ...1G 79
Ryland Pl. BS2: Bris ...6C 48
Rylestone Cl. BS36: Fram C ...6D 28
Rylestone Gro. BS9: W Trym ...3F 47
Rysdale Rd. BS9: W Trym ...2F 47

S

Sabin Cl. BA2: Bath ...1H 121
Sabrina Way BS9: Stok B ...4C 46
Saco Ho. *BA1: Bath ...5G 7*
(off St James's Pde.)
BS1: Bris ...5H 5 (3A 62)
Sadbury Cl. BS22: Wor ...7F 85
Sadlers Ct. BS15: K'wd ...7B 50
Sadlier Cl. BS11: Law W ...7K 33
Saffron Cl. BS5: W'hall ...1E 62
Saffron Ct. BA1: Bath ...3C 100
Saffrons, The BS22: Wor ...7F 85
Saffron St. BS5: W'hall ...1E 62
Sage Cl. BS20: P'head ...4A 42
Sages Mead BS32: Brad S ...6F 27
St Agnes Av. BS4: Know ...7B 62
St Agnes Cl. BS48: Nail ...1J 71
St Agnes Gdns. BS4: Know ...7B 62
St Agnes Wlk. BS4: Know ...7B 62
St Aidans Cl. BS5: St G ...3K 63
St Aidans Rd. BS5: St G ...3J 63
St Albans Rd. BS6: Henle ...4H 47
St Aldams Dr. BS16: Puck ...3B 52
St Aldhelm Rd. BA15: Brad A ...7J 125
St Aldwyn's Cl. BS7: Hor ...7B 36
ST ANDREWS ...5A 48
St Andrews BS30: Warm ...3F 65
BS37: Yate ...6E 30
St Andrews Cl. BS22: Wor ...1D 106
BS48: Nail ...1J 71
BS49: Cong ...7J 87
St Andrews Dr. BS21: Clev ...7A 54
St Andrews Ga. Rdbt. BS11: A'mth ...5F 33
St Andrews Ho. BS11: A'mth ...6E 32
St Andrew's Pde. BS23: W Mare ...1H 127
St Andrews Rd. BS6: Bris ...7A 48
BS11: A'mth ...5F 33
BS27: Ched ...7E 150
BS48: Back ...5K 71
TA8: Bur S ...1D 158
St Andrew's Road Station (Rail) ...3F 33
St Andrews Ter. BA1: Bath ...3F 7 (4B 100)
St Andrews Trad. Est. BS11: A'mth ...5G 33
St Andrew's Wlk. BS8: Clif ...3G 61
ST ANNE'S ...4F 63
St Annes Av. BS31: Key ...4B 78
St Annes Cl. BS5: St G ...3H 63
BS30: C Hth ...5F 65
St Anne's Ct. BS4: St Ap ...4F 63
BS31: Key ...4B 78
St Annes Dr. BS30: Old C ...7G 65
BS30: Wick ...2B 66
BS36: Coal H ...2G 39
ST ANNE'S PARK ...4G 63
St Annes Pk. Rd. BS4: St Ap ...4G 63
St Anne's Rd. BS4: St Ap ...3F 63
BS5: St G ...3K 63
St Anne's Ter. BS4: St Ap ...4G 63
St Ann's Dr. TA8: Bur S ...6C 156
St Ann's Pl. BA1: Bath ...4E 6
St Ann's Way BA2: Bath ...4K 7 (5D 100)

St Anthony's Cl.—Sassoon Ct.

St Anthony's Cl. BA3: Mid N 4E 152
St Anthony's Dr. BS30: Wick 2B 66
St Aubin's Av. BS4: Brisl 6H 63
St Aubyn's Av. BS23: Uph 3F 127
St Augustine's Cl. BS20: P'head 4A 42
St Augustine's Pde. BS1: Bris 4E 4 (3K 61)
St Augustine's Pl. BS1: Bris 4E 4 (3K 61)
St Austell Cl. BS48: Nail 2J 71
St Austell Rd. BS22: W Mare 4K 105
St Barnabas Cl. BA3: Mid N 3F 153
BS4: Know 1B 76
BS30: Warm 2G 65
St Bartholomew's Rd. BS7: Bris 5B 48
St Bede's Rd. BS15: K'wd 6A 50
St Bernards Rd. BS11: Shire 2J 45
St Brelades Gro. BS4: St Ap 4G 63
St Brendans Rdbt. BS11: A'mth 6F 33
St Brendans Trad. Est. BS11: A'mth 5F 33
St Brendans Way BS11: A'mth 6F 33
St Briavels Dr. BS37: Yate 6D 30
St Cadoc Ho. BS31: Key 5D 78
ST CATHERINE 1H 83
St Catherine's Cl. BA2: Bath 4K 7 (5E 100)
St Catherine's Ct. BS3: Bedm 6K 61
St Catherines Hospital BA1: Bath 5G 7
St Catherine's Ind. Est. *BS3: Bedm* 5K 61
(off Whitehouse La.)
St Catherine's Mead BS20: Pill 5H 45
St Catherine's Pl. BS3: Bedm 5K 61
St Catherine's Ter. *BS3: Bedm* 6K 61
(off Church La.)
St Chad's Av. BA3: Mid N 5E 152
St Chad's Grn. BA3: Mid N 5E 152
St Charles Cl. BA3: Mid N 4E 152
St Christopher's Cl. BA2: Bath 4E 100
St Christophers Ct. BS21: Clev 4C 54
St Christopher's Way TA8: Bur S 5C 156
St Clements Ct. *BS2: Bris* 1J 5
(off Wilson St.)
BS16: Soun 5B 50
BS21: Clev 5C 54
BS22: Wor 2E 106
BS31: Key 6C 78
St Clement's Rd. BS31: Key 5C 78
(not continuous)
St David's Av. BS30: C Hth 4E 64
St David's Cl. BS22: W Mare 2K 105
St David's Ct. BS21: Clev 2E 68
St David's Cres. BS4: St Ap 3H 63
St Davids M. BS1: Bris 5C 4
St David's Rd. BS35: T'bry 3A 12
St Dunstans Cl. BS31: Key 4C 78
St Dunstan's Rd. BS3: Bedm 7J 61
St Edward's Rd. BS8: Clif 5A 4 (3H 61)
St Edyth's Rd. BS9: Sea M 2B 46
St Fagans Ct. BS30: Will 7F 65
St Francis Dr. BS30: Wick 2B 66
BS36: Wint 1D 38
St Francis Rd. BS3: Ash G 5G 61
BS31: Key 4A 78
St Gabriel's Bus. Pk. BS5: E'tn 1D 62
St Gabriel's Rd. BS5: E'tn 1D 62
ST GEORGE 1J 63
ST GEORGES 2H 107
St Georges Av. BS5: St G 3H 63
St George's Bristol 4C 4 (3J 61)
St Georges Bldgs. *BA1: Bath* 3C 6
(off Up. Bristol Rd.)
St Georges Cl. BS20: Eas 5E 44
St Georges Ct. BS22: St Geo 7G 85
St Georges Ga. *BS5: St G* 1F 63
(off Church Rd.)
St Georges Hgts. BS5: Redf 2F 63
St Georges Hill BA2: B'ptn 3F 101
BS20: Eas 5E 44
St Georges Ho. BS5: St G 1G 63
St Georges Ind. Est. BS11: A'mth 4F 33
St Georges Pl. *BA1: Bath* 3D 6
(off Up. Bristol Rd.)
St Georges Rd.
BS1: Bris 5B 4 (3H 61)
BS20: P'bry 1C 44
BS31: Key 4B 78
St Gregory's Rd. BS7: Hor 7B 36
St Helena Rd. BS6: Henle 4H 47
St Helens Dr. BS30: Old C 7G 65
BS30: Wick 2C 66
St Helen's Wlk. BS5: St G 7J 49
St Helier Av. BS4: Brisl 5H 63
St Hilary Cl. BS9: Stok B 3D 46
St Ivel Way BS30: Warm 3G 65
St Ives Cl. BS48: Nail 1J 71
St Ives Rd. BS23: W Mare 1J 127
St James' Barton BS1: Bris 1G 5 (1A 62)
St James Cl. BS35: T'bry 1A 12
St James Ct. BS1: Bris 2F 5
BS32: Brad S 3E 26
St James' Pde. BS1: Bris 2F 5 (2K 61)
St James Pl. BS16: Mang 3E 50
St James's Pde. BA1: Bath 5F 7 (5B 100)
St James's Pk. BA1: Bath 1E 6 (3B 100)
St James's Pl. BA1: Bath 1E 6 (3B 100)
St James's Sq. BA1: Bath 1D 6 (3A 100)
St James's St. BA1: Bath 1E 6 (3B 100)
St James St. BS16: Mang 3E 50
BS23: W Mare 5F 105
St John's BA1: Bath 3H 99
St John's Av. BS21: Clev 6D 54
St John's Cl. BA2: Pea J 6B 142
BS23: W Mare 3F 105
St Johns Ct. BA2: Bath 2G 7 (4C 100)
BS16: Fish 5J 49
BS26: Axb 4H 149
BS31: Key 4C 78
St John's Cres. BA3: Mid N 4E 152
BS3: Wind H 7A 62
St Johns Hospital *BA1: Bath* 5F 7
(off Chapel Ct.)
St John's La.
BS3: Bedm, Wind H 6J 61
St John's Pl. BA1: Bath 4F 7 (5B 100)
St Johns Rd. BA1: Bath 3A 6 (4J 99)
BA2: Bath 3G 7 (4C 100)
BA2: Tim 4F 141
BS3: Bedm 7E 4 (5K 61)
(Lombard St.)
BS3: Bedm 6J 61
(St John's St.)
BS8: Clif 7G 47
BS21: Clev 6D 54
BS48: Back 5K 71
TA8: Bur S 1D 158
St John's Steep *BS1: Bris* 3F 5
(off All Saints St.)
St John's St. BS3: Bedm 6J 61
St John St. BS35: T'bry 3K 11
St John's Way BS37: Chip S 4H 31
St Joseph's Rd. BS10: Bren 4H 35
BS23: W Mare 3G 105
St Judes Ter. BS22: W Mare 3A 106
St Julian's Rd. BA2: Shos 2E 154
St Julien's Cl. BS39: Paul 2C 152
St Katherine's Quay BA15: Brad A 7H 125
St Keyna Ct. BS31: Key 5D 78
St Keyna Rd. BS31: Key 5C 78
St Kilda's Rd. BA2: Bath 7A 6 (6K 99)
St Ladoc Rd. BS31: Key 5B 78
St Laud Cl. BS9: Stok B 3D 46
St Laurence Rd. BA15: Brad A 7J 125
St Lawrence Ct. BS11: Law W 7J 33
St Leonard's Rd. BS5: E'tn 6E 48
BS7: Hor 2A 48
St Loe Cl. BS14: Whit 7B 76
St Lucia Cl. BS7: Hor 1A 48
St Lucia Cres. BS7: Hor 1A 48
St Lukes Cl. BS16: Emer G 1G 51
TA8: Bur S 1D 158
St Luke's Ct. BS3: Bedm 7H 5 (5A 62)
St Luke's Cres. BS3: Wind H 5B 62
St Luke's Gdns. BS4: Brisl 7G 63
St Lukes Ho. BS16: Emer G 1G 51
St Luke's M. BS4: Brisl 7G 63
St Lukes Rd. BA2: Bath 1B 122
BA3: Mid N 4D 152
BS3: Bris, Wind H 7H 5 (5A 62)
St Luke's Steps BS3: Wind H 5A 62
St Luke St. BS5: Bar H 2D 62
St Margaret's Cl. BS31: Key 4B 78
BS48: Back 5J 71
St Margaret's Ct. BA15: Brad A 6H 125
St Margaret's Dr. BS9: Henle 3J 47
St Margaret's Hill BA15: Brad A 6H 125
St Margarets La. BS48: Back 5J 71
St Margaret's Pl. BA15: Brad A 6H 125
St Margaret's Steps *BA15: Brad A* 6H 125
(off St Margaret's Hill)
St Margaret's St. BA15: Brad A 6H 125
St Margaret's Ter. BS23: W Mare 4F 105
St Margaret's Vs. BA15: Brad A 6H 125
St Mark's Av. BS5: E'tn 6E 48
St Marks Cl. BS31: Key 4C 78
St Marks Gdns. BA2: Bath 7G 7 (6C 100)
St Mark's Grn. BA2: Tim 3F 141
St Mark's Gro. BS5: E'tn 7D 48
St Mark's Rd. BA2: Bath 7G 7 (6C 100)
BA3: Mid N 4E 152
BS5: E'tn 7D 48
BS22: Wor 7D 84
TA8: Bur S 1D 158
St Mark's Ter. BS5: E'tn 7D 48
St Martins BS41: L Ash 1A 74
St Martin's Cl. BS4: Know 7D 62
St Martins Ct. BA2: Odd D 3A 122
BS22: Wor 1C 106
St Martin's Gdns. BS4: Know 1D 76
St Martins Ind. Pk. BS11: A'mth 2K 33
St Martin's Rd. BS4: Know 7D 62
St Martin's Wlk. BS4: Know 1D 76
St Mary Redcliffe Church 6G 5 (4A 62)
St Mary's Bldgs.
BA2: Bath 6F 7 (6B 100)
St Marys Cl. BA2: Bath 4K 7 (5D 100)
BA2: Tim 3F 141
BS24: Hut 3B 128
BS30: C Hth 3F 65
St Mary's Ct. BS24: W Mare 3J 127
St Marys Gdns. BS40: L'frd 7D 110
St Mary's Gro. BS48: Nail 3E 70
St Mary's Pk. BS48: Nail 2E 70
St Mary's Pk. Rd.
BS20: P'head 4E 42
St Marys Ri. BA3: Writ 4C 154
St Mary's Rd. BS8: L Wds 3D 60
BS11: Shire 1G 45
BS20: P'head 4E 42
BS24: Hut 3B 128
TA8: Bur S 1D 158
St Mary's St. BS26: Axb 4J 149
St Mary St. BS35: T'bry 4K 11
St Mary's Wlk. BS11: Shire 2H 45
St Marys Way BS35: T'bry 3K 11
BS37: Yate 4F 31
St Matthews Av. BS6: Bris 7K 47
St Matthew's Cl. BS23: W Mare 3F 105
St Matthews Pl. BA2: Bath 6J 7 (6D 100)
St Matthew's Rd. BS6: Bris 1E 4 (1K 61)
St Matthias Ho. BS2: Bris 2J 5
St Matthias Pk. BS2: Bris 2J 5 (2B 62)
St Michael's Av. BS21: Clev 1D 68
BS22: Wor 1E 106
St Michaels Cl. BS7: B'stn 4A 48
BS36: Wint 7C 28
St Michaels Ct. BA2: Mon C 4G 123
BS15: K'wd 1K 63
St Michael's Hill BS2: Bris 1C 4 (1J 61)
St Michael's Pk. BS2: Bris 1C 4 (1J 61)
St Michael's Pl. BA1: Bath 5F 7 (5B 100)
St Michael's Rd. BA1: Bath 2A 6 (4K 99)
BA2: Bath 6G 99
TA8: Bur S 1D 158
St Monica Ct. BS9: W Trym 3G 47
St Nicholas Cl. BA15: W'ley 5B 124
St Nicholas Ct. BA2: B'ptn 2H 101
St Nicholas Mkt. BS1: Bris 4F 5 (3K 61)
St Nicholas Pk. BS5: E'tn 7D 48
St Nicholas Rd. BS2: Bris 7B 48
BS14: Whit 6E 76
BS23: Uph 3F 127
St Nicholas St. BS1: Bris 4F 5 (3K 61)
St Nicholas Way BS48: B'ley 1F 89
St Oswald's Ct. BS6: Redl 5H 47
St Oswald's Rd. BS6: Redl 5H 47
St Patrick's Ct. BA2: Bath 4K 7 (5D 100)
BS31: Key 5C 78
ST PAUL'S 1C 62
St Pauls Pl. BA1: Bath 4E 6
BA3: Mid N 4E 152
St Paul's Rd. BS3: Bedm 5K 61
BS8: Clif 2A 4 (2H 61)
BS23: W Mare 7G 105
TA8: Bur S 1D 158
St Paul St. BS2: Bris 1H 5
St Peter's Av. BS23: W Mare 3F 105
St Peters Ct. *BS3: Bedm* 5K 61
(off Bedminster Pde.)
St Peter's Cres. BS36: Fram C 6F 29
St Peter's Ho. BS8: Clif 5B 4
St Peters Lodge BS20: P'head 4F 43
St Peter's Pl. BA2: Bath 5B 6 (5K 99)
St Peter's Ri. BS13: Bis 3G 75
St Peter's Rd. BA3: Mid N 6G 153
BS20: P'head 4F 43
TA8: Bur S 1D 158
St Peter's Ter. BA2: Bath 5B 6 (5K 99)
St Peter's Wlk. BS9: Henle 2H 47
St Philips C'way. BS2: Bris 2C 62
BS4: Bris 2C 62
BS5: Bar H 2C 62
St Philips Central Ind. Est. BS2: Bris 4C 62
ST PHILIP'S MARSH 4D 62
St Philips Rd. BS2: Bris 3K 5 (2B 62)
St Pierre Dr. BS30: Warm 3F 65
St Ronan's Av. BS6: Cot 7J 47
St Saviours Ho. BS4: Know 7B 62
St Saviours Ri. BS36: Fram C 1F 39
St Saviours Rd. BA1: Bath, Swa 2D 100
St Saviour's Ter. BA1: Bath 2D 100
St Saviours Way BA1: Bath 2E 100
St Stephen's Av. BS1: Bris 4E 4 (3K 61)
St Stephens Bus. Cen. *BS30: Old C* 4G 65
(off Poplar Rd.)
St Stephen's Cl. BA1: Bath 2B 100
BS10: S'mead 5J 35
BS16: Soun 5C 50
St Stephen's Ct. BA1: Bath 3B 100
St Stephen's Pl. BA1: Bath 3B 100
St Stephen's Rd. BA1: Bath 1F 7 (3B 100)
BS16: Soun 6B 50
St Stephen's St. BS1: Bris 3E 4 (2K 61)
St Swithin's Pl. BA1: Bath 1G 7 (3C 100)
St Swithin's Yd. BA1: Bath 2G 7
St Thomas Pl. BS1: Bris 5G 5 (3A 62)
St Thomas Rd. BA3: Mid N 4F 153
St Thomas St. BS1: Bris 4G 5 (3A 62)
St Thomas St. E. BS1: Bris 5G 5 (3A 62)
St Vincent's Hill BS6: Redl 6G 47
St Vincents Rd. BS8: Clif 3G 61
St Vincents Trad. Est. BS2: Bris 3E 62
Saint Way BS34: Stok G 3J 37
St Werburghs City Farm 5B 48
St Werburgh's Pk. BS2: Bris 6C 48
St Werburgh's Rd. BS2: Bris 6B 48
St Whytes Rd. BS4: Know 2K 75
St Winifred's Dr. BA2: C Down 2F 123
St Wulfstan Av. BS10: W Trym 7G 35
Salcombe Gdns. BS22: Wor 1E 106
Salcombe Rd. BS4: Know 1B 76
Salem Rd. BS36: Wint 7D 28
SALISBURY 2D 152
Salisbury Av. BS15: K'wd 1K 63
Salisbury Dr. BS16: Down 2C 50
Salisbury Gdns. BS16: Down 3C 50
Salisbury Pk. BS16: Down 2C 50
Salisbury Rd. BA1: Bath 1D 100
BS4: St Ap 4F 63
BS6: Redl 6K 47
BS16: Down 2C 50
BS22: W Mare 3A 106
BS39: Paul 2D 152
TA8: Bur S 1E 158
Salisbury St. BS5: Bar H 3D 62
BS5: St G 2G 63
Salisbury Ter. BS23: W Mare 4F 105
Salisbury Vw. BS39: Paul 2D 152
Sally Barn Cl. BS30: L Grn 7C 64
Sally Hill BS20: P'head 1G 43
Sally Lunn's House 5G 7 (5C 100)
Sallysmead Cl. BS13: Hart 6H 75
Sallys Way BS36: Wint 7D 28
Salmon Cl. BS35: Sev B 7A 16
Salmons Way BS16: Emer G 7E 38
SALTERS BROOK 1F 117
SALTFORD 7J 79
Saltford Ct. BS31: Salt 7J 79
Salthouse Farm Cvn. Pk.
BS35: Sev B 5A 16
Salthouse Rd. BS21: Clev 7B 54
Salthrop Rd. BS7: B'stn 4A 48
Saltings Cl. BS21: Clev 7B 54
Saltmarsh Dr. BS11: Law W 6A 34
Saltwell Av. BS14: Whit 5E 76
Salway Cl. BS40: Chew S 3E 114
Sambourne La. BS20: Pill 3G 45
Samian Way BS34: Stok G 2G 37
Sampson Ho. Bus. Pk. BS10: H'len 7D 24
Sampsons Rd. BS13: Hart 6K 75
Samuel Cft. La. SN14: Hin 2H 53
Samuel Rodgers Cres. NP16: Bulw 1A 8
Samuel St. BS5: Redf 1E 62
Samuel White Rd. BS15: Han 6K 63
Samuel Wright Cl. BS30: Old C 4H 65
Sanctuary, The BS20: Pill 4J 45
Sanctuary Gdns. BS9: Stok B 5D 46
Sandacre Res. Pk. TA9: High 4F 159
Sandbach Rd. BS4: Brisl 5F 63
Sandbed Rd. BS2: Bris 6C 48
Sandburrows Rd. BS13: Bis 4E 74
Sandburrows Wlk. BS13: Bis 4F 75
Sand Cl. BA15: Brad A 5J 125
Sandcroft BS14: H'gro 4B 76
Sandcroft Av. BS23: Uph 3F 127
Sanderling Pl. BS20: P'head 2H 43
SANDFORD 1G 131
SANDFORD BATCH 3F 131
Sandford Cl. BS21: Clev 1B 68
Sandford Rd. BS8: Clif 4G 61
BS23: W Mare 5H 105
BS25: Wins 3F 131
Sandgate Rd. BS4: Brisl 6F 63
Sand Hill BS4: Brisl 5E 62
Sandhills Dr. TA8: Bur S 3B 156
Sandholme Cl. BS16: Down 7C 38
Sandholme Rd. BS4: Brisl 5E 62
Sandhurst BS37: Yate 6D 30
Sandhurst Cl. BS34: Pat 5D 26
Sandhurst Rd. BS4: Brisl 5F 63
Sandling Av. BS7: Hor 1C 48
Sandmead Rd. BS25: Sandf 1G 131
Sandown Cl. BS16: Down 6D 38
Sandown Rd. BS4: Brisl 5F 63
BS34: Fil 4E 36
Sandpiper Dr. BS22: Wor 3D 106
Sandringham Av. BS16: Down 7C 38
Sandringham Ct. BS23: W Mare 7H 105
Sandringham Pk. BS16: Down 7C 38
Sandringham Rd. BS4: Brisl 6F 63
BS23: W Mare 7H 105
BS30: L Grn 7D 64
BS34: Stok G 2F 37
Sand Rd. BS22: Kew 6A 84
Sands Hill SN14: Dyr 4K 53
Sands La. BS36: Fram C 5D 28
Sandstone Ri. BS36: Wint 3C 38
Sandwich Rd. BS4: Brisl 5F 63
Sandy Cl. BS32: Brad S 1G 37
TA9: High 4F 159
Sandy La. BS5: Eastv 5E 48
BS8: Abb L, Fail 7E 44
BS35: Aust 4G 9
(not continuous)
BS39: Stan D 1A 116
BS40: Chew M, Stan D 1J 115
Sandy Leaze BA15: Brad A 6G 125
Sandyleaze BS9: W Trym 1E 46
Sandy Lodge BS37: Yate 6E 30
Sandy Pk. Rd. BS4: Brisl 5E 62
Sarabeth Dr. BA2: Tun 1A 142
Saracens, The BS7: Hor 3A 48
Saracen St. BA1: Bath 3G 7 (4C 100)
Sarah St. BS5: Bar H 2D 62
Sargent St. BS3: Bedm 5A 62
Sarum Cl. BS16: Emer G 2G 51
Sarum Cres. BS10: S'mead 6J 35
Sassoon Ct. BS30: Bar C 4D 64

Satchfield Cl.—Sir Bevil Grenville Monument

Satchfield Cl. BS10: Hen 5F 35
Satchfield Cres. BS10: Hen 5F 35
Satellite Bus. Pk. BS5: St G 2F 63
Sates Way BS9: Henle 2J 47
Saunders Rd. BS16: Stap H 4C 50
Saunton Wlk. BS4: Know 2A 76
Savages Wood Rd.
BS32: Brad S 6F 27
Savernake Rd. BS22: Wor 1D 106
Saville Cres. BS22: W Mare 4A 106
Saville Ga. Cl. BS9: Stok B 4F 47
Saville M. BS6: Bris 1E 4 (1K 61)
Saville Pl. BS8: Clif 3G 61
Saville Rd. BS9: Stok B 5F 47
BS22: W Mare 4A 106
Saville Row BA1: Bath 2F 7 (4B 100)
Savoy Rd. BS4: Brisl 5F 63
Saw Cl. BA1: Bath 4F 7 (5B 100)
Saw Mill La. BS35: T'bry 3K 11
Saw Mills, The *BA15: Brad A 7G 125*
(off Frome Rd.)
Sawyers Cl. BS48: Wrax 7J 57
Sawyers Ct. BS21: Clev 6E 54
Saxby Cl. BS21: Clev 1B 68
BS22: Wor 7F 85
Saxon Ct. BS22: St Geo 1H 107
Saxondale Av. TA8: Bur S 4C 156
Saxon Pl. BS27: Ched 7D 150
Saxon Rd. BS2: Bris 6C 48
BS22: W Mare 4A 106
Saxon St. BS40: L'frd 6F 111
Saxon Way BA2: Pea J 5E 142
BA15: W'ley 5D 124
BS27: Ched 7H 151
BS32: Brad S 5E 26
Says La. BS40: L'frd 7C 110
Say Wlk. BS30: B'yte 2H 65
Scafell Cl. BS23: W Mare 3J 105
Scandrett Cl. BS10: Hen 5E 34
Scantleberry Cl. BS16: Down 6B 38
Scaurs, The BS22: Wor 2D 106
School Cl. BS5: Eastv 5F 49
BS14: Whit 6B 76
BS29: Ban 2B 130
BS34: Pat 6E 26
School Ct. BS34: Stok G 3J 37
School La. BA1: Bathe 6H 83
BS16: Stap 3G 49
BS21: Clev 6E 54
(off Old St.)
BS22: Wick L 4F 85
BS25: Row 4C 132
BS29: Ban 2B 130
BS39: C'wd 3J 117
BS40: Chew S 4D 114
BS40: F'tn 3E 90
BS40: Dar G 5H 73
School Rd. BS4: Brisl 7G 63
BS4: Wind H 6C 62
BS15: K'wd 1A 64
BS30: C Hth 5E 64
BS30: Old C 6F 65
BS36: Fram C 6D 28
BS40: Wrin 2G 111
School Vw. BS48: Wrax 7K 57
School Wlk. BS5: W'hall 7F 49
BS37: Yate 4E 30
School Way BS35: Sev B 7A 16
Scobell Ri. BS39: High L 3A 140
Scop, The BS32: Alm 1D 26
Score, The BS40: Blag 3C 134
Score La. BS40: Blag 4C 134
Scornfield La. BS40: Chew S 5D 114
Scotch Horn Cl. BS48: Nail 7H 57
Scotch Horn Leisure Cen. 7H 57
Scotch Horn Way BS48: Nail 7H 57
Scot Elm Dr. BS24: W Wick 3G 107
BS29: Ban 3G 107
Scotland La. BS4: Brisl 2H 77
BS14: Brisl 4H 77
Scot La. BS40: Chew S 3D 114
Scots Pine Av. BS48: Nail 7H 57
Scott Ct. BS30: Bar C 4D 64
Scott Lawrence Cl.
BS16: B'hll 1J 49
Scott Rd. BS23: W Mare 1J 127
TA9: High 5F 159
Scott Wlk. BS30: B'yte 2H 65
Scott Way BS37: Yate 6F 31
Scumbrum La. BS39: High L 2A 140
Sea Bank Rd. BS20: P'bry 7B 32
Seabrook Rd. BS22: W Mare 3B 106
Seagry Cl. BS10: S'mead 6A 36
SEA MILLS 2C 46
Sea Mills La. BS9: Sea M 4C 46
Sea Mills Station (Rail) 4B 46
SeaQuarium 6F 105
Searle Ct. BS21: Clev 6E 54
Searle Ct. Av. BS4: Brisl 5G 63
Searle Cres. BS23: W Mare 6J 105
Seaton Rd. BS5: E'tn 7E 48
Seavale Rd. BS21: Clev 5C 54
Seaview Rd. BS20: P'head 4B 42
TA8: Bur S 7C 156
Seawalls BS9: Stok B 6D 46
Seawalls Rd. BS9: Stok B 6D 46
Second Av. BA2: Bath 7B 6 (7K 99)
BA3: Mid N 7G 153
BS14: H'gro 3D 76
Second Severn Crossing
BS35: Sev B 5A 16
Second Way BS11: A'mth 6H 33
Seddon Rd. BS2: Bris 6C 48
Sedgefield Gdns. BS16: Down 6D 38
Sedgemoor Cl. BS48: Nail 2F 71
Sedgemoor Rd. BA2: C Down 3B 122
BS23: W Mare 3H 105
Sedgemoor Ter. BA2: C Down 2C 122
Sedgewick Ho. BS11: Shire 1J 45
Sefton Pk. Rd. BS7: B'stn 5A 48
Sefton Sq. BS24: W'ton V 4E 106
Selborne Rd. BS7: Hor 3B 48
Selbourne Cl. BA1: Bath 3G 99
Selbourne Rd. BS23: W Mare 1G 127
Selbrooke Cres. BS16: Fish 2K 49
Selby Rd. BS5: S'wll 7H 49
Selden Rd. BS14: Stoc 5G 77
Selkirk Rd. BS15: K'wd 7A 50
Selley Wlk. BS13: Bis 5G 75
Selwood Cl. BS22: W Mare 5A 106
Selworthy BS15: K'wd 2C 64
Selworthy Cl. BS31: Key 5B 78
Selworthy Gdns. *BS48: Nail 1G 71*
(off Mizzymead Rd.)
Selworthy Ho. BA2: C Down 2B 122
Selworthy Rd. BS4: Know 7D 62
BS23: W Mare 1H 127
Selworthy Ter. BA2: C Down 2B 122
Seneca Pl. BS5: St G 2F 63
Seneca St. BS5: St G 2F 63
Septimus Bldgs. *BS14: Hart 5K 75*
(off Hawkfield Cl.)
Serbert Cl. BS20: P'head 3G 43
Serbert Rd. BS20: P'head 3G 43
Serbert Way BS20: P'head 3G 43
Sercombe Pk. BS21: Clev 1E 68
Serlo Ct. BS22: Wor 7D 84
Serridge La. BS36: Coal H 3G 39
Seven Acres, The BS24: W'ton V 5D 106
Seven Acres La. BA1: Bathe 5H 83
Seven Dials BA1: Bath 4F 7 (5B 100)
Seventh Av. BS7: Hor 6D 36
BS14: H'gro 3C 76
Severn Av. BS23: W Mare 7G 105
SEVERN BEACH 7A 16
Severn Beach Station (Rail) 7A 16
Severn Bridge Vis. Cen. 5A 16
Severn Dr. BS35: T'bry 2K 11
Severn Grange BS10: Hen 4D 34
Severn Gro. TA8: Bur S 3D 158
Severn Ho. BS10: Hen 4D 34
Severn Leigh Gdns. BS9: Stok B 5F 47
Severnmead BS20: P'head 3B 42
Severn Rd. BS10: H'len 6A 24
BS11: Chit 6A 24
BS11: Shire 2H 45
BS20: P'head 3E 42
BS20: Pill 3G 45
BS23: W Mare 7F 105
BS35: N'wick, Piln 6C 16
BS35: Sev B 2A 24
Severn Rd. Bri. NP16: B'ly 2C 8
Severnside Trad. Est. BS11: A'mth 2G 33
Severn Vw. BS11: Law W 6C 34
Severn Vw. Ind. Pk. BS10: H'len 3A 24
Severn Vw. Rd. BS35: T'bry 2A 12
SEVERN VIEW SERVICE AREA 4F 9
Severn Way BS31: Key 6D 78
BS34: Pat 5B 26
Severnwood Gdns. BS35: Sev B 1A 24
Sevier Rd. BS26: Lox, Webb 3G 147
Sevier St. BS2: Bris 6B 48
Seville Ct. BS20: P'head 1G 43
Seville Rd. BS20: P'head 1G 43
Seward Ter. BA3: Writ 4C 154
Sewell Ho. BS25: Wins 5G 131
Seymour Av. BS7: B'stn 4A 48
Seymour Cl. BS21: Clev 6E 54
BS22: Wor 7D 84
Seymour Pl. BS16: Mang 4D 50
Seymour Rd. BA1: Bath 3C 100
BS5: E'tn 7C 48
BS7: B'stn 4A 48
BS15: K'wd 7B 50
BS16: Stap H 4B 50
Seyton Wlk. BS34: Stok G 2G 37
Shackel Hendy M. BS16: Emer G 3G 51
Shackleton Av. BS37: Yate 6F 31
Shadow Wlk. BS24: Elbgh 2G 129
Shadwell Rd. BS7: B'stn 5K 47
Shaftesbury Av. BA1: Bath 4J 99
BS6: Bris 7A 48
Shaftesbury Cl. BS48: Nail 2F 71
Shaftesbury Crusade *BS2: Bris 3C 62*
(off Union Rd.)
Shaftesbury M. BA2: Bath 7B 6 (6K 99)
Shaftesbury Rd. BA2: Bath 7B 6 (6K 99)
BS23: W Mare 4K 105
Shaftesbury Ter. BA3: Rads 3A 154
BS5: St G 2F 63
BS6: Bris 7A 48
(off Ashley Rd.)
Shaft Rd. BA2: C Down, Mon C 2F 123
BS35: Sev B 5A 16
Shakespeare Av. BA2: Bath 7B 100
BS7: Hor 7C 36
Shakespeare Ct. BS23: W Mare 3H 127
Shakespeare Rd. BA3: Rads 5G 153
Shaldon Rd. BS7: L'lze 4C 48
Shallows, The BS31: Salt 7K 79
Shambles, The BA15: Brad A 5H 125
Sham Castle La. BA2: Bath 3K 7 (4D 100)
Shamrock Rd. BS5: Eastv 5F 49
Shanklin Dr. BS34: Fil 4D 36
Shannon Ct. BS1: Bris 4F 5
BS35: T'bry 4B 12
Shannon Wlk. BS20: P'head 2H 43
Shapcott Cl. BS4: Know 1D 76
Shaplands BS9: Stok B 4F 47
Sharland Cl. BS9: Stok B 5E 46
Sharland Gro. BS13: Hart 6J 75
Sharpham Rd. BS27: Ched 7B 150
Shaw Cl. BS5: E'tn 1D 62
BS16: Mang 5F 51
Shaw Gdns. BS14: H'gro 2C 76
Shaw Path TA8: Bur S 2E 158
Shaws Way BA2: Bath 5F 99
Shaymoor La. BS35: Piln 2F 25
Shearmore Cl. BS7: Hor 1C 48
Shearn La. TA8: Bur S 1D 158
Shearwater Ct. *BS16: B'hll 2H 49*
(off Begbrook La.)
Sheaves Pk. BS10: S'mead 5K 35
Sheene Ct. BS3: Bedm 6J 61
Sheene Rd. BS3: Bedm 6J 61
Sheene Way BS3: Bedm 6J 61
Sheephouse Cvn. Pk. BS20: Eas 1C 44
Sheepscroft BS13: Withy 6G 75
SHEEPWAY 3A 44
Sheepway BS20: P'bry, P'head 4H 43
Sheepway La. BS20: P'bry 2A 44
Sheepwood Cl. BS10: Hen 5G 35
Sheepwood Rd. BS10: Hen 5G 35
Sheldare Barton BS5: St G 2K 63
Sheldon Cl. BS21: Clev 7F 55
Sheldrake Dr. BS16: B'hll 2G 49
Shellard Rd. BS34: Fil 5C 36
Shellards La. BS35: Alv 1A 20
Shellards Rd. BS30: L Grn 6D 64
Shelley Av. BS21: Clev 7D 54
Shelley Cl. BS5: St G 1H 63
TA8: Bur S 5C 156
Shelley Dr. TA8: Bur S 5C 156
Shelley Rd. BA2: Bath 7F 7 (6B 100)
BA3: Rads 5G 153
BS23: W Mare 1J 127
Shelley Way BS7: Hor 7C 36
Shellmor Av. BS34: Pat 5D 26
Shellmor Cl. BS34: Pat 5E 26
Shepherds Cl. BS16: Stap H 3C 50
Shepherd's La. TA9: W Hunt 7D 158
Shepherds Wlk. BA2: C Down 3B 122
BS32: Brad S 5F 27
Shepherd's Way BS22: St Geo 2G 107
Sheppard Rd. BS16: Fish 2A 50
Sheppards Gdns. BA1: W'ton 1H 99
Sheppy's Mill BS49: Cong 6K 87
Shepton BS24: W Mare 3J 127
Shepton Wlk. BS3: Bedm 7J 61
Sherbourne Av. BS32: Brad S 1G 37
Sherbourne Cl. BS15: Soun 6D 50
Sherbourne St. BS5: St G 1G 63
Sheridan Rd. BA2: Bath 6F 99
BS7: Hor 6C 36
TA8: Bur S 3E 158
Sheridan Way BS30: L Grn 7E 64
Sherrings, The BS34: Pat 6D 26
Sherrin Way BS13: Withy 6E 74
Sherston Cl. BS16: Fish 3K 49
BS48: Nail 1J 71
Sherston Rd. BS7: Hor 7A 36
Sherwell Rd. BS4: Brisl 6G 63
Sherwood Cl. BS31: Key 5C 78
Sherwood Cres. BS22: Wor 1D 106
Sherwood Rd. BS15: K'wd 7K 49
BS31: Key 5C 78
Shetland Rd. BS10: S'mead 6K 35
Shetland Way BS48: Nail 1J 71
Shickle Gro. BA2: Odd D 3J 121
Shield Retail Cen. BS34: Fil 4C 36
Shields Av. BS7: Hor 5C 36
Shiels Dr. BS32: Brad S 7F 27
Shilton Cl. BS15: K'wd 2D 64
Shimsey Cl. BS16: Fish 2A 50
Shiners Elms BS49: Yat 3G 87
SHIPHAM 5B 132
Shipham Cl. BS14: Whit 5D 76
BS48: Nail 2H 71
Shipham La. BS25: Wins, Star 4F 131
Shipham Rd. BS25: S'ham 7B 132
BS27: Ched 4B 150
Ship Hill BS15: Han 4K 63
Ship La. BS1: Bris 7G 5 (4A 62)
SHIPLATE 1D 146
Shiplate Rd. BS24: B'don 7A 128
BS26: Lox 7A 128
Shipley Mow BS16: Emer G 2F 51
Shipley Rd. BS9: W Trym 7G 35
Shire Gdns. BS11: Shire 7H 33
SHIREHAMPTON 2J 45
Shirehampton Rd.
BS9: Sea M, Stok B 1B 46
BS11: Shire 2K 45
Shirehampton Station (Rail) 3H 45
Shirehampton Swimming Pool 2J 45
Shires Yd. BA1: Bath 3F 7 (4B 100)
Shire Way BS37: Yate 7C 30
Shockerwick La.
BA1: Bathf, Sho 6K 83
Shophouse Rd. BA2: Bath 5H 99
Shoreditch BS40: Chew S 5C 114
Shorland Ho. BS8: Clif 7G 47
Shorthill Rd. BS37: W'lgh 3C 40
Shortlands Rd. BS11: Law W 6A 34
Short La. BS41: L Ash 7A 60
Short St. BS2: Bris 4C 62
Short Way BS8: Fail 6F 59
BS35: T'bry 5K 11
SHORTWOOD 3H 51
Shortwood Hill BS16: Short 3H 51
Shortwood Rd. BS13: Hart 7A 76
BS16: Puck 4K 51
Shortwood Vw. BS15: K'wd 1D 64
Shortwood Wlk. BS13: Hart 7A 76
SHOSCOMBE 7E 142
SHOSCOMBE VALE 1E 154
Showcase Cinema
Bristol 4E 62
Showering Cl. BS14: Stoc 5F 77
Showering Rd. BS14: Stoc 5F 77
Shrewsbury Bow BS24: W'ton V 4E 106
SHROWLE 7H 137
Shrubbery, The BA1: Bath 1E 6 (3B 100)
Shrubbery Av. BS23: W Mare 3E 104
Shrubbery Cl. TA8: Berr 6A 144
Shrubbery Cotts. BS6: Redl 6H 47
Shrubbery Ct. BS16: Stap H 3B 50
Shrubbery Rd. BS16: Stap H 3B 50
BS23: W Mare 3F 105
Shrubbery Ter. BS23: W Mare 3E 104
Shrubbery Wlk. BS23: W Mare 3F 105
Shrubbery Wlk. W. BS23: W Mare 3F 105
Shuter Rd. BS13: Withy 5F 75
Sibland BS35: T'bry 4B 12
Sibland Cl. BS35: T'bry 4B 12
Sibland Rd. BS35: T'bry 3B 12
Sibland Way BS35: T'bry 4A 12
SIDCOT 6H 131
Sidcot BS4: Brisl 7J 63
Sidcot Dr. BS25: Wins 6G 131
Sidcot La. BS25: Wins 6G 131
Sideland Cl. BS14: Stoc 4G 77
Sidelands Rd. BS16: Fish 2A 50
Sidelings, The BS40: Ubl 5H 135
Sidings, The BS16: Sis 6F 51
BS34: Fil 5E 36
Sidmouth Cl. TA8: Bur S 7E 156
Sidmouth Gdns. BS3: Wind H 7K 61
Sidmouth Rd. BS3: Wind H 7K 61
Signal Rd. BS16: Stap H 4C 50
Silas Ct. BS14: Stoc 5E 76
Silbury Ri. BS31: Key 1E 96
Silbury Rd. BS3: Ash V 7E 60
Silcox Rd. BS13: Hart 6J 75
Silklands Gro. BS9: Sea M 2C 46
Silverberry Rd. BS22: Wor 3D 106
Silver Birch Cl. BS34: Lit S 7F 27
Silver Ct. BS48: Nail 7F 57
Silverhill Brake BS35: Rudg 4G 19
Silverhill Rd. BS10: Hen 4E 34
Silverlow Rd. BS48: Nail 7F 57
Silver Mead BS49: Cong 2K 109
Silver Moor La. BS29: Ban 6J 107
Silverstone Way BS49: Cong 1K 109
Silver St. BA3: Mid N, Stratt F 7E 152
BA15: Brad A 6H 125
BS1: Bris 2F 5 (2K 61)
BS20: Wes 7A 42
BS27: Ched 6D 150
BS35: T'bry 3K 11
BS40: Chew M 1H 115
BS40: Wrin 2F 111
BS48: Nail 7E 56
BS49: Cong 2K 109
Silverthorne La. BS2: Bris 4C 62
Silverthorne Wharf BS2: Bris 3C 62
Silverton Ct. BS4: Know 1B 76
Simmonds Bldgs. BS16: Ham 4A 38
Simmonds Vw. BS34: Stok G 2H 37
Simons Cl. BS22: Wor 2E 106
BS39: Paul 1D 152
Sinclair Ho. BS8: Clif 4A 4 (3H 61)
Singapore Rd. BS23: W Mare 2G 127
SINGLE HILL 1G 155
SION HILL 2A 100
Sion Hill BA1: Bath 2A 100
BS8: Clif 2F 61
Sion Hill Pl. BA1: Bath 2A 100
Sion La. BS8: Clif 2F 61
Sion Pl. BA2: Bath 4K 7 (5D 100)
BS8: Clif 2F 61
Sion Rd. BA1: Bath 2A 100
BS3: Bedm 6J 61
Sir Bevil Grenville Monument 1G 81

Sir John's La.—Square, The

Sir John's La. BS5: Eastv ... 4D 48
(not continuous)
BS16: L'lze ... 4D 48
Sir Johns Wood BS48: Nail ... 6F 57
Siskin Cl. BS20: P'head ... 2H 43
Siskin Wlk. BS22: Wor ... 4D 106
SISTON ... 5K 51
Siston Cen. BS15: Soun ... 6E 50
Siston Cl. BS15: Soun ... 6E 50
SISTON COMMON ... 6E 50
Siston Comn. BS15: Sis ... 6E 50
(not continuous)
BS30: Sis ... 6E 50
Siston Hill BS30: Sis ... 7E 50
(not continuous)
Siston La. BS16: Sis ... 4K 51
BS30: W Hth ... 1J 65
Siston Pk. BS15: Soun ... 6E 50
Sixpence BS39: High L ... 3B 140
Sixth Av. BS7: Hor ... 6D 36
BS14: H'gro ... 3C 76
Sixty Acres Cl. BS8: Fail ... 6F 59
Six Ways BS21: Clev ... 5D 54
Skinner's Hill BA2: Cam ... 6J 141
Skinners La. BS25: C'hll ... 1B 132
Skippon Ct. BS15: Han ... 4C 64
Skypark Rd. BS3: Bedm ... 6J 61
Slad, The BS35: Grov ... 6C 12
Sladacre La. BS40: Blag ... 3C 134
SLADEBROOK ... 1J 121
Sladebrook Av. BA2: Bath ... 1J 121
Sladebrook Ct. BA2: Bath ... 1H 121
Sladebrook Rd. BA2: Bath ... 7H 99
Slade Cotts. BA2: Mon C ... 3G 123
Slade La. BS24: Lym ... 5K 145
BS48: Bar G ... 6F 73
Slade Rd. BS20: P'head ... 3F 43
Sladesbrook BA15: Brad A ... 5H 125
Sladesbrook Cl. BA15: Brad A ... 4H 125
Slades Ct. BS48: Back ... 4J 71
Slate La. BS31: Q Char ... 3J 95
BS39: Comp D ... 3J 95
Slaughter La. BS30: Upton C ... 7D 66
Sleep La. BS14: Whit ... 7F 77
Sleight Vw. BA2: Tim ... 2F 141
Slimbridge Cl. BS37: Yate ... 7F 31
Slimeridge Farm Cvn. Pk.
BS23: Uph ... 3E 126
Sloan St. BS5: St G ... 1F 63
Sloe Cl. BS22: W Mare ... 5B 106
Slymbridge Av. BS10: Bren ... 4G 35
Smallbrook La.
BS39: Comp D, Wool ... 5J 95
Smallcombe Cl. BA3: Clan ... 1J 153
Smallcombe Rd. BA3: Clan ... 1J 153
Small Down End BS25: Wins ... 3F 131
Small La. BS16: Stap ... 3G 49
(not continuous)
Small St. BS1: Bris ... 3E 4 (2K 61)
BS2: Bris ... 4C 62
Smallway BS49: Cong ... 5K 87
Smallwood Vw. BA3: Mid N ... 7C 152
Smarts Grn. BS37: Chip S ... 6J 31
Smeaton Rd. BS1: Bris ... 4F 61
Smithcourt Dr. BS34: Lit S ... 1E 36
Smithmead BS13: Hart ... 5H 75
Smith's Forge Ind. Est. BS49: Yat ... 7F 69
Smith Way TA9: High ... 5F 159
Smoke La. BS11: A'mth, Chit ... 1G 33
Smoke La. Ind. Est. BS11: A'mth ... 1G 33
Smurl La. TA9: W Hunt ... 7E 158
Smythe Cft. BS14: Whit ... 7C 76
Smyth Rd. BS3: Bedm ... 6G 61
Smyths Cl. BS11: A'mth ... 6F 33
SNEYD PARK ... 5D 46
Snowberry Cl. BS22: Wor ... 3E 106
BS32: Brad S ... 6G 27
Snowberry Wlk. BS5: W'hall ... 7G 49
Snowdon Cl. BS16: Fish ... 4H 49
Snowdon Rd. BS16: Fish ... 3H 49
Snowdon Va. BS23: W Mare ... 3J 105
Snowdrop Cl. BS22: Wick L ... 6E 84
Snow Hill BA1: Bath ... 3C 100
Snow Hill Ho. BA1: Bath ... 3C 100
Soapers La. BS35: T'bry ... 4K 11
Soaphouse Ind. Est. BS5: St G ... 1G 63
Sodbury La. BS37: W'lgh ... 2E 40
Sodbury Rd. GL12: Wickw ... 2G 23
Solent Way BS35: T'bry ... 5B 12
Solsbury Ct. BA1: Bathe ... 6H 83
BA2: Clav D ... 5H 101
Solsbury La. BA1: Bathe ... 6G 83
Solsbury Vw. BA2: B'ptn ... 2H 101
Solsbury Way BA1: Bath ... 1B 100
(not continuous)
Somer Av. BA3: Mid N ... 4D 152
Somerby Cl. BS32: Brad S ... 7F 27
Somer Ct. BA3: Mid N ... 5F 153
SOMERDALE ... 3D 78
Somerdale Av. BA2: Odd D ... 2J 121
BS4: Know ... 2B 76
BS22: W Mare ... 4A 106
Somerdale Cl. BS22: W Mare ... 4A 106
Somerdale Rd. BS31: Key ... 4D 78
Somerdale Rd. Nth. BS31: Key ... 3D 78
Somerdale Vw. BA2: Bath ... 2J 121
Somer La. BS3: Bedm ... 1J 75
Somermead BS3: Bedm ... 1J 75
Somer Ridge BA3: Mid N ... 3D 152
Somer Rd. BA3: Mid N ... 4D 152
Somerset Av. BS22: W Wick ... 5C 106
BS24: W Wick, W'ton V ... 5C 106
BS37: Yate ... 3F 31
Somerset Cres. BS34: Stok G ... 2H 37
Somerset Folly BA2: Tim ... 3F 141
Somerset Ho. BA2: Bath ... 1K 121
BS2: Bris ... 2K 5
Somerset La. BA1: Bath ... 2A 100
Somerset M. BS23: W Mare ... 7H 105
Somerset Pl. BA1: Bath ... 2A 100
Somerset Rd. BS4: Know ... 6C 62
BS20: P'head ... 3B 42
BS21: Clev ... 6E 54
Somerset Sq. BS1: Bris ... 7G 5 (4A 62)
BS48: Nail ... 7G 57
Somerset St. BA1: Bath ... 6F 7 (6C 100)
BS1: Bris ... 7H 5 (4A 62)
BS2: Bris ... 1E 4 (1K 61)
Somerset Ter. BS3: Wind H ... 6K 61
Somerset Way BS39: Paul ... 7C 140
TA9: High ... 5G 159
Somerton BS24: W Mare ... 3J 127
Somerton Cl. BS15: K'wd ... 2C 64
Somerton Rd. BS7: Hor ... 2A 48
BS21: Clev ... 1E 68
Somervale Rd. BA3: Rads ... 4H 153
Somerville Cl. BS31: Salt ... 1J 97
Somerville Rd. BS25: Sandf ... 2G 131
Sommerville Rd. BS6: Bris ... 5A 48
BS7: B'stn, Bris ... 5A 48
Sommerville Rd. Sth. BS6: Bris ... 6B 48
BS7: Bris ... 6B 48
Soper Gdns. BS4: Know ... 3K 75
Sophia Gdns. BS22: Wor ... 7F 85
Sorbus Cl. BS32: Alm ... 1G 27
Sorrel Cl. BS35: T'bry ... 2B 12
Sorrel Gdns. BS20: P'head ... 3H 43
SOUNDWELL ... 5D 50
Soundwell Rd. BS15: K'wd ... 7A 50
BS16: Soun ... 6B 50
Southampton Gdns. BS7: B'stn ... 3B 48
Southampton M. BS7: B'stn ... 3B 48
South Av. BA2: Bath ... 6A 6 (6K 99)
BS20: P'head ... 2F 43
BS37: Yate ... 5B 30
TA9: High ... 4E 158
Southblow Ho. BS3: Ash G ... 6G 61
Southbourne Gdns. BA1: Bath ... 2D 100
Southbourne Mans.
BA2: Bath ... 5H 7 (5C 100)
Sth. Brent Cl. TA9: Bre K ... 4H 157
Sth. Bristol Bus. Pk.
BS4: Know ... 3A 76
Sth. Bristol Crematorium & Cemetery
BS13: Bis ... 2F 75
Sth. Bristol Retail Pk. BS3: Ash G ... 6F 61
Sth. Bristol Trade Pk. BS3: Ash V ... 6F 61
South Cl. BS24: Lym ... 5K 145
South Combe BS24: B'don ... 7K 127
Southcot Pl. BA2: Bath ... 7H 7 (6C 100)
South Ct. BS32: Brad S ... 3F 27
South Cft. BS9: Henle ... 1J 47
BS25: Wins ... 3F 131
South Dene BS9: Stok B ... 2E 46
SOUTH DOWN ... 1H 121
Southdown BS22: Wor ... 7D 84
Southdown Av. BA2: Bath ... 1H 121
Southdown Rd. BA2: Bath ... 7H 99
BS9: W Trym ... 7F 35
Southdowns BS8: Clif ... 7G 47
Southend Gdns. GL12: Wickw ... 7G 15
TA9: High ... 3G 159
Southend Ho. GL12: Wickw ... 7H 15
Southend Rd. BS23: W Mare ... 1G 127
Southernhay BS8: Clif ... 5A 4
BS16: Stap H ... 4A 50
Southernhay Av. BS8: Clif ... 5A 4 (3H 61)
Southernhay Cres. BS8: Clif ... 5A 4 (3H 61)
Southern Lea Rd. TA8: Bur S ... 7E 156
Southern Ring Path BS21: Clev ... 1C 68
(Braikenridge Cl.)
BS21: Clev ... 7E 54
(Hill Moor, not continuous)
Southern Way BS21: Clev ... 7B 54
South Esplanade TA8: Bur S ... 3C 158
Southey Av. BS15: K'wd ... 7C 50
Southey Ct. BS15: K'wd ... 7B 50
Southey Rd. BS21: Clev ... 7D 54
Southey St. BS2: Bris ... 6B 48
SOUTHFIELD ... 4A 154
Southfield BS27: Ched ... 6D 150
Southfield Av. BS15: K'wd ... 7C 50
Southfield Cl. BS23: Uph ... 3F 127
BS48: Nail ... 6G 57
Southfield Ct. BS9: W Trym ... 1G 47
Southfield Hill BA3: Hem ... 7G 155
Southfield Rd. BS6: Cot ... 7K 47
BS9: W Trym ... 1G 47
BS48: Nail ... 6G 57
(not continuous)
Southfield Rd. Trad. Est. BS48: Nail ... 6H 57
Southfields BA3: Rads ... 4A 154
Southfield Way BS37: Yate ... 2G 31
Southgate BA1: Bath ... 5G 7 (6C 100)
(not continuous)
South Grn. St. BS8: Clif ... 3F 61
South Gro. BS6: Henle ... 3J 47
BS20: Pill ... 4G 45
South Hayes BS5: Eastv ... 4D 48
South Hill BS25: Wins ... 3F 131
Southlands BA1: W'ton ... 1G 99
(not continuous)
BS4: Know ... 1D 76
GL12: Tyth ... 1F 21
Southlands Dr. BA2: Tim ... 4F 141
Southlands Way BS49: Cong ... 6K 87
South Lawn BS24: Lock ... 1D 128
Sth. Lawn Cl. BS24: Lock ... 1D 128
Sth. Lea Rd. BA1: Bath ... 3G 99
Southleaze BS25: Wins ... 7G 131
Southleigh BA15: Brad A ... 7G 125
Southleigh Rd. BS8: Clif ... 1A 4 (1H 61)
Sth. Liberty La. BS3: Ash V, Bedm ... 1E 74
South Lodge BS9: Stok B ... 2D 46
SOUTH LYNCOMBE ... 1B 122
SOUTHMEAD ... 6J 35
Southmead BS25: Wins ... 5G 131
Sth. Mdws. BS40: Wrin ... 2G 111
Southmead Rd.
BS10: S'mead, W Trym ... 1J 47
BS22: W Mare ... 5K 105
BS34: Fil ... 1J 47
Southmead Way BS10: S'mead ... 7K 35
Southover Cl. BS9: W Trym ... 7G 35
Southover Rd. BS39: High L ... 4B 140
Sth. Pde. BA2: Bath ... 5H 7 (5C 100)
BS8: Clif ... 1A 4 (1H 61)
BS23: W Mare ... 4F 105
BS37: Yate ... 5E 30
BS40: Chew M ... 1H 115
South Pde. Cotts. *BA2: C Down* ... *3E 122*
(off Tyning Rd.)
South Quay BS1: Bris ... 4H 5 (3A 62)
Southridge Hgts. BS24: W Mare ... 5J 127
South Rd. BA2: Tim ... 4F 141
BA3: Mid N ... 5E 152
BS3: Bedm ... 6J 61
BS6: Redl ... 6J 47
BS15: K'wd ... 1B 64
BS20: P'head ... 1F 43
BS23: W Mare ... 3E 104
BS24: Lym ... 5K 145
BS32: Alm ... 7F 19
TA8: Berr, Brean ... 5A 144
Southsea Rd. BS34: Pat ... 7C 26
Southside BS23: W Mare ... 4G 105
BS49: Cong ... 6A 88
Southside Cl. BS9: C Din ... 7B 34
SOUTH STOKE ... 5B 122
Southstoke La. BA2: S'ske ... 5B 122
Southstoke Rd. BA2: C Down ... 3B 122
South St. BS3: Bedm ... 6H 61
TA8: Bur S ... 2C 158
South Ter. BS6: Redl ... 6H 47
BS23: W Mare ... 4F 105
TA8: Bur S ... 2C 158
SOUTH TWERTON ... 7A 6 (6K 99)
South Vw. *BA1: Bath* ... *2C 100*
(off Camden Rd.)
BA2: Clav D ... 2H 123
BA2: Mon C ... 3G 123
BA2: Tim ... 3F 141
BA3: Clan ... 1J 153
BS2: Bris ... 1E 4
BS16: Stap H ... 3C 50
BS20: P'head ... 1F 43
BS36: Fram C ... 7F 29
BS39: Paul ... 7C 140
Southview Cl. BS24: Hut ... 3C 128
South Vw. Cres. BS36: Coal H ... 1H 39
South Vw. Pl. BA2: Odd D ... 4J 121
BA3: Mid N ... 4F 153
South Vw. Ri. BS36: Coal H ... 1G 39
South Vw. Rd. BA2: Bath ... 5A 6 (5K 99)
South Vw. Ter. BS49: Yat ... 2H 87
SOUTHVILLE ... 5J 61
Southville Cl. BA15: Brad A ... 7J 125
Southville Pl. BS3: Bedm ... 5K 61
Southville Rd. BA15: Brad A ... 7J 125
BS3: Bedm ... 7D 4 (5J 61)
BS23: W Mare ... 1G 127
Southville Ter. BA2: Bath ... 7D 100
South Wlk. BS37: Yate ... 5E 30
South Wansdyke Sports Cen. ... 5F 153
Southway Ct. BS21: Clev ... 1D 68
Southway Dr. BS30: Old C ... 4H 65
Southway Rd. BA15: Brad A ... 7H 125
Southwell Cres. TA9: High ... 5G 159
Southwell St. BS2: Bris ... 1D 4 (1J 61)
SOUTH WIDCOMBE ... 7H 137
Southwood Av. BS9: C Din ... 7C 34
Southwood Dr. BS9: C Din ... 1B 46
Southwood Dr. E. BS9: C Din ... 7C 34
SOUTH WRAXALL ... 5J 103
Sovereign Shop. Cen.
BS23: W Mare ... 4F 105
Space BS3: Bedm ... 1H 75
Spa La. BA1: Swa ... 1E 100
Spalding Cl. BS7: Eastv ... 5C 48
Spaniorum Vw. BS35: E Comp ... 4F 25
Sparks Way TA9: High ... 5F 159
Spar Rd. BS37: Yate ... 4D 30
Sparrow Hill Way BS26: Weare ... 7D 148
Spartley Dr. BS13: Bis ... 4F 75
Spartley Wlk. BS13: Bis ... 4F 75
Spa Vis. Cen. ... 5F 7
Spaxton Cl. TA8: Bur S ... 7E 156
Specklemead BS39: Paul ... 1B 152
Spectrum Ho. BS2: Bris ... 1H 5 (1A 62)
SPEEDWELL ... 7J 49
Speedwell Av. BS5: St G ... 2F 63
Speedwell Cl. BS35: T'bry ... 2B 12
Speedwell Rd. BS5: S'wll ... 7H 49
BS15: K'wd ... 7H 49
Speedwell Swimming Pool ... 7H 49
Spencer Dr. BA3: Mid N ... 4E 152
BS22: Wor ... 1F 107
Spencer Ho. BS1: Bris ... 7G 5
Spencers Belle Vue
BA1: Bath ... 1F 7 (3B 100)
Spencers Ct. BS35: Alv ... 6K 11
Spencers Orchard BA15: Brad A ... 7H 125
Sperring Ct. BA3: Mid N ... 6D 152
Spey Cl. BS35: T'bry ... 4A 12
Spider La. BS23: W Mare ... 4F 105
Spindleberry Gro. BS48: Nail ... 7J 57
Spinners End BS22: Wor ... 7F 85
Spinney, The BS20: P'head ... 4E 42
BS24: W Mare ... 4H 127
BS32: Brad S ... 7G 27
BS36: Fram C ... 7F 29
Spinney Cft. BS13: Withy ... 5F 75
Spinney Rd. BS24: Lock ... 1H 129
Spinnings Drove BS48: Back ... 7B 72
Spires Vw. BS16: Stap ... 3G 49
Spratts Bri. BS40: Chew M ... 1G 115
Sprigg Dr. BS20: Wes ... 7B 42
Spring Cres. BA2: Bath ... 5H 7 (5C 100)
Springfield BA2: Pea J ... 6C 142
BA15: Brad A ... 6J 125
BS35: T'bry ... 4B 12
Springfield Av. BS7: Hor ... 3B 48
BS11: Shire ... 2H 45
BS16: Mang ... 2E 50
BS22: W Mare ... 3B 106
Springfield Bldgs. BA3: Rads ... 3A 154
Springfield Bungs. BS39: Paul ... 4B 152
Springfield Cl. BA2: Bath ... 6H 99
BS16: Mang ... 1E 50
BS26: Cross ... 4F 149
BS27: Ched ... 6C 150
Springfield Crest BA3: Rads ... 3A 154
Springfield Gdns. BS29: Ban ... 2A 130
Springfield Gro. BS6: Henle ... 3H 47
Springfield Hgts. BA3: Clan ... 2J 153
Springfield Ho. BS6: Cot ... 1J 61
Springfield Lawns BS11: Shire ... 2H 45
Springfield Pl. BA1: Bath ... 2B 100
BA3: Clan ... 2J 153
Springfield Rd. BS6: Bris ... 7K 47
BS16: Mang ... 1E 50
BS20: P'head ... 3D 42
BS20: Pill ... 4G 45
BS27: Ched ... 6C 150
TA9: High ... 4G 159
Springfields BS34: Fil ... 5C 36
Spring Gdns. BS4: Know ... 1C 76
Spring Gdns. Rd. BA2: Bath ... 4H 7 (5C 100)
(Argyle St.)
BA2: Bath ... 6H 7 (6C 100)
(Ferry La.)
Spring Ground Rd. BS39: Paul ... 1C 152
Spring Hill BS2: Bris ... 1K 61
(not continuous)
BS15: K'wd ... 6C 50
BS22: W Mare, Wor ... 2A 106
Springhill Cl. BS39: Paul ... 7A 140
Spring Hill Dr. BS22: Wor ... 3B 106
Spring La. BA1: Bath ... 1D 100
BS41: Dun ... 2G 93
Springleaze BS4: Know ... 1C 76
BS16: Mang ... 1E 50
Springly Ct. BS15: K'wd ... 1E 64
Spring Ri. BS20: P'head ... 5E 42
Spring St. BS3: Bedm ... 5A 62
Spring St. Pl. BS3: Bedm ... 7H 5 (5A 62)
Spring Ter. BS22: W Mare ... 2A 106
Spring Va. BA1: Bath ... 1D 100
Spring Valley BS22: W Mare ... 2A 106
Springville Cl. BS30: L Grn ... 6E 64
Springwater Pk. Trad. Est. BS5: St G ... 2G 63
Springwood Dr. BS10: Hen ... 4D 34
Springwood Gdns. BS24: Hut ... 2C 128
Spruce Way BA2: Odd D ... 4A 122
BS22: W Mare ... 4C 106
BS34: Pat ... 7A 26
Square, The BA2: Bath ... 6E 6 (6B 100)
BA2: Tim ... 3F 141
BA2: Wel ... 4K 143
BS1: Bris ... 5J 5 (3B 62)
BS4: Brisl ... 7F 63
BS4: Know ... 1C 76
BS16: Stap H ... 4C 50
BS25: S'ham ... 6A 132

A-Z Bristol, Bath & North Somerset Atlas 199

Thurston's Barton—Union Rd.

Thurston's Barton BS5: W'hall 7G 49
Thyme Cl. BS20: P'bry, P'head 3H 43
Thynne Cl. BS27: Ched 7H 151
Tibberton BS15: K'wd 1E 64
Tibbott Rd. BS14: Stoc 5F 77
Tibbott Wlk. BS14: Stoc 5E 76
Tichborne Rd. BS5: Redf 2E 62
BS23: W Mare 3G 105
TICKENHAM 5C 56
Tickenham Drove BS21: Tic 7K 55
Tickenham Hill BS21: Tic 5F 57
Tickenham Rd. BS21: Clev 6F 55
Tide Gro. BS11: Law W 7A 34
Tidenham Way BS34: Pat 5B 26
Tiffany Ct. BS1: Bris 6H 5 (4A 62)
Tiledown BS39: Temp C 4H 139
Tiledown Cl. BS39: Temp C 4H 139
Tilley Cl. BA2: F'boro 6E 118
BS31: Key 1E 96
Tilley La. BA2: F'boro 7D 118
Tilling Rd. BS10: Hor 1A 48
Tilling Wlk. BS10: Hor 1A 48
Tilting Rd. BS35: T'bry 2K 11
Timber Dene BS16: Stap 4F 49
Timbers, The BA3: Mid N 7F 153
Timberscombe Wlk.
BS14: Whit 5D 76
Time Machine (Mus.) 4G 105
TIMSBURY 3F 141
TIMSBURY BOTTOM 4D 140
Timsbury Ind. Est. BA2: Tim 2D 140
Timsbury Rd. BA2: F'boro 6E 118
BS3: Know 5A 62
BS39: High L 4B 140
Timsbury Wlk. BS3: Know 7A 62
Timswell Batch BS40: Blag 2C 134
Tindell Ct. BS30: L Grn 5D 64
Tinker's La. BS40: Comp M 6B 136
BS48: Back 7D 72
Tintagel Cl. BS31: Key 6B 78
Tintern Av. BS5: St G 1F 63
Tintern Cl. BS30: Bar C 3D 64
Tippetts Rd. BS15: K'wd 3B 64
Tirley Way BS22: W Mare 2K 105
Titan Barrow BA1: Bathf 1A 102
Tithe Barn 7G 125
Tiverton Gdns. BS22: Wor 2E 106
Tiverton Rd. BS21: Clev 1E 68
Tiverton Wlk. BS16: Fish 6J 49
Tivoli Ho. BS23: W Mare 4G 105
Tivoli La. BS23: W Mare 4G 105
Tobacco Factory, The 5G 61
Tobias Gdns. BS37: Yate 5D 30
TOCKINGTON 4D 18
Tockington Grn. BS32: Toc 4D 18
Tockington La. BS32: Alm 1C 26
Tockington Pk. La. BS32: Alm 5G 19
Toddington Cl. BS37: Yate 6D 30
Toghill La. BS30: Doy 7G 53
Tolland BS24: W Mare 3J 127
Toll Bri. Rd. BA1: Bathe 7G 83
Toll Ho. Ct. BS3: Ash G 5G 61
Toll House Gallery 5C 54
Toll Rd. BS23: B'don 5H 127
Tone Rd. BS21: Clev 1D 68
Top Rd. BS25: S'ham 6B 132
Tor Cl. BS22: Wor 2E 106
Tormarton Cres. BS10: Hen 3F 35
Tormynton Rd. BS22: Wor 2C 106
Toronto Rd. BS7: Hor 7B 36
Torpoint Rd. BS3: Wind H 1K 75
Torrance Cl. BS30: Old C 3H 65
Torridge Rd. BS31: Key 6E 78
Torrington Av. BS4: Know 2B 76
Torrington Cres. BS22: Wor 1E 106
Tortworth Rd. BS7: Hor 3A 48
Tor Vw. BS27: Ched 7E 150
Tory BA15: Brad A 6G 125
Tory Pl. BA15: Brad A 6G 125
Totnes Cl. BS22: Wor 2E 106
Totshill Dr. BS13: Hart 7A 76
Totshill Gro. BS13: Hart 6A 76
Tottenham Pl. BS8: Clif 3A 4 (2H 61)
TOTTERDOWN 5B 62
Totterdown Bri. Trad. Est.
BS2: Bris 5C 62
Totterdown La. BS24: W Mare 5J 127
Totterdown Rd. BS23: W Mare 1G 127
Touchstone Av. BS34: Stok G 2H 37
Tourist Info. Cen.
Bath 5G 7 (5C 100)
Bradford-on-Avon 6H 125
Bristol 3E 4 (2K 61)
Broadmead 3G 5 (2A 62)
Burnham-on-Sea 2C 158
Canon's Marsh 5D 4 (3J 61)
Chipping Sodbury 5H 31
Thornbury 3K 11
Tyndall's Park 3C 4 (2J 61)
Weston-Super-Mare 5F 105
Tovey Cl. BS22: Kew 7C 84
Tower, The BS1: Bris 4G 5 (3A 62)
Tower Cl. BS27: Ched 7H 151
TOWERHEAD 1E 130
Towerhead Rd. BS25: Sandf 2C 130
BS29: Ban 2C 130
Tower Hill BS2: Bris 4H 5 (2A 62)
BS24: Lock 1H 129
Tower Ho. La. BS48: Wrax 4H 57
Tower La. BS1: Bris 3F 5 (2K 61)
(not continuous)
BS30: Warm 3E 64
Tower La. Bus. Pk. BS30: Warm 3F 65
Towerleaze BS9: Stok B 5D 46
Tower Rd. BS15: K'wd 7A 50
BS20: P'head 4C 42
Tower Rd. Nth. BS30: Warm 2F 65
Tower Rd. Sth. BS30: C Hth 3F 65
Tower St. BS1: Bris 5H 5 (3A 62)
Tower Wlk. BS23: W Mare 3F 105
TOWNS END 2C 152
TOWNSEND
BS40, Chew Stoke 4E 114
BS40, East Harptree 6K 137
Townsend BS32: Alm 2B 26
Townsend Cl. BS14: Stoc 5H 77
Townsend La. BS32: Alm 2B 26
Townsend Rd. BS14: Stoc 5H 77
Townshend Rd. BS22: Wor 6E 84
TOWNWELL 2B 14
Toynbe Rd. BS4: Know 2A 76
Tozer's Hill BS4: Know 7E 62
Tracy Cl. BS14: H'gro 3B 76
(not continuous)
Trafalgar Ct. BS23: W Mare 5G 105
Trafalgar Rd. BA1: W'ton 2H 99
Trafalgar Ter. BS3: Bedm 7H 61
Trafalgar Wlk. BS1: Bris 2F 5 (2K 61)
Tralee Wlk. BS4: Know 1K 75
Tramshed, The BA1: Bath 3G 7 (4C 100)
Tramway Rd. BS4: Brisl 6E 62
Tranmere Av. BS10: Bren 3G 35
Tranmere Gro. BS10: Bren 4G 35
Transom Ho. BS1: Bris 5H 5
Tratman Wlk. BS10: Hen 4F 35
Travers Cl. BS4: Know 4K 75
Travers Wlk. BS34: Stok G 2H 37
Trawden Cl. BS23: W Mare 3J 105
Treasure Ct. TA8: Bur S 6C 156
Tredegar Rd. BS16: Fish 5K 49
Treefield Pl. BS2: Bris 6C 48
Treefield Rd. BS21: Clev 7D 54
Treesbanks BS37: Yate 4F 31
Treenwood Ind. Est. BA15: Brad A 7H 125
(off Moulton Dr.)
Tregarth Rd. BS3: Ash V 1F 75
Tregelles Cl. TA9: High 4E 158
Trelawn Cl. BS22: St Geo 2H 107
Trelawney Av. BS5: St G 1F 63
Trelawney Pk. BS4: Brisl 6F 63
Trelawney Rd. BS6: Cot 7J 47
Trelissick Gdns.
BS24. W'ton V 4D 106
Trellick Wlk. BS16: Stap 7G 37
Tremlett M. BS22: Wor 7F 85
Trenchard Rd. BS24: Lock 1H 129
BS31: Salt 7H 79
Trenchard St. BS1: Bris 3E 4 (2J 61)
Trench La. BS32: Alm 4G 27
BS36: Wint 4G 27
Trendlewood Pk. BS16: Stap 4G 49
Trendlewood Way BS48: Nail 7J 57
Trenleigh Dr. BS22: Wor 1D 106
Trent Dr. BS35: T'bry 5B 12
Trent Gro. BS31: Key 6E 78
Trentham Cl. BS2: Bris 6C 48
Trescothick Cl. BS31: Key 4B 78
Trescothick Dr. BS30: Old C 5H 65
Tresham Cl. BS32: Brad S 4F 27
Trevelyan Rd. BS23: W Mare 5H 105
Trevelyan Wlk. BS10: Hen 4F 35
BS34: Stok G 2J 37
Trevenna Rd. BS3: Ash V 1F 75
Treverdowe Wlk.
BS10: Hen 4D 34
Trevethin Cl. BS15: K'wd 2A 64
Trevisa Gro. BS10: Bren 3J 35
Trewartha Cl. BS23: W Mare 4H 105
Trewartha Pk.
BS23: W Mare 4H 105
Trewint Gdns. BS4: Know 2B 76
Triangle, The BS20: P'head 3D 42
BS21: Clev 6D 54
BS39: Paul 7C 140
BS40: Wrin 2F 111
Triangle E. BA2: Bath 6A 6 (6K 99)
Triangle Nth. BA2: Bath 6A 6 (5K 99)
Triangle Sth. BS8: Clif 3B 4 (2H 61)
Triangle Vs. BA2: Bath 6A 6 (6K 99)
Triangle Wlk. BS8: Clif 3B 4
Triangle W. BA2: Bath 6A 6 (6K 99)
BS8: Clif 3B 4 (2H 61)
Trident Cl. BS16: Down 6E 38
Trim Bri. BA1: Bath 4F 7 (5B 100)
Trim St. BA1: Bath 4F 7 (5B 100)
Trinder Rd. BS20: Eas 4F 45
Trinity Cl. BA1: Bath 5E 6 (5B 100)
TA8: Bur S 6C 156
Trinity Ct. BS15: K'wd 1C 64
BS48: Nail 1E 70
Trinity La. BS37: Chip S 4J 31
Trinity M. BS2: Bris 3J 5
Trinity Pl. BA1: Bath 4E 6 (5B 100)
BS8: Clif 3G 61
(off Charles Pl.)
BS23: W Mare 3E 104
(not continuous)
Trinity Quay BS2: Bris 4J 5 (3B 62)
Trinity Ri. TA8: Bur S 6C 156
Trinity Rd. BA2: C Down 2D 122
BS2: Bris 2K 5 (2C 62)
BS23: W Mare 3E 104
BS48: Nail 1E 70
Trinity St. BA1: Bath 5F 7 (5B 100)
BS1: Bris 5D 4 (3J 61)
BS2: Bris 2C 62
Trinity Theological College 4E 46
Trinity Wlk. BS2: Bris 2K 5 (2B 62)
Trin Mills BS1: Bris 6F 5 (4K 61)
Tripps Cnr. BS49: Yat 4K 87
Tripps Row BS41: L Ash 1A 74
Troon BS37: Yate 6E 30
Troon Dr. BS30: Warm 3F 65
Trooper's Hill Rd. BS5: St G 3H 63
Tropical Bird Garden 3B 126
Trossachs Dr. BA2: Bath 3F 101
Trowbridge Cl. TA9: High 4F 159
Trowbridge Rd. BA15: Brad A 6H 125
BS10: S'mead 6J 35
Trowbridge Wlk. BS10: S'mead 6J 35
Trubshaw Cl. BS7: Hor 2B 48
Trumpet La. BS5: St G 2K 63
Truro Cl. TA8: Bur S 1E 158
Truro Rd. BS3: Ash G 6H 61
BS48: Nail 2J 71
Trym Cross Rd. BS9: Sea M 3C 46
Trym Leaze BS9: Sea M 3C 46
Trym Rd. BS9: W Trym 7G 35
Trym Side BS9: Sea M 3C 46
Trymwood Cl. BS10: Hen 5F 35
Trymwood Pde. BS9: Stok B 2D 46
Tucker's La. BS40: Ubl 4J 135
Tuckett Ho. BS16: Fren 1A 50
Tuckett La. BS16: Fren 1A 50
Tuckingmill La. BS39: Comp D 6C 96
Tuckmill BS21: Clev 1B 68
Tudor Cl. BS30: Old C 6G 65
Tudor Rd. BS2: Bris 7B 48
BS5: E'tn 7E 48
BS15: Han 4A 64
BS20: P'head 4G 43
BS22: Wor 7E 84
Tuffley Rd. BS10: W Trym 7J 35
Tufton Av. BS11: Law W 7A 34
Tugela Rd. BS13: Bis 3F 75
Tumps Nature Area, The 5B 26
Tun Bridge 2H 115
Tunbridge Cl. BS40: Chew M 2H 115
Tunbridge Rd. BS40: Chew M 1H 115
Tunbridge Way BS16: Emer G 7E 38
TUNLEY 2A 142
Tunley Hill BA2: Cam 3J 141
Tunley Rd. BA2: Tun 1B 142
Tunstall Cl. BS9: Stok B 4E 46
TURLEIGH 6D 124
Turley Rd. BS5: E'tn 7F 49
Turnberry BS30: Warm 3F 65
BS37: Yate 6E 30
Turnberry Wlk. BS4: Brisl 1F 77
Turnbridge Cl. BS10: Bren 4J 35
Turnbridge Rd. BS10: Bren 4J 35
Turnbury Av. BS48: Nail 1J 71
Turnbury Cl. BS22: Wor 1D 106
Turner Cl. BS31: Key 5E 78
Turner Ct. BS22: Wor 1D 106
Turner Dr. BS37: Yate 5B 30
Turner Gdns. BS7: L'lze 2D 48
Turners Ct. BS30: L Grn 5D 64
Turner's Twr. BA3: Hem 5G 155
Turner Wlk. BS30: B'yte 2H 65
Turner Way BS21: Clev 1B 68
Turnpike Cl. BS37: Yate 4E 30
Turnpike Ga. GL12: Wickw 6G 15
Turnpike Rd. BS25: S'ham 5A 132
BS26: L Wre 7C 148
Turnstone Av. BS20: P'head 2H 43
Turtlegate Av. BS13: Withy 6E 74
Turtlegate Wlk. BS13: Withy 6E 74
Turville Dr. BS7: Hor 2C 48
Tuscany Ho. BS6: Redl 5G 47
Tutton Way BS21: Clev 2D 68
Tuttors Hill BS27: Ched 5E 150
Tweed Cl. BS35: T'bry 4A 12
Tweed Rd. BS21: Clev 1C 68
Tweed Rd. Ind. Est. BS21: Clev 1C 68
Tweentown BS27: Ched 6D 150
Tweeny La. BS30: Old C 3H 65
Twelve O'Clock La. BA2: New L 2B 120
Twenty Acres Rd. BS10: S'mead 5H 35
TWERTON 5A 6 (6K 99)
Twerton Farm Cl. BA2: Bath 5H 99
TWERTON HILL 1G 121
Twerton Pk. 6H 99
Twickenham Rd. BS6: Henle 3J 47
Twinhoe La. BA2: Wel 3K 143
Twinnell Ho. BS5: E'tn 1C 62
Two Acres Rd. BS14: H'gro 2C 76
Two Mile Ct. BS15: K'wd 1K 63
TWO MILE HILL 1K 63
Two Mile Hill Rd.
BS15: K'wd 1J 63
Two Stones La. BS37: Chip S 6J 31
Two Trees BS40: Blag 4B 134
Twynings, The BS15: K'wd 6C 50
Tybalt Way BS34: Stok G 2G 37
Tydeman Rd. BS20: P'head 3H 43
Tydings Cl. BS41: L Ash 1A 74
Tyler Cl. BS15: Han 4C 64
Tyler Grn. BS22: Wor 7F 85
Tylers End TA9: High 5H 159
Tylers Farm BS37: Yate 2F 31
Tylers La. BS16: Stap H 3B 50
Tyler St. BS2: Bris 3C 62
Tylers Way BS37: Yate 1F 31
Tyler Way TA9: High 5F 159
Tyndale Av. BS16: Fish 4K 49
BS37: Yate 3D 30
Tyndale Ct. BS6: Redl 7H 47
(off Chertsey Rd.)
Tyndale Rd. BS15: Soun 6C 50
Tyndale Vw. BS35: T'bry 4K 11
Tyndall Av. BS8: Clif 2C 4 (2J 61)
Tyndall Ho. BS2: Bris 2J 5
Tyndall Rd. BS5: E'tn 1D 62
TYNDALL'S PARK 2B 4 (2H 61)
Tyndalls Pk. M. BS2: Bris 1C 4 (1J 61)
Tyndall's Pk. Rd.
BS8: Clif 1B 4 (1H 61)
Tyndalls Way BS10: S'mead 7A 36
Tyne Gro. BS20: P'head 2H 43
Tyne Path BS7: B'stn 6K 47
Tyne Rd. BS7: B'stn 5K 47
Tyne St. BS2: Bris 6C 48
TYNING
BA2 3E 140
BA3 3A 154
Tyning, The BA2: Bath 7K 7 (6D 100)
BA2: F'frd 7K 123
Tyning Cl. BS14: H'gro 3C 76
BS37: Yate 4E 30
Tyning End BA2: Bath 6K 7 (6D 100)
Tyning Hill BA3: Hem 7J 155
BA3: Rads 3A 154
Tyning La. BA1: Bath 2D 100
BS39: Stan D 2A 116
Tyning Pl. BA2: C Down 2E 122
Tyning Rd. BA2: B'ptn 1H 101
BA2: C Down 2E 122
BA2: Pea J 6C 142
BA15: W'ley 5C 124
BS3: Wind H 6B 62
BS31: Salt 1J 97
Tynings BS39: Clut 2F 139
Tynings, The BS20: Wes 7B 42
BS21: Clev 1A 68
Tyning's La. BS36: Wint 4A 28
Tynings M. BS23: W Mare 1G 127
Tynings Way BS39: Clut 2G 139
Tyning Ter. BA1: Bath 2D 100
(off Fairfield Rd.)
Tynte Av. BS13: Hart 7K 75
Tyntesfield 5D 58
Tyntesfield Pk. 6D 58
Tyntesfield Rd. BS13: Bis 3G 75
Tyrone Wlk. BS4: Know 2A 76
Tyrrel Way BS34: Stok G 2G 37
TYTHERINGTON 7F 13
Tytherington Rd. BS35: Grov 5D 12
GL12: Tyth 5D 12

U

UBLEY 4H 135
Ubley Drove BS40: Blag 7E 134
BS40: Ubl 5G 135
UBLEY SIDELING 5H 135
UDLEY 7E 88
Ullswater Cl. BS23: W Mare 1J 127
BS30: Old C 3H 65
BS37: Yate 3E 30
Ullswater Dr. BA1: Bath 1C 100
Ullswater Rd. BS10: S'mead 6H 35
Uncombe Cl. BS48: Back 3B 72
Underbanks BS20: Pill 4H 45
Underdown Ho. BS1: Bris 7F 5 (4K 61)
Underhill Av. BA3: Mid N 4D 152
Underhill Dr. BS23: Uph 3F 127
Underhill La. BA3: Mid N 5B 152
Under Knoll BA2: Pea J 4E 142
Under La. BS40: Redh 3B 112
Underleaf Way BA2: Pea J 6D 142
Undertown BS40: Comp M 6A 136
Undertown La. BS40: Comp M 6A 136
Underwood Av. BS22: W Mare 3K 105
Underwood Cl. BS35: Alv 1J 19
Underwood End BS25: Sandf 1G 131
Underwood Rd. BS20: P'head 5E 42
Unicorn Bus. Pk. BS4: Brisl 4F 63
Unicorn Pk. Av. BS4: Brisl 4E 62
Union Pas. BA1: Bath 4G 7 (5C 100)
Union Pl. BS23: W Mare 5F 105
Union Rd. BS2: Bris 4K 5 (3C 62)
(not continuous)

Walton Cl.—Westfield Pk.

Walton Cl. BS30: Bit 1G 79
BS31: Key 6B 78
Walton Cres. BS40: Winf 3K 91
Walton Heath BS37: Yate 5F 31
WALTON IN GORDANO 2H 55
Walton Ri. BS9: W Trym 7G 35
Walton Rd. BS11: Shire 2H 45
BS21: Clev 5F 55
WALTON ST MARY 3D 54
Walton St. BS5: E'tn 7D 48
BS21: Walt G 1G 55
Walwyn Cl. BA2: Bath 5G 99
Walwyn Gdns. BS13: Hart 7K 75
Wansbeck Rd. BS31: Key 6E 78
Wansbrough Rd. BS22: Wor 7F 85
Wanscow Wlk. BS9: Henle 2H 47
Wansdyke Bus. Cen.
BA2: Bath 7B 6 (7K 99)
Wansdyke Ct. BS14: Whit 5D 76
Wansdyke Rd. BA2: Odd D 3J 121
Wansdyke Workshops BS31: Key 4E 78
WAPLEY 3E 40
Wapley Bushes Local Nature Reserve
. . . . 1E 40
Wapley Hill BS37: W'lgh 2E 40
Wapley Rank BS37: W'lgh 2D 40
Wapley Rd. BS37: Cod, W'lgh 4F 41
Wapping Rd. BS1: Bris 6E 4 (4K 61)
Warden Rd. BS3: Bedm 5J 61
Wardour Rd. BS4: Know 2K 75
Ware Ct. BS36: Wint 2B 38
Wareham Cl. BS48: Nail 1F 71
Wareham Ct. BS48: Nail 1F 71
Waring Ho. BS1: Bris 7F 5 (4K 61)
WARLEIGH 6A 102
Warleigh Dr. BA1: Bathe 7J 83
Warleigh La. BA1: Warl 3K 101
Warleys La. BS24: W Wick 3G 107
Warman Cl. BS14: Stoc 4H 77
Warman Rd. BS14: Stoc 4H 77
Warmington Rd. BS14: H'gro 2E 76
Warminster Rd.
BA2: Bath, B'ptn, C'ton 2K 7 (3E 100)
BA2: F'frd, Lim S, Mon C 7H 123
BS2: Bris 6C 48
WARMLEY 1F 65
WARMLEY HILL 1D 64
Warne Pk. BS23: W Mare 6J 105
Warner Cl. BS15: K'wd 3D 64
BS49: C've 4C 88
Warne Rd. BS23: W Mare 6J 105
Warns, The BS30: C Hth 5E 64
Warren Cl. BS24: Hut 3B 128
BS32: Brad S 3F 27
Warren Farm Holiday Pk.
TA8: Brean 1B 144
Warren Gdns. BS14: Stoc 5H 77
Warren La. BS41: L Ash 1J 73
Warren Rd. BS34: Fil 4D 36
TA8: Brean 1B 144
Warren's Cl. BS27: Ched 5D 150
Warrens Hill BS27: Ched 5D 150
Warrens Hill Rd. BS27: Ched 3D 150
BS40: C'hse 2E 150
Warrens Holiday Village
BS21: Clev 2C 68
Warren Way BS37: Yate 3E 30
Warrilow Cl. BS22: Wor 6F 85
Warrington Rd. BS4: Brisl 7F 63
Warry Cl. BS48: Wrax 7K 57
Warth La. BS22: Wick L 3E 84
BS35: N'wick 2C 16
Warwick Av. BS5: E'tn 7D 48
Warwick Cl. BS22: W Mare 4A 106
BS30: Will 7F 65
Warwick Gdns. BS39: Clut 2F 139
TA8: Bur S 6D 156
Warwick Pl. BS35: T'bry 3J 11
Warwick Rd. BA1: Bath 4H 99
BS5: E'tn 7D 48
BS6: Redl 7H 47
BS31: Key 6B 78
Warwick Vs. BA2: Bath 6J 99
Washingpool Hill BS35: Rudg 4G 19
Washingpool Hill Rd. BS32: Toc 3D 18
Washingpool La. BS11: Chit 7A 24
Washing Pound La. BS14: Whit 6D 76
BS21: Tic 6D 56
Washington Av. BS5: E'tn 7E 48
Washpool La. BA2: Eng 2F 121
BA2: Stan P 1J 119
SN14: Hin 1G 53
Watch Elm Cl. BS32: Brad S 1G 37
Watch Ho. Pl. BS20: P'head 1G 43
Watch Ho. Rd. BS20: Pill 4H 45
Watchill Av. BS13: Bis 4F 75
Watchill Cl. BS13: Bis 4F 75
Watcombe Cl. BS22: Wor 3C 106
Waterbridge Rd. BS13: Withy 5F 75
Watercress Cl. BS48: Wrax 7K 57
Watercress Rd. BS2: Bris 5B 48
Waterdale Cl. BS9: Henle 1J 47
Waterdale Gdns. BS9: Henle 1J 47
Waterford Cl. BS35: T'bry 4B 12
Waterford Pk. BA3: Rads 6H 153
Waterford Rd. BS9: Henle 2H 47
Waterhouse La. BA2: Lim S 5G 123
Water La. BA3: Mid N 2E 152
BS1: Bris 4H 5 (3A 62)
BS3: Wind H 6B 62
BS4: Brisl 1F 77
(not continuous)
BS20: Pill 4G 45
Waterloo Bldgs. BA2: Bath 5H 99
(not continuous)
Waterloo Ho's. *BS20: Pill* *3G 45*
(off Underbanks)
Waterloo Pl. BS2: Bris 3K 5 (2C 62)
Waterloo Rd. BA3: Rads 4K 153
BS2: Bris 3K 5 (2B 62)
Waterloo St. BS2: Bris 3K 5 (2B 62)
BS8: Clif 2F 61
BS23: W Mare 4F 105
Watermead Cl. *BA1: Bath* *5E 6*
(off Kingsmead W.)
Watermore Cl. BS36: Fram C 7G 29
Watermore Gdns. BS36: Fram C 6H 29
Waters Edge BS20: P'head 1G 43
Watershed Media Cen. 5E 4 (3K 61)
WATERSIDE 5J 153
Waterside Ct. BA2: Bath 5J 99
Waterside Cres. BA3: Rads 5H 153
Waterside Dr. BS32: Alm 5C 26
BS34: Pat 5C 26
Waterside La. BA3: Kil 7K 153
Waterside Rd. BA3: Rads 5H 153
Waterside Way BA3: Rads 5H 153
Waters La. BS9: W Trym 1G 47
BS27: Ched 6E 150
Waters Rd. BS15: K'wd 1A 64
Waters Rd. Bus. Pk. BS15: K'wd 1A 64
Water St. BS1: Bris 2H 5
BS40: E Harp 7K 137
Watery La. BA2: Bath 5G 99
BS30: Doy 1G 67
BS37: Yate 1C 30
BS40: Winf 7B 92
BS48: Nail 7D 56
Wathen Rd. BS6: Bris 5B 48
Wathen St. BS16: Stap H 3B 50
Watkins Yd. BS9: W Trym 7G 35
WATLEY'S END 7D 28
Watley's End Rd. BS36: Wint 7C 28
Watling Way BS11: Shire 1G 45
Watson Av. BS4: Brisl 5F 63
(not continuous)
Watson Cl. TA8: Bur S 5C 156
Watson's Rd. BS30: L Grn 6D 64
Watters Cl. BS36: Coal H 1H 39
Watts La. BS15: K'wd 7C 50
Wavell Cl. BS37: Yate 3D 30
Waveney Rd. BS31: Key 7E 78
Wavering Down Ri. BS26: Cross 3G 149
Waverley Ho. BS1: Bris 6C 4
Waverley Rd. BS6: Cot 7J 47
BS11: Shire 2J 45
BS23: W Mare 1H 127
BS37: Yate 4B 30
BS48: Back 3J 71
Waverley St. BS5: E'tn 7C 48
Wayacre Drove BS23: B'don 7F 127
Wayfield Gdns. BA1: Bathe 6H 83
Wayford Cl. BS31: Key 7E 78
Wayland Ct. *BS16: Fish* *4J 49*
(off Guinea La.)
Wayland Rd. BS22: Wor 1C 106
Wayleaze BS36: Coal H 7H 29
Wayside BS22: Wor 2B 106
Wayside Cl. BS36: Fram C 7F 29
Wayside Dr. BS21: Clev 4E 54
WAY WICK 3J 107
Weal, The BA1: W'ton 1H 99
WEARE 7E 148
Weare Ct. BS1: Bris 7A 4 (4G 61)
Weatherley Dr. BS20: P'head 5B 42
Weatherly Av. BA2: Odd D 2K 121
Weavers Orchard BA2: Wel 4K 143
WEBBINGTON 2J 147
Webbington Rd.
BS26: Comp B, Webb 3J 147
WEBBS HEATH 1H 65
Webbs Heath BS30: W Hth 7H 51
Webbs Mead BS40: Chew S 4D 114
Webb St. BS5: E'tn 1C 62
Webbs Wood Rd. BS32: Brad S 1H 37
Wedgewood Rd. BS16: Down 6B 38
Wedgwood Cl. BS14: Whit 5D 76
Wedgwood Rd. BA2: Bath 6F 99
Wedlock Way BS3: Ash G 6F 61
Wedmore Cl. BA2: Bath 1G 121
BS15: K'wd 2D 64
BS23: W Mare 3H 127
TA8: Bur S 7E 156
Wedmore Pk. BA2: Bath 1G 121
Wedmore Pl. BS3: Know 7A 62
Wedmore Rd. BS21: Clev 1B 68
BS27: Ched 7C 150
BS31: Salt 6H 79
BS48: Nail 2G 71
Wedmore Va. BS3: Know, Wind H 7A 62
Weedon Cl. BS2: Bris 6C 48
Weekesley La. BA2: Cam 5G 141
Weetwood Rd. BS49: Cong 6A 88
Weight Rd. BS5: Redf 2E 62
Weind, The BS22: Wor 2B 106
Weir Cl. BS39: Paul 7C 140
Weir La. BS8: Fail 2H 59
Weir Rd. BS49: Cong 1A 110
Weirside Mill BA15: Brad A 6J 125
Welland Rd. BS31: Key 6D 78
Wellard Cl. BS22: Wor 7F 85
Well Cl. BS24: W Mare 3K 127
BS25: Wins 5G 131
BS41: L Ash 1B 74
Wellesley M. BS10: W Trym 7J 35
Wellgarth Ct. BS4: Know 7C 62
Wellgarth Rd. BS4: Know 7C 62
Wellgarth Wlk. BS4: Know 7C 62
Well Ho. Cl. BS9: Stok B 6E 46
Wellington Av. BS6: Bris 7A 48
Wellington Bldgs. BA1: W'ton 1H 99
Wellington Ct. BS21: Clev 4C 54
Wellington Cres. BS7: Hor 2A 48
Wellington Dr. BS9: Henle 2K 47
BS37: Yate 4B 30
Wellington Hill BS7: Hor 2A 48
Wellington Hill W. BS9: Henle 1J 47
Wellington La. BS6: Bris 7A 48
Wellington M. BS11: Shire 3H 45
Wellington Pk. BS8: Clif 7G 47
Wellington Pl. BS16: Fren 6K 37
BS23: W Mare 5F 105
BS27: Ched 7D 150
Wellington Rd. BS2: Bris 1K 5 (1B 62)
BS15: K'wd 6B 50
BS37: Yate 2E 30
Wellington Ter. BS8: Clif 3F 61
BS21: Clev 4C 54
Wellington Wlk. BS10: W Trym 1J 47
Well La. BS29: Ban 2J 129
BS49: Yat 3J 87
WELLOW 4K 143
Wellow Brook Ct. BA3: Mid N 4F 153
Wellow Brook Mdw. BA3: Mid N 4F 153
Wellow La. BA2: Pea J 6B 142
(not continuous)
Wellow Mead BA2: Pea J 6B 142
Wellow Rd. BA2: Pea J, Wel 6F 143
Wellow Tyning BA2: Pea J 6D 142
Well Pk. BS49: Cong 6K 87
Well Path BA15: Brad A 6G 125
Wells Cl. BS14: Whit 5E 76
BS48: Nail 1K 71
TA8: Bur S 1E 158
Wellsea Gro. BS23: W Mare 5K 105
Wells Hill BA3: Rads 4K 153
Wells Rd. BA2: Bath 7D 6 (6A 100)
BA2: Cor, New L 5J 97
BA3: Rads 5G 153
BS4: Know, Wind H 5B 62
BS14: H'gro, Whit 2D 76
BS21: Clev 1D 68
BS39: Hall 7J 139
BS40: Chew M 2E 92
BS41: Chew M, Dun 2E 92
Wells Sq. BA3: Rads 4H 153
Wells St. BS3: Ash G 5G 61
Wellstead Av. BS37: Yate 5D 30
Wellsway BA2: Bath, Odd D 4K 121
BS31: Key 5D 78
Wellsway Cl. BA2: Odd D 3K 121
Wellsway Pk. BA2: Odd D 4K 121
Welsford Av. BS16: Stap 4F 49
Welsford Rd. BS16: Stap 4E 48
Welsh Bk. BS1: Bris 5F 5 (3K 61)
Welsh Back Squash and Health Club
. . . . 5F 5 (3K 61)
WELTON 4F 153
Welton Gro. BA3: Mid N 3E 152
WELTON HOLLOW 4H 153
Welton Rd. BA3: Rads 4J 153
Welton Va. BA3: Mid N 4F 153
Welton Wlk. BS15: K'wd 6A 50
Wemberham Cres. BS49: Yat 2G 87
Wemberham La. BS49: Yat 4D 86
Wenmore Cl. BS16: Down 6B 38
Wentforth Dr. BS15: K'wd 6A 50
Wentwood Dr. BS24: W Mare 4J 127
Wentworth BS30: Warm 3E 64
BS37: Yate 5E 30
Wentworth Cl. BS22: Wor 1E 106
Wentworth Rd. BS7: B'stn 5K 47
Wescott Gro. BS11: Law W 5C 34
Wesley Av. BA3: Rads 5G 153
BS15: Han 4B 64
Wesley Cl. BS5: W'hall 7F 49
BS16: Soun 5B 50
TA8: Brean 3B 144
Wesley Dr. BS22: Wor 1E 106
Wesley Hill BS15: K'wd 7B 50
Wesley La. BS30: C Hth 4F 65
Wesley M. BS27: Ched 7D 150
Wesley Pl. BS8: Clif 6G 47
Wesley Rd. BS7: B'stn 4A 48
Wesley St. BS3: Bedm 6J 61
Wesley Ter. BS39: Pens 7F 95
Wessex Av. BS7: Hor 1B 48
Wessex Bus. Cen. BS27: Ched 7C 150
Wessex Ct. BS7: Hor 1B 48
Wessex Ho. BS2: Bris 2K 5
(Lawfords Ga.)
BS2: Bris 4H 5 (3A 62)
(Passage St.)
Wessex Rd. BS24: W Mare 3K 127
Westacre Cl. BS10: Hen 5G 35
BS27: Ched 6D 150
Westacre Rd. BS27: Ched 6D 150
West Av. BA2: Bath 6A 6 (6J 99)
TA9: High 4E 158
Westaway Cl. BS49: Yat 4J 87
Westaway Pk. BS49: Yat 4K 87
West Bath Riverside Path 5H 99
Westbourne Av. BS21: Clev 7B 54
BS31: Key 5C 78
Westbourne Cres. BS21: Clev 7B 54
Westbourne Gro. BS3: Bedm 6J 61
Westbourne Ho. BA2: Bath 5H 7 (5C 100)
Westbourne Pl. BS8: Clif 2A 4 (2H 61)
Westbourne Rd. BS5: E'tn 1D 62
BS16: Down 7D 38
Westbourne Ter. BS16: Fren 1K 49
West Broadway BS9: Henle 2K 47
Westbrooke Ct. BS1: Bris 4G 61
Westbrook Pk. BA1: W'ton 1G 99
Westbrook Rd. BS4: Brisl 2F 77
BS22: W Mare 3A 106
Westbury College Gatehouse 1G 47
Westbury Ct. BS9: W Trym 1G 47
Westbury Ct. Rd. BS9: W Trym 1F 47
Westbury Cres. BS23: W Mare 3H 127
Westbury Hill BS9: W Trym 1G 47
Westbury La. BS9: Sea M 1B 46
Westbury M. *BS9: W Trym* *1G 47*
(off Westbury Hill)
WESTBURY ON TRYM 1G 47
WESTBURY PARK 4G 47
Westbury Pk. BS6: Henle 4G 47
Westbury Rd. BS6: Henle, Redl 4G 47
BS9: W Trym 2G 47
Westbury Ter. BA2: Dunk 7E 120
Westbury Vw. BA2: Pea J 5E 142
West Cl. BA2: Bath 6G 99
West Coombe BS9: Stok B 2D 46
West Cotts. BA2: C Down 3E 122
West Country Water Pk. 4H 27
Westcourt Dr. BS30: Old C 5F 65
West Cft. BS9: Henle 1J 47
BS21: Clev 7B 54
BS40: Blag 3C 134
West Dene BS9: Stok B 2E 46
W. Dundry La. BS41: Dun 1E 92
WEST END
BS21 . . . . 7B 54
BS40 . . . . 2C 134
BS48 . . . . 3B 70
GL12 . . . . 7E 14
West End BS2: Bris 1E 4 (1K 61)
BS3: Bris 7D 4 (4J 61)
West End La. BS48: Nail 3B 70
Westend Rd. GL12: Wickw 1E 22
West End Trad. Est. BS48: Nail 1D 70
Westering Cl. BS16: Mang 3E 50
WESTERLEIGH 3B 40
Westerleigh Bus. Pk. BS37: Yate 6B 30
Westerleigh Cl. BS16: Mang 1D 50
Westerleigh Crematorium
BS37: W'lgh 5C 40
Westerleigh Hill BS37: W'lgh 4C 40
Westerleigh Rd. BA2: C Down 3D 122
BS16: Down, Emer G 2C 50
BS16: Puck 2B 52
BS21: Clev 7B 54
BS36: H'fld 6F 39
BS37: W'lgh 1B 40
BS37: Yate 7C 30
Western App. Distribution Pk.
BS35: Sev B 2C 24
Western Av. BS36: Fram C 5E 28
Western Ct. BS21: Clev 6D 54
BS34: Stok G 3J 37
Western Dr. BS14: H'gro 3A 76
Western Rd. BS7: Hor 2A 48
WESTFIELD 5G 153
Westfield BA15: Brad A 5F 125
BS21: Clev 2D 68
Westfield Bus. Pk. BS21: Clev 2E 68
Westfield Cl. BA2: Bath 1A 122
BS15: Han 4B 64
BS23: Uph 3F 127
BS31: Key 5A 78
BS48: Back 4J 71
TA8: Bur S 7D 156
Westfield Ct. TA8: Bur S 7D 156
Westfield Cres. BS29: Ban 2A 130
Westfield Dr. BS48: Back 4J 71
TA8: Bur S 7D 156
Westfield Ind. & Trad. Est.
BA3: Mid N 7G 153
(not continuous)
Westfield La. BS34: Stok G 4G 37
BS40: Chew M 7F 93
Westfield Lawn TA8: Bur S 7D 156
Westfield Pk. BA1: Bath 4G 99
BS6: Redl 7H 47

Willow Cl.—Worle Moor Ga.

Willow Cl. BS23: Uph . . . 3G 127
BS30: Old C . . . 3H 65
BS30: Wick . . . 3B 66
BS34: Pat . . . 7A 26
BS41: L Ash . . . 1K 73
Willowdown BS22: Wor . . . 7C 84
Willow Dr. BS24: B'don . . . 7A 128
BS24: Hut . . . 3C 128
BS24: Lock . . . 7C 106
Willow Falls, The BA1: Bathe . . . 7G 83
Willow Gdns. BS22: St Geo . . . 2H 107
Willow Grn. BA2: Bath . . . 7A 100
Willow Gro. BS16: Fish . . . 6A 50
Willow Ho. BS13: Hart . . . 6K 75
Willow Rd. BS15: Han . . . 6A 64
Willows, The BS16: Fren . . . 6K 37
BS31: Key . . . 4C 78
BS32: Brad S . . . 6F 27
BS37: Yate . . . 4D 30
BS48: Nail . . . 6H 57
TA9: Bre K . . . 5J 157
Willow Shop. Cen., The BS16: Down . . . 2B 50
Willow Wlk. BS10: Bren . . . 4H 35
BS31: Key . . . 6B 78
Willow Way BS36: Coal H . . . 1G 39
WILLSBRIDGE . . . 7E 64
Willsbridge Hill BS30: Will . . . 7E 64
Willsbridge Ho. BS30: Will . . . 7E 64
Willsbridge Mill Countryside Cen. . . . 7E 64
Willsbridge Valley Nature Reserve . . . 7F 65
Wills Dr. BS5: E'tn . . . 1C 62
Wills Hall BS9: Stok B . . . 4F 47
Wills Way BS13: Bis . . . 4K 75
Willway St. BS2: Bris . . . 3K 5 (2B 62)
BS3: Bedm . . . 5K 61
WILMINGTON . . . 3A 120
Wilmington La. BA2: Ing . . . 3C 120
Wilmot Ct. BS30: C Hth . . . 3E 64
Wilmots Way BS20: Pill . . . 4H 45
Wilshire Av. BS15: Han . . . 4B 64
Wilson Av. BS2: Bris . . . 1J 5 (1B 62)
Wilson Pl. BS2: Bris . . . 1J 5 (1B 62)
Wilson St. BS2: Bris . . . 1J 5 (1B 62)
Wilton Cl. BS10: S'mead . . . 7J 35
TA8: Bur S . . . 7E 156
Wilton Gdns. BS23: W Mare . . . 6F 105
Wiltons BS40: Wrin . . . 2F 111
Wiltshire Av. BS37: Yate . . . 3G 31
Wiltshire Music Cen. . . . 5F 125
Wiltshire Pl. BS15: Soun . . . 5C 50
Wiltshire Way BA1: Bath . . . 1C 100
Wilverley Ind. Est. BS4: Brisl . . . 1H 77
Wimbledon Rd. BS6: Henle . . . 3J 47
Wimblestone Rd. BS25: Wins . . . 3F 131
Wimborne Rd. BS3: Bedm . . . 1J 75
Winash Cl. BS14: Stoc . . . 3F 77
Wincanton Cl. BS16: Down . . . 6D 38
BS48: Nail . . . 1K 71
Winchcombe Cl. BS48: Nail . . . 2J 71
Winchcombe Gro. BS11: Shire . . . 3K 45
Winchcombe Rd. BS36: Fram C . . . 6F 29
Winchcombe Trad. Est.
BS2: Bris . . . 5C 62
Winchester Av. BS4: Brisl . . . 6F 63
Winchester Rd. BA2: Bath . . . 6B 6 (6K 99)
BS4: Brisl . . . 6F 63
TA8: Bur S . . . 7E 156
Wincroft BS30: Old C . . . 5G 65
(not continuous)
Windcliff Cres. BS11: Law W . . . 7J 33
Windermere BS10: S'mead . . . 5K 35
Windermere Av. BS23: W Mare . . . 1H 127
Windermere Rd. BS34: Pat . . . 6C 26
Windermere Way BS30: Old C . . . 3H 65
Windmill Bus. Pk. BS21: Clev . . . 3E 68
Windmill Cl. BS3: Wind H . . . 5A 62
TA9: Edith . . . 1K 159
Windmill Farm Bus. Cen.
BS3: Bedm . . . 5K 61
WINDMILL HILL . . . 6A 62
Windmill Hill BS3: Wind H . . . 6K 61
BS24: Hut . . . 3D 128
Windmill Hill City Farm . . . 5K 61
Windmill La. BS10: Hen . . . 4D 34
Windmill Rd. BS21: Clev . . . 2D 68
Windrush Cl. BA2: Bath . . . 7F 99
Windrush Ct. BS35: T'bry . . . 4A 12
Windrush Grn. BS31: Key . . . 6E 78
Windrush Rd. BS31: Key . . . 6E 78
Windsor Av. BS5: St G . . . 3K 63
BS31: Key . . . 6C 78
Windsor Bri. Rd.
BA1: Bath . . . 3A 6 (5K 99)
BA2: Bath . . . 3A 6 (5K 99)
Windsor Castle BA1: Bath . . . 3A 6
Windsor Cl. BS21: Clev . . . 7C 54
BS34: Stok G . . . 2G 37
TA8: Bur S . . . 6D 156
Windsor Ct. BA1: Bath . . . 3A 6 (4K 99)
BS8: Clif . . . 3F 61
BS16: Down . . . 1C 50
BS30: Wick . . . 2C 66
Windsor Cres. BS10: H'len . . . 3C 34
Windsor Dr. BS37: Yate . . . 4D 30
BS48: Nail . . . 7G 57
Windsor Gro. BS5: E'tn . . . 1D 62
Windsor Pl. BA1: Bath . . . 3A 6 (4J 99)
BS8: Clif . . . 3F 61
BS16: Mang . . . 3E 50
Windsor Rd. BS6: Bris . . . 6A 48
BS22: W Mare . . . 2A 106
BS30: L Grn . . . 7D 64
Windsor Ter. BS3: Wind H . . . 5B 62
BS8: Clif . . . 3F 61
BS39: Paul . . . 1C 152
Windsor Vs. BA1: Bath . . . 3A 6 (4J 99)
Windwhistle Circ. BS23: W Mare . . . 2H 127
Windwhistle La. BS23: W Mare . . . 2G 127
(not continuous)
Windwhistle Rd. BS23: W Mare . . . 2F 127
Wineberry Cl. BS5: W'hall . . . 7F 49
Wine St. BA1: Bath . . . 5G 7 (5C 100)
BA15: Brad A . . . 5G 125
BS1: Bris . . . 3F 5 (2K 61)
Wine St. Ter. BA15: Brad A . . . 6G 125
Winfield Rd. BS30: Warm . . . 2G 65
WINFORD . . . 4A 92
Winford Cl. BS20: P'head . . . 4G 43
Winford Gro. BS13: Bis . . . 2G 75
Winford La. BS41: Dun . . . 3B 92
Winford Rd. BS40: Chew M . . . 1E 114
Winford Ter. BS41: Dun . . . 5C 74
Wingard Cl. BS23: Uph . . . 3F 127
Wingfield Rd. BS3: Know . . . 7A 62
Winifred's La. BA1: Bath . . . 2A 100
Winkworth Ho. BS1: Bris . . . 5C 4
Winkworth Pl. BS2: Bris . . . 7B 48
Winnowing End BS25: Sandf . . . 2G 131
Winsbury Vw. BA2: Mark . . . 3F 119
Winsbury Way BS32: Brad S . . . 6E 26
WINSCOMBE . . . 6G 131
Winscombe Cl. BS31: Key . . . 4B 78
Winscombe Drove
BS25: S'ham, Wins . . . 1G 149
Winscombe Hill BS25: Wins . . . 7E 130
Winscombe Rd. BS23: W Mare . . . 5J 105
Winsford St. BS5: E'tn . . . 1K 5 (1C 62)
Winsham Cl. BS14: Whit . . . 5D 76
WINSLEY . . . 5C 124
Winsley By-Pass BA15: W'ley . . . 5B 124
Winsley Hill BA2: Lim S . . . 5J 123
Winsley Rd. BA15: Brad A . . . 5E 124
BS6: Cot . . . 7K 47
Winstone Ct. *BS2: Bris . . . 2D 4*
(off St Michael's Hill)
WINTERBOURNE . . . 1B 38
WINTERBOURNE DOWN . . . 3C 38
Winterbourne Hill BS36: Wint . . . 2B 38
Winterbourne Rd. BS32: Brad S . . . 2J 37
BS34: Stok G . . . 1G 37
WINTERFIELD . . . 2C 152
Winterfield Cl. BS39: Paul . . . 2C 152
Winterfield Pk. BS39: Paul . . . 2C 152
Winterfield Rd. BS39: Paul . . . 1C 152
Winter Gdns. . . . 4F 105
WINTERHEAD . . . 5K 131
Winters La. BS40: Redh . . . 1B 112
BS48: Back . . . 4K 89
Winterstoke Cl. BS3: Bedm . . . 7H 61
Winterstoke Commercial Cen.
BS23: W Mare . . . 6J 105
Winterstoke Ho. BS3: Ash G . . . 6G 61
Winterstoke Rd. BS3: Ash V, Bedm . . . 6F 61
BS23: W Mare . . . 6H 105
BS24: W Mare . . . 3K 127
Winterstoke Underpass
BS3: Bwr A . . . 5F 61
Winter Wlk. BS14: H'gro . . . 4E 76
Winthill BS29: Ban . . . 4A 130
Winton St. BS4: Wind H . . . 5B 62
Wiseman Apartments BS8: Clif . . . 1F 61
Wisemans Ho. BS8: Clif . . . 1G 61
Wishford M. BA3: Mid N . . . 4G 153
Wisley Wlk. BS24: W'ton V . . . 5D 106
Wisteria Av. BS24: Hut . . . 3B 128
BS37: Chip S . . . 5G 31
Witchell Rd. BS5: Redf . . . 2E 62
Witch Hazel Rd. BS13: Hart . . . 7A 76
Witcombe BS37: Yate . . . 7C 30
Witcombe Cl. BS15: K'wd . . . 7C 50
Witham Rd. BS31: Key . . . 7E 78
Withey Cl. E. BS9: W Trym . . . 2F 47
Withey Cl. W. BS9: W Trym . . . 3E 46
Witheys, The BS14: Whit . . . 6E 76
Withies La. BA3: Mid N . . . 7D 152
Withies Pk. BA3: Mid N . . . 7C 152
Withington Cl. BS30: Bit . . . 7G 65
Withleigh Rd. BS4: Know . . . 7D 62
Withy Cl. BS48: Nail . . . 6H 57
WITHYDITCH . . . 2C 142
Withyditch La. BA2: Tun . . . 2C 142
Withymead BS49: Clav . . . 2B 88
WITHY MILLS . . . 6E 140
Withypool Gdns. BS14: Whit . . . 5D 76
Withys, The BS20: Pill . . . 4H 45
WITHYWOOD . . . 6F 75
Withywood Gdns. BS13: Withy . . . 5F 75
Withywood Rd. BS13: Withy . . . 6F 75
Witney Cl. BS31: Salt . . . 7H 79
Witney Mead BS36: Fram C . . . 6F 29
Woburn Cl. BS30: Bar C . . . 4D 64
Woburn Rd. BS5: Eastv . . . 5D 48
Wolferton Rd. BS7: Bris . . . 6B 48
Wolfridge Gdns. BS10: Bren . . . 3G 35
Wolfridge La. BS35: Alv . . . 1H 19
Wolfridge Ride BS35: Alv . . . 1H 19
Wolseley Rd. BS7: B'stn . . . 5K 47
Wolvershill Ind. Est. BS29: Ban . . . 5G 107
Wolvershill Pk. BS29: Ban . . . 2A 130
Wolvershill Rd. BS24: W Wick . . . 4G 107
BS29: Ban . . . 7J 107
WONDERSTONE . . . 7B 128
Woodacre BS20: P'head . . . 1G 43
Woodbine Rd. BS5: W'hall . . . 1F 63
WOODBOROUGH . . . 5H 131
Woodborough Ct. *BS25: Wins . . . 5G 131*
(off Woodborough Rd.)
Woodborough Cres. BS25: Wins . . . 6G 131
Woodborough Dr. BS25: Wins . . . 5G 131
WOODBOROUGH HILL . . . 2C 154
Woodborough La. BA3: Rads . . . 2A 154
Woodborough Rd. BA3: Rads . . . 3A 154
BS25: Wins . . . 5F 131
Woodborough St. BS5: E'tn . . . 7D 48
Woodbridge Rd. BS4: Know . . . 7C 62
Woodbury La. BS8: Clif . . . 6G 47
Woodchester BS15: Soun . . . 5C 50
BS37: Yate . . . 7E 30
Woodchester Rd. BS10: W Trym . . . 1J 47
Woodcliff Av. BS22: W Mare . . . 3A 106
Woodcliff Rd. BS22: W Mare . . . 3A 106
Woodcote BS15: Han . . . 3B 64
Woodcote Rd. BS16: Fish . . . 5K 49
Woodcote Wlk. BS16: Fish . . . 6K 49
Woodcroft BS39: Bis S . . . 2J 137
Woodcroft Av. BS5: W'hall . . . 7F 49
Woodcroft Cl. BS4: Brisl . . . 5G 63
Woodcroft Rd. BS4: Brisl . . . 5G 63
Woodend BS15: K'wd . . . 3B 64
Woodend Rd. BS36: Coal H, Fram C . . . 7F 29
Wood End Wlk. BS9: Sea M . . . 2C 46
Woodfield Cl. TA8: Bur S . . . 3E 158
Woodfield Rd. BS6: Redl . . . 7H 47
Woodford Cl. BS48: Nail . . . 1J 71
Woodford La. BS40: Chew S . . . 4E 114
Woodgrove Rd. BS10: Hen . . . 5D 34
Woodhall Cl. BS16: Mang . . . 2D 50
WOODHILL . . . 1F 43
Woodhill BS49: Cong . . . 5K 87
Woodhill Av. BS20: P'head . . . 1F 43
Wood Hill Pk. BS20: P'head . . . 1F 43
Woodhill Pl. BA2: Clav D . . . 6F 101
Woodhill Rd. BS20: P'head . . . 2F 43
Woodhill Views BS48: Nail . . . 6H 57
Woodhouse Av. BS32: Alm . . . 6F 19
Woodhouse Cl. BS32: Alm . . . 7F 19
WOODHOUSE DOWN . . . 6F 19
Woodhouse Gro. BS7: Hor . . . 2A 48
Woodhouse Rd. BA2: Bath . . . 5G 99
Woodhurst Rd. BS23: W Mare . . . 4J 105
Woodington Ct. BS30: Bar C . . . 5D 64
Woodington Rd. BS21: Clev . . . 1C 68
Wood Kilns, The BS49: Yat . . . 2G 87
Woodland Av. BS15: K'wd . . . 6B 50
Woodland Cl. BS8: Fail . . . 5F 59
BS15: K'wd . . . 6A 50
Woodland Ct. BS8: Clif . . . 1H 61
BS9: Stok B . . . 5C 46
BS16: Fish . . . 2A 50
(off Partridge Dr.)
Woodland Glade BS21: Clev . . . 4E 54
Woodland Gro. BA2: Clav D . . . 6G 101
BS9: Stok B . . . 2D 46
Woodland La. BS31: Q Char . . . 7F 77
Woodland Pl. BA2: Clav D . . . 6F 101
Woodland Ri. *BS8: Clif . . . 3D 4*
(off Cantock's Cl.)
Woodland Rd. BS8: Clif . . . 1C 4 (1J 61)
BS23: W Mare . . . 1F 127
BS48: Nail . . . 6G 57
GL12: Ley . . . 1B 14
WOODLANDS . . . 3E 26
Woodlands BS16: Down . . . 2C 50
BS26: Axb . . . 4K 149
BS32: Brad S . . . 3F 27
GL12: Tyth . . . 6F 13
Woodlands, The BA2: Tun . . . 2K 141
SN13: Kings . . . 1D 102
(off Kingsdown Gro.)
Woodlands Ct. BS32: Brad S . . . 3D 26
Woodlands Dr. BA2: Lim S . . . 6K 123
Woodlands La. BS32: Alm . . . 1G 27
BS32: Brad S . . . 4D 26
(not continuous)
Woodlands Pk. BA1: Bath . . . 1E 100
BS32: Brad S . . . 3E 26
Woodlands Ri. BS16: Down . . . 2B 50
Woodlands Rd. BS20: P'head . . . 1F 43
BS21: Clev . . . 5C 54
GL12: Tyth . . . 6F 13
Woodland Ter. BS6: Redl . . . 6H 47
BS15: K'wd . . . 1C 64
Woodland Way BS8: Fail . . . 5F 59
BS15: K'wd . . . 6A 50
Wood La. BS20: Clap G . . . 2G 57
BS23: W Mare . . . 3H 105
BS49: Cong, Yat . . . 4A 88
Wood Leaze BS37: Yate . . . 5F 31
Woodleaze BS9: Sea M . . . 2B 46
Woodleigh BS35: T'bry . . . 3A 12
Woodleigh Gdns. BS14: H'gro . . . 4E 76
Woodmancote BS37: Yate . . . 6D 30
Woodmancote Rd. BS6: Bris . . . 7A 48
Woodmans Cl. BS37: Chip S . . . 6H 31
Woodmans Rd. BS37: Chip S . . . 6H 31
Woodmans Va. BS37: Chip S . . . 6J 31
Woodmarsh Cl. BS14: Whit . . . 6C 76
Woodmead Gdns. BS13: Hart . . . 6J 75
Woodmead La. BS30: Doy . . . 7G 53
Woodmill BS49: Yat . . . 2G 87
Woodnock, The BS10: S'mead . . . 5J 35
Woodpecker Av. BA3: Mid N . . . 6F 153
Woodpecker Cres. BS16: Puck . . . 4C 52
Woodpecker Dr. BS22: Wor . . . 4C 106
Wood Rd. BS15: K'wd . . . 1B 64
Woods Hill BA2: Lim S . . . 6J 123
Woodside BA3: Mid N . . . 5C 152
BS9: Stok B . . . 5D 46
Woodside Av. BS24: W Mare . . . 3K 127
Woodside Cotts. BA2: Eng . . . 4J 121
Woodside Gdns. BS20: P'head . . . 3A 42
Woodside Gro. BS10: Hen . . . 4D 34
Woodside Rd. BS4: St Ap . . . 3G 63
BS15: K'wd . . . 2A 64
BS16: Down . . . 1A 50
BS21: Clev . . . 4E 54
BS36: Coal H . . . 7H 29
Woodspring Av. BS22: W Mare . . . 1J 105
Woodspring Cres. BS22: W Mare . . . 1J 105
Woodspring Priory Mus. . . . 2A 84
Woodspring Stadium . . . 1J 127
WOODSTOCK . . . 2C 64
Woodstock Av. BS6: Cot . . . 7J 47
Woodstock Cl. BS15: K'wd . . . 1D 64
Woodstock Rd. BS6: Redl . . . 6H 47
BS15: K'wd . . . 1D 64
BS22: W Mare . . . 4K 105
Wood St. BA1: Bath . . . 4F 7 (5B 100)
BA2: Bath . . . 6E 6 (6B 100)
BS5: E'tn . . . 6D 48
Woodview BS21: Clev . . . 6F 55
BS39: Paul . . . 1A 152
Woodview Cl. BS11: Shire . . . 1J 45
Woodview Dr. BS49: C've . . . 3C 88
Woodview Rd. BS27: Ched . . . 7E 150
Woodview Ter. BA2: Bath . . . 5F 99
BS23: W Mare . . . 6J 105
BS48: Nail . . . 7H 57
Woodward Av. BS37: Yate . . . 5B 30
Woodward Dr. BS30: Bar C . . . 5D 64
Woodwell Rd. BS11: Shire . . . 2J 45
(not continuous)
Woodyleaze BS15: Han . . . 3A 64
Woodyleaze Dr. BS15: Han . . . 3A 64
Wookey Cl. BS48: Nail . . . 2H 71
Woolcot St. BS6: Redl . . . 6H 47
Wooler Rd. BS23: W Mare . . . 4G 105
WOOLLARD . . . 6J 95
Woollard La. BS14: Whit . . . 7F 77
BS39: Wool . . . 5H 95
WOOLLEY
BA1 . . . 4B 82
BA15 . . . 5J 125
Woolley Cl. BA15: Brad A . . . 5J 125
Woolley Dr. BA15: Brad A . . . 5J 125
WOOLLEY GREEN . . . 4K 125
Woolley La. BA1: Charl, W'ly . . . 5B 82
Woolley Orchard BA15: Brad A . . . 5J 125
Woolley Rd. BS14: Stoc . . . 5G 77
Woolley St. BA15: Brad A . . . 6H 125
Woolley Ter. BA15: Brad A . . . 5J 125
Woolvers Way BS24: Lock . . . 6F 107
Wootton Cres. BS4: St Ap . . . 3G 63
Wootton Pk. BS14: H'gro . . . 1D 76
Wootton Rd. BS4: St Ap . . . 3G 63
Worcester Bldgs. BA1: Bath . . . 1D 100
Worcester Cl. BA2: Pea J . . . 6D 142
BS16: Fish . . . 6K 49
Worcester Ct. *BA1: Bath . . . 1D 100*
(off Worcester Pk.)
Worcester Cres. BS8: Clif . . . 1G 61
Worcester Gdns. BS48: Nail . . . 2D 70
Worcester Pk. BA1: Bath . . . 1D 100
Worcester Pl. BA1: Bath . . . 1D 100
Worcester Rd. BS8: Clif . . . 1G 61
BS15: K'wd . . . 7B 50
Worcester Ter. BA1: Bath . . . 2D 100
BS8: Clif . . . 1G 61
Worcester Vs. BA1: Bath . . . 1D 100
Wordsworth Cl. TA8: Bur S . . . 5D 156
Wordsworth Rd. BS7: Hor . . . 2C 48
BS21: Clev . . . 7C 54
BS23: W Mare . . . 2J 127
Worlds End La. BS8: Clif . . . 5A 4
BS31: Key . . . 5G 79
WORLE . . . 2D 106
WORLEBURY . . . 2J 105
Worlebury Cl. BS22: W Mare . . . 1K 105
Worlebury Hill Fort . . . 3E 104
Worlebury Hill Rd. BS22: W Mare . . . 2J 105
BS23: W Mare . . . 2H 105
Worlebury Pk. Rd. BS22: W Mare . . . 1J 105
Worle Ct. BS22: Wor . . . 1D 106
Worle Moor Ga. BS24: W'ton V . . . 3F 107

The representation on the maps of a road, track or footpath is no evidence of the existence of a right of way.

The Grid on this map is the National Grid taken from Ordnance Survey® mapping with the permission of the Controller of Her Majesty's Stationery Office.

Copyright of Geographers' A-Z Map Company Ltd.

No reproduction by any method whatsoever of any part of this publication is permitted without the prior consent of the copyright owners.

SAFETY CAMERA INFORMATION

Safety camera locations are publicised by the Safer Roads Partnership who operate them in order to encourage drivers to comply with speed limits at these sites. It is the driver's absolute responsibility to be aware of and to adhere to speed limits at all times.

By showing this safety camera information it is the intention of Geographers' A-Z Map Company Ltd., to encourage safe driving and greater awareness of speed limits and vehicle speed. Data accurate at time of printing.

HOSPITALS, WALK-IN CENTRES and HOSPICES
covered by this atlas.

N.B. Where it is not possible to name these facilities on the map,
the reference given is for the road in which they are situated.

BATH BMI CLINIC 2F **123**
Claverton Down Road
Combe Down
BATH
BA2 7BR
Tel: 01225 835555

BLACKBERRY HILL HOSPITAL 3H **49**
Manor Road
Fishponds
BRISTOL
BS16 2EW
Tel: 0117 9656061

BRISTOL DENTAL HOSPITAL 2E **4** (2K **61**)
Lower Maudlin Street
BRISTOL
BS1 2LY
Tel: 0117 9284383

BRISTOL EYE HOSPITAL 2F **5** (2K **61**)
Lower Maudlin Street
BRISTOL
BS1 2LX
Tel: 0117 9230060

BRISTOL GENERAL HOSPITAL 7F **5** (4K **61**)
Guinea Street
BRISTOL
BS1 6SY
Tel: 0117 9286223

BRISTOL HAEMATOLOGY & ONCOLOGY CENTRE
. . . . .2E **4** (2K **61**)
Horfield Road
BRISTOL
BS2 8ED
Tel: 0117 9282416

BRISTOL HOMOEOPATHIC HOSPITAL (OUTPATIENTS)
. . . . .1J **61**
Cotham Hill
BRISTOL
BS6 6JU
Tel: 0117 9731231

BRISTOL NUFFIELD HOSPITAL AT ST MARY'S . . .3B **4** (2H **61**)
Upper Byron Place
BRISTOL
BS8 1JU
Tel: 0117 9872727

BRISTOL NUFFIELD HOSPITAL AT THE CHESTERFIELD
. . . . .3G **61**
3 Clifton Hill
BRISTOL
BS8 1BP
Tel: 0117 9730391

BRISTOL PRIORY GRANGE HOSPITAL 4D **48**
Heath House Lane
Stapleton
BRISTOL
BS16 1EQ
Tel: 0117 9525255

BRISTOL ROYAL HOSPITAL FOR CHILDREN 2E **4** (2K **61**)
Upper Maudlin Street
BRISTOL
BS2 8BJ
Tel: 0117 342 8461

BRISTOL ROYAL INFIRMARY 1E **4** (1K **61**)
Marlborough Street
BRISTOL
BS2 8HW
Tel: 0117 9230000

BRISTOL SPIRE HEALTH CLINIC 7G **47**
116 Pembroke Road
Clifton
BRISTOL
BS8 3EW
Tel: 0117 3171300

BRISTOL SPIRE HOSPITAL .6G **47**
Redland Hill
Redland
BRISTOL
BS6 6UT
Tel: 0117 9804000

BURNHAM-ON-SEA WAR MEMORIAL HOSPITAL 1D **158**
Love Lane
BURNHAM-ON-SEA
TA8 1ED
Tel: 01278 773118

CALLINGTON ROAD HOSPITAL 1E **76**
Marmalade Lane
BRISTOL
BS4 5BJ
Tel: 0117 919 5600

CLEVEDON HOSPITAL 6E **54**
Old Street
CLEVEDON
BS21 6BS
Tel: 01275 872212

COSSHAM MEMORIAL HOSPITAL 6A **50**
Lodge Road
BRISTOL
BS15 1LF
Tel: 0117 9671661

DOROTHY HOUSE HOSPICE CARE 6B **124**
Winsley
BRADFORD-ON-AVON
BA15 2LE
Tel: 01225 722988

FRENCHAY HOSPITAL 7K **37**
Frenchay Park Road
BRISTOL
BS16 1LE
Tel: 0117 9701212

FROMESIDE 3H **49**
Blackberry Hill
Stapleton
BRISTOL
BS16 1EG
Tel: 0117 958 3678

GROVE ROAD DAY HOSPITAL 6G **47**
12 Grove Road
Redland
BRISTOL
BS6 6UJ
Tel: 0117 9730225

KEWSTOKE CYGNET HOSPITAL 1J **105**
Beach Road
Kewstoke
WESTON-SUPER-MARE
BS22 9UZ
Tel: 01934 428989

NHS WALK-IN CENTRE (BATH) 4D **6** (5A **100**)
Riverside Health Centre
James Street West
BATH
BA1 2BT

NHS WALK-IN CENTRE (BRISTOL - CITY GATE)
. . . . .3F **5** (2K **61**)
33 Broad Street
BRISTOL
BS1 2EZ
Tel: 0117 903 9610

NHS WALK-IN CENTRE (BRISTOL - SOUTH) 1K **75**
5 Knowle West Health Park
Downton Road
Knowle
BRISTOL
BS4 1WH
Tel: 0117 903 0000

PAULTON MEMORIAL HOSPITAL 2D **152**
Salisbury Road
Paulton
BRISTOL
BS39 7SB
Tel: 01761 412315

ROBERT SMITH UNIT DAY HOSPITAL 2G **61**
12 Mortimer Road
BRISTOL
BS8 4EX
Tel: 0117 9735004

ROYAL NATIONAL HOSPITAL FOR RHEUMATIC DISEASES
. . . . .4F **7** (5B **100**)
Upper Borough Walls
BATH
BA1 1RL
Tel: 01225 465941

ROYAL UNITED HOSPITAL .3H **99**
Combe Park
BATH
BA1 3NG
Tel: 01225 428331

ST MARTIN'S HOSPITAL .3A **122**
Midford Road
BATH
BA2 5RP
Tel: 01225 831500

ST MICHAEL'S HOSPITAL 1D **4** (1J **61**)
Southwell Street
BRISTOL
BS2 8EG
Tel: 0117 928 5325

ST PETERS HOSPICE 7C **62**
St. Agnes Avenue
BRISTOL
BS4 2DU
Tel: 0117 9159200

ST PETERS HOSPICE (BRENTRY) 5H **35**
Charlton Road
Brentry
BRISTOL
BS10 6NL
Tel: 01179 159400

SOUTHMEAD HOSPITAL 7K **35**
Southmead Road
Westbury-on-Trym
BRISTOL
BS10 5NB
Tel: 0117 9505050

THORNBURY HOSPITAL 3A **12**
Prowse Close
Thornbury
BRISTOL
BS35 1DN
Tel: 01454 412636

WESTON GENERAL HOSPITAL 3G **127**
Grange Road
Uphill
WESTON-SUPER-MARE
BS23 4TQ
Tel: 01934 636363

WESTON HOSPICECARE .3F **127**
Jackson-Barstow House
28 Thornbury Road
Uphill
WESTON-SUPER-MARE
BS23 4YQ
Tel: 01934 423900

A-Z BRISTOL BATH NORTH SOMERSET

CONTENTS

REFERENCE

Motorway	M5
Primary Route	A4
A Road	A36
B Road	B4055
Dual Carriageway	
One-way Street Traffic flow on A Roads is also indicated by a heavy line on the driver's left.	
Restricted Access	
Pedestrianized Road	
City Centre Loop	
Track / Footpath	
Residential Walkway	
Railway	Station Level Crossing Tunnel Heritage Station
Built-up Area	MILL ST.
Local Authority Boundary	
Posttown Boundary	
Postcode Boundary (within Posttown)	
Map Continuation	86 Large Scale City Centre 4
Airport	✈
Car Park (selected)	P
Church or Chapel	†
Cycleway (selected)	🚲
Bristol Ferry Waterbus Stop	F
Fire Station	■
Hospital	H
House Numbers (Selected roads)	13 8 25
Information Centre	i
National Grid Reference	³60
Park & Ride	Portway P+
Police Station	▲
Post Office	★
Safety Camera (with Speed Limit) Fixed cameras and long term road works cameras Symbols do not indicate camera direction	30
Toilet: without facilities for the Disabled with facilities for the Disabled Disabled facilities only	▽ ▽ ▽
Viewpoint	✳ ✳
Educational Establishment	
Hospital or Healthcare Building	
Industrial Building	
Leisure or Recreational Facility	
Place of Interest	
Public Building	
Shopping Centre or Market	
Other Selected Buildings	

SCALE

Map Pages 8-159	Map Pages 4-7 1:7,454
1:14,908 4¼ inches (10.8 cm) to 1 mile 6.71 cm to 1 km	1:7,454 8½ inches (21.6) to 1 mile 13.42 cm to 1 km

0   ¼   ½ Mile
0   250   500   750 Metres

0   ⅛   ¼ Mile
0   100   200   300   400 Metres

Copyright of Geographers' A-Z Map Company Limited

Fairfield Road, Borough Green, Sevenoaks, Kent TN15 8PP
Telephone: 01732 781000 (Enquiries & Trade Sales)
01732 783422 (Retail Sales)
www.a-zmaps.co.uk
Copyright © Geographers' A-Z Map Co. Ltd.
EDITION 4   2009

Ordnance Survey

This product includes mapping data licensed from Ordnance Survey® with the permission of the Controller of Her Majesty's Stationery Office.
© Crown Copyright 2008. All rights reserved. Licence number 100017302
Safety camera information supplied by www.PocketGPSWorld.com
Speed Camera Location Database Copyright 2008 © PocketGPSWorld.com

Every possible care has been taken to ensure that, to the best of our knowledge, the information contained in this atlas is accurate at the date of publication. However, we cannot warrant that our work is entirely error free and whilst we would be grateful to learn of any inaccuracies, we do not accept any responsibility for loss or damage resulting from reliance on information contained within this publication.

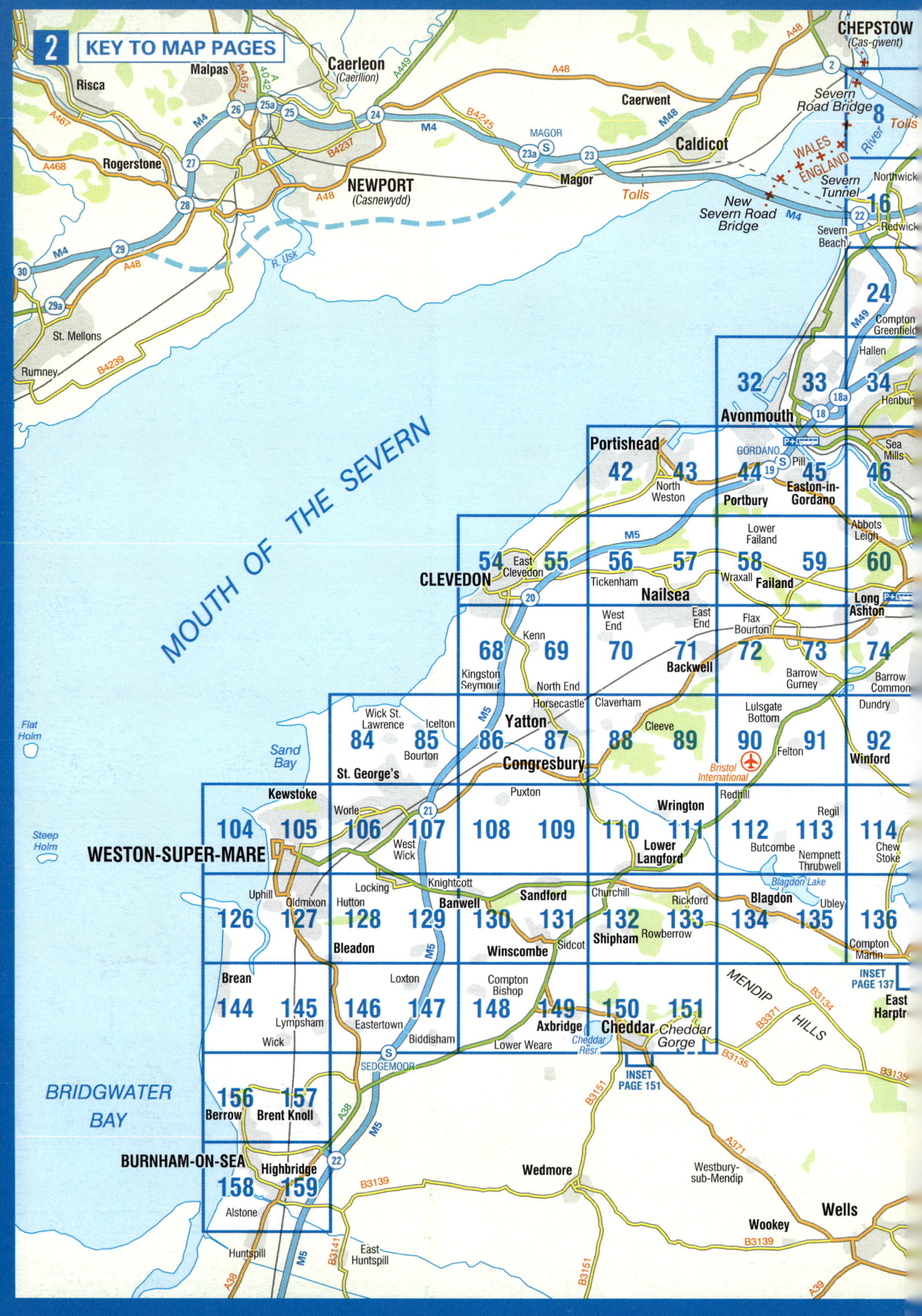